S0-BLL-142

The Philippine Temptation

In the series *Asian American History and Culture,*
edited by Sucheng Chan, David Palumbo-Liu, and Michael Omi

Also in the *Asian American History and Culture* series:

Sucheng Chan, ed., *Entry Denied: Exclusion and the Chinese Community in America, 1882–1943,* 1991

Gary Y. Okihiro, *Cane Fires: The Anti-Japanese Movement in Hawaii, 1865–1945,* 1991

Yen Le Espiritu, *Asian American Panethnicity: Bridging Institutions and Identities,* 1992

Karen Isaksen Leonard, *Making Ethnic Choices: California's Punjabi Mexican Americans,* 1992

Shirley Geok-lin Lim and Amy Ling, eds., *Reading the Literatures of Asian America,* 1992

Renqiu Yu, *To Save China, To Save Ourselves: The Chinese Hand Laundry Alliance of New York,* 1992

Velina Hasu Houston, ed., *The Politics of Life: Four Plays by Asian American Women,* 1993

William Wei, *The Asian American Movement,* 1993

Sucheng Chan, ed. *Hmong Means Free: Life in Laos and America,* 1994

Timothy P. Fong, *The First Suburban Chinatown: The Remaking of Monterey Park, California,* 1994

Chris Friday, *Organizing Asian American Labor: The Pacific Coast Canned-Salmon Industry, 1870–1942,* 1994

Paul Ong, Edna Bonacich, and Lucie Cheng, eds., *The New Asian Immigration in Los Angeles and Global Restructuring,* 1994

Carlos Bulosan, *The Cry and the Dedication,* edited and with an introduction by E. San Juan, Jr., 1995

Yen Le Espiritu, *Filipino American Lives,* 1995

Vicente L. Rafael, ed., *Discrepant Histories: Translocal Essays on Filipino Cultures,* 1995

E. San Juan, Jr., ed., *On Becoming Filipino: Selected Writings of Carlos Bulosan,* 1995

Deepika Petraglia-Bahri and Mary Vasudeva, eds., *Between the Lines: South Asians and Postcoloniality,* in press

The Philippine Temptation

DIALECTICS OF

PHILIPPINES—U.S.

LITERARY RELATIONS

E. San Juan, Jr.

TEMPLE UNIVERSITY PRESS

PHILADELPHIA

Temple University Press, Philadelphia 19122
Copyright © 1996 by Temple University
All rights reserved
Published 1996
Printed in the United States of America

⊛ The paper used in this publication meets the requirements of the American
National Standard for Information Sciences—Permanence of Paper for Printed
Library Materials, ANSI Z39.48—1984

Text design by Erin New

Library of Congress Cataloging-in-Publication Data

San Juan, E. (Epifanio), 1938–
    The Philippine temptation : dialectics of Philippines–U.S. literary
relations / E. San Juan, Jr.
       p.   cm.—(Asian American history and culture series)
    Includes bibliographical references and index.
   ISBN 1-56639-417-1 (cloth : alk. paper).—ISBN 1-56639-418-X
(pbk. : alk. paper)
    1. Philippine literature—American influences. I. Title.
II. Series.
PL5531.S25   1996
809'.89599—dc20   95-47191

For, presently, came the Philippine temptation. . . .

What we wanted, in the interest of Progress and Civilization, was the Archipelago, unencumbered by patriots struggling for independence; and War was what we needed. . . .

And as for a flag for the Philippine province, we can have a special one—Our States do it; we can have just our usual flag, with the white stripes painted black and the stars replaced by the skull and cross-bones.

—*Mark Twain, 1901*

Perhaps the great American republic with interest in the Pacific and without a share in the partition of Africa may one day think of acquiring possessions beyond the seas. It is not impossible, for example is contagious, greed and ambition being the vices of the strong. . . .

Very probably the Philippines will defend with indescribable ardor the liberty she has bought at the cost of so much blood and sacrifice. With the new men that will spring from her bosom and the remembrance of the past, she will perhaps enter openly the wide road of progress and all will work jointly to strengthen the mother country at home as well as abroad with the same enthusiasm with which a young man returns to cultivate his father's farmland so long devastated and abandoned due to the negligence of those who had alienated it. . . . And [Filipinos] will be free once more, like the bird that leaves the cage, like the flower that returns to the open air, they will recover their good old qualities which they are losing little by little and again become lovers of peace, joyful, lively, smiling, hospitable, and fearless.

If there is no permanent condition in nature, how much less there ought to be in the life of peoples, beings endowed with mobility and energy!

—*Jose Rizal, 1889*

We have fought on the conviction that we were bound both in duty and dignity to defend our natural liberties to the extent of our might, for without them the social equality between the ruling caste and indigenous classes would be practically impossible, and so we could not secure full justice among us. . . .

If in the harmony between reason and experience truth is hidden, in the harmony between theory and practice virtue lies concealed. . . .

So be it then; but in the meantime let us strive so that both our mind and heart may become capable of everything worthy and honorable in life, hoping that time shall disclose the veil of the future and let us see the true path of our progress and happiness.

—*Apolinario Mabini, 1899*

Contents

Acknowledgments

It is tempting to state at the outset that all errors are mine and to disclaim any implication of others as "accessory" to the act. But not only is this superfluous and tautological, it is also not accurate. We are always in "situation," as Sartre would say, and "others" are complicitous, whether they like it or not.

The production of any work such as this book is always a collective enterprise, with many collaborators, so that often one is at a loss to account for all the people one should thank. For this occasion, constrained by limitations of space and memory, I want to thank the editors of this series, Sucheng Chan (University of California, Santa Barbara) and David Palumbo-Liu (Stanford University), for their support and advice, and also Director David Bartlett, Executive Editor Janet Francendese, and the editorial staff of Temple University Press for making the book a reality.

I am also grateful to Giovanna Covi of the University of Trento, Eugene Van Erven of the University of Utrecht, Michael Wilding of the University of Sydney, and Arif Dirlik of Duke University, for their warm sympathy and solidarity. I also want to acknowledge here Eric San Juan (University of Chicago) and Karin Aguilar–San Juan (Brown University), both of whom contributed ideas and suggestions that have put me on guard and made me more cautious in expressing unwarrantable if not scandalous propositions. For their encouragement and assistance in various ways, I want to express my gratitude to my colleagues Sam Noumoff, Robert Perry, Karen Gould, James Bennett, Alan Wald, Bruce Franklin, and especially Delia Aguilar.

Some of the materials in this book appeared earlier in different versions in various journals, to whose editors I am grateful: *Minnesota Re-*

view; Philippine Studies; Journal of English Studies; Parenthesis; Diliman Review; Ang Makatao; Philippine-American Journal; Diaspora; Midweek; and *Prisoners of Image: Ethnic and Gender Stereotypes,* published by the Alternative Museum, New York City.

The Philippine Temptation

Introduction

For the first time since the outbreak of the Spanish-American War in 1898 and the fall of Bataan and Corregidor to the Japanese invaders in 1942, the Philippines captured the world's attention for a few days in February 1986: an urban mass insurrection of over a million people overthrew the long-hated dictatorship of Ferdinand Marcos (1972–86) with little bloodshed, in the face of tanks and soldiers armed to the teeth. Scenes of this uprising were televised worldwide, images exuding an aura of the miraculous. Distanced from their original context, those media images and representations which mediated this singular event became an inspiration to the popular rebellions that soon exploded around the world, particularly in Eastern Europe, China, Pakistan, Haiti, and other countries in the Third World.

Less publicized is one epochal achievement of the national-democratic movement, kindled by the "First Quarter Storm" (mass protests and demonstrations against U.S. imperialism and the Marcos client regime) in 1970 and still recklessly alive: in 1992, the U.S. government finally yielded to Filipino nationalist resolve and abandoned its two huge military installations (Clark Air Field and Subic Naval Base), symbols of colonial domination for over half a century. The intervention of nature, in the form of the eruption of Mt. Pinatubo, precipitated the U.S. military's rapid departure. Despite some attenuation, the Philippines has the only viable communist-led and self-rectifying guerilla insurgency in all of Asia and perhaps in the whole world.

But, like most Third World societies plagued by colonial underdevelopment (from the time of its conquest and annexation by the United States in 1898 to the present), the Philippines, although nominally independent today, still suffers the classic problems of neocolonial dependency. Its economy is controlled by the draconian "conditionalities" and impositions of the International Monetary Fund / World Bank (IMF / WB); its politics are run by semifeudal warlords, bureaucrats, and military officials who are beholden to Washington; and its culture is managed by U.S. mass media and the Western information / knowledge monopoly (also known as the culture / consciousness industry).

U.S. direct colonial rule lasted up to 1946, but its cultural and political hegemony persists to this day. When the Reagan administration intervened in 1986 to shore up the ruins of empire by rescuing the dictator Marcos from the wrath of Filipinos in revolt and installing its new set of clients, Corazon Aquino and her successor General Fidel Ramos, it was less nostalgia than a tactical and prudent retreat (see May and Nemenzo; Sison, *Philippine Crisis*; Cingranelli). Desperate maneuvers to salvage the military bases confirmed a long-range strategy of retrenchment. There was definitely no retreat in politics, ideology, and economics, notwithstanding the claim of pundits that such intervention demonstrated U.S. goodwill to preserve its investment in its long-revered Asian "showcase of democracy" following its debacle in Vietnam.

Whatever the status of the national collective memory, the day soon will be here when the U.S. public will celebrate the centennial anniversary of Admiral George Dewey's defeat of the Spanish armada in Manila Bay on 1 May 1898, perhaps not with the usual jingoistic fanfare of yore, but surely with some nostalgia for the days of Empire. We are, after all, inhabiting today a "New World Order" characterized by U.S. triumphalist incursions in the Middle East and its post–Cold War saber-rattling toward Haiti, Libya, Iran, Cuba, and socialist Korea.

Contrary to the claim that the first Philippines-U.S. contact began when Filipino recruits jumped off a Spanish galleon in the seventeenth century and settled in what is now Louisiana, I contend that the inaugural scene was the intrusion of Dewey into Manila Bay in 1898 and the subsequent Filipino-American War (1899–1903), which suppressed the revolutionary forces of the first Philippine Republic. This was the infamous event when "thirty thousand [Americans] killed a million [Filipinos]." And this hegemony continues today in covert, neocolonial forms—proof that what Mark Twain, in his manifesto "To the Person Sitting in Darkness," called the Philippine "temptation" (*Weapons of Satire* 32) persists amid profound mutations in the world system of transnational capital.

But for the moment, I want to cite Twain's comment on the "Philippine temptation," which, in Carey McWilliams' view, prompted the American ruling class to "guide the natives in ways of our own choosing," especially when the "lesser breeds" or "little brown brothers occupied a potentially rich land" (*Brothers* 548). The ironic resonance of this self-proclaimed "civilizing mission" is registered in Twain's distinctive idiom:

> We have pacified some thousands of the islanders and buried them; destroyed their fields, burned their villages, and turned their widows and orphans out-of-doors; furnished heartbreak by exile to some dozens of disagreeable patriots; subjugated the remaining ten millions by Benevolent Assimilation, which is the pious new name of the musket; we have acquired property in the three hundred concubines and other slaves of our business partner, the Sultan of Sulu, and hoisted our protecting flag over that swag. And so, by these Providences of God—and the phrase is the government's, not mine—we are a World Power. (Zinn, *Twentieth Century*, 20)

In his nuanced satire, Twain marveled at the report that thirty thousand American soldiers killed a million Filipinos: *"Thirty thousand killed a million. It seems a pity that the historian let that get out; it is really a most embarrassing circumstance"* ("Thirty Thousand" 62). In February 1899, the Filipino-American War of 1899–1903 began and the U.S. Senate ratified the treaty that formalized the annexation of Spain's former colonies. In that same month was published Rudyard Kipling's poem, "The White Man's Burden." It echoed U.S. Senator Albert Beveridge's claim of "the mission of our race, trustee under God, of the civilization of the world."

This foundational event in the chronicle of the expansion of U.S. coercive sovereignty is not unprecedented, as described and documented by Gareth Stedman Jones, William Appleman Williams, Gabriel Kolko, and others. H. Bruce Franklin remarks in his insightful commentary on the U.S. war machine, *War Stars*: "The warfare waged against the Cuban and Philippine nationalists, for whose ostensible benefit we had defeated Spain, was an export of the genocidal campaigns against the 'savages' and 'redskins' who had inhabited North America" (92).

In a penetrating essay, "Cuba, the Philippines, and Manifest Destiny," Richard Hofstadter delineated the configuration of "psychic crisis" that mixed several elements: the jingoist expansionism of the 1890s, the imperialist ethos of duty and populist self-assertion, the disappearance of the frontier, and the bureaucratization of business amid the economic depression. In his magisterial anatomy of the evolution of the United States as a modern world power, Kolko returns us to Twain's insight in more prosaic but perspicuous and cogent language:

Violence in America antedated industrialism and urban life, and it was initially a product of an expansive rural-commercial economy that in the context of vast distance and a hastily improvised and often changing social structure saw barbarism, violence, and their toleration ritualized into a way of life. Slavery consisted of institutionalized inhumanity and an attack on the very fiber of the black's personal identity and integrity. . . . Against the Indians, who owned and occupied much coveted land, wholesale slaughter was widely sanctioned as a virtue. That terribly bloody, sordid history, involving countless tens of thousands of lives that neither victims nor executioners can ever enumerate, made violence endemic to the process of continental expansion. Violence reached a crescendo against the Indian after the Civil War and found a yet bloodier manifestation during the protracted conquest of the Philippines from 1898 until well into the next decade, when anywhere from 200,000 to 600,000 Filipinos were killed in an orgy of racist slaughter that evoked much congratulation and approval from the eminent journals and men of the era who were also much concerned about progress and stability at home. From their inception, the great acts of violence and attempted genocide America launched against outsiders seemed socially tolerated, even celebrated. Long before Vietnam, that perverse acceptance of horror helped make possible the dominating experiences of our own epoch. (*Main Currents* 286--87)

Unfortunately, this critical framework—an intellectual stance enabled not by Michel Foucault and Friedrich Nietzsche but by the now much-maligned "national liberation" struggles of Third World peoples in the sixties and seventies—has been gradually expunged from textbooks and from civic memory. But despite the neoconservative resurgence of the eighties, it is now being slowly grasped and applied in the canon-revising program of scholars in the humanities, as witnessed by the 1993 volume *Cultures of United States Imperialism,* edited by Amy Kaplan and Donald Pease, to cite one example.

Admittedly, this orientation still is rare, and even taboo, when it comes to understanding the complex cultural and literary relations between the United States and the Philippines. These relations are muddled and constrained by substantial and long-standing military, political, and financial interests, a fact that is easily confirmed by the latest negotiations over Philippine debt to the IMF/World Bank and other transnational investors. Not a few scholarly reputations and chauvinist icons also are at stake.

The major obstacle to any scientific and rigorously nuanced exploration of U.S. imperialist hegemony in the Philippines inheres in the controlling paradigm of philosophical idealism that has founded disciplines and dictated their regimes of truth. In 1992, I reviewed Stanley Karnow's book, *In Our Image: America's Empire in the Philippines* (see my *Reading the West/Writing the East*). As I argued in that review, the dominant schema is the generalizing one of culture—traditional patterns of conduct, norms, beliefs, and attitudes, together with their corresponding practices of symbolic translation and signification. Culture functions as the explanatory key to the inferiorized condition of the Filipino. That constellation of action, nexus of tropes, and *habitus* (in Pierre Bourdieu's terminology) also explains the production/reproduction of dependency relations (see Church). Reduced to a few pivotal notions like *hiya*, "mutual loyalties," internal debt (*utang na loob*), and so on, culture with its symbolic economy is divorced from its worldly or circumstantial anchorage and becomes a universal formula used to unravel affairs of extreme "thickness" and complexity.

The functionalism of deploying the patron-client dyad is not, of course, totally without value in shedding light on specific empirical phenomena. But, lacking a grasp of the historical world-system dynamics involving the asymmetrical relations between exploitative occupiers and subjugated peoples, and being devoid of a multi-sided comprehension of the unequal power relations between contending subjects who necessarily impinge on one another's physiognomies, what we have in such accounts is nothing but a banal exercise in apologetics.

From a more theoretical vantage point, Karnow's historiography may be taken as emblematic of a problem, an almost irresistible syndrome, in defining the Self via representing the Other from the Self's interested position. In this framework, the Filipino becomes both a "real" referent and a construct of invented narratives. Of half a dozen texts that have contrived the received "truths" about the Philippines and Filipinos—texts considered imperative for the constitution of the discipline called "Philippine Studies"—one may cite three that are acknowledged to be influential in informing state policies and popular consensus: William Cameron Forbes, *The Philippine Islands*; Joseph Hayden, *The Philippines: A Study in National Development*; and George Taylor, *The Philippines and the United States: Problems of Partnership*. The latter is generally construed as the Cold War primer for Filipinologists of that period.

These texts, commissioned by U.S. military and political authorities, constructed the object of knowledge and exercised mastery over it. They were, in turn, authorized by a whole panoply of practices (economic, political, cultural, and so on), hortatory and legitimizing, governing the relations between the United States as a colonial sovereign power and the subjugated inhabitants of the territory labeled "the Philippine Islands."

Conceived as one ideological apparatus mobilized for the post-Marcos era of mending "fences" and "bridges," Karnow's narrative is symptomatic. It discloses not only the U.S. Establishment's need to periodically redefine its global mission in tune with the requirements of business and geopolitical rivalries (especially in the light of its economic decline), but also reveals the urge to rewrite the past—precisely, to represent many "other" wills and actions—in order to define the "American Self" anew. Since "notions of white supremacy and superiority are very deeply embedded in all the cultural discourses developed by 'Western' thought" (Bradley 50), this act of U.S. self-definition operates within the epistemological parameter of Western civilizational supremacy. Karnow's discourse can be read as the latest in a long series of Eurocentric efforts to represent the Filipino people as a reflection of Anglo-American "manifest destiny" in its various mutations, particularly urgent at this conjuncture when U.S. ascendancy has eroded and is being challenged or threatened by other states.

Karnow's narrative reflects, of course, the hegemonic outlook, even though it claims to represent the genuine or true Filipino ethos by quoting prestigious Filipino politicians and by invoking the authority of indigenous sources and informants. A claim of impartiality or liberal latitude is subtly disposed with the collaboration of the inarticulate "others." Everyone knows, of course, that not a few subjects of the Empire have volunteered to sanction the authority of their tutors and legitimize such production of knowledge about themselves, in exchange for recognition of their identities.[1] Analysts of imperial metaphysics like Edward Said, C.L.R. James, Frantz Fanon, and others have testified to this paradoxical dependency.

What happened to this much-touted U.S. experiment in colonial entrepreneurship that claimed to produce the "showcase of U.S. democracy" in Asia after World War II? Why did it fail? About five decades ago, the great German philosopher Karl Korsch provided the explanation that everyone since has tried to ignore:

> The history of Philippine independence can hardly be told without constantly making an effort to separate the real facts and conditions from their various more or less ideological representations. It is precisely the latter which are usually considered the true history. . . . The new form of U.S. imperialism can be defined in a much more definite sense than all preced-

ing forms as an imperialism which relies on "friendly governments," puppets, Quislings, and all sorts of collaborators, including certain types of so-called resistance movements. . . . Concessions of political independence are used today for the purpose of considerably increasing, rather than decreasing, the economic and social dependence of the Philippine Republic on its Western creditors. (40, 42)

From the beginning, the entire discursive apparatus of U.S. academic scholarship has been committed to explaining the vicissitudes of this new form of refurbishing imperial suzerainty. Challenged by mounting popular resistance from the late sixties on, the rationale for U.S. support of the Marcos dictatorship for almost two decades—from President Nixon through Presidents Ford, Carter, and Reagan—has drawn its logic and rhetoric from the scholarship of American historians, political scientists, sociologists, and assorted functionaries in other disciplines. Complicit with state policies since the advent of Empire, their intellectual authority in the field of actual implementation remains to be scrutinized and evaluated.

The gravity of the crisis of Philippines-U.S. relations can be gauged by the "axe grinding" of Karnow's book. His tendentious and highly slanted summary of over eighty years of American archival labor, scrutinized to reveal the dynamics of U.S. involvement in the Philippines, has yielded only the most banal (albeit not invidious) conclusion: the effort to Americanize the Filipinos partly succeeded by introducing the *forms* of institutions like electoral democracy, mass public education, and civil service mechanisms, but it completely failed in altering traditional "Filipino" values, in particular those that invariably sanction the ubiquitous patron-client asymmetry.

Now this theme of "imperial collaboration" between the Filipino élite and the U.S. colonial administration has been a recurrent leitmotif in the canonical apologetics of U.S. diplomacy since the aforementioned works by Cameron Forbes, Hayden, and Taylor. Notwithstanding their authors' claims to objectivity, those texts now have been irretrievably compromised by the realities of poverty, social injustice, racism, and exploitation, exposed by Filipino intellectuals and activists. Among these intellectuals are Filipino writers and artists who have courageously dared to speak up and in the process duly suffered the consequences of opposing U.S. imperial oppression, from the time of the forcible annexation of the islands in 1898 through the Marcos dictatorship and its successors, its latest reincarnations.

Logos yields to the immediacy of praxis, transcendence to historical contingency. Given the intensifying menace of Filipino nationalism, which threatens to expunge once and for all the myth of Philippines-U.S. "special relations," the compulsive desideratum of contemporary U.S. scholarship on the Philippines is to reconceptualize the experience of U.S. imperial domination as a transaction of equal partnership between Filipinos and Americans. This is demonstrated by the works of David Steinberg, Theodore Friend, and Peter Stanley, among others. It is essentially an interpretive strategy to revise the canonical narrative of imperial success, based on the ontology of patronage.

This project of revaluation, what I would call a *post hoc ergo* construal of the imperial record or balance-sheet to underscore its status quo instrumentalism, would center on a refurbishing of the patron-client paradigm. The notion of reciprocal obligation that it entails arguably would serve as the theoretical framework within which one could then exorcise the burden of U.S. political and ethical responsibility for what happened in the Philippines from 1898 to 1946. This would be done by shifting the cause of the failure of American tutelage to the putative shrewdness of Filipinos in "manipulating" their masters. "We tried to do our best, but. . . ." This is the basic thesis of Peter Stanley's *A Nation in the Making: The Philippines and the United States, 1899–1921*, an updated sequel to the family of metanarratives and epistemic paradigms cited earlier. It is an argument rehearsed by Karnow and numerous replicative commentaries before and after the 1986 insurrection. A dialectical twist of historical sensibility seems to have occurred. The sharp contrast between these revisionary texts and previous works critical of U.S. imperialism—to cite only the most accessible—may be read as symptomatic of a cleavage in the élite consensus, a change in tactics attuned to the reactionary climate of opinion ascendant since the mid-seventies. (Among the earlier works critical of U.S. imperialism, the most readily available are James Blount's *The American Occupation of the Philippines* 1912, Leon Wolff's *Little Brown Brother* 1961, and Stuart Creighton Miller's *"Benevolent Assimilation": The American Conquest of the Philippines 1899–1903* 1982.)

The argument also can be conceived as a defensive mechanism set into play to counter a resurgent, nomadic movement of anti-U.S. imperialism around the world in the wake of the Vietnam debacle and revitalized popular insurgencies. These are occurring in Latin America, Africa, the Middle East, Oceania, and elsewhere (Chiapas, Mexico is the latest, as of this writing).

The issue needs to be clarified further because of its impact on post-modernist cultural politics and the function of intellectuals in the Philippines. In reviewing a volume edited by Peter Stanley entitled *Reappraising an Empire, New Perspectives on Philippine-American History*, Robert B. Stauffer acutely points to the dogmatic ideological framework employed by the new apologetic historians, cited earlier. The revisionary thrust of scholars employing the paradigm of patron-client linkage is meant to recast the exploitive relationship of dependency into a reciprocal one, wherein responsibility is equalized if not dispersed. They use this instead of a concept like dependency, or even (in the pedantic jargon) "asymmetrical relation" within the capitalist world system, with its uneven and overdetermined cartographic representation.

By downplaying any serious American influence on Philippine social structures and inflating the ingenious duplicity of the subaltern, Stauffer contends, Stanley and his colleagues make "empire" into a romantic ideology: "it is as if to give a Victorian legitimacy to past conquests and in so doing to justify . . . future imperial ventures" (103). Since a seemingly immutable patron-client template determined political life during U.S. colonial ascendancy, Filipino nationalism is relegated to the "manipulative underside of the collaborative empire." This phrase euphemistically reformulates President William McKinley's "benevolent assimilation proclamation" of 21 December 1898, the legitimating rationale of U.S. rule.

Stauffer's reservation is amplified and sharpened by Peter Tarr in another context. Reviewing Karnow's book in *The Nation*, Tarr cogently attributes the fallacy of the new apologetics to the "Immaculate Conception" view of American imperial policy as a glorious and selfless "civilizing mission." This last phrase evokes the period of a socioeconomic transition from European mercantilism to a new monopoly capitalist, international division of labor. In retrospect, one can describe this "civilizing mission" as the ideological impetus behind the march of Anglo-Saxon progress over the conquered territories and subjugated bodies of African slaves, American Indians, Mexicans, Chinese workers, and so on, from the founding of the pilgrim colonies to the closing of the western frontier at the end of the nineteenth century.

A crisis in the logic of representationalism—also known as "Orientalism," *mission civilizatrice*, "Benevolent Assimilation" (in the case of the Philippines), or Eurocentrism in general, already has overtaken this field of inquiry. Still, despite the decades that have passed since the foundational texts of Forbes, Hayden, and Taylor, not to speak of the operations of an entire range of ideological apparatuses like schools, census, civil service examinations, mass media, sports, and so on, we find their categories and repertoire of tropes and syllogisms still operational. Representative texts of recuperation are David Steinberg, *The Philippines: A Singular and a Plural Place; Crisis in the Philippines: The Marcos Era and Beyond,* edited by John Bresnan; and Claude Buss' *Cory Aquino and the People of the Philippines.*

A plethora of books on the February 1986 insurrection has tried to exploit the commercial opportunity opened by those transitional events. Even reportage on the revolutionary National Democratic Front and the New People's Army is competing for attention (for example, William Chapman's *Inside the Philippine Revolution*). Most of these works, however, are flawed by the uncritical or naive acceptance of the narrow functionalist and empiricist culturalist paradigm that claims to represent the "truth" about the dense, richly textured experience of millions of workers and peasants who have been victimized by hypothetical "special relations" that bind the United States and the Philippines.[2]

Lest I be accused of nativist chauvinism or "reverse discrimination," I hasten to interpose here the obvious caveat. I do not claim that accounts by Filipino historians, sociologists, anthropologists, and critics are more authentic and trustworthy, just because they are written by victims or "insiders." That would be patently false, both empirically and theoretically. In fact, recent work by American social scientists, such as James K. Boyce (*The Philippines: The Political Economy of Growth and Impoverishment in the Marcos Era*) and James Putzel (*Captive Land: The Politics of Agrarian Reform in the Philippines*) affords just two examples of excellent, painstaking historical analysis of the political economy of the Philippine social formation. Also noteworthy is George Weightman's critique of sociology in the Philippines. These and other recent works provide a wider and deeper comprehension of what is going on than the previous texts I have cited. An earlier monograph by Robert Stauffer, entitled *The Marcos Regime: Failure of Transnational Developmentalism and Hegemony-Building from Above and Outside,* is a brilliant model of broad and penetrating analysis that I recommend for those disgusted by academic subservience to official doxa and "conventional wisdom."

Further, one can even venture the scandalous proposition that a book originally written for popular consumption, Joseph B. Smith's *Portrait of a Cold Warrior,* affords a survey of the Filipino comprador bureaucrat-capitalist oligarchy and its élite representatives that is arguably more plausible than tomes of statistical data turned out by RAND Corporation experts and researchers for U.S. Congressional committees.

Even the enemy can be granted to possess realism to a degree sufficient to manipulate players that would produce results. Their realism is the pragmatic calculation of those in power, those determined to preserve the status quo. On the other hand, those resolved to alter that situation—one deemed unjust, painful, and inhumane by the world's conscience—would have more reason to be clear-eyed, sensitive, and cognizant of as many factors and forces in play, and on guard lest illusions of success or utopia waylay them. This, of course, is not always the case. Nevertheless, the views of Filipino protagonists (for example, those in the substantial volume *Dictatorship and Revolution: Roots of People's Power*, edited by Aurora Javate-de Dios and others) cannot be dismissed as unreliable, simply because they are partisan and committed to popular democracy, nationalist and egalitarian. What study of social phenomena does not proceed from a certain theoretical framework or set of informing assumptions?

In diametrical opposition to the sentimental and racist patronage of the commentators I cited earlier,[3] it is an immense relief and joy to find splendid accounts of recent cultural developments. These include Eugene Van Erven's *The Playful Revolution*, on the evolution of grassroots theater—the "theater of liberation" network—in the Philippines; Fredric Jameson's infinitely suggestive reading of Kidlat Tahimik's *The Perfumed Nightmare* in *The Geopolitical Aesthetic*; and Mary Bresnahan's pioneering study on the virtues of the vernacular for crosscultural communication, *Finding Our Feet*. With the current transvaluation of Establishment canons and the emergence of "Cultural Studies" with a world-system orientation, I hope that the parochialism and chauvinism of veteran "Filipinologists" (my term for scholars specializing on the Philippines) can be permanently consigned to the museum of colonial artifacts, with little loss to a new generation of students and teachers.

In an insightful and lucid essay on U.S. interventions in the Third World entitled "Political Culture and Foreign Policy," Eqbal Ahmad underscores the tradition of bargaining, cooptation, or management in American political culture for those located within the boundary of the liberal market-centered polity. For those defined outside this boundary (American Indians, blacks, and others), violence and extermination are the chosen modes of maintaining the consensus. Within this authoritarian superstructure exists "a well-defined but extremely permissive infrastructure." Displaced onto a global arena, the practice of liberal discourse (as exemplified in the texts I cited earlier) underwrites the way American experts on the Philippines have sought to reconcile the everyday violence inflicted by "free enterprise" on millions of hard-working peasants, women, and workers in all sectors. Stauffer already has explained the reality of democracy in the Philippines as "that form of intra-élite competition for office via elections during the colonial era, and under conditions where elected officials were given a great deal of symbolic public space but were denied real power which remained firmly anchored in U.S. hands" (36).[4]

Revisionist historians have suggested that the predicament of the "institutional invisibility" of Philippine studies results from the absence of any serious discussion of U.S. "imperialism" or American "exceptionalism" in the academy, as well as in the public sphere. It is widely known that American scholars of Philippine affairs have been marginalized as a function of the low geopolitical status of the Philippines on the U.S. global profit-making horizon, a status fixed by the successful hegemonic strategy of "Filipinization." U.S. President William Howard Taft's ingenious idea of "Filipinization" may indeed be taken as the originary inspiration for the current fashion of holding the victims responsible for their plight.

However, I do not think that this negligible status of American Filipinologists involves simply the question of representation, whether political, semiotic, or ethnographic. I believe that the structural cause has something to do with the persistent failure of those Filipinologists to critique the process of U.S. hegemonic rule in the Philippines that is celebrated by Karnow and his ilk, due to the nature of their training and the narrow conservatism of the profession. This is compounded with the usual compensatory reward in the "gaining mastery over others by the metropolitan intellectual" that is so integral a part of Western racist culture (which David Goldberg has so persuasively demonstrated in *Racist Culture*, 1994).

This, I submit, is the hard lesson that the Philippine "temptation"— the "civilizing mission" that has assumed a new, portentous disguise at every stage of uneven development—must reinculcate for every generation: oppositions and contradictions cannot be converted into a series of differences for the sake of celebrating multicultural or pluralist liberalism, without sacrificing the ultimate goal of socialist liberation. An aesthetics of difference is a poor substitute for a politics of creative, dialectical transformation. What makes a real difference is the moment of recognition by the millions of the powerless and disenfranchised, recognition that the world can be changed if they seize the initiative, and that the future is in their hands. Criticism is a handmaiden to this process of recognition and seizing the initiative.

A more pressing issue needs to be addressed: Is the Filipino intellectual's position one of hybridity, "part of the colonized by ancestry while aligning with the colonizer by franchise," and therefore complicitous? Is the Filipino from this angle simultaneously part of the problem and part of the solution? This putative positionality is tied to the larger problematic of laissez-faire pluralism, of the logic of possessive individualism. In this milieu, a stratified, racialized, and gendered polity is legitimized whenever "freedom" and "democracy" are brandished about. "Hybridity" is a term that one can choose or reject. But the central issue is: what is the actual alignment of power relations and political forces in which we find ourselves inserted? Given the predominance of hierarchical eclecticism, metaphysical nihilism, and other varieties of postcolonial opportunism / careerism, I am afraid the inventory of ourselves that Gramsci once prescribed (in his *Prison Notebooks*) as a preliminary and heuristic imperative might take some time to accomplish.

Meanwhile, a few modest proposals may not be entirely supererogatory. What I think is salutary is the stance of being conscious and critical of one's framework as a point of departure, oriented to analyzing events in terms of their multiple determinants, extrapolating the internal relations that comprise their differentiated and overdetermined unity, and above all demarcating their historical trajectories and assigning responsibility. In this way, the praxis of producing knowledge—one inevitably asks for what purpose? and for whom?—recognizes its determinants, its condition of possibility, in the terrain of popular struggles across class, gender, ethnicity, and so forth. Thus, we come to understand the process whereby the knower becomes an integral part of the known; the educator is educated (to rehearse the old adage) when interpretation ceases to be an end in itself and coincides with the ensemble of acts seeking to transform the world.

The acquisition of such a critical sensibility, transgressive but also simultaneously dialogic and oppositional, is an arduous task for the expropriated sensibility. Paulo Freire once taught us the elementary lesson of decolonization via "conscientization." In the same vein, Frantz Fanon outlined the vicissitudes of this Manichean ordeal in his essay,

"On National Culture," a trial of cunning and resourcefulness and endurance. What any subject of colonial bondage faces in this attempt to liberate his or her life from the mind-forged manacles of servility was poignantly intimated by the great Caribbean revolutionary thinker, C.L.R. James. He wrote how the colonial myth of Western supremacy, so deeply ingrained in the subjugated psyche, is so difficult to disgorge: "It is not that the myth is not challenged. It is, but almost always on premises that it has itself created, premises that (as with all myths) rest on very deep foundations within the society that has created them" ("Colonialism and National Liberation," 109). Demystification of idols and their dethronement then becomes the first order of the day.

Historical experience teaches us that some idols may endure, as long as capitalism and its variants survive their periodic and ineluctable crises. In the spectrum of reactive responses to the ravages of white supremacy, the most common seems to be the nativist glorification of traditional pieties, archaic customs, and tributary rituals, often labeled by well-intentioned educators as "Filipino values." These values are then privileged to be what distinguishes the warm organic community of the pristine countryside as the authentic homeland, counterposed to the alienating, diabolic, and strife-torn Westernized cities. This type of "nationalism" is understandable but scarcely defensible. Of late, that archaic essentialism has given way to the cult of the hybrid and heterogeneous, the indeterminate and fragmented—in short, of the decentered subjectivity.

In this postmodern context, should we Filipinos then make a virtue of the colonial predicament, celebrating hybrid and syncretic subjectivity as our autochthonous sublime? Disavowing the perils of essentialism and Eurocentric "grand narratives," we sometimes succumb to the sirens of postmodern anomie in our endeavor to affirm our dignity, our identity and tradition, our right to self-determination. There is something provocative, self-gratifying, and obscene in the characteristic gesture of "postcolonized" intellectuals embracing their schizoid and amphibious fate as a virtue, or at best as a springboard for future nomadic quests. On the other hand, the transnational corporate system can utilize this posture of sophistication to promote tourism and its profitable exploitation of spectacle.[5]

This valorization of the fissured and sedimented identity of the "Filipino"—of any survivor of imperial tutelage, for that matter—is symptomatic of over four hundred years of colonial oppression and resistance. It may be read as the trademark of intellectuals uprooted from the popular-democratic struggles of the masses of people, whose aspirations for freedom and dignity demand the prior satisfaction of basic needs as a fundamental human right. In this era of flexible, disaggregated capitalism, we as a nation-in-the-making seem still to be on the threshold of modernity, still constructing allegories of the birth of *Pilipinas* (discussed in Chapter 7), a process of collective work and imagination aborted by Admiral Dewey's incursion into Manila Bay.

One is reminded here of how Jose Rizal, martyred for his alleged complicity in the 1896 insurrection against Spain, envisioned the coming of the Americans in that prescient and uncanny polemic he wrote, addressed to the liberal Spaniards of his time, "The Philippines A Century Hence." His prediction was tentative and hesitant, a reflection of his own personal contingencies and a testimony to the role of accidents in history. But he set an example by taking as much of everything into account. In a letter of 27 June 1888 to his compatriot Mariano Ponce, concerning the criteria of literary judgment, Rizal wrote: "... *a veces con una mala literatura pueden decirse verdades grandes*" (Jolipa 338). Put another way, flawed writing can deliver relentless, truth-bearing blows for emancipation.

It is a platitude to say now that, although Rizal was deeply rooted in his time, he was able to transcend it because he always strove to attain a totalizing view of human affairs; he always contextualized any perception, idea, or belief in the thickness of concrete historical circumstances. As illustrated in his novels and in his own life, he pursued this method, mindful of the circulation of social energies in structures and actions, the movement of these energies through contradictions and antagonisms, personified by classes and groups imbricated in the totality of overlapping and changing modes of social production and reproduction.

In the spirit of Rizal's prophetic reconnaissance, I survey in this book the tracks of the Filipino imagination as it bodily crossed the Pacific Ocean and implanted itself in the North American continent—the migrant-worker's dream of success, enacted by individual artists named Jose Garcia Villa, Carlos Bulosan, and so forth. This saga of deracination and exile is still going on, exacerbated, in fact, by the "warm-body export" of Filipino labor. This circulation of bodies is a result of the immense disarticulation of the local economy by the depredations of the Marcos dictatorship and the avarice of its transnational patrons. This global phenomenon of the plight of female domestic contract workers now is epitomized by Flor Contemplacion, recently executed by the

Singapore government; by Sarah Balabagan, accused of killing her rapist master in Saudi Arabia; and by countless victims of flexible, postFordist capital accumulation.

Certainly, this diaspora of Filipinos to the Middle East, Europe, Japan, Canada, and all over the planet has "decentered" the United States from its privileged position as goal and destination of immigrants. But the inaugural narratives of the Filipino experience in these locales have yet to be composed, circulated, and appraised. Meanwhile, we have to sum up the achievement of Filipino writers in the United States and accomplish a cognitive mapping of the archive, as well as the geopolitical space, to overcome the limits of the politics of ethnic identity. After self-affirmation comes solidarity.

Crossing boundaries and frontiers of fear and hope, we return to native ground: free fire zones, contested and compromising terrain of warring hearts and minds, the homeland as permanent battleground.

The legacy of the past centuries of colonialism has proved horrifying and almost insurmountable. Of about sixty-nine million Filipinos today, 72 percent are extremely impoverished, scattered throughout 7,100 islands once endowed with abundant natural resources but now regarded as one almost unrelieved ecological disaster. In 1950, the country had 52 million hectares of tropical forest; now only a million hectares remain (Tauli-Corpuz). In the primate city of Manila, 38 percent live below the poverty line; 40 percent inhabit substandard squatter settlements. Almost 40 percent of the entire work force is unemployed or underemployed. The country has one of the lowest per capita incomes and one of the lowest wage rates in the world. Its people are the second-most malnourished in the whole world, despite the country being a top producer and exporter of food, minerals, and one of the most vital resources for transnational capital: between 4 to 6 million migrant workers. With a per capita income of $2,300 (gross domestic product), the Philippines is easily ranked the poorest in the region. Aside from rising unemployment, inflation and high prices of basic foods, lack of capital goods industries, corruption in government, and a huge foreign debt, the immediate prospect for amelioration of the lot of the majority is practically nil.

The major source of political and economic inequality in Filipino society, all recent studies concur, is the control of land and other resources by an oligarchic minority who also manipulate the bureaucracy, the

legislature, courts, and the military to preserve their power and privileges. (Former President Corazon Aquino's family counts among the
most wealthy.) State power in a disarticulated formation like the Philippines encroaches deeply into the trenches and ramparts of civil society.
Consequently, the sphere of private life, even the recesses of the psyche,
cannot be considered an inviolable refuge of peace, rational communication, and liberty.

It is primarily owing to U.S. support of this parasitic and moribund
élite since the turn of the century that fifty-four million Filipinos, according to human rights lawyer Romeo Capulong, "will never forget
that it was U.S. tanks, guns, bullets, bombs, planes and even chemicals
that the Philippine military used to kill them." Hundreds of political
prisoners still languish in jails, now classified as common criminals,
according to Amnesty International reports. U.S. low-intensity warfare,
initiated by the Reagan administration, proceeds with little impedi-
ment (Klare and Kornbluh 158–82). Senator Wigberto Tañada warned
us recently:

> Despite the demise of the Cold War, nuclear-armed U.S. naval vessels
> continue to make port calls in the Philippines. A prepositioning agreement
> between the Clinton and Ramos governments is quietly being negotiated
> to pave the way for continued U.S. military access to Philippine territory,
> despite the clear-cut prohibition against this kind of deployment of foreign
> forces by the Philippine Constitution. (5)

The much ballyhooed "Philippines 2000" promoted by President Ramos
as a scheme to convert the Philippines into a newly industrialized country (NIC), underwritten by the IMF / World Bank and transnational corporations, is bound to worsen the plight of ordinary working people
and deepen the stagnation all around (see BAYAN International). In
my opinion, transitory reform from above neither can alter deeply entrenched property relations, nor effect a redistribution of wealth and
power, without sustained and voluntary mass participation. Only the
perseverance and sacrifice of popular-democratic forces across the spectrum can give hope to the masses for improvement of their everyday
lives, vindication of their exuberant spirit, and renewal of their integrity
and dignity. These forces include the Moro, Lumads, and Igorots, with
their long record of anticolonial intransigence (Bauzon; Rodil; Scott) in
wars of position and maneuver; the left-wing progressive bloc, the most
durable of which have been National Democratic Front and the Com-

munist Party–led New People's Army; militant women's organizations; national student and youth formations; radical intelligensia; and the volatile petty bourgeois, middle stratum.

Despite the government's claim that insurgent forces had declined from a peak strength of 25,000 armed combatants in the mid-1980s to about 8,000 in the early 1990s, the reality disavows the illusion of peace. The material conditions that fuel oppression and exploitation remain and, as noted, have even worsened. Meanwhile, the old "mole" keeps burrowing, crafting new weapons, drawing up an inventory, planning for the next offensive. There seems to be no alternative but refusal and insurgency, always bearing in mind too that (as Father Edicio de la Torre puts it) "politics is a choice among realities, among possibilities"— a condition of indeterminacy that provokes mass popular-democratic interventions.

The culture of Filipino resistance possesses a long, durable memory, drawing sustenance from four centuries of anti-imperialist rebellion against Spain, the United States, and Japan. We can go back to Father Jose Burgos and the 1872 martyrs, to Rizal and the *propagandistas,* and to Apolinario Mabini's audacity, evoked in this statement from his letter to General J. F. Bell (dated 31 August 1900):

> I hope the Americans will understand that the present state of culture of the Filipino people shall not put up with subjugation by force as a permanent condition. The Filipinos may be vanquished now and again, but as long as they are denied every kind of right, there will not be lasting peace. (99)

Salud Algabre, leader of the 1935 Sakdal uprising, attests to this insurrectionary legacy:

> We did what we ourselves [peasants masses] had decided upon—as free people, and power resides in the people. What we did was our heritage. . . . We decided to rebel, to rise up and strike down the sources of power. I said "We are Sakdals! We want immediate, complete, and absolute independence." No uprising fails. Each one is a step in the right direction. (Sturtevant 165)

I know of only one progressive American writer who succeeded in capturing this irrepressible Filipino desire for liberation. In his 1951 quasi-documentary novel, *Fortress in the Rice,* Benjamin Appel transcribes the underlying "structure of feeling" that inspired and sustained the prodigious ambition of the Hukbalahap rebellion *(People's Army Against the Japanese)*:

For blowing around that bowl of rice there was a sighing wind made up of the whispers, the laments, the passions of generations. A wind that had blown across the rice provinces for half a century. The wind of freedom, Luis Taruc had called it. For who had fought with the Katipuneros against the Spaniards in 1896 but the peasants? Who were the Colorums, years later, swearing that Jose Rizal would return like a second Christ to divide the land? Who the Sakdals of the 1930s, believing that Japan would send her fleets to Manila to liberate her brother Asiatics from the mestizo landlords? A wind of many names, a wind that would never stop. For who could stop the wind could stop the soul of man. (77)

This tradition of revolt, as dramatized and allegorized in literary texts and theoretical discourses inventoried here, refutes the "postcolonial" argument that subaltern identities cannot speak, are paralyzed by permanent psychic crisis, and are hostage to a past of betrayals and missed opportunities. A "negation of negations" is the desideratum here, prior to collective self-affirmation.

The restoration of élite democracy in 1896 ushered in a new stage for the revival of neocolonial apparatuses of domination to which I alluded earlier, agencies of hegemonic rule designed to underwrite the nation's protracted dependency on the accumulation strategy of transnational business. The comprador-oligarchic élite retains the same qualities discerned by Pedro Abad Santos during the thirties: "It is timid because it is aware of its weakness. It is ignorant, for even its intellectual leaders lack understanding of advanced political and economic thought" (Allen 65). Western bourgeois values persist in saturating the mass media, fostering consumerism and the self-indulgent lifestyles glamorized by U.S. music, films, advertisements, and one-dimensional popular culture in general. Patriarchal and authoritarian habits pervade the organs of the state and the institutions of civil society. Commodification is the modernizing engine running over all.

From this perspective, the censorship of films like Lino Brocka's *Orapronobis* can be considered a symptom of the shriveled "democratic space" for oppositional practices (just as the confiscation by the military of Behn Cervantes' film *Sakada* in the seventies signaled the enlarged role of underground cultural activity). However, the cultivation of anti-communist religious fundamentalism that flourished for a while with the Aquino-sponsored "vigilante" groups has been displaced with other forms of "low-intensity warfare" against liberationist formations. Splittist and divisive tendencies in the progressive organizations are being fomented by the counterinsurgency agencies and hirelings of the

government. Ongoing are unwarranted arrests of activists, militarization of villages and towns, and extrajudicial summary execution of suspected subversives. Political prisoners are multiplying, with the courts
functioning as instruments of the military and the oligarchy. Schools
and the mass media continue to shape cultural policy that is geared to
supply cheap labor for the global market, particularly for despotic Middle Eastern sheikdoms as well as for the domestic needs of Singapore,
Hong Kong, and the sex-entertainment industries of Japan.

Meanwhile, the popular forces—sectoral groups of peasants, workers, women, ethnic communities, youth, teachers, religious communities, professionals, government employees, and so on—are inventing
new initiatives to fill the vacuum created by the dissolution of the Cory
mystique and the more flagrant exposure of the bankruptcy of any successor regime. Oligarchic comprador rule, though moribund, still prevails, mainly by virtue of inertia and manipulation of the divisions
among the oppressed. The exhausted logic of cynical compromise formerly indulged by *trapos* (traditional politicians) now is being artifi-
cially revived by its sponsors from Japan, Hong Kong, Taiwan, and
assorted surrogates of the United States. Aquino's victims point the
way to future emancipatory projects far beyond the ironic recuperation
of "people power" for profit and class-conflicted peace, far beyond any
mock-utopian promise of "Philippines 2000."

Everyone by now has realized that Corazon Aquino stood not for real
change but only for the restoration of the status quo—this time much
worse than even before Marcos declared martial law in 1972, because of
the electoral facade that now exists. We thus have reached a turning
point in our itinerary of collective self-discovery. Systematic violation of
human rights and impoverishment of workers and peasants worsened
in the years of the Aquino presidency. With the failure of the Aquino
regime in stabilizing an élite conservative order, the movement for revolutionary socialist transformation has to renew its project of shaping
a national-popular agenda of land reform, autonomy for indigenous
peoples, vindication of the victims of military-landlord abuses, and a
sweeping redistribution of wealth. Whatever strategy is pursued to
achieve such long-range goals—all means are necessary, provided that
the masses support them—the plotting of mass mobilization is itself
overdetermined by the changed landscape of post–Cold War global
alignments.

In my *Crisis in the Philippines* (written before the 1986 February uprising) as well as in subsequent books—*Writing and National Liberation* and *Allegories of Resistance*, to mention only the most recent—I attempted to outline those possibilities for renewal in the face of the dogmatisms of the past, suspicions of the present, and uncertainties of the future. Within this framework, it appears certain that the fate of U.S. cultural hegemony, as well as U.S. business, cultural, and political interests, soon will be decided. The breakthrough in the impasse will transpire with the unfolding of diverse social antagonisms, primarily by the action of the Filipino masses, in the first decades of the twenty-first century.

Meanwhile, democratic socialist thinking inspired by C. L. R. James, Fanon, Gramsci, and others is being "supplemented," enriched, and historicized by post-structuralist modes of analysis, including analytic marxism, socialist feminism, and world-system analysis. The postcolonial or postmodern alternative is arguably one possible route, not the best in my judgment, to arrive at the correct bearing—correct, that is, in the interest of advancing popular-democratic transformations (Dirlik; McClintock). After all the detours and zigzags, the responsibility of cultural activists (literary critics included) and organic intellectuals of the people remains clear: *to participate with the masses in the discovery and charting of the Filipino road to national liberation and socialist reconstruction in the next millennium.*

The Philippines, a country undergoing profound social and political transformations, exemplifies a Third World society where the major contradictions of our time—forces embodying the categories of class, ethnicity, gender, nationality, religion, sexuality, and so on—converge into a fissured and disjunctive panorama (both discursive and practical) that is open for interpretation, critique, and ecumenical exchanges. This book endeavors to survey this field via a radical critique of Philippines-U.S. literary contacts, transactions, and displacements. At the same time, it endeavors to express a Third World perspective on the impact of Eurocentric power (specifically the United States) on a hitherto unexplored indigenous tradition of protest and resistance. This work seeks to elucidate the ruses and stratagems of hegemonic ideology, its encounter with oppositional discourses and cultural practices, foregrounding in the process the creative and critical power of those victimized by the political economy of accumulation and its oppressive racist-patriarchal technologies.

What this counterhegemonic narrative hopes to valorize is the emancipatory project of Filipino artists, incarnating a popular-democratic vision and praxis of national liberation that is attuned to the multilayered struggles of other oppressed, subjugated, and exploited peoples, wherever they are found. With the Philippines as a figure for the revolutionary impulse everywhere, one then can conceive of the cultural production of two-thirds of the planet's inhabitants—people of color in Africa, Asia, and Latin America, as well as the "internal colonies" in the developed industrialized societies—as indivisible from their struggle for empowerment, for self-determination, justice, and the affirmation of dignity.

These heterogeneous projects of resistance and revolt, inscribed in poems, stories, *testimonios,* and other performances of those formerly silenced and made invisible, are what ultimately reproduce the "Third World" as a permanent political-cultural agency of global transformation (San Juan, "Tresspassing Letters"). As I have said with reference to texts like Philip Vera Cruz's autobiography, these performances can be used to fashion emancipatory constituent subjects who are equipped with "a memory of the future," a recollection of hopes and dreams from which the future is extrapolated. They can restore to primacy the value-creating practice of associative labor, the power of the multitude (first theorized by Baruch Spinoza), including the network of productive cooperation that generates society and legitimizes the state. They can help recover the rights of racialized collectivities (especially in the United States and Europe) that are marginalized or excluded by the bourgeois system of contracts, laws privileging private property, and the elaborate network of commodification, so as to renew the revolutionary practice of the masses—the autonomy, productivity, and the constitutive drive (*conatus*) of people of color.

This axiom bears reiteration even when it has become dangerously commonplace, as circumstances warrant: wherever there is imperial domination in any form or disguise, there will always be a "Third World" protagonist fighting for national-popular liberation, whether in Haiti, Somalia, East Timor, Mexico, Hawaii, Palestine, the Philippines, or elsewhere.

1

"Civilize 'em with a Krag":
Errand to the Boondocks[1]

No uprising fails. Each one is a step in the right direction.
  —*Salud Algabre, 1966*

The bourgeois revolution has not been completed and left the feudal landlord
system almost untouched. . . . On our part we are doing everything to arouse
the class consciousness and revolutionary spirit of the masses, especially the
peasants.
  —*Jose Abad Santos, 1937*

The revolution is inevitable. . . . If an armed conflict does arise, we will fight
alongside with the men. . . .
  —*Maria Lorena Barros, circa 1975*

Reconnaissance

In E. L. Doctorow's *Ragtime*, during the expedition to the North Pole, Father tended to agree with explorer Peary who, although he had "adopted the Esquimo way of life" in pursuit of the conquest of Nature by Science and Will, treated the Eskimos "like children." This "suggested a consensus. He recalled an observation made in the Philippines ten years before where he had fought under General Leonard F. Wood against the Moro guerrillas. Our little brown brothers have to be taught a lesson, a staff officer had said, sticking a campaign pin in a map" (83).

Several chapters later, the Black protagonist Coalhouse Walker blows up the Emerald Isle Engine Station House. Father registers his misrecognition of this "tragedy," and a nostalgic reflex unfolds the source of his disintegrating patriarchal control: "He had taken from his bureau drawer his old army pistol from the Philippine campaign" (241). We return to the theme of the historicity of the imagination—both the conqueror's and the conquered's—caught in the dialectics of the well-nigh untotalizable encounter.

Almost a century now after Admiral George Dewey defeated the Spanish flotilla in Manila Bay, and about ninety since Father's castration trauma, the "Fathers" in Washington today (circa 1986) were haunted by an incipient nightmare. They twisted in their sleep at the possible "loss" of those islands in the western Pacific—more specifically, the "loss" of several strategic military bases and installations (for background, see Garcia and Nemenzo 1988). They bewailed President Corazon Aquino's lack of will to mount a massive counterinsurgency campaign against the revolutionary forces that, for over thirteen years, had prepared the February 1986 uprising that toppled the U.S.-backed Marcos dictatorship.[2] Today, the Pentagon is maneuvering to obtain an "Acquisition and Cross-Servicing Agreement" to replace the bases lost in 1991. From all accounts, scholarly and journalistic, over half a century of U.S. cultural hegemony over this erstwhile U.S. colony has not completely eradicated the virus of the desire and drive for popular self-determination. The dogma of laissez-faire business and corporate liberalism is on the defensive.

With the emergence of revolutionary nationalism in the Philippines in the last three decades, the fate of élite-controlled democracy introduced by the United States has hung precariously in the balance. Very few progressive American scholars have preoccupied themselves with a study of the genealogy and vicissitudes of this crisis. It is somewhat of a minor scandal that no American intellectual of stature has expended energy to investigate exactly how "humane letters" were used for over half a century to "Americanize" and pacify the only U.S. colony in Asia. (William Dean Howells, Twain's contemporary, probably was the first and last to take notice of a major Filipino writer.)

In the last two decades, I have proposed numerous research projects—often turned down by foundations and other funding agencies—to inquire into what role U.S. literary practice performed in assisting and enforcing U.S. colonial domination of the Philippines in the first three decades, up to the Philippine Commonwealth and the eve of World War II: which writers? which texts? Before an inventory of the "usable past" can be drawn up, a process of interrogation needs to be charted along this line:

- How did U.S. canonical texts propagate certain beliefs, attitudes, and dispositions that reconciled Filipinos to their subordination?
- How did Filipinos respond to subjectifying modes of U.S. ideological apparatuses, particularly schooling, and various instrumentalities that affected family life, sexuality, religious practices, and so on?
- How and why did U.S. literary values and ideals continue to exert a powerful influence on the Filipino intelligentsia throughout half a century, producing in some an acquiescent or adaptive response, yet in others a critical reaction?
- After the grant of formal independence in 1946, what elements in U.S. cultural theory and practice continued to extract consent (backed by coercive suasion such as jobs, public recognition, and so forth) and collaboration from Filipino intellectual circles?

These key questions target the crucial themes and problematics of intercultural analysis, in particular the nexus and liaison between history and the modern sensibility, which is mortgaged to the absolute centrality of the utilitarian marketplace. Given the historical context outlined earlier, I foreground the dialectical exchange of sensibilities and intellectual horizons crystallized in "diachronic structures" of interhistoricity / intertextuality, which Claudio Guillen privileges as the real object of inquiry for comparatists. Consequently, my research program intends to approximate the paradox of *Weltliteratur* as a plurality of distinct cultural practices characterized by fruitful tensions, disparities, and contradictions (more on this in the concluding chapter).

Given the crisis of a deformed liberal-democratic order and the persistence of an authoritarian ethos that pervades civil society, the fate of U.S. "humane letters" is now being decided in the political arena. Are the writings of Emerson, Faulkner, Hemingway, as well as popularly sanctioned culture-heroes (Elvis Presley, Madonna) a force of repression or a catalyst for liberation?

In the massive sociopolitical upheaval that is overtaking Filipinos, it has become clear that the condition of possibility for U.S. hegemony is the erasure of its imperial history, even as this history continues to erode and undermine the life-chances of people of color everywhere. For example: should Filipino writing in English continue to be judged by Euro-American criteria? Moreover, the intransigent nationalism of the last three decades, though temporarily attenuated, has jeopardized the status and future of English as a literary medium of expression for Filipinos. The crisis of American literature and its influence in this tropic "borderland" is irreversible. Today, when the autotelic text has been displaced by the authorless practice of postmodern *écriture*, this argument is no longer extravagant nor disturbing to the connoisseurs of the multiculturalist and ecletic supermall of ideas.

Although thousands of Filipinos migrate every year to the United States in quest of that fabled Hollywood "dream of success," nearly seventy million Filipinos remain, mostly peasants and workers. The plebeians are not reading *Reader's Digest* or the *New York Review of Books*; they seem innocent of Bellow's novels, of William Bennett's crusade for the return of the Great Books of the Western Tradition, and of the New Pragmatism of the fashionable academic circles, not to speak of the "politically correct" Establishment apologists of the "New World Order." Why has the putative experiment in U.S.-style democracy failed? More to the point, did it ever succeed in the first place? Can American-style deconstruction and new historicist pragmatism shore up the ruins of the Empire by refurbishing the racist and technocratic strategies tested in the Empire days of *Ragtime?* Is a transnational, postmodern version of Benevolent Assimilation being crafted in the guise of "low intensity warfare"?

Tracking the Fault Lines

When "contact" (to use the euphemism) was made with the inhabitants of the Philippines during the Spanish-American War of 1898, the *fin de siècle* protagonists of the metropole experienced a conjuncture of two antithetical trends. These are summed up in a confession by William Allen White in his *Autobiography:* he was bound to his "idols—Whitman, the great democrat, and Kipling, the imperialist." Historian Richard Hofstadter, in his provocative analysis of that milieu, points out the coalescence of the "rhetoric of Duty and Destiny," of *Realpolitik*, and of the Calvinistic sense of mission (Americans as "master organizers of the world") (158).

According to President McKinley, "Duty determines destiny"—that is, the moral imperative sanctioned by U.S. expansionist drive and this "national and 'racial' inheritance" was in turn justified by an invocation of historical necessity, of God (Vidal; see also Nearing and Freeman; Jones). Symptomatic of this metonymy of apocalypse and capital accumulation (an index of the Will to Power with a social-Darwinist inflection) is McKinley's address to a group of Protestant clergy in August 1898. Listen to this portion of the inaugural discourse of Manichean liberalism:

> The truth is I didn't want the Philippines and when they came to us as a gift from the gods, I did not know what to do about them. . . . I walked the floor of the White House night after night until midnight; and I am not ashamed to tell you gentlemen, that I went down on my knees and prayed Almighty God for light and guidance more than one night. And one night late it came to me this way—I don't know how it was, but it came: (1) that we could not give them back to Spain—that would be cowardly and dishonorable; (2) that we could not turn them over to France or Germany—our commercial rivals in the Orient—that would be bad business and discreditable; (3) that we could not leave them to themselves—they were unfit for self-government—and they would soon have anarchy and misrule over there worse than Spain's was; and (4) that there was nothing left for us to do but to take them all, and by God's grace do the very best that we could by them, as our fellowmen for whom Christ also died. And then I went to bed, and to sleep and slept soundly. (Zinn, *People's History* 305–06)

That "sleep of Reason" begot both dreams and nightmares. The quest for empire—for a subject race upon whom to impose civilization, and thus reaffirm one's self-identical rationality—finds an Archimedean point in McKinley's claim of receiving a charismatic assignment. This revelation occurs in the framework of a moral dilemma staged as spectacle and climaxed with a message-laden vision. It accords with the Puritan "errand into the wilderness"—conceived as a divinely mandated mission to redeem fallen, profane humankind.

Whatever vagaries and ambiguities surrounded subsequent U.S. negotiations with General Aguinaldo, then president of the embattled first Philippine Republic, U.S. policy required military force to destroy the Filipino revolutionary army and to suppress the subsequent guerilla insurgents that sustained the anticolonial resistance until the end of this century's first decade. In the same breath, promises of future independence after a period of tutelage were regularly offered (Miller; Sheridan). Violence was thus the midwife of Philippine dependency and underdevelopment.

In the first thirteen years of U.S. rule, the preeminent task was to build the administrative machinery of the colonial state over what was perceived, in the anthropological wisdom of that time, as the tribal and kinship particularisms of traditional society. For this purpose, the major instrument harnessed was the ideological apparatus of mass education. The colonial administration imposed compulsory public education and sponsored a *pensionado* system to train natives for the lower echelons of the bureaucracy. U.S. tutelage also established a juridical system based on "free labor," procedural-judicial review of contracts, restricted civil service examinations, and an entrepreneurial ethos premised on the right of private ownership of the means of production. Exchange value began to displace use value, even while serfdom or tributary relations persisted throughout the islands.

But in the implementation of colonial policy, contradictory tendencies surfaced—symptoms of the overdetermined imperial formation. We encounter the Jeffersonian outlook of David Barrows, Ph.D. in anthropology from the University of Chicago, who served as Philippine Secretary of Education from 1903–09, juxtaposed with the vocational orientation of succeeding administrators who prevailed from 1910 forward. Barrows candidly espoused a premonopoly vision rooted in the agrarian past, a bias uncannily resurrecting itself in the programatic New Criticism of John Crowe Ransom and Allen Tate, theoreticians of the antebellum Southern legacy (more on this in the succeeding chapters). Barrows argues for a patrician authority exercised by a managerial élite:

> The [Filipino] race lends itself naturally and without protest to the blind leadership of aristocracy. . . . I believe we should . . . seek to develop in the Philippines, not a proletariat, but everywhere the peasant proprietor. . . . Wherever we find the Filipino the possessor of his own small holding there we find him industrious and contributing largely to the productive industry of the islands. (May 98; Veneracion 58–66)[3]

While this view allowed the works of the "Fireside Poets" (Longfellow, Holmes, Whittier, Lowell, Bryant) to spread a diluted eighteenth-century rationalism mixed with romantic Puritanism, it fostered chiefly a literary curriculum that laid the foundation for liberal ideological practices in the Filipino élite sensibility. An individualistic ethos was deployed to counter the collective project of inventing the Filipino nation.

After seven years of this belletristic curriculum under Barrows, the colonial administration returned to a distinctly utilitarian pedagogy more directly synchronized with the need to produce skilled and semi-skilled workers for the development of extractive industries and infrastructures, particularly means of communication and transportation. It was also necessary to staff the lower ranks of the bureaucracy with natives who would reproduce the *habitus* of hierarchical social relations. One commentator evaluates the effect of U.S. educational policy and program in this period: "The tragedy of the U.S. educational effort was that, despite benevolent intentions, the Bureau of Education prepared Filipinos neither for citizenship nor for productive labor" (May 99).

One survivor of this period, Fernando Leaño (born 1905) recounts the writers assigned in the grade schools: Shelley, Arnold, Elizabeth Barrett Browning, Amy Lowell, Longfellow, "all the Horatio Alger and Pollyanna books" (Alegre and Fernandez 121–29).[4] To be sure, neither Mark Twain's anti-imperialist fables nor Herman Melville's ironic allegories, much less the satire and criticism of the Naturalists (Norris, Crane), were broadcast by the first Peace Corps volunteers who came years later, elementary and high school teachers from all parts of the United States. Pedagogy dovetailed with state policies and market mechanisms of the first three decades. The ideological state apparatus of the primary and intermediate schools mainly functioned to imprint and reinforce the image of Americans as masters in command of a language, together with the knowledge and power invested in it, that the natives must learn to measure up to the colonizer's superior standards. Orthodox historians refer to this process of linkage between metropolitan state and peripheral civil society—that is, the interpellation of natives so as to identify them as colonial subjects—as "tutelage."[5]

One tactic of U.S. hegemonizing strategy can be cited at this point. The appropriation of Jose Rizal (1861–96), his personality, and his writings by the U.S. ideological apparatus exemplifies how the transition from a tributary or quai-feudal formation to a capitalist setup (or more exactly, comprador system) converts texts into sites of political contestation. U.S. consensus-building undermined the nationalist opposition by assimilating parts of its world view and using them to legitimize imperial ascendancy.

While Rizal attacked religious dogmatism and Spanish tyranny, he stressed the ideals of the European Enlightenment that already had become the proclaimed doctrine of Yankee business evangelism and world commerce—the ideals of individual effort, rational calculation, material progress, and civic virtue. U.S. administrators then constructed an image of Rizal as totally committed to Westernization from the heterogeneous materials at hand, circulating this image as the representation of the enlightened, autonomous, self-respecting Filipino. He was thus constructed as "the national hero." This worked versatilely within the cooptative machinery of Taft's "Filipinization," drawing elements of the nationalist intelligentsia and defusing any anti-imperialist resentment.

During the same period when Rizal was thus made to serve as an instrument of colonial legitimation, two documents, purportedly from the pre-Hispanic period (the Code of Maragtas and the Code of Kalantiaw) were released and publicized for local consumption. Doing so claimed for the precolonial tributary culture a purchase on practically all the puritanical virtues of restraint, hard work, hierarchical decorum, family piety, and so forth. (An analogous pedagogy is being purveyed currently by proponents of authentic Filipino "family values," a populist or folkloric essentialism with dire regressive implications.) Widely propagated in school textbooks and government propaganda, these documents were later revealed to be forgeries. But no public debate or national self-examination ensued. Whether genuine or fraudulent, they fulfilled their role in helping to discipline the natives to conform to the new configuration of power relations.

Here we confront a nexus of seemingly antithetical or deterritorializing trends: on the one hand, Rizal the heretical subversive becomes public property, his writings codified into precepts for good law-abiding citizens. And on the other, forgeries initially authenticated by the Filipino élite and its U.S. patron gradually become an integral component of the national heritage. Exchange of fetishes produces the subaltern subject in which elements of the revolutionary past are incorporated by the state and sublated to function as the rationale for citizenship. This status of ideological subjugation is actualized by the selling of one's privately owned labor power, for the alienation of body and spirit under the aegis of local comprador and U.S. monopoly accumulation. In the context of U.S. tutelage, the phantasmal identity of Filipino intellectual production coincides with the reification of social relations in the general exchange of cultural commodities: Rizal, the aforementioned Codes, textbooks on hygiene and sexual decorum, and so on.

The strategy of tutelage thus normalized colonial relations as a learning process of accommodation or adjustment. What is this tutelage but a euphemism for the self-reproducing apparatus of colonial discourse, conforming to the requirements of capital accumulation? Its goal was to implant an entrepreneurial rationality in colonial subjects in response to the demand for efficient, functionally literate workers needed for the production of surplus value and the reproduction of dependency norms. But this disciplinary regime had to be modified for the uneven terrain of a Third World formation with basically tributary social practices, oriented by ritual and organic kinship and client-patron ties.

A hybrid mutation materialized. The prevailing production relations, based largely on tenancy and plantation agriculture, plus the patronage network they entailed, subverted any claim of the colonial administration that it promoted individuals on the basis of merit, skill, and performance. What resulted throughout this period of direct U.S. rule was the entrenchment of an oligarchy, a conglomerate of cacique-dominated clans. Their electoral success was premised on property ownership (ground rent, landed estates of patrimonial domain) and their access to the channels of colonial privilege. This structural imbalance was aggravated by the self-perpetuation of a native bureaucracy whose functionaries were supplied by the schools founded precisely to accomplish the homogenizing and regulatory imperatives spelled out earlier.

In this context, the imposition of English as the official medium of instruction, business, and government, ostensibly to make Filipinos "citizens of the world," formed part of an elaborate machinery of pacification and the installation of hegemony. Secretary Barrows explained the value of the knowledge of English as a force contributing "to the emancipation of the dependent classes . . . which is necessary to the maintenance of a liberal government" (May 110). Unfortunately, he failed to take into account the constraints of economic and social inequalities generated by the very educational mechanisms he commanded.

Behind the facade of a civil service system presumably based on merit, a half-century of learning English (1900–46) yielded only the perpetuation of serfdom in the countryside, where seventy-five percent of the population still live. It brought about the disintegration of the nationalist confluence of people and intelligentsia that had been achieved temporarily during the 1896 revolution and the Filipino-American War. It promoted the alienation of the English-using intellectuals from workers and peasants who spoke the demotic vernacular. By the time of formal independence in 1946, the instrumentality of English as a non-neutral means of imperialist domination had already demonstrated its pedagogical efficacy precisely by this spurious claim to bestow the privilege of access to [Western] civilization. At the same time, it concealed its effect of continuing to disintegrate the fragile identity of the native, fragmenting the nationalist-popular culture in the process of emergence, and reinforcing illusions of progress and democracy within the framework of "U.S.-Philippines special relations."

Just as the French language became for France's overseas departments (colonies) the self-legitimizing vehicle for the reproduction of colonial relations, English and its mormalized usage became the indispensable mechanism by which the United States subordinated the Filipino masses to the profit-making operations of corporate business, the policy of "free trade" supervised by U.S. finance capital. When the U.S. transport *Thomas* left San Francisco for the Philippines in July 1901 with its cargo of six hundred teachers (precursors of Peace Corps, AID experts, and other secular evangelists), that event offered cogent proof of the primacy of institutions that control knowledge-production and circulation of information in the service of the necolonial state.

In the first two decades, state construction enjoyed high priority. The immediate problem was suppression of guerilla resistance and sporadic revolts throughout the islands, together with the training of functionaries to facilitate the export of the islands' cash crops (sugar, hemp, tobacco) and extracted minerals. Thus, the colonial schooling apparatus accordingly mobilized elements from the ideology of social Darwinism and the ideal of private self-cultivation (glorified in puritan homilies on individual perseverance and hard work) toward the goal of pacification.[6] The substance of U.S. civil religion began to take root in erstwhile inhospitable ground.

Mapping the Tropical Arcadia

In 1927, the founding of the University of the Philippines Writers' Club marked the end of the period of "grammar and rhetoric" for a whole generation that was the first to be "Americanized." This stage of cultural development abruptly severed young Filipino intellectuals from the anti-oligarchic, egalitarian inspiration of the 1896 revolution against Spain. The radical orientation of Rizal and the propagandists was eclipsed by U.S. "genteel" letters. The First World War, of course, not only buried Longfellow and Bryant but also ushered the "specter" of the Bolshevik Revolution. Such rumblings were registered in the vernacular sensorium. Amid persisting peasant agitation and uprisings in the countryside, the eve of the 1929 Wall Street crash saw the growth of a sense of professionalism in writing that coincided with the ascendancy of an aestheticist, craft-oriented sensibility among Filipino writers, centered around the personality of Jose Garcia Villa.

Meanwhile, the Jones Act of 1916, which promised independence to the Filipino people "as soon as a stable government can be established," channeled intellectual energies to a series of "Independence Missions" that led eventually to the establishment of the Philippine Commonwealth in 1935. One can discern a parallel or homologous progression between the nationalist rhetoric of chief oligarchs Quezon and Osmeña (who headed the Commonwealth government) and the assertion of autonomy by English-using writers who were alienated from the charismatic politics and philistine vacuity of the élite milieu during the 1920s and early 1930s.

From this, we can conclude that the practice of Euro-American literary discourse and its diffusion caused in a systematic way the alienation of the Filipino artist from the Filipino masses through its semiotic strategies of deflection, catharsis, and sublimation. Consider this asymmetrical development: while the university curriculum and public libraries purveyed the writings of O. Henry, Edna St. Vincent Millay, Edgar Allan Poe, and Amy Lowell, the self-conscious writers who first articulated the platform of an expressive, organicist aesthetic modeled their works on Wilbur Daniel Steele, Ring Lardner, Bret Harte, William Saroyan, and Sherwood Anderson, with Hemingway becoming predominant later through the mediation of French examples, chiefly Flaubert and Maupassant.

We thus confront an overdetermined conjuncture in the maturation of the native sensibility. Fused with the writer's technicist obsession, which is motivated in part by a typical American prejudice claiming that Filipinos lack a sense of form and craft, is a sublimated impulse of revolt and an implicit valorization of naiveté and spontaneous intuition. Note that the 1896 revolution was already a synthesis of classic Enlightenment discipline and autochthonous hubris. I think this explains the fascination with Saroyan and Anderson and the enthusiastic response to the experiments of e.e. cummings and Gertrude Stein. It was not until the thirties—beginning in 1933, up to the establishment of the Philippine Writers' League in February 1939—that the questioning of fetishist avant-gardism began (its genealogy harks back to Poe's "The Philosophy of Composition"), signaling the resumption of the interrupted sequence of revolt that sought to reconcile the artist with the historically determined needs of a national-popular constituency.

While U.S. Naturalism sustained Twain's questioning of genteel conventions, and H. L. Mencken (in the *American Century* circa 1923–24) had begun a trenchant propaganda for Anderson, Dreiser, Sandburg, Masters, and Sinclair Lewis, a gap or lacuna haunted the imagination of the Filipino writers in the first two decades of U.S. rule. Whereas the vernacular writers in Tagalog and other native languages continued their exploration of alternatives initiated by the 1896 propagandists (Rizal, Jaena, del Pilar) in dialogue with Fourier, Bakunin, Zola, Spencer, and Marx, the practitioners of English nourished themselves to a large extent with Washington Irving, Whittier, and Longfellow's *Evangeline*. Excluded from the pedagogy of McKinley's "Benevolent Assimilation" rationale were the writings of Whitman, Thoreau, Melville, Twain, and Jack London, not to mention writers who were female or black.

The transformation of the native intellectual into the cosmopolitan bohemian who would end up in Greenwich Village in the forties is exemplified by the cult figure of Jose Garcia Villa (see Chapter 6). Villa is the only Filipino writer so far who has succeeded in insinuating himself into the "good graces" of the exclusive New York coterie that safeguards bourgeois "High Culture." He personifies the Filipino "lost generation" (if an analogy can be forced) of post–World War I.

Villa's youthful rebellion against his father, a doctor and army chief of staff of the revolutionary Philippine Republic, sublimates the nationalist revolt into the fictive gesture of challenging patriarchal authority. This genre of self-identification serves to mimic the epiphany-hounded protagonists of Anderson's *Winesburg, Ohio* (1919), a paradigm for the assorted *Bildungsroman* of the twenties and thirties. Such assertion of atomized individuality derives its logic from Anderson's principle that "the true history of life is but a history of moments," first enunciated in *A Story-Teller's Story*.

During the first decade of U.S. colonization, the student apprentices published in the *College Folio* (circa 1910) of the state-run University of the Philippines were criticized for "strained and stilted style" by editors like A.V. H. Hartendorp of the *Philippine Magazine*, who encouraged "local color" in fiction. Soon afterward, Villa and his contemporaries discovered the American "lost generation" and corrected their style. While Villa and his clique did not acknowledge the influence of the anti-Establishment polemics of Randolph Bourne, Van Wyck Brooks, and Mencken, nor the aestheticism of James Huneker, James Branch Cabell, and J. E. Spingarn, it is clear that the counteracting pressure of the "New Humanism" (Babbit, Brownell, More) subtly informed the quasi-Kantian transcendentalism of Villa and his epigones.

Documentation of influences and filiations needs to be mediated through examining the pedagogical practices in the University of the Philippines and the circulation of books and periodicals in the first two decades. Villa's creed, given definitive shape in the forties, may be said to encapsulate the triumph of "Manifest Destiny," with its peculiar ensemble of essentialism, a romantic rejection of historical reification, and the myth of the autonomous ego in liberal thought:

I am not at all interested in description or outward appearance, nor in the contemporary scene, but in *essence*. A single motive underlies all my work and defines my intention as a serious artist: the search for the metaphysical meaning of man's life in the Universe—the finding of man's selfhood and identity in the mystery of Creation. I use the term *metaphysical* to denote the ethico-philosophic force behind all essential living. The development and unification of the human personality I consider the highest achievement [possible]. (Kunitz 1036)

Villa negotiated his identity as a Filipino writer in New York by seeking the recognition and receiving the patronage of an exclusive circle of American literati. His status as cosmopolitan author was therefore fashioned by the regulative norms of U.S. knowledge-production, centered on the New Critical orthodoxy and its affiliations with elitist tendencies in the late thirties and forties (Sitwell, Marianne Moore). When the capitalist world system was being reorganized into a Keynesian order amid the turmoil of the Cold War (locally the Magsaysay / CIA suppression of the Huk insurgency in the early 1950s), Villa's novelties had already become devalued as idiosyncratic, quaint mannerisms redolent of *fin de siècle* bohemians. Negation of the colonized subject and assumption of a cosmic subjectivity defined by Angle-Saxon arbiters and codes: this archetypal pattern is what tokenistic liberalism and the clientelist ethos of a Third World formation then offered to people of color who aspired to self-validation and confirmation of worth.

In Chapter 6, I discuss Villa more fully as an instructive example of how the artist from the "boondocks" resorts to syncretic artifice, to cannibalizing of Western texts, and to bricolage, so as to invent an ersatz, syncretic modernism. Villa's representative stories, collected in the volume *Footnote to Youth*, are rightly credited with the articulation of a new if monadic subjectivity that would crystallize a "political unconscious" opposed to the tributary-cum-utilitarian ethos that pervaded the colonial milieu of the twenties. Villa indigenized the themes and styles of the avant-garde iconoclasts (Anderson, Stein, and others) while revolting against the official grammar, taste, and sentiment of U.S. tutelage. Invoking European aestheticism and its alibis, Villa's antibourgeois stance emerged before and during the collapse of finance capitalism in 1929. This individualist rebellion, parasitic on Eurocentric models, would become more narcissistic and paranoid during the Depression and eventually become monumentalized in his "comma poems": "It is the „I„ I write about, the I of Identity . . ." of *Volume Two* (1949).

Villa claimed in the forties—about ten years after his arrival in the United States—that he had experienced an "intellectual transition: he was trying to forget that he was a foreigner." It may be that Villa has escaped the fate of commodification—though he made himself marketable to the decadent blandishments of the Marcos dictatorship, lionized by Imelda Marcos and indulged by the Makati élite—at the expense of acting out his own self-caricature where pathos and bathos merged: the southeast Asian mestizo passing for a Latino exiled artist and damning all those who refused to acknowledge his unique properties now, alas, possessing potential exchange value only for antiquarians and collectors of Filipiniana (on patronage and commodity-fetishism, see Rafael, "Patronage and Pornography").

Signs of Dislocation

One can sum up what I have argued so far: of all the varied instruments mobilized by the United States to subjugate the Philippines after the violent suppression of the popular revolutionary forces in the Filipino-American War, culture was the most powerful and enduring. In general, I define culture here as that sphere of representations, actions, and discursive practices in which hegemony is defined, organized, destroyed, and reconstructed. (Hegemony, in Gramsci's terms, is the moral-intellectual leadership of a social bloc that generates legitimacy and consensus, through negotiating compromises and hierarchies.)

Culture subsumes all social practices that construct human identities and reproduce a hierarchy of differences in the modalities of class, gender, race, nationality, and so on. In its quest for hegemony, U.S. imperialism harnessed the educational system as the chief vehicle of "benevolent assimilation," of acculturation. Within the educational sector of what Althusser calls "the ideological state apparatus" and other disciplinary regimes of the colonial formation, it was the English language that forged the chains of consent and allegiance to the "superior" alien occupier.

Thus, English-writers and intellectuals then served as the most effective mediation or relay between the colonizing power and the subjugated populace. The first Filipino writers in English (for example, Paz Marquez-Benitez and Jose Garcia Villa) were educated in the state's University of the Philippines, founded in 1908; their writings were first published by institutional organs. The idiom of American English displaced both Spanish and the vernaculars as the primary symbolic system through which Filipinos represented themselves—that is, constituted themselves as disciplined subjects with specific functions (rights, duties) in the given social order. It was through this hegemonic medium that the colonized subjects, especially the organic intellectuals of the emerging middle strata (merchants, professionals, rich peasants), represented their subordination and warranted their serviceability to U.S. systemic designs.

Renato Constantino emphasizes this use of the ruler's language as the root cause of the Filipino's inveterate self-alienation:

> The first and perhaps the master stroke in the plan to use education as an instrument of colonial policy was the decision to use English as the medium of instruction. English became the wedge that separated the Filipinos from their past and later was to separate educated Filipinos from the masses of their countrymen. (*Neocolonial Identity* 47)

In short, the implantation of U.S. imperial ideology in the Filipino psyche and the routine of everyday life cannot be dissociated from the use of English in business, government, education, and media. This instrumentality of language acted as the force that unified a repertoire of social practices through which the public and private identity of the Filipino as "bearer" of a commodity (labor-power) was constituted and subsequently valorized.

But what I think transformed Filipinos into the ideal self-regulated subjects was not just their Americanization through language, but with it their internalizing of a decorum of submission—an imaginary relation to the real conditions of existence—which at the minimum guaranteed survival. That decisive conversion occurred with William Howard Taft's policy of "Philippines for the Filipinos," a slogan more revealing for its disingenuous opportunism than for its diplomatic substance. It was really a strategy of cooptation, articulated in terms of equal exchange, as manifested, for example, in Taft's words:

> and when the Filipino, in seeking a position in executive offices where English is the only language spoken, fits himself, as he will with his aptness for learning languages, in English, he will have nothing to complain of, either in the justice of the examination and its marking or in the equality of salaries between him and Americans doing the same work. (Veneracion 61)

What this strategy performed with finesse is its formal conversion of a relation of domination into a relation of exchange, an exchange of ser-

vices, a contractual relation. Maurice Godelier observes that "no domination, even when born of violence, can last if it does not assume the
form of an exchange of services" (161). With this mode of representing
colonial oppression as a service rendered by the powerful—a form of
exchange carried out in the colonizer's language, which establishes a
reciprocal commitment (analogous to a voluntary compact) between
the parties involved—the consent to be subordinated is won, and the
once-indeterminate fate of the Filipino becomes sealed. In short, subjugation is transcoded into freedom—albeit freedom to dispose of one's
body in the reifying marketplace.

In the symbolic exchange of the liberal polity, the stigmata of bondage
can circulate as freely as tokens of autonomy. Nothing could be more
emblematic of this paradox than what a leading *ilustrado* of that time,
T. H. Pardo de Tavera, advocated in his campaign for rapid assimilation.
De Tavera expressed an opinion that, though initially disclaimed by the
"nationalist" bloc, deserves to be honored as the implicit principle of the
comprador élite's platform of achieving independence via gradual and
incremental reform:

> After peace is established, all our efforts will be directed to Americanizing
> ourselves; to cause a knowledge of the English language to be extended
> and generalized in the Philippines, in order that through its agency, the
> American spirit may take possession of us, and that we may so adopt its
> principles, its political customs, and its peculiar civilization that our re-
> demption may be complete and radical. (Veneracion 60)

Viewed from this perspective, the question of language—of replacing
English with a Filipino "national" language—appears today as the most
crucial site of cultural-political struggle in the Philippines. This has been
the case ever since the converted cattle ship *Thomas* brought the first
teachers of English into the country. Despite the intervention of so-
ciolinguistic experts and well-meaning Philippine Congressional committees, this problem of a "national" language will remain unresolved
for the neocolonial government. Meanwhile, the clandestine and outlawed New People's Army is unimpeded in popularizing "Filipino" (a
modified Tagalog; also called "Pilipino") among millions in its liberated
zones across provincial boundaries.

In many Third World countries where massacres have occurred over
language, this foundational question cannot be detached from its complicity with major political issues. In their respective societies, writers
like Ngugi Wa Thiong'o and Chinua Achebe (Africa), Edward Braith-

waite and Wilson Harris (the Caribbean), and Raja Rao (India) have rehearsed the sociocultural context and ideological resonance of the debate over language as the medium of imaginative expression and intellectual reflection (see Ashcroft, Griffiths, and Tiffin 38–115). In the Philippines, the dispute over one "national language" has been sublimated into the politics of affirming—or more precisely, during U.S. colonial rule, gesturing toward—popular self-determination. Because of its history of separatist resistance, the following never have been considered viable options in the Philippine setting, for reasons already outlined: the aesthetic mode of syncretism conceived as a process of abrogation and appropriation of the alien tongue, together with the alternative choice of inventing hybrid interlanguages. The postcolonial illusion of an "in-between, " a borderland space of ludic plenitude is replaced, in the Philippines, with a resistance practice that challenges global capitalism and "transcultural" machinations (see Harlow).

Over the years of anti-imperialist struggle, the sign 1982 has invariably become the site of what Deleuze and Guattari call "deterritorializations"—the index of "minor" disruptive discourse (*Anti-Oedipus*, 280). In the nineties, the "language problem" cannot be dissociated anymore from the quest for popular self-management and democratic sovereignty. After heated exchanges in public forums and special hearings, including threats of boycott and sabotage from non-Tagalog speakers, the Constitutional Convention of 1986 agreed to reaffirm "Filipino" (testimony to shifting class alignments) as the evolving national language of the land. This was the sequel to a political-cultural battle that had been waged by antagonistic classes and regions since the early decades of this century.

Although English continues to be used predominantly in business and in government, "Filipino"-in-the-making, as propagated by the mass media—TV, films, radio—has practically become the *lingua franca* throughout the islands. Counter-insurgency propaganda in the vernacular and in Filipino attests to this trend. The ongoing sociopolitical transformation of property and power relations harbors a reality-effect immanent in verbal performance, in the speech-acts of everyday life. A systematic program of replacing English with Filipino in all universities is now under way so that within the next two or three decades, the use of English as the traditionally sanctioned medium of intellectual communication gradually will be phased out. Eventually, despite setbacks, writing in English will be relegated to the museum for tourists and archaeologists.

In the meantime, it may be instructive for those engaged in Third World cultural studies to inquire: what are the deeper implications in the larger society of this struggle over English as the language of aspiration and artistic expression?

Subterranean Explorations

At the climax of capitalism's crisis in 1929 and the outbreak of peasant insurrections and workers' strikes throughout the thirties, the once fairly homogeneous collective of English-using intellectuals split. The year 1935 marked the inauguration of the Philippine Commonwealth (a status somewhat similar to that of Puerto Rico's today). That year also witnessed the rediscovery of the revolutionary heritage of the 1896 Propagandists, a mutation that in turn exposed writers to the European radical-populist tradition, which had been suppressed by various U.S. disciplinary apparatuses. We should recall here the fact that the national hero, Jose Rizal, in his novels and essays, selectively assimilated the European Renaissance and Enlightenment legacy—from Cicero, Dante, and Cervantes to Voltaire, Schiller, Walter Scott, Galdos, Chateaubriand—to the point where William Dean Howells, in his celebrated review of Rizal's novels, marveled at Rizal's synthesis of moral and aesthetic concerns in his narratives.[7]

The project of theorizing the foundations of Philippine socialist realism began earnestly in the thirties in the criticism of Salvador Lopez, Angel Baking, and others. Their allusions to Gorki and Plekhanov were mediated by oppositional writers like Upton Sinclair, John Steinbeck, Erskine Caldwell, Robert Cantwell, Clifford Odets, Granville Hicks, and Albert Maltz. The polemical thrusts of John Dos Passos, James Farrell, Theodore Dreiser, and the Hemingway of *For Whom the Bell Tolls* soon effectively displaced the banalities of Saroyan and Dorothy Parker. The major novelist of the Cold War years, N.V.M. Gonzalez, listed his prewar models: Flaubert, Proust, Heine, Dostoevsky, Hardy, Chekhov, Ivan Bunin. Most were enshrined in the New Critical pantheon. Symptomatically, it would take the interregnum of World War II and the granting of formal independence in 1946 for U.S. "High Culture"—in the form of New Criticism, *Encounter,* and the handouts of the Congress of Cultural Freedom (fronting for the CIA)—to be deployed as the new instrumentalities of a *pax Americana* dispensation.

I remember my undergraduate years at the University of the Philippines in the late fifties, the heyday of the New Criticism. We studied the canonical texts of Cleanth Brooks, Robert Penn Warren, John Crowe Ransom, and, of course, the scriptural pronouncements of T. S. Eliot, Ezra Pound, and other high priests of the Cold War in the ideological front. We all received our indoctrination from Filipino graduates of Iowa, Stanford, Michigan, and other American "institutions of higher learning." One diehard exponent of reactionary aesthetics, Edilberto Tiempo, confessed that he served his apprenticeship in 1946 at the University of Iowa under Paul Engle and Austin Warren. Neocolonial tutelage disguised itself as the passage to self-enlightenment and recognition by a world audience. American Fulbright professors in the next two decades reinforced the endeavors of their Filipino counterparts in propagating the New Criticism's gospel, adding variants like Chicago neo-Aristotelianism, Frye's archetypal criticism, end-of-ideology existentialism, and lately the rudiments of eclectic structuralism.

Occluding the more overt political implications in Eliot's critique of predatory capitalism, the native New Critics pontificated on the notion of the artwork as a "metaphysical maneuver" (Ransom) and the critic's principal task as the perception of the "object as it really is." While Matthew Arnold and Longinus may be quoted to support a conservative agenda, the Filipino homegrown critic's invocation of the "affective" and "intentional" fallacies led to an impasse of self-righteous idealism. Its import could be deciphered in three ways: first, as a protective defense against the threats of the raging conflicts of the time (Korean war, Huk uprising); second, as a recuperation of the professionalizing mystique of the modernist avant-garde, first broached in the twenties; and third, as a reaction to the putative "Caliban complex" of the Third World subject, overly compensating for a cultural lag between the homeland and the metropolis.

The play of power infiltrated all modes of communicative action in unsuspected ways. Certain institutions played pivotal roles. The Fulbright and Rockefeller Foundation fellowships that enabled American academics and artists to lecture in the Philippines; the numerous scholarships given to Filipino intellectuals to attend Iowa, Kenyon, and Breadloaf; and the support of the Asia Foundation and other Cold War conduits for writers' workshops and journals where Cold War platitudes dominated—all these and more insured the persistence of subaltern, neocolonial discourse from the fifties to the mid-sixties. Only the explosion of international protest against U.S. aggression in Vietnam, combined with the revolts of blacks, women, and youth in the late sixties and early seventies, could break the stranglehold of New Critical dogmatism among the fanatics of the "cult of the Word" in the Philippines.

I recall the visit (circa 1955) of William Faulkner in Manila under U.S. Embassy auspices, an event now conceivable as one hegemonic tactic of trying to revitalize a triumphalist classical humanism already frayed by the bombing of Korean villages and massacre of Filipino peasants. Memorable also is the visit of Sidney Hook, whose lecture then brought the tidings of end-of-ideology instrumentalism, in the service of neither Allen Tate's pious humanism nor Yvor Winter's morality, but of corporate profitmaking. In this context, one can suggest the view that the intrinsic/extrinsic dichotomizing of formalist discourse, which privileges the "intrinsic" of the binary opposition between form and content, produced a universalism that precisely allegorized the United Nations intervention in Korea to save democracy and the "free world" from the communist monolith. (For the larger geopolitical background, see Friedman and Selden). This strategy is replicated today by postcolonial and postmodernist theory and practice (Callinicos; Parry). One may ask today whether Eurocentric postmodernism is performing the same function for U.S. interventions in Panama, Iraq, Peru, and other contested territories in the "New World Order."

But, even during the reactionary tide of the fifties, the space of political contestation—the public sphere for the interrogation of consensus— was not completely sealed off from the unconventional impulse, from the dissident and seditious agencies of change. The velocity of historic shifts then was problematizing the discourse of imperial power, revealing the cracks and fissures of apparently stable institutional bulwarks. Imperialist knowledge-production, authorizing the locus of meaning and power, could not totally eradicate the stratagems of the oppressed. Beleaguered subalterns constantly devised and reproduced tactics of resistance, thwarting the seductions of the Symbolic Order, the siren hymns to Western affluence and consumerism.

By "tactics of resistance" I refer specifically to the nationalist, radical democratic discourse that from the beginning had alarmed U.S. policymakers, inducing them to concentrate once more on coopting the Filipino élite who acted as the historic transmission-belts of the hegemonic world view. History repeated itself in the eighties when President Aquino and her extended family became the target of Washington's diplomatic and public-relations offensive.

In the twilight of *pax Americana* in 1964, George Taylor's *The Philip-*

pines and the United States: Problems of Partnership was written to provide the chief organon for hegemonic reconsolidation. Taylor's paradigm of modernization epitomizes the functionalist conceptualization of the value system and the *habitus* of the native élite as central to the preservation of U.S. supremacy. His Cold War discourse inaugurated the master narrative for charting the trajectory of future U.S. foreign policy strategy in the Philippines, laid out previously by Taft, Worcester, Forbes, and Hayden mentioned earlier. Such a strategy actually was crafted for two purposes: to marginalize alternative modes of consensus (pluralist or relatively egalitarian) and to outlaw the oppositional (the orthodox left, as well as the nationalist critique of U.S. domination voiced by Recto, Tañada, and the Huks in the fifties). The strategy has been retooled in the post–Cold War mutations of capital.

Meanwhile, other peoples—ethnic or tribal "minorities" like five million Moros and a million Igorots—were subsumed by the incorporative figures of Christian lowland politicians. In effect, Taylor conserved and rehabilitated the policy of reform first enunciated by the early civil governors (Taft and Harrison). At the same time, he displaced the themes of social justice and popular democratization as marginal tasks, constrained by the imperatives of political stability and profitmaking through Filipino entrepreneurship and U.S. business. (Both Marcos' putative goal of expanding the middle class and the Aquino/Ramos program of privatization trace their lineage to Taylor's diagnosis.)

In the process of emphasizing "free enterprise," U.S. policy would neutralize adversarial nationalism by placing it under the leadership of a well-tutored élite. The entrepreneurial middle class, according to Taylor's schema, is the definer of Filipino identity and national purpose— a representation that also fulfills the U.S. quest for self-definition as the model of global progress and leader of the "free world." Taylor recommended to policymakers that the U.S. buttress the "middle classes" in their former Asian colony, for their belief in "the strong property concepts of classic liberalism, as well as the doctrines of natural law of the American revolution and a Hamiltonian view of the relation between government and business" (George Taylor 178), which the West needs to combat neutralism and communism.[8] This convergence of knowledge-production and power, of discourse and the will to dominate, has characterized U.S.-Philippines "special relations" since the turn of the century when the first American volunteer teachers, replacing the soldiers' Krag rifles, introduced the ABC of American business to certain pacified zones of the tropical wilderness.

Sometime in the late seventies, when the Marcos dictatorship intensely promoted the "warm body export" of Filipinos to boost the Gross National Product (per advice from the IMF/World Bank), an American-born critic imprisoned in the Philippines, Dolores Feria, described the disastrous shock that faced seventy-five thousand Filipino immigrants in the West Coast in 1929 (1957). She alluded to "the wide-eyed version of American life compiled from U.S.-produced *Osias Readers* and the Sears and Roebuck Catalog." Such a phenomenon testified to the reality effect induced by the popularized version of *inter alia* pragmatism, Weber's "iron cage" of generalized exchange, Puritan philanthropy, and individualist uutilitarianism (now known as "rational choice" theory) all of which helped legitimize the U.S. colonial experiment in imperial democracy.

Before 1946, the Filipino languished in an "occult zone of instability" (Fanon) where boundaries shifted and labor power suffered in quest of the cash-nexus. Defined as a "national" but denied the citizen's right to vote, the Filipino from 1899 to 1946 had the option to replicate the immigrant paradigm, then made attractive by its conflation of dreams of freedom with fantasies of affluence and acceptance. A complex and multivalent mythology of the pioneer-immigrant—the self-reliant, resourceful, rugged individual glamorized in colonial-era textbooks—had kept Filipinos suspended between the degrading reality of exploitation in the "promised land" and the "chimerical and utopian America" envisioned by expatriate writer Carlos Bulosan.

But Bulosan, unlike the first generation of Filipino intellectuals nurtured in Longfellow and Poe, had already neutralized the social Darwinism of the *fin de siècle* passage with a historical-materialist critique of U.S. monopoly capitalism, absorbed from his readings of the socialist classics of nineteenth-century Europe and the American proletarian writers of the thirties. Bulosan thus was saved from the blessings of "High Culture" because, apart from his gift of historical counter-memory, he helped unionize a multi-ethnic array of competing migrant workers in California during the Depression.

The death of the world-famous Carlos P. Romulo, (who served as president of the U.N. General Assembly in the early Cold War years) in December 1985 marked the end of classic tutelage. It signaled the passing away of three generations of Filipino intellectuals, from the *pensionados* of the first two decades to the Fulbright scholars of the fifties and sixties. Romulo's generation was distinguished for exalting the stigmata of the colonial apprentice/initiate, forever subservient to the possessor of the secrets of the English language.

Linked with this mystique of Shakespeare's tongue is, as I have noted earlier, the guild consciousness of the pariah craftsman. For example, both Santos and Gonzalez, two survivors of the pre-World War II upheavals, still cling to a petty-commodity/artisanal conception of literary production. Exiled in the U.S. during the years of martial law, they still seek roots in a bygone pastoral milieu seen through the eyes of Katherine Anne Porter or Chekhov—a rural space no longer mapped by anthropologists like Alfred Kroeber and Felix Keesing but by the insurgents of the New People's Army. Their epigones, simulating the prose styles of Nabokov, Pynchon, Updike, and others, reproduce in the sphere of self-referential signifiers the illusory "undecidable" aura of the neocolonial subject whose image they both love and hate.

Some old New Critical Filipinists are still active, of course, sources of validation for hoary veterans of the fifties. They carry on a rear-guard apologetics for art's compartmentalized sanctity vis-à-vis the almost universal commodification of life in the Philippines, thanks to microchips, PX goods from the military bases, and remittances from the Filipino diaspora in the Middle East, Japan, Hong Kong, and elsewhere. Ideology has always lagged behind the rapid transformations of social life, as instanced by the collapse of developmentalist or modernization schemas in the sixties following the failure of the notorious CIA Phoenix program of assassinating suspected communists in Indochina.

Despite its now-exposed tautological and self-serving character, U.S. academic discourse still exerts a powerful influence on the Filipino élite and their organic intellectuals, who are unaware of its biased predeterminations. Owing to the insistence by American "Orientalists" on the undying supremacy of English, one scholar concludes his survey of Philippine writing in 1962 with this now refuted doxa: "It is, then, in this vigorous and sophisticated literature in English that the hope of Philippine literature chiefly lies" (Vreeland 142). Such an assertion can only be possible because of an enabling presupposition: the normative priority of Western culture throughout the planet.

In other words, the canonical texts of Anglo-Saxon literature serve as the originary matrix that guarantees the legitimacy of native expression: "Political and economic, as well as cultural, events in Europe were largely responsible for the cultural awakening that now took place in the Philippines" (Bernad, "Literature in the Philippines" 447). Thus, the

Filipino experience is always configured as an effect of a primordial act by a Western subject who, as proof of his plenitude, authorizes the intelligibility of his lowly interlocutors.

When U.S. aggression in Indochina peaked in the mid-sixties, there was a rapid shift of interest among students and traditional intellectuals: *Partisan Review* gave way to *Monthly Review* and *Peking Review.* Trilling and Schlesinger were superseded by Malcolm X, Frantz Fanon, George Jackson, and Che Guevara. The imposition of martial law in 1972, backed by then-president Nixon and by subsequent administrations (regardless of party), was needed to put a brake on the erosion of U.S.-comprador hegemony. It was indeed a holding operation, as the explosions since 1983 (after Benigno Aquino was assassinated) and beyond clearly demonstrate.

Taking Our Bearings in Terra Incognita

We may sum up briefly the harvest of half a century of U.S. pacification of the "boondocks" at this pivotal conjuncture. In the thirties and fifties (World War II constituted a cathartic rupture, as remarked earlier), Filipino intellectuals were coopted by the U.S.-controlled media, silenced in the cage of the bureaucracy, or neutralized in the academy. Many surrendered to the illusion of sharing power as ghost writers and publicists of the oligarchs. In the sixties, the emergence of a revitalized worker-peasant movement created an intellectual ferment among students, media professionals, and writers, catalyzing a militant self-awareness hitherto submerged, and precipitating a renewed critical interrogation of U.S. cultural practices. It sparked a questioning of imperial ideology on the terrain of institutions like the family, church, schools, and media, among others. Because the popular uprisings of the late sixties and early seventies polarized the intelligentsia and radicalized the bulk of the writers in English, the ideological state apparatuses (following Althusser's conceptualization) had to be purged of grassroots contamination through an authoritarian coup.

During the thirteen years of the U.S.-subsidized Marcos dictatorship, U.S. cultural domination suppressed any open radical discussion of public issues. It censored all publications and sought to revive various forms of metaphysical speculation, functional empiricism, and assorted positivisms informed by a mystifying instrumentalism in which statistics are manipulated to confirm preconceived official *diktat*. A return of the repressed, however, transpired: the liberal arts orientation of higher learning in the Philippines was slowly being transformed by schemes hatched through the IMF/World Bank and other philanthropic agencies to a narrow vocational one, in order to supply semiskilled and lower-echelon personnel to the corporate assembly plants, while the mass media and bureaucracy remained tightly controlled by technocrats and military officers graduated from Stanford, MIT, Harvard Business School, and the Wharton School in Philadelphia.

It is, however, difficult to conceive of a single contemporary American writer like Poe or Hemingway whose signifying practice can be said to complicitly dovetail with World Bank/IMF formulas designed to prolong and deepen the nation's under-development. American literature has been supplanted by the flood of commercial television shows and films. During the Marcos regime, underground periodicals tried to use the anarchist discourses of Chomsky, Howard Zinn, E. L. Doctorow, and other anti-Establishment critics, amid the ersatz Hollywood-cum-pornography spectacles promoted by Imelda Marcos as substitutes for Gothic romances, television epics, and other "circus" happenings. If Rev. Jerry Falwell's rescue mission to rehabilitate Marcos' international reputation in 1985 represents a pathetic throwback to McKinley's mockagon over "Manifest Destiny," it is possible to interpret that scenario as a farcical retort to Ernest Hemingway's stopover in 1940 in Manila, ostensibly to drum up support for the antifascist resistance in Spain and China.

Further interaction between Filipino intellectuals in exile around the world and progressive thinkers in the metropoles hopefully may prefigure a much-needed reversal of Francis Ford Coppola's exploitation of Filipinos not so long ago in order to lend a veneer of authenticity to *Apocalypse Now.* Such incursions always evoke scenes of American soldiers civilizing pacified hamlets with their Krag rifles, unconscionable episodes documented by Peter Davis' film *Bloody Blundering Business.*

In 1951 Wallace Stegner, a distinguished novelist and professor at Stanford University, visited the Philippines and published his findings in the *Saturday Review of Literature* (4 August 1951). Although Stegner commits the same ethnocentric prejudice as other "Filipinologists" of denigrating vernacular writing (none of which he was able to read in the original), he discerns "the economic and cultural dependency" of the Philippines on the United States, as well as the alienation of the Filipino writer in English from the most urgent political and moral predicament of his people:

> The brutal terrorism of the Huks may silence some protest because responsible people do not want to attack their government when it has its hands full, or because they do not want to be branded as sympathizers. The shadow of violence and fear hangs over even well-policed Manila. It is a strange experience for an American lecturer to see a guard with a carbine outside the hall as he talks and to enter and leave the national university through a roadblock manned by a squad of constabulary. In Manila these are commonplaces. . . . But literature ignores them. (52)

Stegner, however, ignores the causes of peasant uprisings, their durable tradition of resistance to oppression, the role of U.S. colonialism, and so on. These are all peripheral to his mission as one harbinger of progress in the "free world," anticipating the visits of Faulkner and Hook. Stegner's mind focuses on the surface phenomena, oblivious to fifty years of U.S. repression. Without explicit assent he endorses Cold War apologetics: the Huks are bandits who "manipulate" the "disgruntled and underprivileged." We are reminded of how, in the first decade of U.S. rule, Macario Sakay and other beleaguered insurgents were ostracized as "bandits," and how in the recent past revolutionaries were branded by the Marcos regime and his U.S. overseers as "criminals" or "NPA terrorists."

What about the highly touted social conscience of the artist? Stegner offers this opinion:

> Disinterest, caution, fear, disgust—whatever the causes, Filipino writers avoid politics and regard the whole spectacle of government with veiled bitterness. . . . I think the writers as a group are not likely in their present mood to be involved in either muck-racking or reform or revolution. Their attitude is very like that of American writers in the Twenties: they scorn to dirty their hands; politics is always dirty; the writer's interests lead him elsewhere. . . . I suspect that uninterrupted cultivation of the Muse may have to wait until Philippine roads are safe for travelers and Philippine villages exhibit more pastoral peace than they presently do. ("Renaissance" 52–53)[9]

It may be an understatement to say that Stegner's obvious political naiveté reflects a Cold War partisanship he is unable to comprehend, much less surpass. But his uncanny evocation of the "lost generation" of the twenties at that time now exudes the pathos of ironic doubling when we take into account the killing of innocent civilians suspected of being "communists" by paramilitary death squads underwritten by desperate officials and CIA-Pentagon operatives. In the atmosphere of McCarthyite witchhunting in the Philippines, torture of progressive intellectuals like Amado V. Hernandez and Jose Lansang, brutalization and massacre of thousands of peasants and workers, blanket repression—all these escaped Stegner's sophisticated learning.

Less than twenty years after Stegner's 1951 visit, our writers have begun to take up arms (literally and figuratively), in collaboration with millions of workers, peasants, and professionals from the middle strata in a nationwide struggle against U.S. hegemony and its local servitors: compradors, landlords, and bureaucrats entrenched in the military, government, church, and other sites of civil society. The vigorous cultural renascence sweeping the cities and countryside has resurrected the "specter" of 1896 glimpsed by Howells in Rizal's allegorical fictions. It was a specter also intuited by Mark Twain as he contemplated the fierce resistance of the barefoot folk against the Yankee invaders in 1899, a specter rising to foil Stegner's hope that Filipino writing will at best become a minor tributary of the great mainstream of American literature, a specter reborn to challenge what Senator Albert Beveridge said at the turn of the century—"Whips of scorpions could not lash the Filipinos to this land of fervid enterprise, sleepless industry, and rigid order" (Schirmer and Shalom 26). Enterprise, industry, order—telltale stigmata of the Filipino initiation-ordeal into the twentieth century.

After the brief but mesmerizing spotlight focused on the Philippines in 1986, the archipelago has lapsed again into limbo . . . except when the volcano Mount Pinatubo disturbs the stratosphere, as it did in 1991, sending both ecologists and stock market prophets from North to South back to their drawing boards (see *Barron's*, 23 August 1993); or when the "Iron Butterfly" (Imelda Marcos) and her entourage of sycophants grab the headlines with their now-legendary exhibitionism; or when Filipinos explode over the brutalization of millions of contract workers abroad for alleged "crimes"—the latest being Flor Contemplacion, mother of four children, hanged in Singapore.

It has been a long time indeed since the great Russian writer Ivan Goncharov visited the islands and surveyed the "always already" exotic landscape. Intrigued by the chiaroscuro of moods and tones, opaqueness and transparency, he left with a reminiscence of his genial surprise:

On my way to Manila I thought, truth to tell, that the spirit of a fallen, impoverished power would blow on me, that I should see desolation and a lack of strictness and order—in a word, the poetry of disintegration. But I was amazed by the well-organized appearance of the town and its cleanliness; signs of care and even of abundance were to be seen everywhere. (12)

Today this far-flung "outpost of the empire" no longer strikes the American imagination as a breeding ground for the race of "turbaned Fedallah," one of Ahab's personal companions in Melville's *Moby Dick*, whose friends "were of that vivid, tiger-yellow complexion peculiar to some of the aboriginal natives of the Manillas." The pathos of distance in time—from a glimpse of that ferocious and almost inscrutable visage, to its domestication—may be measured by its brief reappearance in F. Scott Fitzgerald's last, uncompleted novel, *The Last Tycoon:* "The Philippino boy brought in a carafe of water and bowls of nuts and fruit, and said good night" (116). The orientalist aura vanishes in the last snapshot of the Other's presence.

Before the collapse of the Marcos regime, the country and its inhabitants impressed the travel writer of *The Guardian* (20 September 1982) in this way: "The price the Philippines has paid for this mutual intoxication with the west is that, as a holiday destination, it cannot offer the magic of Thailand or Indonesia; it is Asia sanitized: its highways are straighter, its sunsets blurred rather than bloody; its religion Christian." The stark indexes of poverty, violence, and prostitution all over Manila have not, however, deterred those seeking a simulacrum of paradise.

Reality, however, opens its secrets to illusion if we view the Philippines as the elaborate stage prop of director Coppola's 35-million-dollar-extravaganza, *Apocalypse Now,* filmed in Baler, Quezon province, featuring a cast of hundreds of Vietnamese "boat people," Filipino extras, and specimens of the immortal "water buffalo" (the carabao) that William Howard Taft once honored with his buttocks. Supposed to condemn U.S. imperialism in Vietnam, the film actually collaborated with imperial policy in promoting the Pentagon's version of the "foreign invasion" of South Vietnam and also aided the Marcos dictatorship in fighting the New People's Army combatants led by Marxist-Leninist cadres. Coppolla's manic consumerism also corrupted the local environment with prostitution, racist treatment of Vietnamese and Filipino participants, and other con games that usually gravitate around Hollywood big-time spending (Sussman 19).

In retrospect, Conrad's vision penetrating the "heart of darkness" seems to have materialized again in these islands, subjected since Magellan's fateful intrusion in 1521 to the violence and perverse fantasies of travelers, missionaries, and conquerors who have produced knowledge and images of the "Philippines" and "Filipinos" for everyone's profit and delight—except for the Filipinos themselves.

2

Discourse of Hegemony, Projects of Critique and Resistance

> Whoever does not recognize and champion the equality of nations and languages and does not fight against all national oppression or inequality is not a Marxist, he is not even a democrat.
> —*V. I. Lenin, 1916*

> On the Asiatic coast, washed by the waves of the ocean, lie the smiling Philippines. . . . There, American rifles mowed down human lives in heaps.
> —*Rosa Luxemburg, 1900*

> The Philippine landscape is familiarly tropical and East Indian. But the world into which you have stepped is unlike anything of which you have yet had experience in the Orient. It is Spain—diluted, indeed, distorted, and overlaid with Americanism.
> —*Aldous Huxley, circa 1930–35*

In the official biography of Ernest Hemingway, Carlos Baker recounts what strikes him as the impact of Philippine reality on the fabled inventor of modernist American prose style:

> On the 11th [of May 1941] Hemingway attended a "ghastly" dinner given by the Philippine Writers Association where everyone's attempt to be gaily informal bored him so much that he got too drunk to care. . . .
> In Manila Hemingway made a few more notes and explored some of the Spanish bars of Intramuros. Otherwise his sole gain from the Philippine stopover was a good short summer haircut. (364–65)[1]

In Hemingway's fiction and journalism, no reference of any importance is made to the Philippines.

In July 1961, the leading Filipino writer in English, Nick Joaquin, recollected Hemingway's two visits (February and May 1941) in elaborate quotation-filled scenarios. Every utterance of the author of *For Whom the Bell Tolls* was transcribed like an apocalyptic message from the guru/avatar of avant-garde Western modernism (*Manila: Sin City?* 49–64). Joaquin recalled how Hemingway emphasized the political commitment and devotion to the truth that writers must cultivate, and how he praised the Spanish and Chinese people's resistance to fascism. But what struck the intimate group of Filipino writers who conversed with him was Hemingway's generous concern for his fellow-practitioners in the craft, his unpretentious bearing, his simplicity and candor. It was in truth, however, an equivocal performance susceptible to plural interpretations.

What this juxtaposition of past event and "present" modes of assessment foregrounds is precisely the complex and overdetermined transaction between metropolitan culture and colonized native sensibilities, between hegemonic center and the decentered periphery, which has been construed often in a one-dimensional positivistic manner. It is, of course, indisputable that so long as the Philippines remains a disguised U.S. satellite or neocolony politically, economically, and culturally, Filipino writing in the English language cannot but be a minor, regional, or subordinate extension of the main body of British and American writing.

I propose here, in contrast, a dialectical interpretation that might elucidate more adequately the nonsynchronous development of the U.S. racializing ideology that inhabits the Philippine social formation. The Baker/Joaquin juxtaposition reveals two opposing perspectives: one, the typical Orientalizing discourse of Western consciousness (Baker) that fabricates and marginalizes its alien object for its own ends; and the other, the native response (Joaquin) that filters, selects, and organizes the raw material it imports according to its own local/national imperatives.

Despite the then-deepening involvement of the U.S. in suppressing revolutions in Indochina and elsewhere, Baker reflects the primitive and parochial consciousness of the intelligentsia here vis-à-vis liberation struggles of people of color. Joaquin, on the other hand, exemplifies a long and vigorous tradition of Filipino cultural producers deeply engaged in radical political and social criticism, a tradition springing from the propagandist reformers of the 1896 revolution against Spain—exponents of Enlightenment ideals that were taken up, refined, and further developed by the vernacular writers of the first two decades, the radical democratic writers of the thirties, and the insurrectionary generation of the sixties and seventies.

Bearing in mind the subtle and complex distinction between reception and influence, as explored by comparatists such as Mineke Schipper, Claudio Guillen, and others, we can argue that the Philippine version of Hemingway is not only historically valid in itself, but probably more true than the biographer's résumé—although it may be granted that each reflects polar ends of a dialectical totality, for each reveals the symptomatic lacunas and silences of the purportedly veridical and authoritative biography.[2] Contexts and intentionalities overdetermine each other across divergent cultural fields and traditions.

In analyzing the problems of influence, reception, and exchange between the imperialist metropole and the peripheral dependencies of the Third World, we must emphasize the concrete specificity of the social relations of production and reproduction, the function of the state and its subordination to transnational capital, together with their reciprocal dynamics, that characterize the neocolonial formation. Our focus is on overdetermined conjunctures of uneven and combined development that syncopate center and periphery, core and margin.

What is needed is an ecological-historical approach that registers the nuances of shifting background and foreground. I contend that, relative to the self-serving hegemonic approach, this is the correct and adequate method to map the vicissitudes of Philippines-U.S. literary exchanges from its inception, to evaluate its social effects, and to demarcate its prospects. For texts to speak, they must be contextualized in a global space consisting of contradictory institutional practices. Whose language is the medium for playing the game—tactical gambits, strategic maneuvers? Who writes for whom? Who is speaking? Who, if anyone, is listening or reading?

In my book, *Toward a People's Literature: Essays in the Dialectics of Praxis and Contradiction in Philippine Writing*, as well as in earlier treatises—*Balagtas: Art and Revolution*, and *The Radical Tradition in Philippine Literature*—I elaborated upon what Gilles Deleuze refers to as the three discernible lines constituting any sociocultural phenomenon: the nomadic, the migrant, and the sedentary lines (Deleuze and Guattari, *On the Line*). They intersect, diverge, run parallel, and metamorphose in various ways. Here I restrict my argument to the native popular discourses marginalized by U.S. cultural hegemony, for it is the hegemonizing process that I chiefly address in this essay.

Disrupting the sedentary line of medieval Christian evangelism introduced by the Spanish colonizers (1635–1898), which segmented into the molar codes of religious ritual and patriarchal familialism, were the agitprop writings of revolutionary, decolonizing democrats like Jose Rizal, Marcelo del Pilar, Emilio Jacinto, and later Apolinario Mabini. Targeting specific mobilized audiences (in either Spanish or Tagalog), their praxis integrated aesthetics and politics and generated the migrant or molecular line that effectively subverted the hierarchical organizations maintained by the Church and the colonial bureaucratic machinery. The writings of these pioneers were proscribed, their bodies incarcerated or destroyed.

But it was principally the nomadic line of vernacular writing that displaced the molecular, reformist politics of Rizal and his contemporaries. One can cite here the productions of "seditious" playwrights like Aurelio Tolentino and the founders of the native *zarzuela*, Severino Reyes, Patricio Mariano, and Hermogenes Ilagan; novelists like Lope K. Santos and Iñigo Ed. Regalado; and poets like Jose Corazon de Jesus and Pedro Gatmaitan. Eventually, a popular-nationalist discourse emerged, using the vernacular languages and exposing the impossibility of an illusionist, ego-centered representation through a consistent allegorical-didactic figuration of political and social questions. We have entered at this point the era of Amado Hernandez, Carlos Bulosan, and Salvador Lopez.

This contestation characterizes the period from the U.S. invasion of 1898 to the consolidation of English as a viable literary medium in the early 1930s. Instead of indigenizing the notions of Faustian *virtù* and Puritan individualism propagated by Europeanized intellectuals like Rizal and Isabelo de los Reyes (perhaps the first Filipino socialist thinker, although for a time he, like his contemporary Lope K. Santos, was an exponent of a modified Proudhonian anarcho-syndicalism), vernacular discourse articulated a process of dissolving the interiority of the co-herent, unitary subject. Circa 1900–10, the Filipino was being interpellated by U.S. racist imperial ideology. In response, vernacular cultural practice tried to represent the breakdown of familial codes, the collapse of binary structures (male / female, urban / rural, and so forth), and the release of a "rhizomatic" desire mistakenly condemned as sentimentalism or pathos by formalist critics who were then inventing Philippine literary history. Exemplary here are the virtuoso performances of Leona Florentino (in Ilocano), Magdalena Jalandoni (in Ilonggo), and Liwayway Arceo (in Tagalog), among others (Feria, *Stag Party*). An analogy to the temper of the pre-romantic "sensibility" in late eighteenth-century

Europe can be discerned in this trend, provided the local contexts and specific life-experiences are not ignored.

A turning point occurred before the Philippine Commonwealth was set up in 1935. Vernacular writing, with the cooptation of the migrant line by U.S. entrepreneurial discourse and the emasculation of the sedentary line, became temporarily hegemonic, dramatizing intensities, quanta of affects immune from the overcoding machine of bourgeois aesthetics. This is the autochthonous tradition suppressed, marginalized, or refunctionalized by the encroaching U.S. colonial-ideological apparatus, the operations and effects of which I attempt to outline here.

Like other colonized formations, the Philippine precapitalist or tributary mode of production which evolved during three hundred years of Spanish rule was disarticulated and reworked by U.S. political-military power when it suppressed the Filipino revolutionary forces in the Filipino-American War of 1899–1903. This event harnessed the natural and human resources of the archipelago to the imperatives of accumulation of U.S. finance capital. But, while U.S. imperial diktat altered the economic-juridical mechanisms and adapted the feudal institutions to serve the paramount goal of extracting surplus value, the Philippines did not metamorphose into a full-fledged industrial state.

The political economy of culture inheres in the dynamics of profit-making. Following Hamza Alavi's formulation, the circuit of commodity circulation needed the metropolis to complete it, and the surplus generated in the colony was not reinvested there to develop generalized commodity production and an independent, expanding internal market, but instead the surplus was transferred to the metropolis.[3] Given these two salient characteristics of peripheral capitalism, which entailed damaging consequences in the cultural sphere, we can understand how Philippine writing in English is constrained to find its self-confirmation and continuity in the larger circumscribing parameter of official Anglo-Saxon literature.

When the United States annexed the Philippines at the turn of the century, it encountered an already highly stratified, uneven formation with a considerable landlord class, differentiated peasantry, emergent working class, and an educated stratum of intellectuals called *ilustrados* attached to the rich peasant and mercantile sectors. To attain its imperialist objective, the new colonial dispensation employed a dual policy of force and persuasion. It violently crushed the revolutionary partisans and coopted/bribed the *ilustrados* who then were subsequently in-

stalled in the lower echelons of the bureaucracy, provincial and munici-
pal administrations, and other consensus-generating agencies of the
colonial government. The institution of the public schools and the town
administrations were the primary ideological state apparatuses during
the first two decades of pacification. They cooperated in establishing the
groundwork for the incessant reproduction of capitalist social relations
centered on the market (the contractual exchanges of juridically free
and equal individuals) and on the striving for rational efficiency in the
operations of petty-commodity business and comprador enterprises.

Within this schematic formulation of the base or infrastructure, the
Philippines "received" U.S. nineteenth-century culture with its contradictions. It was dominated by a pseudo-scientific racism (documented
by historians Gabriel Kolko, Thomas Gossett, and others) and heavily
permeated by a popularized "social Darwinism" and the unifying ethos
of "Manifest Destiny." All these forces converged to gradually rationalize the suppression of the Reconstruction, the populists, the American
Indian nations, anarchists, and socialists during the period following
the Civil War. The ideological themes of reaction were all reworked in
the mass-media propaganda of the Spanish-American War, at which
time the Philippines entered the warring class discourses and camps of
the U.S. public sphere.

Couched in President McKinley's rhetoric of "benevolent assimilation"—the U.S. version of the European apologia of *mission civilizatrice*—
bourgeois ideology was transmitted to the younger generation of Filipinos through the imposition of English as the official language. This
world view was further renegotiated through various educational
and administrative policies that were geared to a reformist neocolonial
strategy. Somewhat anachronistically (a signal proof of uneven development), the literary culture introduced by the American teacher-
volunteers reflected the "genteel" and elitist milieu of a preindustrial
era—Irving, Longfellow, Bryant, and others—quite bereft of any overt
social criticism. In her pioneering study of American literary influence
in the first three decades, Lucila Hosillos notes the following exclusions from the curricula, among others: George Washington Cable, Joel
Chandler Harris' folktales of American and Indian origins, and Mary
Wilkins Freeman's fiction (55–56).[4]

Such exclusions were less conspiratorial than they were indicative
and symptomatic. As a rule, U.S. policymakers judged the Filipinos
quite uncivilized and at best "children" requiring "tutelage"—the code-

word of imperialist apologetics, from McKinley's Proclamation of December 1898 to U.S. State Department pronouncements and mainstream academic scholarship on the Philippines. Consequently, texts embodying the conservative didacticism of New England patriarchs were used to illustrate American English grammar and idiom and to convey an image of idealized U.S. social harmony to the natives.

For an entire generation of Filipino intellectuals who participated in the 1896 revolution and who were reared in or exposed to the writings of Balzac, Zola, Galdos, Tolstoy, Chekhov, Flaubert, and Maupassant, the moralizing of Longfellow, Holmes, and Lowell seemed a useless curiosity, distracting them from the urgent challenge of a drastically changed political environment. Not even the British humanist-liberal trend of Macaulay, Arnold, and George Eliot—standard textbook fare— could deflect the Tagalog novelists and dramatists or the poets using Spanish from invoking the Enlightenment ideals of plebeian-subaltern liberties, equality, and social justice absorbed from Spanish anarchist and French socialist publications that had been widely disseminated in the two decades before Admiral George Dewey intruded into Manila Bay.[5]

Only with the maturation of a generation of intellectuals born during the first two decades of the twentieth century did nineteenth-century American culture begin to be accepted and assimilated, with qualifications. This generation was effectively distanced from the radicalizing impact of the Filipino-American War, was ignorant or contemptuous of the dissident culture that had been suppressed in its aftermath, and was ultimately channeled into reformist political collaboration by being allocated a niche in the bureaucracy and other ideological apparatuses of civil society. The diplomatic and journalistic career of Carlos Romulo epitomizes this generation, a cohort condemned to an unwittingly parodic mimesis of Anglo-Saxon chauvinism and puritanical barbarism.

Others thwarted mimesis by allegorical maneuvers and inversions. The American naturalist/realist revolt against the "Genteel Tradition" and the provincial conformity of the twenties would elicit a sympathetic response from Jose Garcia Villa and his coterie, who found themselves alienated from the vulgar commercialism of Manila and the "nationalist" polemics of the oligarchy. By the late twenties, those Filipinos who had chosen to write in English also acquired a sense of caste distinction (even though most worked for newspapers and weekly magazines, or taught in college), insofar as they thought of themselves as a group privileged to be speaking the master's language. To this attitude corresponded an equivalent world-outlook, a cult of aesthetic form, the metaphysics of the sovereign Word.

Orthodox literary historians still argue that the obsession of Villa's generation with form and technique supposedly accounts for their interest first in O. Henry, Ring Lardner, Poe, Wilbur Daniel Steele, and later with Gertrude Stein, e.e. cummings, and even the untutored Saroyan. This predilecton arguably stemmed from the sensitivity of these writers to the criticism of their teachers and editors on the grammatical and stylistic "defects" of their works (one influential arbiter was A.V. H. Hartendorp of *Philippine Magazine*).

But I suggest that a more adequate and viable explanation of the emergence of aestheticism in a colonial society must be sought in the convergence of multiple factors, the most decisive of which are the following: (a) the traditional or organic function of the writer / intellectual relative to class fractions, (b) the level of nationalist consciousness and anti-imperialist struggle, (c) opportunities for popular democratic participation, and (d) the constellation of cultural modes and social practices in conflict, all of which constitute the historical specificity of any cultural formation.[6] A combination of these factors occupies the foreground of any historical-materialist inquiry.

How else can one explain adequately the phenomenon that, instead of the uncompromising critique of predatory capitalism and racism found in Melville, Thoreau, and Twain (to cite only the canonical authors), it was Sherwood Anderson's vision of discontinuity, fragmentation, and grotesque psychodrama (in *Winesburg, Ohio* and *A Story Teller's Story*)—plus its corresponding syntax—that would exercise such a catalyzing spell on Villa, Arcellana, and their embattled clique? Any democratic or populist impulse that might have survived, albeit dormant, in the inaugural productions of American modernism was transmogrified into elitist renunciation or naive anarchist individualism when imported into America's only Asian colony.

From 1946 (when the Philippines gained formal independence) up to the late 1960s (with the rediscovery and renascence of Marxist critical theory and its underground flourishing after 1972), the cornerstone of the dominant aesthetic ideology may be said to derive from the peculiar function and location of Filipino intellectuals in the sphere of the reproduction of social relations. Writers like Villa, Romulo, A. E. Litiatco, Arcellana, and others, whether employed in the universities or in private business, understood themselves as privileged, superior intellects who would assimilate "the best that has been thought and said" in

Western civilization and thereby purge the culture of the stigma of Otherness. They patterned their careers after the Eurocentric model of the romantic artist sulking or fulminating at the margins of society.

Not to question or undermine the hierarchical order of authority and property-relations, but to affirm and reinforce them on the level of spiritual-ethical discriminations: such was the role defined for artists, whether they recognized it or not, in the historically determinate colonial structure.[7] To transcend their uprooting and alienation, they invoked a cosmopolitan and eclectic humanism inferred from archetypal myths or extrapolated from the Cold War liberalism of Lionel Trilling, Sidney Hook, *Partisan Review, Encounter,* and other cultural imports, such as existentialism and varieties of religious fads.

The first generation of "English" writers was in general removed from the sufferings and struggles of the laboring masses of impoverished peasants and workers, handsomely subsidized by the state or living off rentals and inheritances. They may be categorized as products of U.S. tutelage and the mock "Filipinization" movement promoted by William Howard Taft, the first American civil governor, and subsequently by Francis Burton Harrison, whose administration (1913–21) provided the seductive simulacra of neocolonial self-determination. During the late thirties, the aestheticist faction opposed the short-lived Philippine Writers' League (1939–41). They also opposed the latter's cogent advocacy of a committed art and the writer's civic responsibility, foregrounding instead the primacy of the artist's subjective inwardness. Such developments transpired at the time of fascist aggression in Europe and the advance of Japanese militarism in Asia.[8]

Consonant with intensifying contradictions in the economic and ideological spheres, the Philippine Commonwealth era (1935–42) witnessed the polarization of the "English" writers. This conjunctural phenomenon illustrates my thesis that the Philippine cultural formation should be construed as an articulation process of several modes of practices / discourses in various stages of conservation, stasis, and dissolution. Following Raymond William's theory of cultural dynamics (*The Country and the City*), we need to distinguish the complex interaction among residual, dominant, and emergent tendencies. What was being conserved was a personalistic or metaphysical outlook (coeval with feudal or tributary caciquism) that inflects public predicaments into personal dilemmas. While one strand of this quite banal attitude may be traced to the medieval Christian deformation of Philippine culture—the sedentary line alluded to earlier—its immediate provenance includes as well the romantic transcendentalism of American literature. This organic metaphysics was mediated by editors like Hartendorp and Edward J. O'Brien and reinforced by the instrumentalized craft-specific dicta of Flaubert, Chekhov, and other modernists, but devoid of their anti–status quo impulse.[9]

What was being dissolved or neutralized was the organic fusion of the public and the private, which has thus far materialized in three moments of the nomadic alternative I discussed earlier: the 1896 revolution and the resistance against U.S. pacification during the first two decades of this century; the eve of World War II, with the merger of the urban worker-based Communist party and the Socialist party of peasants in Central Luzon in 1938; and the explosion of the national-democratic movement in the early seventies.

No longer linked to indigenous resistance like the guerilla insurgency of the first decade, which precipitated the rise of the Tagalog novel and the grassroots popularity of the seditious drama in the vernaculars, the "English" writers could neither harness the subtle idiomatic nuances of dialogical representation (Bakhtin) nor exploit the rich generic potential of allegory and ritual available to the vernacular practitioners. Thus, rather than being a direct mechanical reflection or transposition of U.S. imperial ideology, Philippine writing in English before World War II manifested the ambiguous positioning of the middle-level intelligentsia, with its plebeian roots between the rebellious masses and the colonial state. Whether the indigenous revolutionary tradition or the *ilustrado* opportunism and vacillation parasitic upon it will materialize at a certain conjuncture depends crucially on the level or intensity of the masses' opposition to exploitation—as in the Colorum and Sakdalista insurrections of the twenties and thirties. Hence, we witness the emergence and flourishing of Marxist-oriented thought and expression, together with the crystallization of the national-popular will in a vast array of oppositional discourses and practices.

The onset of the Cold War and the McCarthyism-inspired climate of total suppression of dissent that accompanied the U.S. Central Intelligence Agency (CIA)–directed counterinsurgency campaigns against the Huks and their sympathizers in the late forties and early fifties laid the groundwork for the rapid and thorough dissemination of American New Criticism dogmas. These had variants like neo-Aristotelianism, myth criticism, existentialist idealism, pragmatism, functionalism, and others. While surviving left-wing critics of the thirties had been either coopted by the bureaucracy and private business or imprisoned and killed, the aesthetes continued to espouse the primacy of aristocratic taste, combined with fashionable avant-gardism, bohemian styles imitating those of the Parisian Left Bank or New York's Greenwich Village, and consumer cosmopolitanism.

Meanwhile, during the traumatic postwar recovery, in the classrooms of Paul Engle and Robert Lowell at the University of Iowa and in sessions at Breadloaf, Stanford, Kenyon, and elsewhere, a generation of New Critical evangelists was being reared. They would later spread their toxic gospel in the classrooms of the University of the Philippines, Silliman University, and the Ateneo de Manila University, or pontificate in the columns of Manila weekly supplements and journals funded by CIA conduits like the Asia Foundation, the Congress for Cultural Freedom, United States Information Service (USIS), and others.

How can we explain the appeal of the New Criticism when the problem and focus, according to consensus, was no longer the imitation of models but the alignment of language with experience? In the context of the North American institutional setup, Terry Eagleton ventures an explanation:

> New Criticism's view of the poem as a delicate equipoise of contending attitudes, a disinterested reconciliation of opposing impulses, proved deeply attractive to sceptical liberal intellectuals disoriented by the clashing dogmas of the Cold War. Reading poetry in the New Critical way meant committing yourself to nothing. . . . It drove you less to oppose McCarthyism or further civil rights than to experience such pressures as merely partial, no doubt harmoniously balanced somewhere else in the world by their complementary opposites. It was, in other words, a recipe for political inertia, and thus for submission to the political status quo. (50)[10]

In the Philippine context, there really was no credible danger or temptation that the majority of intellectuals, suffering from unemployment, poverty, and paralysis of the will, would incite students or agitate peasants and workers to overthrow the neocolonial power relation. Years of their dependence upon U.S. charity plus habitual subservience to the oligarchy enabled the uninterrupted reproduction of elitist arrogance, narcissistic withdrawal, and cynical temporizing. Stagnation pervaded the ranks of the élite artists and their entourage of court jesters. Having internalized the logic of dependent rationality, the Americanized writer on the whole defended and justified his marginality and irrelevance with the cliché of universalism, technocratic specialization, or an obscurantist mania initially meant to counteract the commodifying stranglehold of programmed corporate modernization. The avant-garde detachment had become time-serving apologists of the iniquitous system.

In 1951, with the Huk rebellion extirpated, the critic Manuel Viray attempted to summarize the transitional curve of the writer's odyssey, from the quest to discover the technical secrets of Sinclair Lewis' *Main Street* and Carl Sandburg's *vers libre* to the mission of exploring thematic-cultural issues in Steinbeck's *In Dubious Battle,* Dos Passos' *USA,* and in the novels of Theodore Dreiser and Thomas Wolfe. In retrospect, it appears that the writer's appropriation of method or technique gravitates to the moment of inquiring: method for whom? technique to accomplish what purpose? Given the global crisis of monopoly capitalism during the thirties, and the internalization of modernist revolt (via the example of the "lost generation"), Filipino intellectuals began to recognize that neither formalist reductionism nor mythical determinism could yield satisfactory answers to those urgent questions. They felt a need to contextualize and indigenize.

From a distance of twenty years, Viray in "Certain Influences in Filipino Writing" reflects that his generation failed to develop or mature as artists with integrity capable of synthesizing moral vision with intelligible form, victimized by, as he puts it, the "dehumanizing influence [of Western hegemony] on culture which started with the machine age and which has, with World Wars I and II, forced almost every man of sensibility to retreat into his inner self and write about his private experience" (298).[11]

This predicted withdrawal into a supposedly pristine and liberated interior space to which Viray alludes no longer entailed, as in the fifties, the anarchist stance of *épatér les bourgeois* (displayed by Villa and his juvenile epigones). Instead it fostered a pseudo-objectivist attitudinizing and a narrow craft-oriented moralism which might be considered the local analogue of the end-of-ideology trend in the West. One obvious example of utilizing New Critical machinery to interpret and evaluate Philippine writing are the two introductions by Edith Tiempo and Edilberto Tiempo to the 1953 anthology *Philippine Writing,* edited by T. D. Agcaoili. With their methodology and criteria of judgment derived from the founding texts of Cleanth Brooks, Robert Penn Warren, John Crowe Ransom, and Allen Tate, the Tiempos fetishized "the organic evolution of a universal truth or experience which represents the story's theme." They apotheosized the ideal of "internal consistency" and the "artistic congruence of denotative and associational elements" derived from New Critical orthodoxy (Agcaoili xi, xxii).

In another essay, Edith Tiempo repeats her adherence to a metaphysical notion of the artist "in thrall only to his art and to his deeply personal commitments" that still informs the thinking of a few diehard reactionaries. Amid the massive brutality inflicted by an authoritarian regime, she conceives of the artist maturing "beyond any chauvinistic-nationalist framework" in order to "continue to celebrate the profoundly human, the exultantly and tragically persisting themes in the heart of man" (26–27).

Meanwhile, in her own backyard, massacres of sugar-cane cutters and innocent civilians by the military had multiplied to the point where Amnesty International, the U.N. Commission on Human Rights, and the World Council of Churches were forced to alarm the international community to help stop such barbarism. Unaffected by such excesses, the English-writing sensibility continued to contemplate the universally human, the perennially true, good, and beautiful.

Probably the most thoroughly "brainwashed" proponent of New Critical dogmatism is Ricaredo Demetillo, whose arsenal of ideas dates back to his stint in a Baptist seminary and brief sojourn at the University of Iowa. Demetillo's mimicry lacks the pedestrian pedantry of Edilberto Tiempo and the pop sociology of Filipiniana expert Leonard Casper (of whom more later), but it makes up for it by an indiscriminate trumpeting of slogans glorifying Eurocentric humanism that would eventually become standard fare for Imelda Marcos' unconscionable exhibitionist stunts. Demetillo writes:

> All these men [Joyce, Gide, Faulkner] project the human condition of their time in all its manifold aspects, not merely the political. . . . This capacity to illuminate the human condition is the reason, too, why we think Dostoevsky and Tolstoy, along with Cervantes, the greatest novelists. No theory of class conflict or social change can do justice to the works of these geniuses. (63)[12]

This fetishism of an abstract "human condition" has been canonized and codified by the Marcos regime's speechwriters (most of whom used English "of a sort," to quote Senator Jose Diokno). With the opportunistic permutation of Third World themes meant to render U.S. acquisitive individualism antithetical to the native "despotic" heritage, the cultural practice of the Marcos apologists exacerbated the paradoxes and ironies of a moribund "New Society" and its sequel, Aquino's caciquism and its military caretakers (now under the patronage of President and ex-General Fidel Ramos).

Compatible with, and in fact complementary to, the New Critical universalism is the minor scholastic brand of casuistry espoused by those educated in colleges owned by the religious orders. The conservative function of this group may be discerned in one Jesuit critic's insistence on "Christian humanism as second nature to the Filipino mind." How this inference was arrived at remains a mystery. The author then exhorts writers to "seek cultural unity with Shakespeare and his cultural heritage," a tautology that betokens a pathetic last-ditch stand to delay the inevitable collapse of the hegemonic culture sustained by the use of English and its prophylactic efficacy.[12]

The subsequent inflection of New Critical formalism into archetypal and anthropological modalities may be grasped as an adaptive modification of the function of academic criticism in the epoch of late capitalism, a response to the crisis of U.S. global ascendancy beginning with the Korean stalemate, the victories of the Cuban and several African anti-imperialist revolutions, and the technological-economic breakthroughs of Germany and Japan. A scandalous conjuncture began to rupture the old dispensation. Besieged by historical-materialist interrogation and other radical interventions, writing in English became contested terrain. In effect, the linguistic space contoured by political and economic constraints no longer could be so openly proclaimed as a neutral, value-free medium for extolling Madison Avenue consumerism and the glory of "free elections" and individual "free play." With autotelic form deconstructed by its internal inconsistences and contextual untenability, there occurred a gradual and uneven shift to a relativist mutation of its concerns, thus rendering more plausible its inherent ahistorical, cosmic claims.

We can perceive this mutation clearly in the novelist N. V. M. Gonzalez's series of ad hoc speculations on the limits and possibilities of the Filipino imagination. In a lecture of May 1952, Gonzalez observes that Filipino writers experience difficulty achieving "integrity of personality," much less nationalistic conviction, because of the temptations of the "materialistic spirit" (by which is meant the acquisitive or possessive drive of the buyer/seller of commodities such as labor power). Gonzalez tries to sketch in the historical coordinates within which the practice of writing has been performed in the local scene. He cites his contemporaries' awareness of the "raw and unrelieved realism of

Erskine Caldwell and Steinbeck," "the hard-boiled Hemingway prose," and the stockpile of techniques appropriated from Henry James, Faulkner, Henry Green, and others. But then he peremptorily exorcises history and valorizes the ego: "art ceases to be art if impelled by historical self-consciousness . . . its fullness of growth is attained only through some independent artistic experience" (Agcaoili 328). Gonzalez's assertion that the only useful literary theory conceives literature as an "act of discovery" attests more to a stark impoverishment of thought than to any presupposed originality of insight. This is surely the last gasp of artisanal petty bourgeois production.

In 1955, Gonzalez called attention to the high prestige enjoyed by writers using English over those using the vernaculars. But because these writers did not have a significantly large informed audience, a critical mass, they had to seek recognition and validation in the U.S. before they could really feel secure or at home in the language, just as Nigerian writers did in London and Senegalese writers in Paris. Bienvenido Lumbera appropriately notes that Gonzalez accepts "economic fact" but elides "history" altogether (74).

In a talk at the Cultural Center of the Philippines in July 1987, Gonzalez summed up the collective experience as "four hundred years of servitude" and described writers like himself as those living "in a world thriving with illiterates" where artists with their claims to élite partisanship and privilege don't count except occasionally as "hewers of wood and drawers of water for the national community's occasional presentations and obligatory fiestas." During the Marcos dictatorship, notable writers in English openly prostituted themselves, reinforcing the idea that the vacillating middle stratum is basically unreliable and opportunistic. Exceptions, of course, abound: Lino Brocka, Maria Lorena Barros, Emmanuel Lacaba, Ed Jopson, and hundreds more.

In pursuing the ordeals of the "English" artist, Gonzales (in a USIS symposium of March 1964) portrays him as a heroic protagonist of the Ibong Adarna myth—the only one of three sons who succeeds in redeeming his ailing father, through his self-laceration and self-sacrifice. Rather than elaborating on the central cognitive thrust of the myth and its collective, decentered subject, Gonzalez narrows his concern to the Filipino writer's irresoluble predicament, expressed as an individual *agon*. Such insight springs from a peculiar blindness. A sudden tremendous upsurge of mass demonstrations, strikes, and widespread peasant revolts against the neocolonial exploitative system characterized the period from 1964 to 1968. But Gonzalez fails to apprehend the rich condensation of such upheavals in popular culture and other social "texts" of that period when, in an essay on "The Filipino Novel" published in 1968, he repeats platitudes drawn from the depleted, well-nigh bankrupt treasury of the New Criticism. For example, he presents the view that the manifold density of social experience is only "an aspect of self-consciousness" and other received doxa. Unlike his academic colleagues, however, Gonzalez spices his makeshift metaphysics with a sprinkling of assorted guidebook statistics to produce an eclectic commentary which, for all its claim to objectivity, nonetheless fails to disguise its basic essentialist presuppositions.

This metaphysics of the hegemonic ideological formation in the first twenty years of the Philippine Republic (1946–66) has evolved, as I noted earlier, from the social division of intellectual labor in a neo-colonial milieu, with the "English" practitioners allowed to invest linguistic capital drawn not from the autochthonous popular tradition but from a narrow, safe region of Anglo-Saxon culture. Such a privilege of "drawing rights," however, imposed the penalty of conformism. A highly effective agency in the inculcation of this conformity was the Fulbright exchange professorships, sponsored by the U.S. government and various private foundations.

One exchange professor during the fifties, perhaps the most fanatical missionary of Cold War orthodoxy, was a certain Leonard Casper. His model and standard of judgment for Philippine writing were derived explicitly from U.S. "southern agrarian ideals and rural actualities," realized in the works of Robert Penn Warren and other ideologues of white supremacy. His opinions and judgments, epitomized in *New Writing from the Philippines*, employ hackneyed social science functionalism to lend pseudoscientific credence to "Christian-agrarian humanism." His pronouncements are replete with the customary underscoring of rhetorical schemes like irony, autonomous form, and mystifying revelations, occluding what is disruptive, heterogeneous, and discontinuous in the national experience vis-à-vis U.S. hegemony. This last category of "experience" is defined by Casper as intrinsically conservative, "essentially defensive, self-conserving" (21).

In effect, what is claimed to be universal or humanist turns out to be a crudely empiricist and prejudiced misreading of the complex dialectics of Philippine reality in accordance with the norms of U.S. Southern plantation aristocracy. To this typically apologetic regress, the corresponding response by militants during the late sixties was the popularization of black expression by Malcolm X and George Jackson and the propagation of the emancipatory ideals of Aimé Cesaire, Amilcar Cabral, C. L. R. James, and especially Frantz Fanon.

In his contribution on "Philippine Poetry" to the *Encyclopedia of Poetry and Poetics* (1965 edition), Casper demonstrates a refurbished strategy of evaluation. New Critical dogmatism by this time had been qualified and supplemented by phenomenology, Northrop Frye schematism, and Cold War sociological platitudes. His revision fabricated an arbitrary chronological grid to deliver scarcely concealed political judgments. Not only does one find factual distortions—for example, "English served to help unify an archipelagic nation divided among nine major dialects"—but also supercilious and presumptuous claims like the following:

> Zulueta da Costa's *Like the Molave* is in the declamatory tradition of Whitman, badly imitated—the pseudo-epic style so attractive to chauvinistic writers substituting enthusiasm for art. More recent poets in English, often trained and published in the United States, have achieved coalescence of native traditions . . . New Critical formalism . . . and personal vision. . . . Even if Tagalog succeeds in becoming the language of literature as well as of elementary communication, American emphasis on the dramatic and concrete has at least hastened the decline of the romantic abstract and essays-in-rhyme in Philippine poetry. ("Philippine Poetry" 614)

When one can so easily assert that Tagalog is not "the language of literature"—whose literature?—it is not difficult to realize whose chauvinism is on trial. In a 1993 revision, Casper deploys a binary opposition ("socially committed" versus "resplendently self-expressive") to evince latitude; but his patronizing tone, ignorance of the vernacular texts, and highly biased inventory together compound the mistakes of the earlier version.

Virtually colonizing (in the passage quoted) the ideals of Western modernism under the aegis of an exhausted and moribund *pax Americana,* Casper is undeterred by the slowly intensifying U.S. aggression in Indochina. In his essays he seeks to revalidate the apriorist outlook implanted during the twenties: First, he ascribes solely to U.S. domination the effect of homogenizing disparities and unifying a presumed schizoid native sensibility. Second, he invents his own version—more precisely, caricature—of the vernacular tradition, purged of its radical, communitarian historicity, thus marginalizing it as a critical force.

Third, he authorizes the hegemonic if precarious supremacy of the English language with its putative monopoly over the "dramatic and concrete," an honorific rubric for the gross empiricism which today governs the "conditionality" ultimatums of the International Monetary Fund/World Bank and their corporate accomplices. Ironically, this formalist sacralization of art legitimizes both capitalist reification (the conversion of all social relations into exchange value, into commodities) and that administered mode of "repressive desublimation" imputed by Herbert Marcuse and others to "affirmative" bourgeois culture.[13]

To what conditions and factors, then, can we attribute the insidious and preemptive influence of New Critical doctrines before the First Quarter Storm of 1970, which marks its long anticipated demise? I can suggest here the outline of a diagnostic analysis, on three interconnected levels—socially, psychologically, and aesthetically.

Socially, in a milieu of political repression and economic harassment, the "English" writers strove hard to maintain their role as defenders/ apologists of the status quo for the sake of jobs, scholarship, amenities, and perquisites. This is assuredly not a conspiracy but the logic of a caste *habitus* (Bourdieu and Passeron). Recall that at this stage the educational institutions and publishing networks still privileged English as the most prestigious medium of communication. With exacerbated class conflict threatening their middling status, these traditional intellectuals repudiated commercialized and degraded mass culture (confusing it with popular, indigenous culture), which automatically was identified with the unlettered strata.

Psychologically, this Americanizing cohort retreated to a frozen, abstract realm of the intellect—a monadic private space guaranteed by the uneven, overdetermined formation. With few exceptions, they denied the ethical imperatives of class struggle. They refused history for myth, conjuring in fantasy a permanent equilibrium or synaesthesia (reminiscent of the early theorizing of I. A. Richards) of the passions. Their plight may also be described as an abortion of Fanon's paradigm of the evolution of the Third World intellectual toward emancipation.

Aesthetically, the disciples of Villa and sycophants of Romulo exalted the virtues of symbolic form, the space for hypostatizing images and impulses into a unified self-contained structure. With progressive critical thought suppressed, neutralized, or incorporated in the secular resistance then mounting against religious/sectarian propaganda (for example, the controversy over the legislative move to include Rizal's novels in the college curriculum), New Criticism preempted and monopolized the field of hermeneutics and aesthetic judgment by max-imizing its Orientalizing scope, intensity, and persistence.[14]

Having charted the constellation of interanimating forces and actors in this field, and having triangulated the political, ideological, and eco-nomic instances to define the concrete phenomenon "Philippine writing in English," it might be instructive, before concluding, to articulate the postwar literary situation with corresponding U.S. perceptions. Long before the Philippines surfaced in the horizon of Hemingway's con-sciousness, the U.S. occupation of the islands—its military commanders fresh from exterminating the American Indians on the western frontier, and pacifying the insurgent Cubans and Puerto Ricans—had aroused the consciences of luminaries like William James, Mark Twain, George Santayana, and William Dean Howells. Their anti-imperialist critiques demystified to some extent the missionary rationale that in overt and covert forms has continued to vitiate U.S. scholarship on the Philippines to the present day.[15]

The distinguished novelist Wallace Stegner, professor at Stanford University, visited the Philippines at the peak of Huk insurgency in 1951 and subsequently assessed the outcome of half-a-century of Amer-ican tutelage. Within the limits of his liberal sympathy, Stegner depicts the country's "economic and cultural dependency" and the Filipino "cultural inferiority complex" arising from what he believes to be the lack of any literary tradition. Stegner's complacent ignorance here does not deviate from the stereotype of the American tourist's overnight expertise. He notes the absence of political consciousness among the "English" writers—"a disturbing evasion of the hard realities" (such as landlord exploitation, usury, and poverty) by intellectuals whose voca-tion strikes him as that of "chroniclers of the nostalgic barrios of their childhood." (Bulosan was then labeled by reviewers as "the genial satir-ist of barrio corruption.")

Stegner goes on to claim that literature produced by Filipinos ignored "the shadow of violence and fear [that] hangs over even well-policed Manila." Whether "living in a dream or a hole," the "English" writ-ers are thus defeated by "the sense of being an extra, unwanted, un-regarded fringe on their national life, an irrelevancy." While Stegner is entirely correct in ascribing irrelevance to the exercise of an alien language, he is completely mistaken in alleging that the vernaculars (which he was unable to read) have no "tradition" (52).[16] His implicit conclusion that Philippine writing is only a minor emerging "branch of

English literature" has been echoed many times by foreign as well as local commentators.

Our last intertextual exhibit comes from John Leonard, reviewer for the *New York Times*, who visited the Philippines in 1978. This testimony of an East Coast liberal, bemused at the sociocultural enigma he encounters, may remind us of Stegner's patronizing expertise and, before him, the skeptical wonder of nineteenth-century European travelers like Jagor and Goncharov:

> And the American visitor is sick of his own lazy generalizations on American culture. His "imperial self" is missing the point. . . . Why—in a nation where English, after 50 years of American rule, is an "official language"— do they want to convert Tagalog into the dominant vernacular? Why, in a nation—7,000 islands, really, and 87 languages, and 300 dialects—where students have enough trouble understanding a sonnet of Shakespeare or a chapter of Dickens, or distinguishing in English between a subject and predicate, are the faculty all trained in American New Criticism? R. P. Blackmur? John Crowe Ransom? Yvor Winters? In the country of Leyte and Corregidor? What has Percy Lubbock or Cleanth Brooks or Rene Wellek to do with little bananas and active volcanos and nipa huts and caribou? (48–49)

Leonard seems to have crawled from a Neanderthal hole: since the sixties, Filipino students are no longer reading Shakespeare or Dickens as part of the general curriculum. In any case, "caribou" speaks volumes. Caribou, anyone? What these rhetorical questions betray, aside from their tone of chic Manhattan ennui, is the fatal deficiency in all American attempts from W. Cameron Forbes to Stanley Karnow to make sense of the Philippine conjuncture: the failure to comprehend the Filipino people's history as a process of national liberation and self-affirmation. Underlying Leonard's view is the incapacity to perceive the difference and understand the Filipino's "Otherness" as the intransigent negation of U.S. racism and imperialism. Like so many well-meaning visitors, he can only see the Filipino "in our image," to quote the title of Karnow's refurbished apologia.

The resurgence of progressive art and criticism in the period 1967–72 exposed the fragility of U.S. ideological supremacy and in turn disclosed the subterranean vitality of the radical democratic Enlightenment program broached in 1896 and articulated during the thirties and forties toward socialism. However, the residual attachment of activist intellectuals to notions of "organic form" and to mechanical, class-reductionist formulas prevented organizations like PAKSA (*Literature for the People*) from forging and consolidating what Gramsci calls "a national-popular bloc" of discourses and practices. Consequently, one will still find today U.S.-trained humanities teachers, together with technocrats graduated from MIT, Stanford, or the Harvard Business School, preaching the tenets of philosophical idealism and pragmatism.

In the seventies, the Marcos regime's state apparatuses (among them the Cultural Center, Writers Union, National Media Center, and assorted journals, TV and radio programs) attempted to contrive nativist revivals couched in the spurious lexicon of development and "Third World liberation." A peculiar innovation may be the slogan "Humanism: The Ideology." The dictator Marcos himself proclaimed that his vision "is mankind as the purpose, the heart and the center of development," a move to preempt or muffle whatever cries of protest about human rights violations may be launched by the United Nations, Amnesty International, and other monitors (64).[17] This invocation of a "humanist ideology," meant to assuage the conscience of bureaucrats and Western diplomats, sounded like an unintentional parody of Wallerstein's paradigm of the capitalist world system and the ubiquitous dependency *problematique*. But its affinity with and descent from the self-legitimating apologetics of William Howard Taft and the New Criticism's agrarian racism seemed fairly evident.

Authoritarian *diktat* did not completely succeed in turning the tide of revolutionary cultural practice. The reason is chiefly because it did not have a coherent, tested, all-encompassing theory that could totalize the complex, diverse relations of a dependent society and interpellate individuals toward collective action. Nationalist militants continued to operate in legal organizations and underground, in the folds and interstices of civil society. What "national security" authoritarianism accomplished was the provision of official channels for the already obsolete or anachronistic aestheticism of younger writers and its updated variants in the controlled media. One example is the article by Cirilo Bautista, "Conversations with Jose Garcia Villa," in the government publication *Archipelago*, where Villa is exalted as the logocentric guru *par excellence:* "Form is art; art is form. . . . It is not the idea that is important but the form" (30). After recording Villa's acknowledged indebtedness to e.e. cummings, Bautista then endorses Villa as the paragon of "New Society" artists:

> In the late 1960s, Villa's poetry provided an alternative to the blood-and-bullet rhetorics of the Proletarian writers. . . . While theirs spoke of physical transformation to restore civil order, his spoke of spiritual transformation to restore sanity to a dehumanized world; while theirs raged in street parlance about economic statistics, social deprivation and fascist tactics, his enlightened in a noble language about the innate dignity of man, moral liberty, and the uses of religion. (31)

The obvious strategy here is to split the unity of theory and practice achieved by Filipino writers—the most exemplary is Bulosan, a worker-exile in the United States during the Philippine Commonwealth and the Cold War era—at those decisive conjunctures triangulated earlier. Because his sensibility was deeply rooted in the proletarian struggles of his time, Bulosan was able to register the latent subversive impulses in his milieu as well as the emancipatory vision in what V. L. Parrington once called the realist, populist tradition in U.S. writing: from Whitman to Twain, Dreiser to Richard Wright (San Juan, *Bulosan*). Challenged by the Philippine counterpart of that tradition, Villa and his disciples can only gesture toward, or even parody, U.S. neoconservative styles and banalities ranging from the compromised liberalism of the welfare state to religious fundamentalism, *laissez-faire* utilitarianism, and packaged postmodern fads fresh from American corporate publicity mills.

One last development in U.S.-influenced cultural theorizing relevant here is a brand of specious historicism intended to supplement or rectify New Critical tendentiousness. One example is Nick Joaquin's widely quoted lecture, "The Filipino as English Fictionist," over which the ghost of Marshall McLuhan tantalizingly hovers. Joaquin argues that in contrast with vernacular writers—not really writers to him but "oral fictionists" devoid of a historical sense—the "English" practitioners participate in a visual culture (that is, literate and historically minded), proving themselves the authentic heirs of Western civilization (both Spanish and Anglo-Saxon).

Like the deposed autocrat of Malacañang Palace, Joaquin is not averse to issuing arbitrary decrees sanctioned only by the force of prejudice or ignorance: "For good or ill, our literature in English is that standard against which our literature in the vernacular will have to measure itself" ("The Filipino as English Fictionist" 46).[18] But Joaquin's apologetics, self-deconstructed by its unwitting aporias and non sequiturs, can be more pertinently characterized as a cathartic figure, a therapeutic emblem for the passing of an epoch in which U.S. cultural ascendancy (neocolonial standards masquerading as universal and absolute) was taken for granted—was, in fact, deemed normal, right, and natural.

Contrary to what Joaquin and his coterie claim about the "English" writers' cultivation of the Western patrimony, it was actually the vernacular artists of the first two decades—and, during the thirties, the socialist principles and precepts of the Philippine Writers' League—that preserved and revitalized the Enlightenment project of *prodesse-delectare* (Arguilla). The vernacular artists encompassed the agitprop theater of Abad and Tolentino and the exuberant Horatian poetics of Lope K. Santos, Jose Corazon de Jesus, and others. This performative strategy was initiated by Rizal's allegorical fabulations (particularly *Noli Me Tangere* and *El Filibusterismo*), the polemics of Isabelo de los Reyes and Claro Recto, and the encyclopedic scholarship of Jaime de Veyra and Epifanio de los Santos, among others (Lopez).

In general, I contend that the "English" practitioners have, as a group, never represented the nation in the process of emergence, much less the people constituted as the victims of U.S. domination and exploitation. And I would also argue that the authentic organic intellectuals who sought to organize the spontaneous national-popular energies and infuse them with conscienticizing purpose rooted in the notion of justice in an egalitarian community are the *vernacular* writers. Examples include Amado Hernandez and Magdalena Jalandoni; the anonymous artificers of the Moro epics (*parangsabil*); committed novelists and dramatists in Cebu, Ilocos, Pampanga, and other regions; the collaborators of *Hulagpos*; the contributors to *Mga Tula ng Rebolusyong Pilipino*; and Jason Montana and the clandestine partisans of ARMAS (Artists and Writers of the People).

The unprecedented debacle of U.S. imperialism in Indochina during the mid-seventies, the summing-up of the lessons of the Proletarian Cultural Revolution in China, the upsurge of worldwide rebellions against capital in Iran, Nicaragua, Palestine, South Africa, and elsewhere involving new historic agents such as women, youth, gays and lesbians, ethnic communities, and the urban poor—all these signaled an acceleration of the process of collapse of U.S. cultural suzerainty in the Philippines in the seventies and eighties. The once-celebrated image of the United States championing freedom, democracy, and equality—the originary and obsessive rationale of its interventionist policy—had been shattered by its brutalizing counterinsurgency in Vietnam, Cambodia, and Laos; by the U.S.-instigated military coup in Chile; by the systematic violence inflicted on the domestic opposition (Black Panthers, antiwar dissenters, resistance by people of color); and by outright cynical brutalization of ordinary citizens at the hands of the U.S.-subsidized Marcos clique.

With the killing of Benigno Aquino in 1983, which climaxed over two decades of U.S.-assisted repression, U.S. complicity in "national security state" abuses demolished its claim of guardianship of democratic principles, despite the last-minute machinations of the Reagan administration to salvage its reputation in February 1986—a classic scene replayed in the Bush administration's intervention of December 1989 to save its disintegrating client regime.

Once lauded as an antidote against the generally acknowledged capitalist perversion of humanist values, New Criticism had exposed its partisanship by its toleration of corruption and state terrorism, grown rampant since the imposition of martial law in 1972, and in its reflex rehashing of anticommunist slogans to deflect attention from the systemic causes of poverty, injustice, and oppression. Aquino's paltry dispensation, which succeeded that of Marcos, compensated for its lack of any reform program by allowing the amoralism of "low intensity" warfare to buttress the logic of the market and to indulge the punitive raids of the IMF/World Bank. In business, media, and schools, U.S. social science methodologies (functionalism and empiricism in particular) harmonize neatly with formalist aesthetics in their ahistorical valorization of feudal familialism, patronage or reciprocity patterns (*hiya, pakikisama*) and the authoritarian scheme of state-guided development (made academically respectable by invoking Hobbes, Weber, Samuel Huntington, and other "latter-day saints" of modernization).

In the new U.S. post–Cold War strategy of more tightly integrating the periphery to the industrial needs of the center, the mediation of IMF/World Bank agencies has replaced the primacy of parliamentary institutions with that of the corporatist state.[19] Except perhaps in El Salvador and other places, the redemocratization trend of the eighties has only succeeded in resurrecting the trappings of civilian government to conceal violence as the ultimate prop of structural inequality and the daily reproduction of oppressive relations. Large-scale exploitation of workers by transnational capital, the exodus of domestics and workers to the Middle East and elsewhere, and U.S.-funded "low-intensity" warfare in the countryside persist; it is "business as usual."

In the wake of the worsening disaster inflicted by the Mt. Pinatubo eruption, the spectacle broadcast around the world in 1991 was not only the eruption, but also the collapse of the myth of "people power." This toppling was dramatized by Aquino's flagrant sellout of the nation's sovereignty when the Philippine Senate, for the first time in the Republic's history, rejected the infamous 1947 treaty that extended the lease of U.S. military bases for 99 years.

With the precipitous obsolescence of English as the medium of instruction and social communication in the Philippines, the growth of progressive forces in all sectors, and the rapid disintegration of the traditional oligarchic ruling bloc as we approach the end of this millenium, the rupture of U.S. hegemony and its supersession by a resurgent national-popular consensus will become finally irreversible. One clear indication is the Senate's aforementioned repudiation of "special relations" with the U.S., an unprecedented decision to affirm Filipino sovereignty in the face of threats to withdraw aid and other help. This surely would not have been possible without the ideological remolding and nationalist mobilization of the middle strata, particularly professionals and business people, by various organized sectors, among them associations of revolutionary writers and artists, militant youth, and enlightened women cadres during the decades of resistance against the Marcos dictatorship and its predecessors.

With its "total war" policy, ineptitude, and corruption, Aquino's refeudalizing state (retooled by Fidel Ramos) has intensified various social contradictions since the collapse of peace talks with the National Democratic Front in 1987. Culture also has become subtly instrumentalized, as in the past, to serve oligarchic rule and transnational corporate interests. The ensemble of signifying practices—ranging from petit bourgeois writing, to feminist mobilization, to cultural resistance practiced by the beleaguered Moro and Igorot peoples—is now envisaged as heavily contested terrain, fulfilling Voloshinov / Bakhtin's hypothetical premise that "the sign becomes an arena of class struggle" (23).[20]

This sign, of course, encompasses not just texts and discourses, but also institutional practices in civil society and the state. Neo–social Darwinist values and the "colonial mentality syndrome" (the contemporary tropes of which are the Free Trade Zones, warm body exports, prostitution-tourist industry, and certain NGO shenanigans) continue to be fostered in the mass media. But, simultaneously, an oppositional trend has evolved throughout the islands before and after 1986, via underground publications, teach-ins, music, poster art, quasi-Brechtian theater, and videofilms, recuperating the vitality of the submerged genealogy of national-popular culture. This trend seeks to fuse the mimetic-cognitive function of art (where, by nuanced sublimations, "the imaginary resolution of real-life contradictions" is inscribed) with its ethical-pedagogical power, for the purpose of inventing new subject positions, contesting dominated sites hitherto pacified, mobilizing mass energies, and inciting emancipatory subversions in all areas of life. This agenda of nomadic, subversive, deterritorializing forces continues to fuel the struggle for a Filipino national-popular culture in the nineties and beyond.

At this pivotal juncture, our paramount decolonizing project—an integral component of the ongoing anti-imperialist struggle—is the construction of a national-popular canon of discourses and practices that would release energies and catalyze wills, ushering the stage for a dialectical transaction between past and future, between folklore / common sense and scientific socialism with a distinctly Filipino orientation, between tradition and the creation of "the new person." It may be neither premature nor anticlimactic to announce here that we have long passed the stage when the rhetorical juxtaposition of texts by Jefferson and Schlesinger with those by Jose Maria Sison, Francisco Nemenzo, Father Edicio de la Torre, and other Filipino socialist intellectuals can be a useful ecumenical game, the gambit of a neopragmatic conversation. Such intertextuality would neither entertain nor deceive anyone. And proposing for the nth time that we re-read the Anglo-American classics (Henry James, Faulkner, and others) as well as politically correct sermons of cultural-literacy experts like Hirsch and assorted neoconservatives, only serves to lend moral credence to IMF / World Bank directives for the more intense exploitation of Filipino peasants, women, students, workers, national minorities, and so on.

In the long run, such "friendly" advice only helps legitimize U.S. political, economic, and military support for developmental subalternity and neo-imperialist repression. Given this unremitting complicity of U.S. administrations with the daily brutalization of the Filipino masses by its well-tutored clients (the native élite in government and military), perhaps Hemingway himself would be painfully surprised and even outraged, if he could revisit now.

Today the praxis of writing in the Philippines manifests itself in its unrelenting and experimentally versatile drive to Filipinize historical materialism and the legacy of Eurocentric socialist thought by purging them of Orientalizing elements and productivist, racializing constraints. Applying the method of materialist dialectics to the analysis of multilayered and overdetermined contradictions, we can liberate our people's transformative genius in a profound popular-democratic cultural renaissance—a permanent recovery and affirmation of our national identity in the process of historic becoming, of exercising informed responsible agency for the construction of a just and egalitarian society in our part of southeast Asia. That, indeed, would be our singular contribution to the advance of all people of color in their revolutionary conquest of their dignity and freedom on this planet.

3

Masks of the Filipino in the "New World"

> Less swart in aspect, the companions of this figure were of that vivid, tiger-yellow complexion peculiar to some of the aboriginal natives of the Manillas;— a race notorious for a certain diabolism of subtility, and by some honest white mariners supposed to be the paid spies and secret confidential agents on the water of the devil, their Lord, whose counting-room they suppose to be elsewhere.
> —*Herman Melville*, Moby Dick, *1851*

Smiling pink round face, gold-rimmed designer spectacles adding intellectual veneer to Corazon Aquino's winsome look as she props her chin, poised proudly to look at readers of *Time, Newsweek, MS., New York Times*—this media phantasy, now slightly frayed, has come to dominate the world's attention since February 1986. In that month, the "People Power" insurrection in the Philippines overthrew the fourteen-year-old dictatorship of Ferdinand Marcos. President Aquino promptly displaced the legendary "Iron Butterfly," Marcos's wife Imelda, in the pantheon of the mass media, even as the scandal of billions of dollars looted from the Philippine treasury, the parade of court indictments, underworld shenanigans, secret assassinations, and so on, continued to define the Filipino stereotype for the U.S. public. Since Aquino's term ended in 1992, the Philippines is virtually under martial rule again, courtesy of General Fidel Ramos, Marcos's former protegé, and the archipelago has returned to the obscurity of the back pages of the world's metropolitan newspapers.

In the October 1986 article on Aquino in *MS.*, a Filipina journalist with "left-wing" pretensions (by not so deft quotes) tried to convince the U.S. audience that "Tita" (Auntie) Cory, by virtue of being a woman, would save all 56 million Filipinos (the population at the time) from being crushed "between the gun [military brutality] and the crucifix [religious sexism]." But, after less than a thousand days of Aquino's regime, the image of the Filipino in the international media remained nebulous, at best a cross between two stereotypes, those of the romantic Mexican bandit and "the inscrutable Oriental."

Even as this is written, on the eve of the twenty-first century, the media still offer the spectacle of the Filipino running amok in contested villages in the Philippines, the "warm body export" of Filipino workers to the Middle East; Filipinas as "mail-order brides," ubiquitous prostitutes around enclaves formerly occupied by U.S. military bases; and "hospitality girls" in Tokyo, Bangkok, Okinawa, and Taipeh. Rumor once broadcast to all and sundry that the *Oxford English Dictionary* defined the "Filipina" as "domestic." Reality, however, revealed dossiers of varying roles.

Meanwhile, in Hong Kong, dolls of Filipino women dressed as maids, complete with passport and labor contract, compete as toys in the department stores (Escoda). Just last year, in 1995, the cruel hanging of contracted maid Flor Contemplacion, beaten by Singapore authorities until she confessed to a double murder, has exploded into a national crusade to redeem the honor of thousands of such "martyrs." (Virtually every issue of the Manila newspapers, or the San Francisco–based *Philippine News*, reports the victimage of Filipino overseas workers with sensationalizing élan.) This is the latest stage in the ongoing metamorphosis of our brothers and sisters: the Filipina not as tourist but as transnational subaltern, virtually a new caste of "postcolonial" serfs— certainly not Goethe's world citizen but a wandering proletariat roaming the global village.

It was not so long ago that Filipino villages sheltered guerrillas of the beleaguered first Philippine Republic. Fresh from routing American Indians, Cubans, and Puerto Ricans, the U.S. military killed over a million insurgent Filipinos in that little-known episode in U.S. history, the Filipino-American War, at the turn of the century. In spite of that "first Vietnam," the U.S. public's early notion was that Filipinos were, in Samuel Gompers' words, "a semi-barbaric population, almost primitive in their habits and customs." This suspicion found visual confirmation in a "scientific" / cultural event, the 1904 Saint Louis World's Fair, where Igorot, Negrito, and Moro tribal specimens were displayed (Robinson 94–95).

Shades of American Indians in the court of Louis XIV? Not quite. We are now in the stage of finance capitalism. A carnival of mass commodification, mass consumption. That now-historic exposition may be said to have fleshed out, in a pseudoscientific bazaar, the rhetoric of William McKinley, Theodore Roosevelt, Henry Cabot Lodge, and the jingoists of "Manifest Destiny" who then felt called to defend the mandate of Anglo-Saxon imperial supremacy.

Over half a century of U.S. tutelage has made many Filipinos entrenched fanatics of "the American dream of success." More than 20,000 Filipinos (not counting the TNTs, Filipinos without legal visas, otherwise known as "undocumented aliens") immigrate to the United States annually, accepting low-income jobs even though they are educated and skilled professionals (dentists, engineers, lawyers, and other "brain-drain" cadres). This repeats a gesture of sacrifice made by their predecessors. The early immigrants were, of course, not college graduates; they were recruited peasants hired to work in the sugar plantations of Hawaii, victims of inflated advertisements of wealth supposed to be acquired through honest manual labor.

Needless to say, the Filipino recruits (more sojourners than migratng settlers) learned quickly the reality of U.S. business society. Experiencing the truth of exploitation in a regime of possessive / acquisitive individualism, Filipinos joined the Japanese plantation workers in fierce strikes in the twenties, thirties, and forties: at Hanapepe, Kauai, fifteen workers were massacred. Visiting the "Plantation Village" at Waipahu, Hawaii, during March 1995, I was reminded how the International Longshoremen's and Warehousemen's Union (ILWU) was born when, in the multiracial strike of 1949, six thousand workers from the Philippines recruited as scabs joined the union and foiled the planters' schemes. The tactic of divide-and-rule failed miserably. Right from the start, the image of the Filipino as militant striker has seized the headlines.

But it was during the worldwide Depression of the early 1930s that Filipinos turned out to be the scapegoats of choice, the targets for lynching. One instance is the January 1930 killing of two Filipinos and the beating of scores in Watsonville, California, by a mob of 500 white vigilantes. It seemed a repeat of Yankee soldiers conducting systematic slaughter of Filipino peasant families in insurgent villages in Samar, Batangas, and other provinces in 1899. One witness of this harrowing collective ordeal was Carlos Bulosan, whose testimony, in *America Is In the Heart* speaks for all the dispossessed and disinherited: "The mockery of it all is that Filipinos are taught to regard Americans as our equals. Adhering to American ideals, living American life, these are contributory to our feelings of equality. The terrible truth in America shatters the Filipino's dreams of fraternity."

One recalls here the story of Maria Ofalsa as an exemplum: she arrived in California in 1926 and was hospitalized after two years of grueling work. Her family suffered horrendous prejudice, racially motivated harassment, and eviction, all of which they quietly endured. After getting her citizenship in 1952, this victim of unrelenting racism advised her compatriots: "When you come here to the United States remember this is not our country, so you try to be nice and don't lose your temper and try to be friendly and don't put on a sour face" (Aguilar–San Juan 208). For obvious reasons, her advice has not been completely heeded. But in truth, we meet her every day.

The "dream of fraternity" has awakened the Filipino into prosaic reality. As far as I know, the solidarity and sacrifice of Filipinos who fought side by side with Americans in Bataan and Corregidor during World War II has not been cited in order to improve the situation of 9,000 stewards in the U.S. Navy during the sixties. Still called "boys," these "model minority" servants have also staffed the kitchen of the White House and other official residences or government quarters. In the sixties, Filipinos became visible as nurses and doctors, with imported nurses sometimes acting as scabs and performing work shunned by whites, servicing nearly entire hospitals.

During this period, the case of two Filipina nurses accused of killing patients in a Veterans Hospital in Michigan became a sensational story. It buttressed the old impression of Filipinos as "devious" and "inscrutable," disturbers of the peace, and so on, so that despite their acquittal, the stigma of wrongdoing still contaminates the atmosphere. The stereotypical persona endures in our crisis-ridden milieu. Meanwhile, the generation of Filipino farmworkers in California who spearheaded union organizing in the thirties and forties had finally merged their patient struggles with the more numerous Chicanos in 1965, with their leader, Cesar Chavez, eclipsing the figures of Filipino veteran labor leaders Larry Itliong and Philip Vera Cruz in the formation of the United Farm Workers of America (Scharlin and Villanueva).

With the exposure of the Marcos regime's corruption and complicity with U.S. reactionary elements in the late sixties, the Filipino acquired rebel status. Political exiles like Benigno Aquino, husband of President Corazon Aquino, and other dissidents (not exactly anticommunist emigres idolized by the Establishment) graced the front pages of metropolitan dailies. They were juxtaposed with pictures of New People's

Army guerrillas and Moro National Liberation Front freedom fighters, the latter resurrecting in the popular memory their heroic ancestors, who up to the late twenties defied the Gringo intruders led by Leonard Wood and John Pershing, veterans of the wars to exterminate the American Indians and to pacify Latino insurgents. Together with the Igorots of Exposition fame, the Moro combatants, joined by a coalition of aboriginal groups in the Mindanaw Lumad, are today mounting attacks on numerous oppressive institutions underwritten by transnational business and the International Monetary Fund / World Bank (Rodil).

One hopes that the insurrection of February 1986 has erased in the U.S. collective memory any lingering vestiges of the 1904 St. Louis Exposition. For this new generation, "Filipino" would translate into images of the striking militants of the Hawaiian canefields (one of whom [Pedro Calosa] returned to the Philippines to lead the "Colorum" peasant uprising in the thirties), the Huk guerrillas of World War II, and the ILWU activists Chris Mensalvas and Ernesto Mangaong who resisted McCarthyism and won (de Vera). We hope that the ritual symbolism of "people power" in 1986 has finally replaced the outworn stereotypes in the white majority's consciousness with the scenario of millions of urban workers, peasants, women, and Filipinos from all walks of life surrounding tanks and soldiers in the streets of Metro Manila. The unprecedented 1986 insurrection, treading closely in the wake of those gory details of Benigno Aquino's cadaver bloodying the tarmac of the Manila International Airport, has prompted Filipinos to reconnect once more with their national demotic origin. I cite a letter from a Connecticut newspaper, the *Hartford Courant:*

> I was born a Filipino. That may seem like an easy statement to make, but even as I write it, I am amazed at the embarrassment I used to feel. Ever since my parents brought me to the United States, I had been ashamed of who I am, and ashamed of my nation. . . .
>
> I was ashamed (as my brother was) of being different. When friends at school said it was disgusting to see my mother serve fish with the head still intact, or for my father to eat rice with his hands, or to learn that stewed dogs and goats were some examples of Filipino delicacies, I took their side. I accused my own of being unsanitary in their eating habits. . . . When Marcos flaunted his tyranny and declared martial law in 1972, . . . I accused Filipinos of lacking the guts to fight for themselves. . . . But everything changed for me when that man [Aquino] I had laughed at landed in my homeland and died on the airport tarmac.

For the first time, I accused myself of not having enough faith in, and hope for, my own people. In the past, I felt that I had no right to be proud of my people. Now, with the cruel Marcos regime tottering, I have finally awakened. Filipinos all over the world need the strength that comes with pride, now more than ever. . . .

Of course, it is clear that this Filipina teenager had not heard of the April 1924 strike of 31,000 Filipinos in Hawaii, nor all the other acts of protest and agitation up to the San Francisco International Hotel saga of resistance that have colored (what an appropriate if paradoxical term!) the white American's perception of Filipinos. Yet the past is there for each generation of Filipinos to rediscover and perhaps revitalize, including the fact that as "nonwhites" (up to 1946) they could be refused service in restaurants, barbershops, swimming pools, moviehouses, and could not marry white / caucasian women because, as one California state prosecutor said, Malays are prone to "homicidal mania" called "running amuck." Antimiscegenation was the name of the game then. The figure of the amok, however, cuts both ways: as derogatory ideologeme for the potboiler *Ghosts of Manila* by James Hamilton-Paterson; and as emancipatory trope in Nick Carbo's laconic poem "Running Amok":

In the slums of Tondo, people live
in shacks of cardboard, bits of bamboo,
corrugated metal, and a few cement blocks.
They come from all the provinces. . . .

The highest incidence of men
running amok is in Tondo. . . .
During the Filipino-American War
from 1900 to 1902, the Colt .45 pistol
was *refined* to kill crazed
Moro fighters who ran amok
and would not stop attacking
when shot with bullets of lesser caliber.

Some superstitious old women say
that no rice, no shoes, and no work
breed beetles and violence.
They say that small black beetles
can lay eggs in a man's ear,
and this is what makes
a man run.

White Men's Burden

Confusion about the racial category to which Filipinos should be assigned has run rampant in the mind of the white imperial élite ever since the colonization of the Philippines, from President McKinley up to the ordinary citizen in suburbia who is unable to tell whether the Malay is a Mongolian; whether the Filipino is an African, Chinese, Japanese, or what. Even today, because of my slant eyes, nose, and other facial features, I am mistaken for being a Japanese or Chinese at the university, in the desolate malls of New England, along small-town streets of the Midwest, almost everywhere. And when I tell the curious observer I am from the Philippines (an original, as they say, "born in the islands"), indeed, the image of an island in the Caribbean immediately flashes in their minds, especially because my name (and those of most Filipinos) is Spanish in origin.

If it is of any consolation for would-be settlers, one can say that we Filipinos are no longer strangers to U.S. immigration officials. For when the Filipino national hero Jose Rizal arrived in San Francisco in transit to Europe in 1888, he was promptly quarantined and fumigated by customs officials (together with 643 Chinese coolies) on the pretext that they were carriers of typhoid, cholera, leprosy, and other "Yellow Perils." Meanwhile, 700 bales of precious Chinese silk were unloaded from the ship without much ado. In 1908, a Hawaiian farmowner ordered farm supplies in which he listed after fertilizer the item "Filipinos." Today, the most valuable commodities from the islands are no longer hemp, sugar, or coconuts, but mail-order brides followed by domestic help and "hospitality" girls. Our status as "model minority" badly needs emergency rectification.

Before the end of this century, there will be an estimated 2.1 million Filipinos (Min 142) in the U.S., the fastest growing community of former colonial subjects (many, of course, still colonized inside, without the slightest suspicion). This population is concentrated in the West Coast, in Chicago, New Jersey–New York, and, of course, in Hawaii and Alaska. A volume of family-and-kin pictures published in 1983 was entitled *Filipinos: Forgotten Asian Americans*. Forgotten? Not quite, as long as TV and mass media and everyday conversation feed off the notorious Marcos dynasty, marvel at Mount Pinatubo's fireworks, and worry about the danger of a "Communist" takeover in the Philippines or some equivalent calamity that might hobble business operations. Forgotten Filipinos, indeed! Millions of Filipino domestics, brides, and bar entertainers, mixing with average citizens, politicians, crooks, and fugitive adventurers of all sorts circulate around the planet—forgotten? Or misbegotten?

As long as the Philippines supplies cheap labor, power, its people will never be forgotten (Villones). The period of the eighties has, in fact, generated a new semantics of racial categorization that expands to cover the whole Third World: Marcos joins the ranks of the unsavory Duvalier of Haiti, Somoza of Nicaragua, the Shah of Iran, Panama's Noriega, and other "not quite civilized" despots to reinforce once again the myth of the West as the virtuous, enlightened *homo sapiens*, civilizing the benighted natives. Unfortunately, internationally acclaimed films—by the innovative Kidlat Tahimik (Eric de Guia), like *The Perfumed Nightmare, Turumba*, and *Who Invented the Yoyo and the Moon-Buggy?* (the Pinoy, of course) or by the late Lino Brocka—have not succeeded in displacing the Hollywood/Madison Avenue stereotypes of Filipinos. We are still categorized as lowly denizens who occupy the boundaryline between China and Latin America, an enigmatic and heterogeneous zone that seems to defy neat pejorative labeling or subtle erasure.

Despite recent efforts at canon revision, Bulosan and other Filipino writers domiciled here remain excluded from the academic textbooks, while the legendary Jose Garcia Villa (not to be confused with Pancho Villa, the Mexican general), who was at one time a minor celebrity of the New York intellectual coterie, languishes in anonymity somewhere in Greenwich Village, waiting for the apocalypse.

While meditating on this conjuncture between apocalypse and genesis, between the fall of the Berlin Wall ("Evil Empire," in neoconservative demonology) and the Indian uprising in Chiapas, Mexico, I want to quote a passage from one of Bulosan's letters (written in the forties) to recapture and perhaps recuperate the force of the Filipinos' submerged and ambiguous history. Consider this a thought-experiment that remains emblematic of the way Filipinos (and perhaps other immigrants from the "periphery") articulate the ethical-ideological core of their predicament as exiles, immigrants, expatriates or refugees. They are not quite "world citizens," as the European Enlightenment dreamed of their peripatetic entrepreneurs. Bulosan outlines the germ of his decisive textual adventure:

> I have been wanting to do something of great significance to the future of the islands. I will probably start one of the most important books in my life

soon, maybe sometime next week. . . . It concerns racial lies: the relations between Pinoys [short for Fili*pinos*] and white Americans. Here it is: Suddenly in the night a Filipino houseboy kills a friend and in his attempt to escape from the law he stumbles into his dark room and bumps against the wall. When he wakes up he is confronted by a veiled image in the darkness who reveals to him that he has become white. It is true, of course, that he has become a white man. But the image tells him he will remain a white man so long as he will not fall in love with a white woman! And that is the tragedy because he has already fallen in love with a white woman. Get that? So long as he will not fall in love with a white woman! Then, according to the warning of the image, he would become a Filipino again, ugly, illiterate, monster-like, and vicious.

This is a parable, of course, an American parable. Some elements in America gave us a gift of speech, education, money, but they also wanted to take away our heart. They give you money but deny your humanity.

This dilemma has been rehearsed and acted interminably over and over, in the waking experiences, deliriums, and nightmares of millions of blacks, Latinos, Asians, and Native Americans. Repetition breeds truth, as Nietzsche once warned us; but how can we finally break the cycle and construct our identity on the edge of negation? Not to make a mystique of the Other's subservience, of difference itself as a virtue, but to identify our desire for recognition via the gaze of the Other? We have had the testimonies of inverse self-development and its impasse: Fanon's *Black Skin, White Masks*, George Jackson's *Soledad Brother*, Rigoberta Menchu's witnessing memoir or *testimonio*, among others. Do we need another diary from the ashes of the Asian holocaust?

For the Filipino, I venture to propose a challenge: *the answer is not to multiply documents in the labyrinthine archive but to liberate the homeland from imperial domination and free our psyches from the racial manacles forged about a hundred years ago in the unforgotten trenches of the boondocks, and still being tempered in the alienating, exploitative practices of everyday life in this belly of the dying beast.* This leviathan is a postmodern descendant of Moby Dick, to allude to the Orientalizing myth of the epigraph above. Of course, this is not just a Filipino project but that of everyone whose humanity remains locked in the prisons of race, sexuality, gender, ethnicity, and class. We may repose our previous questions: Who will rescue the aboriginal tribes from that prison of the 1904 St. Louis Exposition? What is at stake is not just our souls, but more crucially our bodies and those of our children. Can the mass media, universities, and bureaucracy, as well as our foundational scriptures of tolerance and pluralism welcoming "the toiling millions," purge themselves of the poison of racism and fanatical chauvinism under the aegis of the new discourse of postmodern multiculturalism?

[The preceding section, composed for the most part in 1986, rehearses key themes and perennial questions subtending the plight of Filipino immigrants in the United States. The following section, drafted substantially in the early nineties, elaborates certain motifs and contested topics broached earlier. The linkage of these two reflections seeks to provide a contrapuntal orchestration of heterogeneous elements (history, polemics, analysis, personal experience, and empirical data, as well as conjecture) in order to plot the future—a constellation of ideas and figures that might offer justice to all victims and modicum hope to those still struggling.]

"Never the Twain Shall Meet"

An article in the *New York Times Book Review* (d'Alpuget 1, 38) on Jessica Hagedorn's novel, *Dogeaters*, may have contributed to reviving an old impression of Filipinos as "dogeaters" inhabiting an irredeemably debauched society where greed, corruption, and chaos rule. Hagedorn is, however, an "American" author who has never customarily eaten dogmeat. A mestiza claiming Spanish, German, and Malayan blood, she grew up in California as part of the "Filipino national identity movement" (Pajaron 20) in the sixties. Later, as a student in the American Conservatory Theater, she confessed that she would get roles only as maid or hooker.

Hagedorn's contemporaries—the writers included in one of the first Asian-American literary anthologies, *Aiiieeeeee!* (Chin) —bewailed "the years of racism, identity crises, and subsequent ethnic rejection" of the postwar milieu. Exposing the fraud of the "American Dream," these young Filipino-American artists (still hyphenated then) confessed how confused and dismayed they were at the "Oriental" Filipino back in the home islands who adopted and imitated anything American ("brown faces with white minds"). But how many have read their writings?

Extrapolating from the 1990 census, the Filipino community is forecast to become the largest segment of the Asian-American category, 21.5 percent, followed by the Chinese and the Vietnamese (Patel 112). By the year 2000, there will be over two million Filipinos in the United States. In recent surveys of Asian-American literature sponsored by the Modern Language Association of America (MLA) and other professional organizations, however, there is a notable absence of any serious attention to Filipino writers, either those born here in the United States or self-exiled. In scholarly discourse and curricular offerings, "Asian-American" usually designates writers who are Chinese (like Kingston or Chin) or Japanese (like Yamamoto or Okada); customarily, Filipinos are tokenized with allusions to Bulosan or Hagedorn. At the turn of the century William Dean Howells reviewed the novels of Jose Rizal, the national hero; Bulosan had to wait until World War II to be discovered, while the rest have to bide their time in the ethnic ghetto or, if you like, plantation.

MLA president Houston Baker's 1982 edition of *Three American Literatures* privileged the Chinese and Japanese components of the category "Asian-American," perhaps a form of editorial reverse discrimination repeated by A. LaVonne Ruoff and Jerry Ward's expanded survey *Redefining American Literary History*. This has no doubt vitiated the honorably ecumenical intent of an emergent canonizing, if revisionary, scholarship. Why were such well-known authors as Bulosan, Jose Garcia Villa, Bienvenido Santos, and others not considered on par with Maxine Hong Kingston or Toshio Mori? Why this "ethnic" / multicultural marginalization, or even occlusion?

In general, U.S. public perception cannot distinguish Filipinos from other Asians, or even from Latinos (perhaps in part because the majority of Filipinos have Spanish names). The term "Asian-American" continues to inflict semantic violence on the Filipino, even as statistics confirm that Filipinos in the United States as a group receive the lowest income among Asians and occupy low-status jobs incommensurable with their advanced educational attainment (Nee and Sanders 85). Is this either a cause or a result of the failure of Filipinos to project their identity, to assert their ethnic uniqueness?

Apart from the usual scholarly exigencies and the endemic racism in U.S. society, I believe this perception of Filipinos is due to the historically unassimilable character of the Filipino cohort in the Asian-American constituency. This unassimilability, to be sure, is not an aberration but a political effect. While the essentializing notion of "identity politics" has been quarantined by Asian commentators in favor of "heterogeneity, multiplicity, and nonequivalence" (Lowe 30–31), this has nevertheless generated the equally reprehensible binary opposition of "nationalism" versus "assimilation," in which nationalism seems reduced to a species of "fanatical nativism." For example, R. Radhakrish-

MASKS OF THE FILIPINO IN THE "NEW WORLD"

nan posits a binary world "between the politics of an overarching and repressive Identity and the self-defeating strategies of 'difference' that lead to more and more painful fragmentations," the only escape from which is what he calls "a carefully nuanced historical reading of the predicament of ethnicity" (112). From this "post-Marxist" perspective, however, all nationalisms look alike in their complicity with the elitist state. Either nationality is just one historical form—like class, gender, or sexuality—or else it is categorized as a negative (because totalizing) narrative of identity. Anthony Appiah even goes so far as to charge that Black Nationalists of the sixties "responded to their experience of racial discrimination by accepting the racialism it presupposed" (11).

In short, if these pundits are correct, the militant response to U.S. racism from an oppressed nationality like the Filipinos is bound to reproduce the evils of which it is the victim. Such authors to whom I have alluded presumably accept the primacy of historical specificity and the need for flexible, all-sided negotiation with the contingencies of representation, power, and multiple spaces; but few honor these complex desiderata in practice.

Given the genuine historical, political, and cultural differences between the Filipino nationality and other Asian ethnics, one cannot help but discern how scholars have articulated "Asian-American" in a selective and exclusivist direction, translating "Asian" as either Chinese or Japanese, rendering it useless as a totalizing signifier. (For example, recent arrivals like Hmong refugees have had no participation in the disciplinary constitution of the term "Asian-American," even though they are bureaucratically subsumed in it.) Within the field of Asian Studies in the U.S. academe, the holy trinity of China, Japan (with Korea included in the space between the first two) and India still dominate, with Southeast Asian countries (mainly Indonesia) occupying the periphery. The Philippines then constitutes the margin or fold within the periphery, better known as the "Pacific Rim," despite the fact of its being the only Asian colony of the United States (perhaps its "mirror stage" prior to entry into the Symbolic Order of what Lenin called the "imperialism" of finance capital). Geopolitics, however, has superseded historical memory in the present realignment of historical capitalisms after the demise of the Soviet Union and Japan's economic ascendancy.

In line with the recent interrogation of the hegemonic claims of a unitary American "common culture," I propose that Filipinos and their practice of cultural production no longer be subsumed under the rubric of "Asian-American" (this has, de facto, taken place through exclusion anyway). Instead, we Filipinos and our communal existence should be recognized as distinct and different, even incommensurable. By the latter term, I mean a "freak" or sport of historical circumstances. While this accords with what Charles Taylor calls a postmodern "politics of recognition" via difference (38–44), the fundamental rationale is that the Filipinos' homeland (unlike China or Japan) was an emergent sovereign territory when it was forcibly colonized by the United States and its "natives" were subjugated as aliens. They were then recognized or validated as "unfree labor." From 1898 to 1946, Filipinos in the continental United States thus were not immigrants in the conventional sense, but colonial subjects whose bodies were transported or exiled from the periphery to the metropolis, their physiognomies studied and their cultures classified by the appropriate ideological apparatuses (including Protestant missionaries) in order to legitimate the supremacy of U.S. knowledge and power.

The entry of Filipinos into U.S. territory in sizable numbers began in 1908, when 141 workers were recruited by the Hawaii Sugar Planters Association. From then to 1946, when formal independence was granted to the islands, at least 125,000 Filipino workers exchanged their labor-power as a commodity with the sugar planters (McWilliams, *Brothers* 235). By 1930, some 108,260 Filipinos were recorded as being all over the United States, but mostly as farmworkers concentrated in the West Coast.

These Filipinos bore the stigmata of an indeterminate status—neither protected wards nor citizens. Consequently, labelled as "nationals"— veritable floating signifiers!—they were subjected to various forms of racist discrimination and exclusion, circumscribed by (among others) laws of antimiscegenation and prohibited from employment in government and ownership of land. Deterritorialized in this way, Filipinos in the process of affirming their human rights and dignity forged a culture of resistance linking their homeland and place of expatriation. Parallel to the incessant revolts of peasants in the colonized islands, Filipino workers organized one of the first unions in Hawaii in 1919, the Filipino Federation of Labor, which spearheaded industrywide multiracial strikes against sugar planters in 1920, 1924, and 1937. In 1934, the Filipino Labor Union was organized in California with 2,000 active members. It mounted the historic strike of 1934 in Salinas, California, and set the stage for the Filipino Agricultural Workers Organizing Committee, which spearheaded the grape strike of 1965, matrix of the United Farm Workers of America (UFW) (Catholic Institute for International Relations).

When Japanese labor was restricted by the Gentlemen's Agreement of 1908 and then barred in 1917 and 1924, Filipino males in vast numbers were admitted to the country. But, contrary to expectations, they did not blaze a new path of white toleration; they followed the beaten track of the Chinese (excluded in 1882) and the Japanese pioneers. In her chronicle *Asian Americans*, Sucheng Chan remarks on the changing landscape of the United States in the mid-1920s due in part to the decline of the Japanese population: "Filipinos provided most of the agricultural labor force in the islands [Hawaii] and all along the Pacific Coast. Not surprisingly they became the main Asian immigrant group to engage in labor militancy" (87).

Even though they numbered only about 30,000 in California, the Filipinos at that time were seen by American nativists as an enigmatic horde with enormous sexual appetite, ready to impregnate Caucasian women and multiply. The locus of antagonism was the dance hall, where Filipinos congregated and patronized white women. Panicked at the prospect of Filipino fertility, the California legislature rushed to amend the antimiscegenation law to include "the Malay race" in the ban (Daniels and Kitano 67–68). This myth of Filipino sexuality departs from the Anglo-Saxon conception of "Oriental" male sexuality and can be traced to the media and popular identification of Filipinos with Africans during the Filipino-American War of 1898–1903. This perception of Filipino sexual aggressiveness accounts for the rabid anti-Filipino violence that erupted in 1928 in Yakima Valley, Washington, and in 1930 in Watsonville, California, to cite only two of numerous cases.

Forbidden from owning land, refused government jobs, stigmatized by antimiscegenation laws, harassed and persecuted, these "nationals" from southeast Asia woke up in the thirties to find that, as Bulosan memorably put it in one of his letters, "In many ways it was a crime to be a Filipino" in America since "we were stopped each time . . . patrolmen saw us driving a car. We were suspect each time we were seen with a white woman" (*Writings* 144). With the 1934 passage of the Tydings-McDuffie Act, which promised eventual independence to the Philippines and the halting of Filipino immigration, the obsessive anxiety over Filipino sexuality dissipated—only to live an underground existence, metamorphosing into the shape of G.I. brides at the end of World War II and then in the commercialized "mail order bride" syndrome that, beginning with the seventies, heralded the advent of a new racial dynamics of North-South relations.

The world system of the international division of labor thus mapped the libidinal economy of the Filipino psyche, which was caught between two worlds: the underdeveloped hinterland and the center of finance capital. This hinterland, however, was haunted and saturated by a deeply rooted popular tradition of revolutionary resistance. U.S. domination of the insurgent Filipinos in the first three decades of this century required the harnessing of its entire knowledge-production apparatus to create the pacified subaltern subject. Social scientists in anthropology, political science, sociology, education, psychology, linguistics, literature, and other fields were mobilized for the purpose of constructing the appropriate disciplinary regimes to induce consensus and the consent to be ruled—at least from the native élite of landlords and comprador capitalists, whose "nationalism" masked the client-patron relations between them and the imperial authority, even as it sanctioned their legitimacy in the eyes of the compatriots they ruled.

This "special relation" between the U.S. and the Philippines—élite "democracy" (more precisely, oligarchic rule) backed by U.S. military and economic power guaranteeing the ascendancy of the propertied few and the poverty of 80 percent of the masses—has prevailed since then. This state of affairs was maintained through the "national security state" of the Marcos dictatorship (1972–86). And it remains the status quo, with the Philippines as faltering debtor-nation whose major policies are largely managed by directives from the IMF/World Bank, the Pentagon, the CIA, and U.S.-based transnational conglomerates.

More than six million Filipinos are today scattered around the world, with the bulk in the Middle East, Europe, and Asia. They earn on the average $3.5 billion a year for the Philippine government—the government's biggest dollar-earner, and enough to bail it out of its recurrent bankruptcies. Not only foreign debt but also unemployment, hunger, and endemic dissatisfaction with quotidian life-chances are temporarily eased. For about a century now, Filipinos have remained subjugated bodies interpellated by a market-centered panopticon, dispersed as "warm body export" into the fetishized and commodifying space of international trade, their memories of the injustice done to them temporarily suspended under the illusionary force of promised freedom and material success which that space imposes. But this amnesia is fast evaporating.

According to *International Liberation*, the organ of the National Democratic Front of the Philippines, "Filipinos overseas are organizing themselves, studying the Philippine situation and are linking themselves with the progressive and revolutionary movement in the homefront"

(Gomez 11). The Filipino diaspora is peculiar in this organic inter-dependency between the plight of contract workers abroad and the vicissitudes of workers at home, debunking the logic and topos of post-coloniality by this spatial configuration of reproducing class antago-nisms in the First World and doubling subalternity in enclaves of the Third World. The new term for this nomadic commodity is "overseas Filipino contract workers" who are engaged in what government apolo-gists call "alternative livelihood."

Exceptional throughout the world in the persistence of a nationalist and Marxist-inspired guerilla insurgency rooted in the peasantry since the thirties, the Philippines remains a dangerous challenge to U.S. global hegemony (somewhat attenuated in the post–Cold War era). About two million Filipinos in the U.S. resonate to the fortunes of this insurgency. During the Marcos dictatorship, Filipinos here periodically denounced Washington for its collusion with the massive atrocities, still unpunished, committed by the Philippine military, which was managed chiefly by the Pentagon's "low-intensity warfare" experts. Today there are no Americans killed or endangered by guerrillas in China, Japan, Korea, or anywhere in Asia; but in the Philippines, "U.S. imperialism" and its local caretakers remain the enemy.

Hence, Filipinos may be perceived as dangerous in proportion to the workings of this strangely contrafactual dialectic, in which the logic of dependency sustains the Filipino exodus from Manila to Hawaii, San Francisco, Los Angeles, Seattle, Chicago, and New York City. If Fil-ipinos indeed played the role of troublemakers in numerous strikes in Hawaii and California, and led the epoch-making 1965 grape strike in the West Coast, any recuperation of this communal history might serve as the redemptive *Jetztzeit* (to use Walter Benjamin's notion) that will blast the continuum of U.S. history. It might be better then (from the viewpoint of corporate capital) to stabilize the neocolony's political and economic conditions and to reinforce U.S. hegemony in the psyches of Filipinos in order to insure the "free flow" of global labor, surplus value (profit), and symbolic capital.

Over 7,000 Filipinos joined the U.S. armed forces in World War II; those who survived and their families formed the second wave of Fil-ipino immigrants (1945–60). Their children were the politicized com-panions of Hagedorn in California and New York City. Almost twenty years divide that wave from Hagedorn's allegory of the Marcos era and the early stirrings of the Rainbow Coalition, a time when second-gener-ation Filipinos initiated a process of self-conscientization in a racist society with a history of subjugating their parents and the community to which they belonged.

In the seventies, amid the civil rights and antiwar movements, this generation discovered the lost world of the "Manongs," the generation of farmworkers and adventurous Pinoys memorialized by Manuel Buaken, Santos, and Bulosan. The 1973 reprinting of Bulosan's classic ethnobiography, *America Is in the Heart*, was a catalyst in the education of a whole generation kept ignorant of the heroic struggles of Filipinos—from the resistance to American aggression during the Filipino-American War of 1899–1903, to the strikes of 1920 and 1924 against Hawaiian plantation owners; from the 1934 strike in Salinas, California, to the 1965 Delano sit-ins that led to the founding of the UFW. Bulosan captured both the shock of recognizing that it was "a crime" to be a Filipino in America and the pride of being a Filipino that he felt in 1942 fighting in the ranks of the international popular front against fascism, as shown in his testimonial essay "My Education." The sacrifice of more than a million Filipino lives in the resistance against Japanese fascism from 1941 to 1944, in fact, engendered a fantasy of Filipino solidarity with America's rulers (registered in Bulosan's title) that weakened or sublimated the energies of the anti-U.S. imperialist resistance born from the Filipino-American War at the turn of the century.

The Subaltern Speaks

The recent publication of Philip Vera Cruz's biography marks the end of that era of colonial subalternity. Vera Cruz not only reaffirms his fellow expatriate's vision of the Filipino inhabiting two worlds—the dependent/peripheral formation of his homeland and the imperial metropolis—but also extends it to a critique of the U.S.-supported Marcos dictatorship and the authoritarian leadership of the UFW (of which he was a founding member). Unfortunately, UFW leaders fell victim to manipulative bureaucratic temptations: the Marcos regime's bureaucrats offered material and political rewards that Chavez was unable to refuse (Vera Cruz 112-17).

The Filipino community-in-the-making in the United States passed through three stages, encompassed by Vera Cruz's autobiography. The first "wave" (a misleading but common metaphor) of migrants (1903–30) consisted chiefly of males, mostly Filipino youth recruited for agricultural and cannery work in Hawaii, Washington, and Alaska. Also, a minuscule band of upper-class Filipino migrants called *pensionados* were given scholarships and returned home with graduate degrees to fill the lower echelons of colonial bureaucracy. The second "wave" came by way of war marriages and naturalization through service in the U.S. Army and Navy during and after World War II. The third "wave" began to arrive after the 1965 liberalization of U.S. immigration law, and is still continuing. With the influx of skilled workers and professionals through family reunification, this third stream of the Filipino diaspora has now reshaped the community as 70 percent foreign-born and 60 percent female, a demographic imbalance that may spell certain consequences in advocacy politics and cultural politics (Cariño). Vera Cruz remaps familiar territory that was surveyed by Bulosan and encapsulated in sociological accounts by Carey McWilliams, Emory Bogardus, H. Brett Melendy, and others.

In his autobiography, Vera Cruz reminds us of the enduring effects of antimiscegenation and other discriminatory laws dating from the time when Filipino males were virtually indentured by recruiters for the Hawaii plantations (from where they moved to the U.S. mainland). Living in barracks, isolated from other groups, they were allowed only the sociality afforded by taxi dance halls, gambling resorts, and the pool rooms of Chinatown, their ostracized lives punctuated by the terror of racist violence. It was not until 1946, after Philippine independence, that these pioneering survivors were allowed to petition for naturalization. Floating in the limbo of indeterminacy, the Manongs ("Manong" is the Ilocano term for "brother") decided not to reveal to their folks back home the pain of alienating work and exploitation by contractors and hustlers. Both their pathos and craft of survival are distilled in this statement: "It was always an emergency and I was never ready to go back" (Vera Cruz 24).

Though the growth of class consciousness is the theme of Vera Cruz's "remembrance of things past," this experience, a microcosm of the group's plight, is always rendered in historically complex and concrete ways. This is the crucial lesson of his narrative of self-knowledge via solidarity with multiracial coworkers and associates, not just Filipinos. In this manner, the subject of the class-for-itself acquires concrete identity as a Filipino in that the dominant racist society perceives him as a "native," a colonized entity with non-Western "racial" peculiarities. *It is thus primarily through national and racial subjugation that class oppression becomes a lived experience, inscribed within the disequilibrated power relations of a commodifying world-system.*

From his responsible insider's position, Vera Cruz criticized Mexican chauvinism in the UFW (indeed, the privileging of the slogan "Viva La Raza"—"long live the race"—excluded blacks, Arabs, and Filipinos in the union) while at the same time he acknowledged the indispensable contribution of Mexican workers and Euro-American supporters. For Filipinos like Vera Cruz, the *problematique* of difference-in-unity is thus not just a question of symbolic positionality or a rhetorical discursive pretext for postcolonial theorizing. It is a practice with enabling/disabling effects in bodies and psyches. Vera Cruz's practice of internationalism, his belief in an egalitarian democracy (132), is firmly anchored in the *habitus* of a subjugated and dominated people, as the "Epilog" to his life history testifies. When he returns to the Philippines after sixty years of absence, he is dismayed to find his family completely apolitical. He is a "nobody" in his homeland; no one cares about what he presents or represents. This is due to what I have been characterizing here as the Filipino predicament of thwarting assimilation and eluding integration.

Despite this, Vera Cruz reiterates the fact of his self-sacrifices for his family: he asserts that he made it "possible" for his brother and sister to keep ignorance and poverty at a distance. He hopes this knowledge can be communicated to them and others so that they also can make those sacrifices—"to use his or her intellect for the good of their people," especially youth who need to become involved in the "issues of social justice" (146). Concluding the 1977 section of his memoir, Vera Cruz hopes that his readers will "understand who I am and the things I stand for" (145). The fact that only a handful of Filipinos fully and genuinely understand who Vera Cruz is and what he represents is symptomatic of the primitive level of ethical and political consciousness that afflicts the Filipino *ethnos* as a whole. A diagnosis of this malaise as a reflection of ethnic anomie in late capitalist society requires another occasion for full elaboration.

Vera Cruz's claim implicates not only his personal identity and principles but those of an entire community now totaling over two million persons. If Filipinos today count as the largest component of the Asian-American category, and perhaps as one of the most marginalized and misrecognized ethnic and racial constituencies in North America, it is because certain historical specificities of the Filipino incorporation into the U.S. racial formation distinguishes the Filipino diaspora from its Chinese, Japanese, or Korean counterparts. Distinguishing it in particular are the hegemonic domination of U.S. market ideology and neoliberal paradigms in Philippine society and the cultural subjugation of individual Filipinos. Because the early armed resistance in the Philippines to U.S. colonial supremacy and persistent oppositional nationalism have functioned as a sedimented experience that motivates Filipino initiatives in labor-organizing and cultural practices, Filipinos as an oppressed nationality cannot just be lumped beneath the assimilative rubric of "Asian-American." I submit that a new representation of the Filipino community in the U.S. is needed to rectify years of misunderstanding based on assimilationist narratives and acculturation strategies now proved fallacious or untenable.

Rise of the "Brown Peril"?

One source of this misunderstanding may be traced to the U.S. academic and official producers of knowledge about the Filipino, of information and value judgments that have become the circulating doxa of public opinion or "common sense." Take, for example, an often-reprinted article, "Anti-Filipino Race Riots," by Emory Bogardus. According to him, one cause of the 1930 vigilante attack on Filipinos in Watsonville, California, was racial: the Filipino is an outsider, belonging to the "outgroup" because of his "different color and culture" (59). Economic competitiveness and the preponderance of Filipino males were also causal factors, but Bogardus, undeterred by his tautologies, in the end faults the lack of "sane" Filipino leadership! (61)

Since Bogardus premises his research on the assumption that human nature around the world is "one organic unity" (51), he fails to comprehend the differential power relations that characterized the Watsonville riots. In particular, he fails to grasp the ideology and practice of white supremacy materialized in state and civil society apparatuses that mediate and condense economic and political dimensions of social reality. Structural inequality does not appear in the fragments of culture and personal experience that the sociologist investigates. To rectify this positivism, the antidote to date has been a phenomenological and even Weberian account of the lived experience of immigrant alienation by historians like Ronald Takaki and Barbara Posadas—a regress from the dialectic of class, nation, and race thematized by Bulosan, Vera Cruz, and other participant witnesses.

It is ironic to find Bogardus's account reproduced in a 1976 collection, *Letters in Exile*, the chief merit of which is its attempt to restore a historical perspective to the study of the condition and status of the Filipino community in the United States. In the same volume, we find also a contribution by the leading fabricator / purveyor of knowledge about the Filipino in the United States, H. Brett Melendy. Melendy's entry on Filipinos in the *Harvard Encyclopedia of American Ethnic Groups* sums up his more detailed studies, found in *Asians in America* and elsewhere. In some exorbitant fashion, this entry has become the source of most quotations regurgitated as unquestioned truths by Filipino and American scholars.

We cannot fault Melendy for lacking a historical perspective. But his version of history is an empiricist accumulation of "facts" culled from early and now-dated anthropological reports. For example, he derives from the linguistic diversity of the Philippines a judgment about the inhabitants' political consciousness: "Local and regional identification are more important to members of these groups than the notion of being a Filipino; for some, a national identity is not even relevant; too often, such an identity has been superimposed on the Filipinos' other loyalties by outsiders unaware of linguistic and other ties among groups" (355). Here, Melendy employs a functionalist paradigm to explain the Filipino community's lack of unity and direction, but at the expense of historical veracity.

This functionalist framework of knowledge-production subordinates all elements, including the conflicts and tensions in any social formation, to a self-equilibrating order that legitimizes the norms of the ascendant group, in this case the Spanish and American colonizers. Hence the oppositional "deviations" of the natives, whose asymmetrical communities continued to resist foreign rule, are discounted as "lack of unity" and direction (362). Summarizing the *compadrazgo* or client-patron relations in the Philippines, Melendy uses this belief system, which pivots around kinship and local alliances, as a springboard to indict a whole people's "exclusiveness" (that is, their reluctance to assimilate to the individualist ethos of a market economy), their abstention from electoral politics, their civic inertia, and political immaturity. Melendy follows the mainstream social science methodology of diagnosing the behavior of the native / immigrant and its capacity for adaptation by superimposing on the native / immigrant the colonial structure that has determined the behavior. Thus he resorts to a crude determinism in his gloss on the alleged docility of Filipino workers in the Hawaiian plantations in the twenties: "For a long time the young Filipinos, separated from more militant groups and already indoctrinated to submission by the barrio political system known as *caciquismo,* made no attempt to rebel against the plantation system" (358). Given this emphasis on system maintenance and value consensus, the only way for Melendy to account for the Filipinos' bold, militant initiative in the strikes is to allude to the influence of other national groups. "Disappeared" or rubbed out is the centuries-long tradition of Filipino revolutionary opposition to colonial oppression and imperial exploitation.[1]

In conceptualizing the modality of Filipino behavior in the constrained parameters of plantations and other workplaces, Melendy remains unaware of his theoretical blind spots. For one, he forgets the crucial distinction between social exchange based on reciprocity and that based on complementarity. This point is worth underscoring: "Reciprocity is recognized as exchange where giving and receiving are *mutually contingent* . . . [and] *each* party has rights *and* duties. This mutuality is lacking in exchange based solely upon complementarity (as would be the case between master and slave or jailor and jailed) so that 'one's rights are another's obligations, and vice versa' " (Paine 8). This caveat also applies to the limitations of transactional, symbolic interactionist, and other ethnicity-centered research and policy programs that ignore the colony / metropolis asymmetry of power.

It may be instructive to emphasize here that the functionalist approach (as illustrated by Melendy) "conceives race relations as a problem of integration and assimilation or adaptation of minorities in a society that is fundamentally based on a widely shared system of common values" (Berting 183). By implication, the paradigm of ethnic assimilation to the dominant society and its normative code becomes the measure of group legitimacy and success. Studies like Antonio Pido's *The Pilipinos in America,*[2] a typical compendium of data and doxa, are vitiated by an inadequate theoretical grasp of the interplay of class, race, and gender in a history as conflicted as those of European settlers and Native Americans, Mexicans and Euro-Americans, and Euro-Americans and African Americans.

Pido's inconsistencies are symptomatic of empiricist and functionalist reductionism. One example may suffice: After asserting that "the Pilipino community in the country is more of a community of consciousness, located in social space, rather than a definite locality-based physical phenomenon," he immediately qualifies this "community" as true "only in the most abstract sense" because "intraethnic conflicts among Pilipinos and the tendency to identify with smaller groups [kinship or provincial factions] rather than with ethnicity, as well as the pre-immigration heterogeneity of the Pilipinos, is still a basic reality" (121). Another empiricist-oriented study of Filipino group behavior today, however, generates this thesis: "Factionalism [among professional Filipinos] arises where larger than personal relationships are at stake, where friendship and mutual respect end, and prestige and hierarchy begin" (Requiza 28).

I would argue, then, that given the mixture of banality and uncritical, one-sided assumptions informing such speculations on race relations, the sociology of minority-majority relations, as well as the theory of immigration based on push/pull factors, prove themselves unable to grasp the complex racialized subordination of the Filipino in the U.S. and its articulations of race with class and nationality at specific conjunctures. In the same measure, they occlude the Filipino culture of resistance that has accompanied the process of subaltern incorporation or assimilation.

An attempt was made by Bruce Occeña and his associates in *Line of March* quarterly to render such articulations in an article entitled "The Filipino Nationality in the U.S.: An Overview." Occeña should be credited for his insistence in grounding the specific oppression of the different cohorts of Filipino immigrants in their race, class, and nationality determinants (for background data, see Catholic Institute for International Relations). Not only are Filipinos distinguished from other Asians by their collective experience of U.S. imperial oppression at home, but each "wave" of Filipino migration manifests distinctive characteristics rooted in the unequal relations of power between the Philippines and the United States. Occeña appropriately formulates the defining quality of the Filipino presence in the U.S.: "Taken as a group, Filipinos have been integrated into U.S. society on the basis of *inequality* and subjected to discrimination due both to their race and nationality" (31).

My reservation regarding Occeña's inquiry concerns its naively economistic bias (defining the majority of the "third wave" as "concentrated in the lower strata of the U.S. working class" does not automatically endow them with a proletarianized consciousness) and its neglect of the forces of gender and sexuality. As noted earlier, 60 percent of this new cohort of immigrants is female and is equipped with a more sophisticated awareness of gender politics, if not of feminist thinking (Beltran and De Dios; Evasco et al.). Moreover, Occeña still clings to a static and monolithic conception of the extended family as constitutive of the social and political dynamics of the Filipino diaspora today.

Given the severely depressed economy of the Philippines today and the deteriorating condition of its resources due to their unimpeded exploitation by transnationals, assisted by IMF/World Bank conditionalities, over twenty thousand Filipinos emigrate every year to the United States. The Philippine élite partly owes its continued supremacy to emigration and the artificial diaspora of redundant Filipino labor in that the latter's average earnings of over $3.5 billion a year (remitted to the homeland every year) serve to ease the balance of payments for more than $30 billion owed to the World Bank and other foreign financial consortiums. This allows the comprador bourgeoisie and its representatives in the state apparatuses (both coercive and ideological) to sustain their increasingly beleaguered exploitation of the present sixty-six million Filipinos (including five million Moros and about a million indigenous citizens).

Hundreds of thousands of Filipinos swarm the world's airports, going back and forth to the Middle East, Europe, and Asia as contract workers, domestics, "hospitality workers" (mostly in Japan), and every conceivable kind of employment. The traffic in Filipino women via "mail order brides" proceeds unabated alongside sex tourism (more than one hundred thousand prostitutes were displaced when the U.S. military bases closed in 1992) (Villapando). At least twenty thousand Filipinos work in the U.S. Navy—an anomalous situation for citizens of a sovereign nation-state. But this fact only functions as a synecdoche for the true geopolitics of U.S.-Philippines relations since Spain ceded the islands to the U.S. for twenty million dollars at the Treaty of Paris in December 1898 without consulting the representatives of the first Philippine Republic. As long as this geopolitics of Philippine dependency dictates the contingencies of development for the majority of Filipinos, we can expect the transplantation of Filipino bodies into the U.S. to continue and with it the corresponding recolonizing of sensibilities for the complex needs of a service and information-oriented economy (San Juan, "Mapping the Boundaries").

Census data indicate that the Filipino diaspora in the U.S. will total over 2.1 million at the beginning of the twenty-first century. Most of the new immigrants are professionals (nurses, scientists, technicians of all sorts) and skilled workers. Despite their educational achievement, they will not be spared the violence of a racial formation whose discourses and institutional practices have virtually segregated them into low-paying niches and assigned them a subordinate and tokenized status in the class and ethnic hierarchy (U.S. Commission on Civil Rights 17).

I have argued that certain historical specificities of the Filipino nationality in the U.S. distinguish it from other Asian communities—in particular, the colonial/neocolonial position of the Philippines and the hegemonic power of the U.S. Imaginary, a network of fantasies programmed in Filipino psyches by a massive influx of U.S. media/ideological products to promise the fulfillment of dreams for every Filipino. I have also addressed here the heterogeneous, contingent forces that have contributed to the process of defining the emergent subjectivity (or subject-position) of the Filipino nationality, which is caught in the vicissitudes of U.S. racial politics. In the context of identity formation, the following testimony from the mainstream media attests to the power of a persisting libidinal *dispositif* or "desiring machine" (to use Deleuze-Guattari's term) attached to the acqisitive individualist ethos:

> For most the climb is frustrating but ultimately successful. Antonio Cube, 49, a Filipino attorney, immigrated with his wife and two children in 1970. Accustomed to the services of three maids and a driver at home, but unqualified to practice law in the U.S., Cube found work instead as a computer encoder in a bank. "I almost went home," he says now. "But the bank sent me to technical schools and moved me up little by little. For five years my wife and I worked two full-time jobs." Today Cube is a supervisor for Seattle's Rainier Bank and owns not only his own home but three other houses in the metropolitan area. Two of them, now rented, are earmarked for his children, both university students. "We feel that life is about saving for the future," says Cube. "We live for our children." (Doerner 43)

Displaced, and at the same time renewed, by this fantasy is the Other tradition of resistance and revolt against this racist violence and the reassertion of a racial/ethnic subjectivity that is just beginning to find articulation in the texts of young Filipino artists like Hagedorn and her contemporaries. It is prefigured by the undecidable protagonists of *Dogeaters,* by the spectacle of Moro rebels kidnapping American or Japanese businessmen in Mindanao, and by the presence of women and Filipino priests leading the guerrillas of the New People's Army.

After a painstaking analysis of interviews with second-generation Filipinos living in the San Diego area, Yen Le Espiritu concludes that ethnic identification "is, in fact, a more dynamic and complex social phenomenon than has been predicted by either the assimilationist or pluralist model" (268). Accordingly, she contends that identity is not bipolar (torn between nativism and assimilation) but fluid, negotiating multiple and simultaneous identities, multilinear, "in dialogue with and in opposition to the racist ideologies and practices within the

United States." I am sympathetic with her intent to privilege "invented cultural practices"—both resistance to and acceptance of class and racial hierarchy. But, like some cultural-studies scholars afflicted with a postmodern obsession with the tactical and versatile "weapons" for coping used by the poor, Espiritu's orientation is rigorously individualist and also grossly empiricist. One may ask, what strategies of collective opposition can be inferred from stressing flux rather than continuity?

One recent testimony appears to refute Espiritu's generalization. Leny Strobel dramatizes the agony of a schizoid and fragmented consciousness embodied in the process of her growing up in neocolonial Philippines, but concludes her narrative with an affirmation of an essential indigenous virtue that redeems the Filipino tragicomic situation in the United States—kapwa, or shared identity constituting one's humanity, according to the late psychologist Virgilio Enriquez. In almost every exchange I have had with Filipinos in various parts of the islands for the last three decades, I have discovered a strong family resemblance among local experiences that manifest something analogous to Strobel's patterned discontinuities, a syntagmatic chain of intentionality that binds random and dispersed "noises," aleatory impulses, and happenstance. Is this evidence of a counterhegemonic Filipino collective consciousness in the making, in response to what has displaced Cold War antagonisms—namely, the demonization of the immigrant as susupicious "undocumented alien" and threat to the "American Way of Life"?

Dialectics as the determinate flux of unity and contradiction can help correlate tactics with strategy. Historicizing the politicization of ethnicity is imperative. Other strategies of intervention by the uprooted and dislocated people of a disintegrating nation-state may soon erupt in places that the diaspora has marked as sites of oppression and also of empowerment. For example, after the 1991 war by the United States against Iraq, we read stories of contract workers defying their abusive Middle Eastern employers. One Lourana Crow Rafael reportedly killed Sheikha Latifa Abdullah Al-Jaber Al-Sabah (a member of the ruling clan of Kuwait) in Cairo in February 1992 after she refused Rafael's request for permission to return to the Philippines (Kelley 1A). The ecology of the struggle for self-determination is much more complex and unpredictable than the limited texture of such incidents, but any mapping of the diasporic trajectory is bound to implicate the volatile and highly surveilled urban spaces in the United States.

Limitation of space does not allow me to explore the rise of a Filipino style of feminist, gay, and lesbian politics (see Urian), the active participation of Filipinos in the campaign for reproductive rights, and a host of local issues (for example, the right to speak Tagalog in the workplace versus the campaign for English Only in some states). These all signify overdetermined traces of a genealogy of interventions marked within the last two decades by the 1977 campaign to defend Leonora Perez and Filipina Narciso, two nurses scapegoated for the mysterious deaths of patients in a veterans' hospital, and the successful prosecution of Marcos agents responsible for the murder of Seattle union activists Silme Domingo and Gene Viernes (Churchill). One also can cite recent initiatives in electoral politics and in campaigns to stop the traffic in mail order brides and domestic labor (San Juan, *Racial Formations*). We cannot understand the predicament and destiny of the Filipino diaspora here unless we place it in its global context and its unique historical specificity as a relation between U.S. hegemony and the resistance of a people struggling for national and popular self-determination. Analyzing the paradoxes, aporias, and duplicities of this relation, which offers opportunities for the exercise of popular democratic agency, remains the agenda of the ongoing collective project of emancipation that is uniting people of color everywhere.

4

Overseas Writing: Toward a Political Economy of the Diasporic Imagination

... Fertilizer ... Filipinos ...
—*From a letter by H. Hackfield and Company to George Wilcox, Grove Farm Plantation, Hawaii, 5 May 1908*[1]

It must be realized that the Filipino is just the same as the manure that we put on the land—just the same.
—*From an interview of an agricultural association secretary, 1930*[2]

Ever since the United States annexed the Philippine Islands in 1898, the discourse of capital (as the quotes above testify) has always been reductive, monological, and utilitarian. Although luminaries such as Mark Twain, William James, and William Dean Howells denounced the slaughter of the natives during the Filipino-American War of 1899–1903, the Filipino presence was not registered in the public sphere until their singular commodity, labor-power, appeared in large numbers on Hawaii and on the West Coast between 1907 and 1935. Until 1946, when formal independence was granted to the islands, Filipinos in the metropolis (numbering around 150,000) occupied the limbo of alterity and transitionality: they were neither slaves, wards, nor citizens. Carey McWilliams believed that these "others" belonged to "the freemasonry of the ostracized" (*Brothers* 241). How should we address them, and in what language? Can they speak for themselves? If not, who will represent them?

Called "little brown brothers," barbaric "yellow bellies," "scarcely more than savages," and other derogatory epithets, Filipinos as subjects-in-revolt have refused to conform to the totalizing logic of white supremacy and the knowledge of "the Filipino" constructed by the Orientalizing methods of American scholarship. Intractable and recalcitrant,

Filipinos in the process of being subjugated have confounded U.S. disciplinary regimes of knowledge-production and surveillance. They have challenged the asymmetrical cartography of metropolis and colony, of core and periphery, in the official world-system. Interpellated within the boundaries of Empire, Filipinos continue to bear the stigmata of three centuries of anticolonial insurgency.

Given this indigenous genealogy of resistance, which I have traced elsewhere (*Crisis; Only by Struggle; Writing and National Liberation*), the Filipino writer has functioned not simply as *porte-parole* authorized by the imperium's center but more precisely as an organic intellectual (in Gramsci's sense) for a people whose repressed history and its "political unconscious" remain crucial to the task of judging the worth of the American experiment in colonial "tutelage" and to the final settling of accounts with millions of its victims.

Up to now, however, despite the Philippines' formal independence, the texts of the Filipino interrogation of U.S. hegemony remain virtually unread and therefore unappreciated for their "fertilizing" critical force. Not demography, but a symptomatic reconnaissance of contested territory seems imperative. An inventory of the archive (by a partisan native, for a change) is needed as an initial step toward answering questions such as I raised earlier. Foremost among these is: why for so long has the Filipino intervention in the U.S. literary scene been ignored, silenced, or marginalized? Quantity has so far not translated into quality to make a significant difference. In the U.S. Census Bureau's ethnic category, "Asian–Pacific Islander," the Filipino component now has become the largest—1,419,711 persons as of 1990 (Kitano and Daniels 91; Gonzales 181; O'Hare and Felt 2). In the next decade, it will surpass the combined total of the Chinese and Japanese population. But the import of this statistic so far has not been calculated in the existing baedekers of U.S. High Culture.

Literary surveys drawn up in this era of canon revision ignore the Filipino contribution. As noted in the preceding chapter, in the 1982 MLA (Modern Language Association) survey of *Three American Literatures*, the Asian-American section deals only with Chinese and Japanese authors. This omission is repeated in the 1990 MLA guide, *Redefining American Literary History*; no reference is made to Filipino writing except in a meager bibliographic listing at the end under the rubric, "Philippine American Literature" (Ruoff and Ward 361–62). In this quite erroneous citation of ten authors' "Primary Works," three writers would not claim at all to be Filipino-American: Stevan Javellana, Celso Carunungan, and Egmidio Alvarez.[3] Nor would Jose Garcia Villa, the now "disappeared" inventor of modern Filipino expression in English, who is a permanent U.S. resident but not a citizen.

The classification "Philippine-American" may appear as a harmless conjunction of equal and separate terms. But, in fact, it conceals subsumption of the former into the latter. In everyday life, the combinatory relay of American pragmatic tolerance easily converts the "Philippine" half into a routinized ethnic phenomenon, normalized and taken for granted. How then do we account for the absence, exclusion, and potential recuperability of Filipino writing in this society—at least that portion conceded recognition by institutional fiat?

Palimpsests of the "Lovely People"

In general, the production, circulation, and reception of texts are necessarily determined, though not sufficiently, by the dynamics of class and race. Everyone agrees that, in this system, numbers don't really count unless the community exercises a measure of economic and political power. Filipinos in the U.S. remain an exploited and disadvantaged group, not at all a "model" minority. A 1980 study of income distribution among Filipinos found that young men received only about two-thirds of the income of white males, and women and older men get only half. In California, 80 to 86 percent of young males are employed in the low-paying secondary sector (manufacturing). Such income disparities persist, despite comparable investments in human capital (education, work experience, and so forth) which generate low returns "suggestive of race discrimination" (Cabezas and Kawaguchi 99).

Filipinos rank third among Asian-Americans in median household income, behind Japanese and Asian-Indians. Another survey (Nee and Sanders 75–93) concludes that, although Filipinos have a higher educational attainment than whites or recent Chinese immigrants, their average income is lower than Japanese-Americans and Chinese-Americans because they are confined to low-skilled, unremunerative jobs.

Except in the last few years, Filipinos in the United States have not participated significantly in electoral politics (notwithstanding recent breakthroughs in California and Hawaii). Mainstream sociologists attribute this to the inertia of "provincial allegiances and personality clashes" (Melendy, *Asians in America* 362). Collective praxis, however, is not an a priori given but a sociohistorical construct, the fruit of intelligence, foresight, and the courage to take risks. This implies that we have to reckon with the tenacious legacy of four centuries of Spanish and U.S. colonial domination to understand the Filipino *habitus*.

What passes for indigenous music or architecture turns out to be a mimesis of western styles, while the refined skills of reading and writing, which are needed for the production and distribution of the knowledge monopolized by the élite (compradors, landlords, bureaucrat capitalists), serve only narrow business interests. In brief, cultural literacy is geared to soliciting the recognition of American arbiters of taste and brokers of symbolic capital. We may have talented writers, but certainly we have had no sizeable and responsive audience of readers and commentators up to now.

And so this predicament of the community's powerlessness, together with its largely imitative and instrumentalized modality of cultural production / reception, may shed light on the invisibility of Filipino writing in the academy and in public consciousness. But its exclusion and / or marginalization cannot be grasped unless we take fully into account the irreducible historical specificity of the Philippines as a former colony—and at present as a virtual neocolony—of the United States, and Filipinos as subjugated and conflicted subjects.

This dialectical perspective explains the irrepressible centrality of Carlos Bulosan's *oeuvre* in the shaping of an emergent pan-Filipino literary tradition that affiliates the U.S. scene of writing. What distinguishes Bulosan's role in this field of Filipino-American intertextuality is his attempt to capture the inaugural experience of uprooting and bodily transport of Filipinos to Hawaii and the North American continent. In Bulosan's life-history, the itinerary of the peasant / worker-becoming-intellectual unfolds a narrative of collective self-discovery in the womb of the occupying power (the United States). Here, the traumatic primal scene of deracination is reenacted in the acts of participating in the multiracial workers' fight against U.S. monopoly capital and valorized in interludes of critical reflection (San Juan, *Carlos Bulosan* 119–43). And this solidarity, forged in the popular-democratic crucible of struggle, together with whites and people of color against a common oppression, stages the condition of possibility for the Filipino writer in exile.

In effect, writing becomes for the Filipino diaspora the transitional agency of self-recovery. It facilitates a mediation between the negated past of colonial dependency and a fantasied, even utopian, "America" where people of color exercise their right of self-determination and socialist justice prevails. Bulosan's historicizing imagination configures the genealogy of two generations of Filipinos bridging the revolutionary past and the compromised present. He maps a passage from the tributary formation of the periphery to the West Coast's "factories in the fields" and canneries in *America Is in the Heart* (hereafter *America*) which figure as a blank, an absence or silence that cannot be found in the sentimental memoirs of his compatriots.

History, for Bulosan, is what is contemporary and prophetic. In "How My Stories Were Written," he evokes the childhood of Apo Lacay, the folk sage who inspired his vocation of allegorical remembering. Apo Lacay made this choice during "the age of great distress and calamity in the land, when the fury of an invading race impaled their hearts in the tragic cross of slavery and ignorance" (*If You Want to Know What We Are: A Carlos Bulosan Reader* 25). The allusion here is to the scorched-earth tactics of U.S. pacification forces during the Filipino-American War and the ruthless suppression of a nascent Filipino national identity. This is often presented as a foreign policy "aberration" in most textbooks, but it was vindicated without much scruple recently by Stanley Karnow's apologia, *In Our Image*.

In stories like "Be American," in the quasi-autobiographical *America*, and in his novel *The Power of the People* (originally titled *The Cry and the Dedication*), Bulosan renders in symbolic forms of fabulation how the U.S. conquest exacerbated feudal injustice in the Philippines. He also demonstrates how the United States accomplished, on a global scale, an iniquitous division of international labor that transformed the United States into a metropolis of industrial modernity and the Philippines into an underdeveloped dependency: a source of cheap raw materials and manual/mental labor with minimal exchange-value.

It is impossible to ignore Bulosan's works in dealing with Filipino "ethnicity": recall how his essay "Freedom from Want" (*Saturday Evening Post*, 6 March 1943), commissioned to illustrate President Roosevelt's "Four Freedoms" declaration, was subsequently displayed in the Federal Building in San Francisco. So how does the Establishment handle the threat posed by this radical attack on greed and private property? In other words, how is Bulosan sanitized and packaged to promote pluralist American nationalism? Instead of rehearsing all the possible ways, it will suffice here to give an example of a typical recuperative exercise from *The American Kaleidoscope* by Professor Lawrence Fuchs:[4]

The life of Bulosan, a Filipino-American, illustrates the process by which the political struggle against injustice and on behalf of equal rights often turned immigrants and their children into Americans. . . . Disillusioned, Bulosan considered becoming a Communist; at another time, he became a thief. But his principal passions were American politics and American literature, and these stimulated him to organize the Committee for the Protection of Filipino Rights, and to start a small school for migrant workers where "I traced the growth of democracy in the United States" . . . recalling that his brother had told him "America is in the hearts of men." . . . When, after months of illness and debility, he finished his autobiography, he called it *America Is in the Heart*, using words similar to those of President Roosevelt to Secretary of War Stimson, "Americanism is simply a matter of the mind and heart," and those of Justice Douglas, that "loyalty is a matter of the heart and mind."

. . . Bulosan, the Filipino migrant worker, much more than Dillingham, the scion of an old New England family, had proved to be a prescient interpreter of American nationalism. Those who had been excluded longest from membership in the American civic culture had rushed to embrace it once the barriers were lifted. (237–38)

Earlier, Fuchs paternalistically ascribes to Bulosan the fortune Blacks didn't have of being befriended by a half-dozen white women. Somehow Bulosan also was endowed with the exceptional gift of having access to a secret knowledge denied to other minorities:

When he spoke of the American dream he wrote of his migrant-worker students that "their eyes glowed with a new faith . . . they nodded with deep reverence." . . . Bulosan identified with the experience of the Euro-Americans who had come to this country as immigrants. (147–48)

Shades of Andrew Carnegie, Horatio Alger, the Godfather? As if that were not enough, Bulosan is lined up with "Carl Schurz, Mary Antin, and tens of thousands of other self-consciously Americanizing immigrants" (357).

Bulosan is thus appropriated by official discursive practice to hype a putative "civic culture" of "voluntary pluralism" by occluding the historical specificity of his anti-imperialist politics. Both his materialist outlook and his paramount commitment to genuine national sovereignty for the Philippines and to socialism are buried in the abstraction of a "political struggle against injustice." The strategy of containment here is one of tactical omission, calculated redeployment, selective emphasis, and, more precisely, decontextualization. Its mode of uprooting certain words and phrases from their historical habitat of political antagonisms recapitulates President McKinley's policy of "Benevolent Assimilation" and the duplicitous discourse of pacification from William

Howard Taft to the latest scholarship on U.S.-Philippines relations. It also can be read as a textual analogue to the raid of peasant male bodies from occupied territory between 1906 and 1946 by the HSPA (Hawaiian Sugar Planter's Association).

Through such ruses of displacement and complicity, Bulosan is recruited by his enemies, the imperial patriots. They celebrate his romantic naiveté at the expense of his egalitarian principles and his repudiation of chauvinist-fascist apartheid founded on wars of conquest and the dehumanization of people of color.

We would expect a less-distorting treatment of Bulosan from the revisionist anthology edited by Paul Lauter and others: *The Heath Anthology of American Literature* (1841–43). Unfortunately, this textbook disappoints us. Instead of using a more representative text about migrant workers, the editor selects one rather precious, introspective sketch that gives the impression that Bulosan is a neurotic existentialist from the tropics, a brown-skinned Wallace Stevens conjuring verbal fetishes from his head. Moreover, Amy Ling's prefatory note (1840–41) compounds the problem by reproducing factual errors and misleading inferences derived from Elaine Kim's guide to *Asian American Literature.*

Kim might be chiefly responsible for the defusion of Bulosan's insurrectionary aesthetics by ignoring the vicious subjugation of the Filipino masses. This happens because she subscribes to the immigrant paradigm of Euro-American success (criticized long ago by Robert Blauner and others) when she claims that Bulosan "shares with the Asian goodwill-ambassador writers a sustaining desire to win American acceptance" (57). (Because the term "America" denotes a complex overdetermined—but not indeterminate—relation of peoples and nationalities, I urge that its use should always be qualified, or replaced by other terms.)

Despite her good intentions, Kim's pedestrian conformism disables her from perceiving the deviancy of Bulosan's text. Like Fuchs, she fosters the instrumentalist prejudice that *America* is unilaterally "dedicated to the task of promoting cultural goodwill and understanding" (47), an opinion induced by her completely uncritical endorsement of the patronizing banalities of reviewers (46) and the damaged mentalities of her native informants (47). Indeed, Kim's prophylactic handling of Asian-American authors for systemic recuperation and fetishism proceeds from the assumption that ethnic texts are produced by the minds of lonely, disturbed, and suffering immigrants, helpless and lost, but somehow gifted with inner resources capable of transcending their racial oppression and sundry adversities by way of hard work, genius, and circumstantial luck. At best, in the spirit of a philanthropic liberalism shared by apologists of Anglo missionaries, Kim says that, to become part of American society, one can always rely on "the urge for good, for the ideal" which is "lodged permanently in the human heart" (51).

Reading (as Fuchs and his ilk practice it) turns out to be an act of violence in more ways than one. What all these reappropriations of Bulosan signify is the power and limits of the hegemonic consensus and its apparatuses to sustain its assimilative but ultimately apartheid-like strategy to absorb the Asian "Other" into the fold of the unitary hierarchical racial order. In the case of Filipinos settling in the United States, it forgets the original deed of conquest and elides the question: how did Filipinos come to find themselves in "the belly of the beast" (as Jose Marti puts it)?

From a world-system viewpoint, it is the continuing reproduction of unequal power relations between the Philippines and the United States that is the matrix of the disintegrated Filipino. As a result, the Filipino's subjectivity (more exactly, potential agency) is dispersed in the personas of migrant worker, expatriate intellectual (the major actant in Bienvenido Santos' fiction), cannery or service worker, U.S. Navy steward, and solitary exile. We should remind ourselves that, when Filipinos first appeared in large numbers in the landscape of an expansive military power, they came not as fugitives from eighteenth-century Spanish galleons (the few "Manilamen" of the Louisiana bayous) but as recruited laborers transported by the HSPA.[5] Reinscribed into this context of differential power relations, the Filipino imagination pursuing its genealogy thus acquires its fated vocation of disrupting the economy of "humanist" incorporation by transgressing willy-nilly the boundaries of interdicted times and tabooed spaces.

Deciphering the "Inscrutable Oriental"

What is at stake is nothing less than the question of Filipino self-representation, of its articulation beyond commodity reification, postmodern narcissism, and paranoia. In lieu of the usual atomistic and hypostatizing view, I submit this principle of world-system linkage—the colony integrally situated as the double of the imperial polity—as the fundamental premise for establishing the conditions of possibility for apprehending Filipino creative expression in the United States. Lacking this cognitive / reconstructive mapping, one succumbs to sectarian fallacies that are vulnerable to the "divide-and-rule" policy of laissez-faire liberalism.

An instructive case may be adduced here. In their foreword to the anthology *Aiiieeeee!*, Oscar Peñaranda, Serafin Syquia, and Sam Tagatac fall prey to a separatist adventurism and thus inflict genocide upon themselves:

> No Filipino-American ("Flip"—born and / or raised in America) has ever published anything about the Filipino-American experience. . . . Only a Filipino-American can write adequately about the Filipino-American experience. (37–54)

The early seventies were a time when Filipinos born here during or after World War II were undergoing the proverbial "identity crisis" in the wake of Third World conscientization movements that swept the whole country. Our Flip authors, caught in the maelstrom of change, contend that Santos and Bulosan, because of birth, carry "Filipino-oriented minds," whereas "the Filipino born and reared in America writes from an American perspective" (50). But, what exactly is "an American perspective"? Flawed by a crudely chauvinist empiricism, this position of identifying with the hegemonic order and its transcendent claims to validate the "exclusively Filipino-American work" betrays servitude to white Anglo supramacy. It becomes supremacist when it dismisses Philippine literature produced in the former colony as inferior, lacking in "soul" (510).[6]

In contrast to this Flip manifesto, the singular virtue of the volume *Letters in Exile* (published two years later; Quinsaat 1976) lies in confirming the deconstructive / reconstructive force of the premise of colonial subjugation I propose here. Its archival and countervailing function needs to be stressed. When the Philippine Islands became a U.S. colony at the turn of the century, its inhabitants succeeded the Africans, Mexicans, and American Indians as the "White Man's Burden," the object of "domestic racial imperialism" carried out through brutal pacification and cooptative patronage (Kolko 41–43, 286–87).

The first selection in *Letters in Exile*, "The First Vietnam—The Philippine-American War of 1898–1902," provides the required orientation for understanding the Filipino experience of U.S. racism, which culminated in the vigilante pogroms of the thirties. Neither Chinese, Japanese, nor Korean history before World War II contains any comparable scene of such unrestrained unleashing of racial violence by the U.S. military (of course, Vietnam later would exceed all precedents). Without taking into account the dialogic contestation of U.S. power by the Filipino imagination, which judged its exorbitance and "weak links" (mediated in American English, as discussed earlier), the critique of U.S. cultural hegemony worldwide remains incomplete.

Until 1934, when Filipinos legally became aliens under the Tydings-McDuffie Independence Act, their status was anomalously akin to that of a "floating signifier" with all its dangerous connotations. Wallace Stegner described the breathing of their fatigued bodies at night as "the loneliness breathing like a tired wind over the land" (*One Nation*, 20). This index of otherness, difference incarnate in the sweat and pain of their labor, is the stigma Filipinos had to bear for a long time.

Like it or not, we still signify "the stranger's" birthmark. Only in 1934 did the Filipino "immigrant" really come into existence (at first limited to fifty). Hence, neither Bulosan nor Villa were immigrants. Nor were the laborers enraptured by dreams of success who were rigidly bound to contracts. In this context, the hyphenated hybrid called "Filipino-American" becomes quite problematic, concealing the priority of the second term (given the fact of colonial/racial subordination and its hallucinatory internalizations) in what appears as a binary opposition of equals.

If the writings of Bulosan and Santos do not represent the authentic Filipino experience, as the Flips self-servingly charge, and such a privilege of "natural" representation belongs only to those born or raised in the U.S. mainland (which excludes territorial possessions), then this genetic legalism only confirms the Flips' delusions of exceptionality. It reinforces "the thoroughly racist and national chauvinist character of U.S. society" (Occeña 35) by eradicating the rich protean history of Filipino resistance to U.S. aggression. It thereby expropriates what little remains for purposes of Euro-American legitimation.

By contrasting the polarity of ideological positions in the two texts cited, I intended to demonstrate concretely the dangers of systemic recuperation and the illusion of paranoid separatism. Even before our admission to the canon is granted, as Fuchs shows, the terms of surrender or compromise already have been drawn up for us to sign. Who, then, has the authority to represent the Filipino and his or her experience? The answer to this question and to the problem of how to define Filipino cultural autonomy and its vernacular idiom cannot be explored unless historical parameters and the totalizing constraints of the world-system are acknowledged, that is, unless the specificity of U.S. imperial domination of the Philippines is foregrounded in the account.

From 1898 to the present, the production of knowledge and ethicopolitical judgments about the Filipino as a people different from others has been monopolized by Euro-American experts like W. Cameron Forbes, Dean Worcester, Joseph Hayden, and others. Consider, for example, H. Brett Melendy's discourse on "Filipinos" in the *Harvard Encyclopedia of American Ethnic Groups*. It offers the standard functional-empiricist explanation for Filipino workers' subservience to the Hawaii plantation system, due to their indoctrination "to submission by the barrio political system known as caciquismo" (358). Melendy claims that their kinship and alliance system inhibited social adaptation and "militated against their achieving success in American politics" (362). Thus the Filipino becomes a "social problem." Not only does this expert blame the victims' culture, but he also acquits the U.S. state apparatus and its agents of responsibility for deepening class cleavages and instituting that peculiar dependency syndrome which has hitherto characterized U.S.-Philippines cultural exchange.[7]

One of the first tasks of a decolonizing Filipino critical vernacular is to repudiate the putative rationality of this apologia and replace it with a materialist analysis. I have in mind exploratory inquiries like Bruce Occeña's synoptic overview "The Filipino Nationality in the U.S."[8] Occeña's attempt to delineate the historical, social, and political contours of the Filipino in the U.S. as a distinct nationality can be considered a salutary point of departure (except for its patent economistic inadequacies).[9] According to Occeña, two basic conditions have decisively affected the development of a unique Filipino nationality in the United States: first, the continuing oppression of the Filipino nation by U.S. imperialism, and second, the fact that as a group, "Filipinos have been integrated into U.S. society on the bases of inequality and subjected to discrimination due both to their race and nationality" (31).[10]

What follows is a broad outline of the sociopolitical tendencies of three "waves" of migration, as sketched by Occeña. This is needed to clarify the unfixed and dismantled character of the Filipino nationality in the United States:

1. The first "wave" (1906–46) covers 150,000 workers concentrated in Hawaii and California, mostly bachelor sojourners—crippled "birds of passage"—forced by poverty, ill health, and such to settle permanently.

2. The second "wave" (1946–64) includes 30,000 war veterans and their families, conservative in general because of their relative privilege.
3. The third "wave" (1965–84) is comprised of about 630,000 people. It is the most numerous and complexly stratified group, due to the fact that they have moved at a time when all sectors of Philippine society were undergoing cataclysmic change. This latest influx harbors nationalist sentiments that help focus their consciousness on multifaceted struggles at home and keep alive their hope of returning if and when their life-chances improve (although, of course, some will stay).

Given the collapse of distance by the greater scope and frequency of modern communication and travel, links of the Filipino diaspora to the islands (linguistic, cultural, and social) have been considerably reinforced, enough to influence the dynamics of community politics and culture here. This is a situation "quite different from the previous period when the Filipino community was in the process of evolving a conspicuously distinct subculture which was principally a reflection of their experiences in U.S. society and alien in many ways to the national culture of the Philippines itself" (Occeña 38).[11] Contradictory networks of thought and feeling traverse this substantial segment of the Filipino community, problematizing the evolution of a monolithic "Filipino-American" sensibility not fissured by ambivalence, opportunism, and schizoid loyalties.

Recent immigrants are composed of (1) urban professionals, strata exhibiting a self-centered concern for mobility and status via consumerism, and (2) a progressive majority who occupy the lower echelons of the working class exposed to the worst forms of class, racial, and national oppression. Occeña posits "the prospect that the life options of many of these Filipino-Americans are grim—the 'poverty draft' will push them into the front lines of the U.S. war machine or the life of low paid service workers. Consequently, this emerging generation promises to be the most thoroughly proletarianized section of the third wave" (41) and thus ripe for mobilization. I think the last inference is mechanical and does not allow for the impact of changing political alignments, ideological mutations, and other contingencies in the "New World Order" of late "disorganized" capitalism. But Occeña does emphasize the unifying pressure of racial and national marginalization and serves to rectify the narcosis of identity politics that posits a mystifying "Filipino-American" essence. In addition, a focus on the overlay and coalescence of the key sociological features of the three "waves" in the extended family networks should modify the schematic partitioning of this survey and intimate a more dynamic, hospitable milieu within which Filipino heterogeneity can be further enhanced and profiled.

It becomes clear now why, given these nomadic and deterritorializing circuits of exchange between the fertilizing margin and parasitic center the use of the rubric "Filipino-American" can be sectarian and thus susceptible to hegemonic disarticulation. Should we then bracket "American" (not reducible to heart or mind) in this moment of analysis, mimicking the antimiscegenation law of the thirties? In the hope of resolving the predicament of the intractable temper of Filipino subjectivity, (I hesitate to use "subject position" here because it may suggest a shifting monad, a disposable lifestyle unanchored to specific times and places), one may be tempted to unduly totalize the heterogeneous trends of writing styles, while at the same time preserving the fragmentation of writers into the easy categories of "oldtimers," activists of "identity politics," and assorted expatriates. But for analytic purposes, my present discourse seeks to articulate constellations of tropes, ethical postures, and idioms of *habitus* within a differentiated and provisional totality.

I think it is facile, if not falsifying, to lump the multiplicity of incompatible cultural productions into a putative phenomenology of "exile and displacement." Such an approach may be superficially provocative. On one hand, it invites us to test the validity of Edward Said's conceptualization of exile as a reconstitution of national identity ("Reflections" 359). On the other hand, it asks us to contextualize Julia Kristeva's psychoanalysis of every subject as estranged, the "improper" Other as our impossible "own and proper" (*Strangers* 191–95). But how does it really protect us from the internal colonialism at work in High Culture's idealizing of the worldwide division of mental / manual labor? Such a critical stance may foreground the fact of dependency and its libidinal investment in an archetypal pattern of exile and redemptive return. But it indiscriminately lumps together migrant workers, sojourners, expatriates, pseudo-exiles, refugees, emigres, and opportunists at the expense of the nuanced and creative tensions among them.[12] The hypothesis of exile is heuristic and catalyzing, but it fails to discriminate the gap between Bulosan's radical project of solidarity of people of color against capital and the integrationist "melting pot" tendencies that vitiate the works of N.V.M. Gonzalez, Bienvenido Santos, and their epigones.

Subjugation of one's nationality cannot be divorced from subordination by means of racial and class stigmatizing. Only Bulosan and some Flip writers are able to grapple with and sublate this complex dialectic of Filipino subalternity and bureaucratic closure. In a typical story, "The Long Harvest," Gonzalez easily cures the incipient anomie of his protagonist by making him recollect the primal scene of his mother suturing his narcissism with artisanal commodity production at home (28). As long as those sublimating images of an archaic economy survive, the petit bourgeois expatriate can always resort to a conciliatory, accommodationist therapy of mythmaking and need never worry about class exploitation, racism, and national oppression.[13] Of course, this is the easy path to ethnic self-aggrandizement and a compensatory, ghettoized *ressentiment*.

This is the caveat I would interpose: unless the paradigm of exile is articulated with the global division of labor under the *diktat* of U.S. finance capital (via IMF / World Bank, the United Nations, and private foundations), it simply becomes a mock-surrogate of the "lost generation" avant-garde and a pretext for élite ethnocentrism. The intellectual of color can even wantonly indenture himself to the cult of exile, à la Joyce or Nabokov. Bulosan also faced this tempting dilemma: stories like "Life and Death of a Filipino in the USA" and "Homecoming" (San Juan, *Bulosan* 25–30, 105–11) refuse commodity fetishism by fantasizing a return to a healing home, which is a seductive catharsis indeed:

> Everywhere I roam [in the United States] I listen for my native language with a crying heart because it means my roots in this faraway soil; it means my only communication with the living and those who died without a gift of expression. (Bulosan, *Writings* 153–54)

But he counters this nostalgic detour, this cheap Proustian fix, by reminding himself of his vocation and its commitment to the return of symbolic capital expropriated from his people:

> I am sick again. I know I will be here for a long time [Firland Sanitarium in Seattle, Washington]. And the grass hut where I was born is gone, and the village of Mangusmana is gone, and my father and his one hectare of land are gone, too. And the palm-leaf house in Binalonan is gone, and two brothers and a sister are gone forever.
>
> But what does it matter to me? The question is—what impelled me to write? The answer is—my grand dream of equality among men and freedom for all. To give a literate voice to the voiceless one hundred thousand Filipinos in the United States, Hawaii, and Alaska. Above all and ultimately, to translate the desires and aspirations of the whole Filipino people in the Philippines and abroad in terms relevant to contemporary history.
>
> Yes, I have taken unto myself this sole responsibility. (Kunitz 145)

Bulosan's transplantation from the empire's hinterland to the agribusiness enclaves of the West Coast coincides with his transvaluative mapping of the future as the space of everyone's desire and emancipated-but-still-embodied psyche—not the "America" of corporate business or of Fuchs' fantasy (San Juan, *People's Literature* 119–43; "Beyond Identity Politics" 1991: 556–58). When the patriarchal family disintegrates, the narrator of *America* (unlike Melendy's "Filipino") discovers connections with Chicano and Mexican workers, finds allies among white middle-class women, and taps the carnivalesque life-energies of folklore in *The Laughter of My Father,* Bulosan's satire of a money-obsessed society. He encounters the submerged *genius loci* of anti-imperialist solidarity in gambling houses, cabarets, labor barracks. These are sites of loss, excess, and expenditure that found a new social bond; they are points of escape that circumscribe the power of the American "dream" of affluence. Bulosan's strategy of displacement anticipates the insight that "a society or any collective arrangement is defined first by its points or flows of deterritorialization" and by jump-cuts, syncopations, and scrambling of positions (Deleuze and Guattari, *Plateaus* 220).

Borderlines, of course, include by excluding. It might be surmised that Bulosan suppresses history, when the conclusion of *America* reaffirms the narrator's faith in "our unfinished dream," an "America" diametrically opposed to the nightmares of history, which comprise the verisimilitude of quotidian existence. One might suspect that he infiltrates into it a "jargon of authenticity" and forces art to fulfill a compensatory function of healing the divided subject. But David Palumbo-Liu cogently puts the case against this kind of closure into ethnic textuality as capitulation to, and recapitalization of, the dominant ideology: "In ethnic narrative, the transcendence of the material via an identification with the fictional representation of lived life often suppresses the question of the political constitution of subjectivity, both within and without the literary text, opting instead for a kind of redemption that short-circuits such questions" (4). Likewise, as Marilyn Alquizola has shown, a probing of *America*'s structure will disclose an ironic counterpointing of voices or masks, with numerous didactic passages and exempla critical of the system. These undercut the naive professions of faith, compelling the reader to judge that "the totality of the book's contents contradict the protagonist's affirmation of America in the conclusion" (206). Beyond this formalist gloss, an oppositional reading would frame the logic of the narrator's structuring scheme with two influences: first, the routine practice of authors submitting to the publisher's market analysis of audience reception (wartime propaganda enhances a book's saleability) and, second, the convention of the romance genre in Philippine popular culture, which warrants such a formulaic closure.

Further metacommentary on the subtext underlying *America*'s mix of naturalism and humanist rhetoric would elicit its Popular Front politics as well as its affinity with Bulosan's massive indictment of capital. These are found in "My Education"; in the 1952 ILWU *Yearbook* editorial; and in numerous letters. All belie his imputed role of servicing the behemoth of American nationalism. Ultimately, we are confronted once again with the masks of the bifurcated and even duplicitous subject disseminated in the text, traces of his wandering through perilous contested terrain.

Forgotten after his transitory success in 1944 with *The Laughter of My Father*, Bulosan remained virtually unknown until 1973. Then the University of Washington Press, convinced of Bulosan's marketability and impressed by the activism of Filipino-American groups who were opposed to the "U.S.-Marcos Dictatorship," reissued *America*. My current acquaintance with the Filipino community, however, confirms Bulosan's lapse into near oblivion and the unlikelihood of the Establishment initiating a retrieval to shore up the ruins of the "model minority" myth. This immunity to canonization, notwithstanding the possibility that the fractured discourse of *America* can lend itself to normalization by disciplinary regimes, is absent in the works of Bienvenido Santos, whose narratives cultivate a more commodifiable topos: the charm and hubris of victimage.

Santos' imagination is attuned to an easy purchase on the hurts, alienation, and defeatism of *pensionados*, expatriated ilustrados, petit bourgeois males marooned during World War II in the East Coast and Midwest, and other third-wave derelicts. His pervasive theme is the reconciliation of the Filipino psyche with the status quo.[14] Since I have commented elsewhere on Santos' achievement (*People's Literature* 171–73; *Crisis* 182–83), suffice it to note here its power of communicating the pathos of an obsolescent humanism such as that exemplified, for instance, by David Hsin-Fu Wand's celebration of the universal appeal of ethnic writing, its rendering of "the human condition of the outsider, the marginal man, the pariah" (9), in his introduction to *Asian-American Heritage*.

The patronage of the American New Critic Leonard Casper might be able to guarantee Santos' efficacy in recycling the ethnic myth of renewal, the born-again syndrome which is the foundational site of the hegemonic American identity. Casper's technique of assimilation differs from Fuch's in its reactionary essentialism. He first bewails Filipino society's alleged loss of "agrarian ideals that guaranteed cultural uniformity and stability" ("Introduction" xiv), a loss that supposedly aggravates the traumatic impact of the "America of individualism" on poor tribal psyches. Then, Casper superimposes his antebellum standard on his client: Santos is "offering an essentially timeless view of culture, which transcends history limited to the linear, the consecutive, and the one-dimensional" (xv). But read against the grain, Santos' *Scent of Apples,* and possibly his two novels set in San Francisco and Chicago, derive their value from being rooted in a distinctive historical epoch of Filipino dispossession. As symptomatic testimonies of the deracinated neocolonized subject, they function as arenas for ideological neutralization and compromise. They mount serious obstacles to any salvaging operation and any effort to thwart recuperation, because they afford what Brecht calls "culinary" pleasure, a redaction of the native's exotic susceptibilities for tourist consumption and patronage.

So far, we have seen how Fuch's extortive neoliberalism can hijack the transgressive speech of Bulosan into the camp of "American nationalism" (!) and how Casper's paternalistic chauvinism can shepherd Santos up to the threshold of the western manor of polite letters. Appropriated thus, our authors don't really pose any threat to the élite proprietorship of administered learning. Does that also apply to Villa, the avant-garde heretic now *desaparecido* who once scandalized the colony's philistines?

Villa: Orphic Legerdemain

When Jose Garcia Villa arrived in the United States in 1930, he was already acclaimed as a modernist master by his contemporaries. His stature was reinforced with the publication of his two books of experimental, highly mannered poems: *Have Come Am Here* and *Volume Two.* Both earned praise from the mandarins of the Anglo-American literary establishment, among them Edith Sitwell, Marianne Moore, e. e. cummings, Richard Eberhart, and Mark Van Doren. Villa's poems then were anthologized by Selden Rodman, Conrad Aiken, and W. H. Auden (although, as far as I know, no textbook of American literature has included Villa). In addition to receiving American Academy of Arts and

Letters Award and the Shelley Memorial Award, he was nominated for
the Pulitzer Prize in 1943. Villa claims that he was denied a Bollingen
Prize because he was not an American citizen. On 12 June 1973, the
Marcos government bestowed on Villa its highest honor, "National Artist of the Philippines." After the publication of his *Selected Poems and
New* in 1958, however, Villa immediately sank into obscurity. One can
speculate that enigmatic disappearance can be explained plausibly
(apart from rapid change in taste and fashion) by the immense reifying
and integrative power of mass-consumer society to flatten out diverse
or antithetical visions and philosophies.[15]

Villa had no problems being hailed as an "American" poet by the
celebrities mentioned earlier, including the editor of *Twentieth Century Authors* (Kunitz). For this reference guide, Villa confessed the reason why his poems were "abstract" and lacked feeling for detail and
particularity:

> I am not at all interested in description or outward appearance, nor in
> the contemporary scene, but in essence. A single motive underlies all my
> work and defines my intention as a serious artist: The search for the meta-
> physical meaning of man's life in the Universe—the finding of man's self-
> hood and identity in the mystery of Creation. I use the term metaphysical
> to denote the ethic-philosophic force behind all essential living. The de-
> velopment and unification of the human personality I consider the highest
> achievement a man can do. (1035–36)

Thirty years later, Werner Sollors tries to smuggle Villa back into the
limelight by focusing on the poet's reactive idiosyncracy, not his metaphysical selfhood, to substantiate the myth of U.S. exceptionalism in
which the languages of consent (to assimilation) and descent collabo-
rate to Americanize almost any immigrant. Villa's indeterminate status
in the United States motivated his fabrication of a new poetic language
of "reversed consonance" (253–54). Positing the imperative of syncretic
belonging, Sollor's pastiche of ethnic genealogy thoroughly cancels
Villa's descent. Meanwhile, S. E. Solberg "naturalizes" Villa and so annuls Filipino collective self-determination, labeling the poet's spiritual
quest a "personal and idiosyncratic fable, a protean version of the 'making of Americans'" (54).

Elsewhere I have argued that Villa's poems can be properly appraised
as "the subjective expression of a social antagonism" that constitutes
the originality of the lyric genre (Adorno 376; San Juan, *Reading the
West*). What preoccupies Villa is the phenomenology of dispossession

or lack in general. This malaise translates into the double loss of the poet's traditional social function and of the audience, once exile overtakes the Filipino artist. What is staged in Villa's texts are scenarios for overcoming these losses by the discovery and ratification of the imagination as a demiurgic logos that expresses the poet's godhood, a process which also reciprocally evokes the forces of alienation and reification with which the poet is wrestling. In short, both the reality-effect and the domination-effect (Balibar and Macherey 91–97) are fused in the grammar of poetic enunciation. Such contradictions, which pivot around the themes of revolt against patriarchal power, psychomachia, negativity, and bodily uprooting, elude the neocolonizing maneuvers of Villa's critics and the parodic mimicry of his epigones.

It is not too much, I think, to suggest that Villa has refused the "ethnic" trap (at the expense of denying an entire horizon of alternatives). He has done so by challenging imperial authority to recognize his authentic artist-self and so validate his equal standing with his white peers. But this also spelled his premature redundancy, since reconciliation via aestheticism is nothing but the hegemonic alternative of healing the split subject in a transcendental restoration of plenitude of meaning.

We can observe this in the way that the crisis of exile is dissolved by metaphoric sublimation when rendered as metonymic displacement in "Wings and Blue Flame: A Trilogy" and "Young Writer in a New Country" (in *Footnote to Youth*). In Villa's visionary representation of the primal loss (exile as castration; expulsion by the father), the antinomic discourses of place, body, inheritance, and need converge in the self-exiled native being reborn in the desert of New Mexico, where the Oedipal trauma (the loss of the mother's / *patria*'s body) is exorcised by a transcendent trope of the imagination. Art then functions as the resolution of the conflict between solitary ego and community, unconscious drives and the fixated body, symbolic exchange and the imaginary fetish, between subjugated people and despotic conqueror.

In his sympathetic introduction to Villa's stories, Edward J. O'Brien intuits a "Filipino sense of race" or "race consciousness" embedded in the text, but senses that this consciousness swiftly evaporates in the "severe and stark landscape of New Mexico" (*Footnote* 3). Such a gesture of alluding to difference acquires a portentous modality when Babette Deutsch, again with the best of intentions, apprehends something anomalous in Villa's situation, only to normalize it as strange: "The fact that he is a native of the Philippines who comes to the English language as a stranger may have helped him to his unusual syntax" (56).

But the stigmata of the alien is no hindrance to Villa's creation of "luminous and vibrant" poems "concerned with ultimate things." This is a sacrificial rite, whose anti-utilitarian telos may not be so easily instrumentalized as Bulosan's idealism for the sake of vindicating the ethos of the pluralist market. Even if difference as plurality is granted, it is only at the expense of its subsumption in the sameness/identity of the artist. His self-contained artifices, which are predicated on the organic reconciliation of ego and alter, transcend the exigencies of race, nationality, class, gender, and all other segmentations integral to profit accumulation in the planetary domain of the late bourgeoisie.

At this juncture, the quest for Filipino self-representation reaches an impasse. Villa's "abject" response to the world of commodities and the cash-nexus combines both acquiescence and nausea, given our hypothesis that the lyric form harbors social antagonisms and yields both reality-effects and domination-effects. His work might be read as a highly mediated reflection of the vicissitudes of the conscienticized Filipino, who is driven from the homeland by economic crisis, alternatively nostalgic and repelled, unable to accommodate himself to his new environment.

Villa's "disappearance" is but one episode in the allegory of the Filipinos' pre-postcolonial ethnogenesis. The group's persistently reproduced subordination arises from its belief that it owes gratitude for being given an entry visa, and that by imitating the successful models of Asians and other immigrants who made their fortune, it will gradually be accepted as an equal. Yet, at the same time, Filipinos cherish the belief that they originated from a distinct sovereign nation that enjoys parity with the United States. To salvage Villa, then, we have to read his work symptomatically for those absent causes that constitute its condition of possibility, even as those very same ruptures and silences betray the manifold contradictions that define the "American civic" consensus. Villa's agenda is integration of the personality. Ours is the reinscription of our subject-ion, our transformative agency, in the revolutionary struggle to forge an independent, self-reliant Philippines and in the resistance of people of color everywhere to the violence of white supremacy.

From "Dogeaters" to Warm Body Export

In this emancipatory project to build the scaffolding of our cultural tradition, we can learn how to safeguard ourselves from the danger of reclamation by a strategy of retrospective mapping (performed above) and anticipatory critique. To advance the latter, I comment on two modes of narrating Filipino self-identification: Jessica Hagedorn's *Dogeaters* and Fred Cordova's *Filipinos: Forgotten Asian Americans.*

Conflating heresy and orthodoxy, Hagedorn's novel possesses the qualities of a canonical text in the making—for the chic multiculturati. She unfolds the crisis of U.S. hegemony in the Philippines through a collage of character types who embody the corruption of the Americanizing oligarchic élite (see San Juan, "Mapping the Boundaries" 125– 26). In trying to extract some intelligible meaning from the fragmentation of the comprador-patriarchal order that sacrifices everything to acquisitive lust, she resorts to pastiche, aleatory montage of diverse styles, clichés, ersatz rituals, hyper-real hallucinations—a parodic bricolage of western high postmodernism—the cumulative force of which blunts whatever satire or criticism is embedded in her character portrayals and authorial intrusions (for an alternative view, see Covi).

This narrative machine of the novel converts the concluding prayer of exorcism and *ressentiment* into a gesture of stylized protest. Addressed mainly to a cosmopolitan audience, Hagedorn's trendy artifice is undermined by postmodern irony: it lends itself easily to consumer liberalism's drive to sublimate everything (dreams, eros, New People's Army, feminism, anarchist dissent) into an ensemble of self-gratifying spectacles. At best, *Dogeaters* measures the distance between the partisanship of Bulosan's peasants-become-organic-intellectuals and the pseudo-yuppie lifestyles of recent arrivals. As a safe substitute for Bulosan and as one of the few practitioners of Third World/feminine "magic realism," Hagedorn may easily be the next season's pick for the Establishment celebration of its multicultural canon.[16]

Examining Cordova's photographic montage in *Filipinos: Forgotten Asian Americans,* we encounter again our otherness or supplementarity as "fertilizer" and "little brown brother." We discern here a symptom of the conflicted subaltern compensating for his lack by impressing the public with an overwhelming multiplicity of images. These evoke family/communal togetherness, a simulacra of smiles and gestures which animate the rituals of the life-cycle and whose repetition seems enough to generate illusions of successful adjustment and progress. Filipinos turn out to be "first" on many occasions. Despite the negative witness of parts of the commentary, the surface texture of those images serves to neutralize the stark evidence of a single photo (on page 42) that captures stooping, faceless workers caught in the grid of a bleak imprisoning landscape. Nothing is mentioned of why or how these alien bodies were transported and smuggled in.

What is suppressed here can be gleaned from a comparable, though abbreviated, photographic discourse made by another outfit, *Pearls* (Bock 38–47). Its section on "Pinoy" offers an apologetic history and the usual documentary exhibits of Filipinos adapting to their new habitat, but the inclusion of newspaper cutouts headlining anti-Filipino riots serves to demystify the ideology of adjustment and compromise that informs officially funded enterprises such as Cordova's.[17] *Pearls* records a vestigial trace, a lingering effect, of what *Letters in Exile* (Quinsaat) strove to accomplish: a reconstruction of the historical conditions of possibility of the Filipino presence in the metropolis and their struggle to affirm their humanity by acts of refusal, solidarity, and remembering.[18] It is one way of arming the community spirit for impending battles.

The Marcos interlude in Philippine history (1972–86) brought a flood of exiles and pseudo-refugees to the United States at the same time that Washington amplified its military and economic aid to the national security state. This period has foregrounded again the reality of U.S. domination of the homeland, a fact that distinguishes the Filipino nationality from other minorities. Our neocolonial stigmata renews the signifiers of difference.[19] I reiterate my thesis that the creation of the vernacular résumé of the Filipino's experience of limits and possibilities here can only be theorized within the process of comprehending the concrete historical particularity of their incorporation in the U.S. empire and the ecology of this unequal exchange.

In the context of recent demography, Bulosan seems a "rural" misfit. The transplantation of recent Filipino immigrants to the urban wilderness of Los Angeles, San Francisco, Seattle, Chicago, and New York City has impelled young writers to conjecture the emergence of an "urbane" sensibility, adoptive and adaptive at the same time, born from the clash of cultures and memories. The trajectory of the proletarian imagination from Hawaii's plantations to California's Imperial Valley to Washington's Yakima Valley no longer crosses the paths of "dogeaters" and "Flips." Recent subaltern anxiety, however, seeks legitimacy from the universal archetypes found in archaic folklore and myth—an ironic aporia, indeed. How can this resort to mystification recover from the "backwaters" the writings of Serafin Malay Syquia, for example? And how can it valorize the paradigm of the *sakada*'s redemptive agon in

Istorya ni Bonipasyo: Kasla Gloria Ti Hawaii (Bonipasyo's Story: Hawaii Is Like Paradise) for its lessons of inventing "history from below"?[20]

Only disconnect and recontextualize—that's our motto. What makes such disparate events as Fermin Tobera's killing in 1930 and the murder of Domingo and Viernes in 1981 the condensed turning points of the Filipino odyssey in the U.S.?[21] You have to conceive of both events occurring in the space of the heterogeneous Other occupied by U.S. "civilizing" power. The texts of the nationality's autochthonous tradition are interred in the imperial archive, which cries for inventory and critique—I am thinking of the oral histories of the "Manongs"; interviews of veterans of union organizing; testimonies in letters and journals of immigrant passage; reportage and videofilms of various struggles such as that over the International Hotel in San Francisco; and other nonverbal signifying practices. Unfortunately, there are few discerning and astute commentaries or informed reflections for these circumstantial texts. We need to disconnect them from the hegemonic episteme and recuperation of Fuchs and Melendy; we need contextualize them in the resistance narrative of peasants and workers, and then reconfigure them in the punctual lived experiences of Filipinos today.

Therefore, I consider the production of transformative critical discourse a priority in the task of identifying, generating, and selecting the anti-canon[22] of Filipino agency and praxis that in varying degrees have resisted cooptation and incorporation. Toward realizing this agenda of searching for our "representative" speech, I propose Bulosan's corpus of writings as central touchstone and researches like *Philip Vera Cruz: A Personal History of Filipino Immigration and the Farmworkers Movement* as crucial linkages between popular memory and individualist dissidence. In this syllabus, we include Santos' and Gonzalez's fiction on the diaspora as loci for renegotiation, together with Villa's entire production as salvageable for counterhegemonic rearticulation in spite of his status as a legendary classic. Meanwhile the prodigious creativity of a "third wave" generation—among them Jessica Hagedorn, Marianne Villanueva, Fatima Lim-Wilson, R. Zamora Linmark, Peter Bacho, and many more who participated in the annual exodus from the Philippines in the last decade—remains a reservoir of practices for future hermeneutic appraisal and reader/writer empowerment.

To accomplish this project of discovery, rescue, and affirmation of Filipino agency against recolonizing strategies from above, we need a radical transformation of grassroots consciousness and practice. This task is addressed by Marina Feleo-Gonzalez's playbook, *A Song for Manong*. What is at stake here is a recovery of the inaugural scene of Filipino subjectification and insurgency as a dialectical process. We find this event dramatized here when the script unfolds the figure of Pedro Calosa, a leader of the Tayug uprising in the Philippine province of Pangasinan, as one who learned the craft of resistance from the Hawaii inter-ethnic strikes of the twenties. (It is from this milieu of sedition and dissidence that Bulosan emerged.) Feleo-Gonzalez chooses to circumvent any easy return to a pristine homeland by concluding the performance with the solidarity-in-action of Euro-Americans and Third World peoples in the campaign to preserve the site of the International Hotel from corporate modernization.[23] Feleo-Gonzalez's intervention aims to reawaken the community's conscience and redeem its "collective assemblage of enunciation" (to use Deleuze and Guattari's phrase) from the fate of recoding by the celebrated "melting pot" religion.

One such assemblage is Manuel Buaken's neglected book *I Have Lived with the American People*. Indeed, Buaken returns to haunt us with a powerful lesson: no fable of dredging up a coherent and synchronized identity through memory alone, no privileging of the therapeutic power of art, no sacred ceremony of reminiscence by itself, can cement together the fragments of our uprooting from the ravished homeland and repair the tragic disintegration of the nation's spirit. In the breakdown of Buaken's "goodwill autobiography" as a teleological fable, we find a counterpointing discourse: our quest for linkage and autonomy encounters the testimonies of such early migrants as Francisco Abra (117–20) and Felipe Cabellon (121–24), soliciting empathy and justice, interrupting our pursuit of wholeness.

With the Filipino nationality in the United States still mind-manacled and the islands convulsed in the fire of people's war for liberation, the practice of writing by, of, and for Filipinos in the United States remains nomadic, transitional, hybrid, metamorphic, discordant, beleaguered, and embattled, "always already" in abeyance. Such a genre of "minor" writing, which I define as a praxis of becoming-what-is-other-for-itself, is "the revolutionary force for all literature" (Deleuze and Guattari, *Kafka*).

5

Violence of Exile, Politics of Desire: Prologue to Carlos Bulosan

Of the Asian American population in the United States, the Filipino community is now the second largest constituency, and the largest in the state of California (based on the 1990 Census). By the year 2000, it is estimated that there will be over two million Filipinos in this country (Patel). But in the study of contemporary U.S. culture and society and in the multi-ethnic literary canon, Filipinos either do not exist or else they are tokenized and subsumed within the larger official racializing category of Asian-American. However, there are genuine historical, political, and cultural differences between Filipinos and other Asian ethnic groups. In the context of the current interrogation of the hegemonic claims of a unitary "American common culture," I propose that Filipinos and their practice of cultural production now should be appraised as a force in its own right, in its difference and integrity, in its complex dialectical relation with the distinctive histories of other peoples of color in the United States, with the dominant consensus, and especially with the power alignment within the present globalized world-system of late capitalism.

One approach to this task of retrieving the Filipino presence in the United States—of locating the space for a process or project called "becoming Filipino"—may be accomplished by examining the life and writings—their singular intertextuality as practices in the field of cultural production (to use Bourdieu's term)—of Carlos Bulosan.

Long forgotten since his brief success in the 1940s, Bulosan was rediscovered in the 1960s by a generation of Filipino American youth who had been radicalized by the anti–Vietnam War and civil-rights struggles. This self-awakening of Filipinos born in the United States arose in counterpoint with the worldwide resurgence of "Third World" national-liberation movements, particularly in the Philippines. Coincid-

ing with this was the climax in 1965 of the Filipino farmworkers' movement led by Larry Itliong and Philip Vera Cruz, as well as the founding
of the United Farm Workers of America (Scharlin and Villanueva). Initially sparked by an identity crisis, the Filipino youth movement inaugurated the birth of political self-reflection—the intensity of "becoming"
a subject claiming to be "Filipino." The reissuance of *America Is in the
Heart* in 1972 (originally published in 1946) catalyzed this process of
recuperating the past, interrogating the present, and revisioning the
future. I address the contours of this process in the next sections.

With the downfall of the Marcos dictatorship in 1986 and the ascendancy of a neoconservative trend in the United States, however, the energies mobilized by this process have been rechanneled once more into
either hedonist or neo–social Darwinist preoccupations. This leaves a
sizeable number of young Filipinos growing up into the twenty-first
century with no alternative but hedonistic lifestyles, crass consumerism, and a generally unreflective conformity to the official dispensation.
Are these symptoms of the decadence of the Empire at the end of this
millennium?

This impasse in the evolution of the U.S. Filipino community is then
the conjunctural pretext for this new reappraisal—the fourth after those
in my previous works: *Toward a People's Literature, Writing and National
Liberation*, and *Reading the West/Writing the East*. What does Bulosan,
with his unique sensibility shaped by the Depression, and the circumstances of the 1940s and 1950s, have to offer in articulating that still intractable and anarchic desire called "becoming Filipino"? Given the dis-
parity between his peasant / working-class background and the petty
bourgeois cosmopolitan milieu of recent immigrants, what in Bulosan's
writings can help us understand the unresolved predicament—the
powerlessness and invisibility—of being labeled a "Filipino" in post–
Cold War America?

My intervention here aims less to provide answers than to initiate a
forum for exploring the pertinacity and resonance of these questions. I
wrestled with these pursuits, in their initial formulations, when I wrote
the first scholarly treatise on Bulosan in 1972 (*Carlos Bulosan and the
Imagination of the Class Struggle*) and while editing several collections of
his works over the last two decades. The publication of Bulosan's novel,
The Cry and the Dedication (hereafter *The Cry*), in 1995 also seeks to open
the space for a dialogue between the first "wave" of Filipinos in the
United States and those migrant professionals who have arrived since
1965. This exchange has been made more necessary and urgent by the

unprecedented resurgence of racism in the United States and the intensification of civil war in the Philippines. Whatever our personal biases and situational contingencies, Bulosan will not ignore us, even if we remain indifferent or pretend to be unconcerned.

Return of the Repressed

Our destiny
To find our path once again to the heart of the earth. . . .
For it is the power to see beyond ourselves,
And to give ourselves. . . .
—*"Five Poems for Josephine"*

When Bulosan was born on 22 November 1911, in the village of Binalonan, in the northwestern province of Pangasinan, the Philippines already was a full-fledged U.S. colony. He was born in the aftermath of Spain's defeat in the Spanish-American War of 1898 and the disastrous Filipino-American War of 1898–1903; the latter killed an estimated one million Filipinos and several thousand Americans. With territorial conquest in hand, the United States then proceeded to transform this Southeast Asian archipelago into a classic colonial dependency, a source of raw materials and cheap labor power (Constantino, *Neocolonial Identity*). After almost half a century of nationalist resistance (both peaceful and violent) plus three years of savage rule by the Japanese military during World War II, the Philippines finally gained political independence in 1946.

Unlike China or Japan, the homeland of the Filipino people was an emergent sovereign territory when it was forcibly invaded and annexed by the United States. With the destruction of the first Philippine Republic, Filipinos were subjugated as "natives," "a semibarbaric population" (Samuel Gompers' phrase) soon destined to be "civilized." While white-supremacist ideology informed President William McKinley's policy of "benevolent assimilation," the logic of U.S. liberal capitalism dictated a recognition of the long-enduring tradition of indigenous resistance to colonialism; hence Filipinos remained aliens. In 1903, William Howard Taft, the Philippines' first civil administrator, proclaimed "Filipinos for the Philippines," inaugurating the advent of the neocolonial order, under which, up to now, thousands of Filipinos continue to migrate to the United States every year.

Except for a few hundred *pensionados* or scholars sent by the colonial government to the United States to be trained for bureaucratic positions, the entry of Filipinos into U.S. territory in sizeable numbers first began in 1907. In that year, one hundred and fifty workers were recruited by the Hawaii Sugar Planters Association (Chan). From then until 1946, at least 125,000 Filipino workers sold their labor power as commodity to the Hawaiian plantation owners and alienated their bodies to the Alaskan canneries and agribusiness of the West Coast.

From 1900 to 1946, Filipinos in the United States thus were not immigrants in the conventional sense, nor were they settlers. Rather, they were, in today's parlance, "economic refugees." They were colonized "subalterns" (in Gramsci's sense of ideologically subjugated groups) whose bodies were transported from the hinterland to the metropolis, their physiognomies studied and their customs classified by the appropriate ideological mechanisms (which included school teachers and Protestant missionaries) to legitimize the supremacy of U.S. knowledge/power and its disciplinary regime over an entire nation.

Thus, unlike the Chinese and other Asian groups, whose first experience of victimization was mediated by the immigration authorities, Filipinos may be considered exceptional precisely because of their origin as the object of colonial subjugation, at once coercive and consensual. In general, the Filipino was the product of what Louis Althusser calls the machinery of "interpellation." In this process, individuals (addressed by the ideological apparatuses of race, class, and gender) become the subjects/bearers of specific functions within the framework of an overdetermined, uneven, and combined modes of production and reproduction that are geared for worldwide capital accumulation.

Driven by poverty and feudal oppression at home, Filipinos under imperial tutelage began traveling to the United States to pursue the "dream of success" via thrift, hard work, and unrelenting self-sacrifices (Buaken; Pido). By 1930, there were 108,260 Filipinos countrywide—mostly farmworkers in the West Coast. They had indeterminate status: neither protected wards nor citizens, they were subjected to various forms of racist discrimination and exclusion, circumscribed by laws of antimiscegenation (among others) and prohibited from employment in government and from land ownership (McWilliams, *Brothers*).

Being neither citizens nor strictly aliens, Filipino "nationals" (mostly males) suffered class, national, and racial oppression directed by agribusiness functionaries or administered by technocratic state bureaucracies—the legislature, the courts, and the police. Categorized in this irrec-

oncilable alterity, Filipinos endured as victims of exploitation, perpe-
trated by labor contractors, farmers, gamblers, racist vigilantes, by state
laws, and so on (Melendy, *Asians in America*; Takaki, *Strangers*). Deterritorialized in this way, members of this "internal colony" fought to survive and affirm their human rights and dignity. In doing so, they forged
a rich and complex culture of resistance linking their homeland (site of
dispossession) and the metropolitan power (site of commodification).

Examples may be cited here. Parallel to the endemic revolts of peasants in the colonized islands, Filipino workers organized one of the first
unions in Hawaii in 1919, the Filipino Federation of Labor, which spearheaded industrywide, multiracial strikes in 1920 and 1924 (Chan). In
1934, the Filipino Workers Association was established in California
with 2,000 active members; it organized the strikes of 1934 in Salinas, El
Centro, Vacaville, and the cotton fields of the San Joaquin Valley, California (referred to in *America Is in the Heart*). This reservoir of experience eventually enabled the Filipino Agricultural Workers Organizing
Committee to lead the historic grape strike of 1965, the matrix of what
became the United Farm Workers of America (Catholic Institute for
International Relations).

Bulosan landed in Seattle, Washington, in 1930, equipped only with
textbook stereotypes of American society and its affluence. He arrived
during the worst crisis of the twentieth century: the Great Depression.
Fierce class wars raged throughout the land. Laboring in restaurants
and farms in those years of poverty, homelessness, and racial antagonisms, he was exposed to the suffering of migrant workers scattered
from California to Alaska and, in the process, learned their survival
craft. The Depression inflicted on Filipinos (100,000 in Hawaii, 30,000 in
California) severe unemployment, intense labor exploitation, and rampant vigilante violence. In 1928 and 1930, Filipinos were attacked by
racist mobs in Yakima Valley, Washington; Watsonville, California; and
other towns (Bogardus). Filipinos also were threatened with deportation. On top of this, in 1935, immigration from the Philippine Commonwealth was limited to fifty persons per year. From the 1898 annexation
of the islands to 1946, Filipinos in the United States (called "Pinoys")
inhabited a limbo of indeterminacy: neither citizens nor complete for-
eigners, they were "nationals" without a sovereign country.

With that background, we can grasp the historicity of Bulosan's imagination. His apprenticeship as an organic intellectual of the masses (in
Gramsci's sense of leaders who conceptualized their coherent identity)
started with the trials of his family to overcome feudal tyranny in a

colonized social formation. Bulosan followed his two brothers, Aurelio and Dionisio, to California to escape the hopeless destitution of his village, where unequal property relations were sanctioned by U.S. colonial power. His life on the West Coast exposed him to the hazards of itinerant work (Kunitz). In the early 1930s, he became involved in union-organizing through his friendship with Chris Mensalvas of the United Cannery, Agricultural, Packing and Allied Workers of America (UCAPAWA). He also participated in activities of the CIO (Congress of Industrial Organization).

As editor of *The New Tide,* a bimonthly workers' magazine, in 1934, Bulosan came into contact with progressive writers Richard Wright, William Saroyan, William Carlos Williams, Louis Adamic, and others. He also wrote for the *Philippine Commonwealth Times* and two other newspapers in the Stockton and Salinas areas.

When Bulosan was confined in the Los Angeles General Hospital for tuberculosis and kidney problems, it was Sanora Babb and her sister Dorothy who helped Bulosan discover through books a new "world of intellectual possibilities—and a grand dream of bettering society for the working man" (this from his poignant testimony in *America Is in the Heart*). From 1936 to 1938, the convalescent Bulosan read voraciously the works of Neruda, Dreiser, Farrell, Nazim Hikmet, Steinbeck, Gorky, Marx, Whitman, Agnes Smedley, Hellman, Nicolas Guillen, Edgar Snow, Gandhi, Shaw, Rizal, and others, plus periodicals like *New Masses, The New Republic,* and *Nation* ("Carlos Bulosan" 1957). His further adventures in the Los Angeles Public Library completed his rudimentary high school education, endowing him with a working knowledge of human behavior and a grasp of world history.

But it was his partisan experience as journalist and union activist that actually laid the groundwork for his becoming a committed "tribune" of the Filipino people (in Lenin's sense of collective spokesman). The responsibility of the tribune involved the twin tasks of critique and prophecy. Even while in the hospital, Bulosan began composing vignettes that indicted patriarchal despotism (both religious and domestic) and the tyranny of the feudal / comprador élite. He depicted the life-worlds of plebeian rebels and outcasts, outlawed subalterns who bore the stigmata of inhabitants from a dependent economy. These comic-satiric fables later would be collected in the best-selling *The Laughter of My Father* (hereafter *Laughter*). Its aesthetic decorum is elaborated in the article "I Am Not a Laughing Man. "

Contrary to the philistine dismissal of *Laughter* as commercialized folk humor and mere local "exotic" color, Bulosan himself emphasized its allegorical thrust:

> My politico-economic ideas are embodied in all my writings. *The Laughter* is *not* humor; it is satire; it is indictment against an economic system that stifled the growth of the primitive . . . making him decadent overnight without passing through the various stages of growth and decay. (*Sound of Falling Light* 273)

Other more trenchant stories attacking the predatory excesses of the oligarchy and the horrors of profit accumulation in the first three decades of U.S. rule now are available in *The Philippines Is in the Heart*. By mobilizing folk/plebeian memory and the carnivalesque resources of his heritage, Bulosan devised a strategy of cultural resistance that would subvert the Eurocentric representation of Filipino "Otherness," an alterity captured in the perception that it was "a crime to be a Filipino in America."

Bulosan's art thus was born in the gap between colonial bondage and capitalist "freedom." His obsessive theme revolves around the Filipino people's project of attempting to deconstruct their anonymity/subordination and thus gain autonomy, the power of self-determination. To help perform a cognitive-ethical mapping of the future as a space of national emancipation and attainment of full "species being" (Marx's term), Bulosan's works seek to harness ideas, dreams, memories, and images flashing in moments of danger to reconstitute the ideals of the aborted 1896 revolution and numerous insurrections thereafter.

In this process, he memorializes the figure of the resolute, strong, persevering mother associated with planting/harvest rituals (see, for instance, "Passage into Life" or the first part of *America Is in the Heart*). He celebrates the beauty and fertility of the homeland which, amid his panicked flight from lynchers and police, become symbolic of an immanent harmony, relics of a fugitive but incarnate happiness. This cathexis of the soil/mother imagery (transposed to the geography of the U.S. West Coast) serves as a counterpoint to the linear rhythm of historical development and generates the tension of semantic horizons in Bulosan's narratives.

When the mystique of kinship dissolves and the promise of security and heirs vanishes, the Filipino workers discover multiple affinities with their compatriots. And they recuperate the submerged impulse of racial/national solidarity in the wasteland of capitalism: gambling houses, labor barracks, union halls, and brothels. While exploding the illusion of mobility, the mythical "dream of success," these tabooed, peripheral sites become the matrix of Bulosan's historical imagination. This imagination in turn extrapolates from the past, from the determinisms of loss and expenditure, the emerging free play of mutual recognitions. Eventually the Filipino finds allies and collaborators among white workers, middle-class women in particular, and other nationalities and races participating in picket lines, strikes, and other militant struggles for justice and equality.

Before the end of the Great Depression—that apocalyptic crisis of global capitalism—Bulosan already had plotted his long-range program of anatomizing the political economy of the colonized psyche. His mandate was to "interpret the soul of the Filipinos. . . . What really compelled me to write was to try to understand this country, to find a place in it not only for myself but my people" (*Selected Works and Letters* 81). "Self" here does not mean the paranoid denizen of Lacan's (1978) Imaginary register, that phase of psychic development characterized by identifying the self with illusory models. It does not allude exclusively to the Filipino ethnic particularity or its constrained ethnogenesis. It also envisages a nascent collective agency of all subordinated people, inventing new forms of subjectivity. Such a place in the U.S. cultural canon and public consciousness has yet to be claimed and staked out by all people of color who follow in Bulosan's wake.

Traversing the Frontlines

And all will move forward
On the undiscriminate course of history that never
Stops to rectify our tragic misgivings and shame.
—*"Letter in Exile"*

We are not pure in blood but one in living deed.
—*"Meeting with a Discoverer"*

On the eve of Pearl Harbor, Bulosan summed up his years of experience as union propagandist-agitator and nomadic exile:

Yes, I feel like a criminal running away from a crime I did not commit. And the crime is that I am a Filipino in America. . . . It was now the year of the great hatred [1941]; the lives of Filipinos were cheaper than those of dogs. (*Sound* 199)

This moment signals the birth of the writer's dialectical sensibility. We observe a totalizing urge on Bulosan's part to inventory what has been achieved in the Philippines by popular resistance to the oppression of the first three decades of U.S. colonial rule. In a time when "life was swift and terrible," Bulosan had to repudiate liberal individualism and the hubris of the intellect. He was compelled to realize that without the organized resistance of the working masses and the discipline of cooperative labor, the individual is condemned to recapitulate the ignominy of the past: the painful vicissitudes of colonial servility and self-contempt, as well as the atrocities of the 1930s when Filipinos in the United States were stigmatized, quarantined, and lynched.

The exemplary text of such a counterhegemonic strategy is *America Is in the Heart* (hereafter *AIH*), Bulosan's novelistic synthesis of Filipino lives, written in the middle of World War II. Because of its centrality in the Bulosan canon, its popularity, and its problematic challenge to critical consensus, I would like to sketch here an approach to this text that would serve also as a framework or point of departure for appreciating the art and craft of his stories, poems, essays, and letters.

Originally acclaimed as a classic testimony of immigrant success when it appeared in 1946, *AIH* presents a massive documentation of the varieties of racism, exploitation, alienation, and inhumanity suffered by Filipinos in the West Coast and Alaska during the decade beginning with the Depression and ending with the outbreak of World War II. Scenes of abuse, insult, neglect, brutalization, and outright murder of these colonial "wards"—natives of the only direct Asian colony held by the United States—are rendered with naturalistic candor, alongside depiction of their craft of survival and resistance.

America Is in the Heart is a magnificent polyphonic orchestration of events from the lives of the author and his generation of compatriots. Except for part one (12 chapters), the remaining three parts (chapters 13 to 49) of this ethnobiography chart the passage of the youthful narrator (who also doubles as protagonist and witness of events) in a land of privation, terror, and violence. It begins with his victimization by corrupt labor contractors on his arrival in Seattle (99–100), his anguished flight from lynch mobs, his first beating by two policemen in Klamath Falls, Oregon (156–57), and his desperate flirtation with Max Smith's cynicism (164–65)—vicissitudes punctuated in the middle of the book when his testicles are crushed by white vigilantes (208). A hundred pages after this episode, replete with more degrading ordeals, "Allos"— the fictional representative of about 30,000 Filipinos resident in Califor-

nia—concludes by reaffirming his faith in "America," now the name for
a metaphoric space, "sprung from all our hopes and aspirations" (327).

How do we reconcile this stark discrepancy between reality and
thought, between fact (the social wasteland called "United States") and
ideal ("America," land of equality and prosperity)? Is this simply an
astute ironical strategy to syncopate naive narrator with subversive
author, thus multiplying polyvalent readings and celebrating the virtues of schizoid *jouissance* (Roland Barthes' term for the unique pleasure
of reading)?

One way to approach this aporia, this impasse of divergent views, is
to reject the conventional thesis that *AIH* belongs to "that inclusive and
characteristic Asian-American genre of autobiography or personal history" (Kim 47) designed to promote assimilation or cooptation. Challenging received doxa, *AIH* invents a new genre, the antithesis to the
quest for Americanization. The address to the "American earth" at the
end is cast in the subjunctive mood, sutured in an unfolding process,
the future of which is overshadowed by Pearl Harbor and the defeats in
Bataan and Corregidor. The concluding three chapters reiterate the bit-
terness, frustration, loneliness, confusion, "deep emptiness," and havoc
in the lives of Filipinos in America (315–25). This explains the paradox
of the ending vis-à-vis the caustic naturalism of what precedes it. Whatever the pressures of the Cold War and marketing imperatives, to construe Bulosan's chronicle of the Filipino struggle to give dignity to their
spoiled or damaged lives in the U.S. as a plea for patriotism or imperial
"nationalism" is quite unwarranted. Such a construal is surely meant
to erase all evidence of its profoundly radical, popular-democratic
inspiration.

Critics have alleged that pressures from the Cold War and the publisher's marketing ploy forced Bulosan to disseminate in the text praises
of American democracy that are sharply at odds with his message of
almost total victimization. I suspect there is some truth to this charge.
What demands clarification is how we are able to perceive the discrepancy and assay the text's "cunning" in using alternating perspectives to
convey something more complex. But to construe Bulosan's chronicle of
the Filipino endeavor to salvage dignity from damaged lives as an ad-
vertisement for majoritarian "nationalism" (Fuchs) or an exhibitionist
pluralism (Lim) is simply wrongheaded, if not deliberately perverse.
This publicity, however well-intentioned, works to erase all evidence of
the book's profoundly radical, anti-Establishment motivation.

Perhaps the easiest way to elucidate this crux is to highlight Bulosan's trope of personification, the wish-fulfilling Imaginary of this artifact. Who is "America"? The text replies: Eileen Odell, one of Bulosan's companions and mentors, "was undeniably the *America* I had wanted to find in those frantic days of fear and flight, in those acute hours of hunger and loneliness. This America was human, good, and real" (235; on Bulosan's relations with American women, see Evangelista). If "Eileen" and other surrogates function as a synecdoche for all those who demonstrated comradeship to a stranger like Bulosan, then the term should not to be conflated with the abstract referent "U.S.A." as a whole. Overall, the caring maternal figure with her multiple personifications (the peasant mother, Marian, the Odell sisters, Mary, and others who serve as icons of mutual recognition) is the singular desire thematized as "America."

Viewed from another angle, the idiomatic tenor of the title may be read as a metaphor of an inward process of self-becoming, more precisely of parthenogenesis: it is in Bulosan's "heart"/sensibility that "America" (the text) germinates. By metonymic semiosis, the trope of containment gestures toward deliverance: discovering that he could write after striking back at the white world and feeling free, Bulosan translates his life into the text of *AIH*. Of crucial importance is the equation of "heart" with "one island" (323), the Philippines. Literally and figuratively, then, the "heart" becomes a polysemous vehicle that signifies either inclusion or exclusion. "Heart" becomes a fantasy/romance metaphor (what Mikhail Bakhtin calls a "chronotope" or space-time configuration) integral to the task of adumbrating a community within the treacherous, alienating, heartless metropolis.

This utopian theme of imagining a home, an extraterritorial enclave, within the fold of a disintegrated polity explains the didactic portions of *AIH*. The climax of Bulosan's project of educating his countrymen about the unifying trajectory of their fragmented lives allows him to displace their hopes into the vocabulary of America as "our unfinished dream" (312). Purged of his narcissistic malaise, he writes, "I was rediscovering myself in their lives." This counters the Robinson Crusoe motif of individualism and replaces it with the Moses/mother motif of collective concern. The narrator's private self dissolves into the body of an enlarged "family"—recall that he originally traveled to America to find his brothers and to reconstitute the broken family. The members of this extended family are affiliated by purpose or principle, anticipating what Bulosan calls "the revolution . . . the one and only common thread that bound us together, white and black and brown, in America" (313).

The ideal of fraternity among races (nurtured by the fight against a common global enemy, fascism) grounds the virtues of patience and hope underlying his "prophecy of a new society." It can be conceived as a "structure of feeling" that motivates the obsession with the Spanish Civil War (1936–39), the key historical conflict that polarized events and characters, and a touchstone of authentic solidarity. Framed by Bulosan's cathartic discovery of his ability to write and his acquisition of a socialist vision of "the war between labor and capital" (Bulosan, "Labor and Capital: The Coming Catastrophe" 1), the apostrophe to the multiracial masses as "America" gravitates around a cardinal principle: unity of all the oppressed across class, gender, and racial lines, which precedes the restructuring of state power. This appeal to "America"—a word whose meaning (can one still doubt it?) is subject to constant renegotiation—is better grasped as part of Bulosan's strategy to rearticulate the liberal discourse of civil rights toward a socialist direction. This, of course, incurs risks and liabilities; hence the quoting of "America" as a double bind.

So far, the theme of popular-front democracy-versus-fascism at the outbreak of World War II (Japanese aggression in the Philippines evokes the earlier aggression there by the United States) may be used to resolve the tension between naive idealism and realist mimesis. This is the utopian resolution that mediates the idea of "America" as a classless society and the actuality of racism and exploitation. It is achieved at the expense of extinguishing the historical specificity of what is indigenous or autochthonous, which is the primal event of colonial subjugation and deracination.

A dialectic of compensatory fulfillment is offered here when the fact of colonial domination becomes the repressed, the "political unconscious," of the text. Bulosan himself points out that as exiles "socially strangled in America," rootless Filipinos find it easier "to integrate ourselves in a universal ideal" (241). It is personified by Felix Razon, who connects the peasant uprising in Tayug, Pangasinan, with the Loyalist cause in Spain (240). This is the thrust of the autobiographical schema of the narrative, oriented around the development or education of a young man who matures into an artist. The vocation of writer should be conceived not so much as a status with prestige—a possibility foiled by circumstance—but as a consciousness able to comprehend the world through ideas and a broad and impassioned knowledge of other cultures, transcending locale and origin (246).

This theme of growing up, of initiation into adult reality, is the most commonly emphasized feature of *AIH*. From the time he learns the facts of landlord exploitation and sexist corruption in part I to the abuses of labor contractors (101), repeated racist violence (110, 129), and his discovery that it was "a crime to be a Filipino in California" (121), together with the terror, hunger, and loneliness of the "alien" in a dehumanizing milieu, the narrator-becoming-antihero undergoes a test of character. He succeeds in his initial objective of linking up with his brothers Amado (123) and Macario (129). This search for deracinated kins, ostensibly to reconstitute the broken family, counterpoints the usual immigrant story of labor recruitment. Eventually, the brothers' fighting at the end (304) dissolves the mystique of kinship and impels Bulosan's entry into an emergent community whose festival is suggested in chapter 46. But this fulfillment of a vow to unite the dispersed family serves to provide the occasion for writing, for the composition of the narrative itself.

In effect, the condition of possibility for art is imperial racist violence. This occurs in the exact middle of the book, the end of chapter 23. Struggling to communicate to his brother, the protagonist narrates his own life and gains release from the prison of his silence to "tell the world what they've done to me." This is repeated later in chapter 41, where he laments his brother's suffering and tries to piece together "the mosaic of our lives" (289). This discovery of the capacity for expression comes after he revolts against his employer at the Opal Cafe two chapters earlier: "I had struck at the white world, at last; and I felt free" (163). When he meets the socialist lawyer Pascual, Bulosan assumes his role as witness / spokesperson for the union movement (he helps edit *The New Tide* and later *The Philippine Commonwealth Times*). He envisions literature as the allegory of his death / rebirth, betokening a social type of the ongoing metamorphosis of social formations. However, this theme of the native's development as wordsmith, literally letter-writer, is quickly displaced by another narrative schema when Pascual, the first Filipino identified as a socialist, dies at the end of part II and the first half of the book culminates in the rhetoric of "We are all America . . ." (189).

The apprenticeship with Conrado Torres in the Alaskan cannery, and with Julio, Luz, Pascual, Max Smith (whose exploits mirror the duplicity of the system), and particularly Jose (whose mutilation becomes the stigmata of the outlaw / rebel) is, of course, a composite of many lives. Its chief function is to indicate what the potential is for ethnic Filipino unity. Partly sublimated in the act of writing, Bulosan's fear of the barbarian and sentimentalist in himself, his anger at social injustice, and his desire for synthesis and participation in a "dynamic social struggle" are registered in the vicissitudes of union activism in part II.

What any reader would have noticed at this point is that the realistic style of this memoir and its affinities with picaresque naturalism (recurrent scenes of petty crimes, squalid surroundings, raw violence, rough language) are frequently disrupted by lyricized memories of the homeland (108, 114, 123, 127, 132, especially 139, 155, 166, 172, 187). By this time, the generic conventions of the memoir and autobiography, with their drive for chronological verisimilitude and linear plotting, already have been eroded by a strongly emergent comic rhythm of repetition and uncanny resourcefulness. Characters appear and disappear with inexhaustible gusto, incidents multiply and replicate, while the narrator's comments and the dialogue he records are recycled, quoted, and redistributed in a carnivalesque circulation of energies in the narrative. The crisis of hegemonic representation arrives at this juncture.

In part III, a decisive break occurs. It permanently nullifies the model of the successful immigrant or the ethnic "melting pot" archetype: Bulosan's "conspiracy" or dream of making "a better America"—a forgetting of himself—is suspended by the breakdown of his body, a product of the years of hunger, brutality, and anguish. History or the past materializes in the return of the "child" as invalid, the time of drifting and wandering displaced by the stasis of physical breakdown.

We discover contained within the disfigured bosom of "America" representatives of its other, its negative. The introduction of Marian signals the establishment of dialogue and empathy: she resurrects the "good" side of America that has been ruined by the treachery of Helen and the patriarchal debasement of women (159). The prostitute Marian, the ambiguous embodiment of commodification and self-sacrificing devotion, resurrects all the other images of maternal / feminine care from the peasant mother, Estelle (108), the nameless girl raped in the train (113), Judith (173), Chiye (184), all the way to the most important influences in his life, Alice and Eileen Odell and Dora Travers, followed by other lesser maternal surrogates like Mary Strandon, Harriet Monroe, Jean Doyle, Anna Dozier, Laura Clarendon, and Jean Lawson. The mysterious Mary of chapter 44, the last fleeting incarnation of American "hospitality" (the term is used as a pun on Bulosan's hospitalization, which converts him into a reading / writing subaltern), assumes iconic significance as "an angel molded into purity by the cleanliness of our thoughts," giving Bulosan "a new faith in myself" (301).

In retrospect, Bulosan's illness is not a gratuitous interruption but a functional device. Not only is his confinement at the hospital the point where the notion manifests itself of a community larger than the male-bonding of Filipino bachelors in gambling and dance halls. It also halts the spatial discontinuity, the alleged "Necessitous mobility" (Wong 133), of the narrative line. His illness ushers him to a realization (the numerous recognition scenes in the book comprise the comic refrain that belies individualistic fatality and environmental determinism) of his new vocation: he is not so much the ignored author of *The Laughter of My Father* (the index of Bulosan's acknowledgment of the folk sources of his art, 260) as he is the historian / guardian of collective memory and covenant with the "associated producers" of the islands, the peasantry as matrix of production.

What should be given a close symptomatic reading is the structure of the dream Bulosan records in chapter 40. Mislabeled as "the Filipino communist" strike leader, he flees from the police and falls asleep on a bus. He dreams of his return to his hometown of Mangusmana in the Philippines, where he rejoices at seeing his mother and the whole family eating (280–81); awakened by "tears of remembrance," he asks himself how the "tragedy" of his childhood had returned in a dream "because I had forgotten it" (283). This dream functions as the crucial synecdoche for what is repressed—not only by the text but by the scholarly archive. It is the whole of part I, in particular the resourcefulness, insurgent courage, and strength of the peasantry epitomized by the mother (chapters 4–9), that virtually most critics and scholars have forgotten, and this is bound to haunt them.

Here I underscore the desideratum of an interpretive framework that necessarily structures all possible "horizons of expectation." The framework is centered on this insight: what the bulk of this narrative wants to forget but cannot—what is, in fact, the absence or lacuna, the manifold traces of which everywhere constitute the text—is U.S. colonial violence. This refers to the Filipino-American War of 1899–1903 and its aftermath in the neocolonial system, which subjugated the natives, reinforced the semifeudal structure called "absentee landlordism," and drove Bulosan and his brothers to permanent exile. The other name for U.S. colonial violence is "fascism," and its genealogy includes Spanish Falangists and Filipino sympathizers, American racist vigilantes and police, and Japanese aggression—this last evoking what the text dares not name: U.S. invasion of the islands at the turn of the century.

I cannot overemphasize this point: what the text's archaeology of repetitions seeks to capture, above all, is the time of the islands, of the mother and other producers, of all the women who have been victimized by patriarchal law and exchanged without the singular value of their desires acknowledged. What this narrative attempts to seize is "woman's time," the surplus or excess value of which is measured, calculated, and dispersed into the derelict space of "America." It is in "America," the symbolic turned real, where Filipino men—including the witnessing, conflicted sensibility named Bulosan—found themselves "castrated" under its regime of violence, premised on the rationality of white supremacy, the logic of capital, and commodity-reification.

The project of *AIH*, then, is the reinscription of this inaugural moment of colonial dispossession in the hegemonic culture by a text that violates all generic expectations and foregrounds the earth, the soil, and the maternal psyche / *habitus* as the ground of meaning and identity. This text, viewed as cultural practice, valorizes both the oppositional and the utopian, as negated by the dominant ideology. What is needed is to elucidate the process whereby the unity of opposites (such as individual rationality versus tradition) shifts into the protagonist's trial or agon of unearthing duplicities (147) and multiple causalities, and discriminating what is fraudulent from what is genuine.

Finally, the text interrogates all readers with the ethico-political reflection in the penultimate chapter: "Our world was this one, but a new one was being born. We belonged to the old world of confusion; but in this other world—new, bright, promising—we would be unable to meet its demands" (324). Bulosan's species of "magical" or "fantastic" realism allegorizes this radical transformation from the old to the new—that is, from colonial bondage redeemed via analysis / critique to witness / testifier of that history of decolonization: the project of becoming-Filipino. This task is accomplished by *AIH* without the luxury of consolation afforded by the blandishments of traditional aesthetic form.

What makes *America Is in the Heart* the first example of a new genre, a popular-front allegory which articulates class, race, nation (ethnicity), and gender in a protean configuration, is its *narrative schema*. The stages of Bulosan's awakening follow a path away from a focus on "workerist" unionizing to a concern with broader social issues in a force-field of diverse collectivities.

This is the thrust of the plot of becoming-Filipino, the odyssey of a young native who matures into an artist: the vocation of writer is realized through imperial, racist violence that paradoxically also is the condition of possibility for his art. By the time Bulosan joins the socialist-oriented union movement and helps edit *The New Tide*, he already has acquired a consciousness able to comprehend the world through a historical-materialist optic, a philosophy of revolutionary praxis transcending family, ethnic chauvinism, and bourgeois nation. Against the tribalism of government representatives, Bulosan counterposed a socialist outlook, informed by the ecology of heterogeneous civilizations. He is cured of the symptoms of the Hegelian "Unhappy Consciousness" exemplified in *AIH*.

As I noted above, Bulosan's dream of making "a better America," a forgetting of the Filipino unconscious, is suspended by the breakdown of the body. His hospitalization concretizes U.S. hospitality. History, the incommensurable waste of injustice, materializes in the return of the "child" as invalid; the time of wandering metamorphoses into physical immobility. In retrospect, Bulosan's illness is not a sleight of hand interruption but a functional device. It inaugurates his new vocation as the ventriloquist of collective memory and guardian of the covenant with the "associated producers" of the islands. We encounter finally the limit of liberal idealism.

But what I think constitutes the originality of the text, something no one else has commented upon thus far, is its rendering of what Julia Kristeva calls "woman's time." This is virtually the subtext of the self-constitution of Filipino nationality, the subject of the internal colony of the metropolis. Comedy and the flows / flights of the unconscious interact with the realist code in defining this new genre. The fundamental *mythos* of comedy, the alternation of death and rebirth in "monumental" time, organizes the allegory of a transported native who "died many deaths" in his itinerary of exile and fantasized return. The suicide of the writer Estevan precipitates a mutation, a turnaround: "I began to rediscover my native land, and the cultural roots there that had nourished me, and I felt a great urge to identify myself with the social awakening of my people" (139). Those deaths impregnate the psyche, inducing the self-production of the text noted earlier, recovering the ruins of archaic plenitude in the language of dreams.

Earlier I called attention to how the theme of popular-front democracy-versus-fascism (Japanese aggression in the Philippines eclipses the earlier one by the United States) at World War II's inception is deployed to negotiate the tension between naive idealism and realist mimesis. It is also utilized to induce amnesia of U.S. imperial conquest of the Philippines. This alliance with bourgeois democracy is achieved at the expense of almost forgetting the primal event of colonial conquest and deracination—hence the compulsive repetitions of scenes/events in the narrative. Bulosan testified that as exiles "socially strangled in America," rootless Filipinos find it easier "to integrate ourselves in a universal ideal." But a dialectic of compensatory fulfillment insinuates itself when the fact of colonial domination registered in feudal and comprador rule becomes the repressed, the hermeneutic sine qua non, of the text.

Indeed, what most readers of *America* have ignored, by virtue of dogmatism or inertia, is the whole of part I, in particular the resource-fulness, perseverance, and courage of the peasantry, which could not be fitted into an implicit Asian-American canonical paradigm. U.S. impe-rial subjugation of the Philippines is what even scrupulous scholars have forgotten, an omission that is nonetheless bound to haunt them. What the rhetoric of the book wants to elide but cannot, the absence or lacuna whose manifold traces everywhere constitute the text, is U.S. co-lonial violence—the Filipino-American War of 1899–1903 and its legacy, as manifested in the patronage system—that subjugated the natives, reinforced the oppressive structure Bulosan called "absentee landlord-ism," and drove him and tens of thousands of Filipinos to permanent exile. Its other name is "fascism," phallocentric law driven to violence, whose personifications include Spanish Falangists and their Filipino sympathizers, American racist vigilantes and police, and Japanese ag-gressors—the last evoking what the text dares not name: U.S. invasion of the islands at the turn of the century.

This is what the text's archaeology of reiterations seeks to capture: the scenario of beginning and apocalypse, of loss of independence and its promised recovery. What Bulosan's *testimonio* attempts to transcribe is "woman's time" whose exorbitance reaches the fault lines of the Ameri-can landscape where derelict Filipinos found themselves "castrated" under its regime of violence.

What Bulosan strove to accomplish then is the reinscription of the Filipino experience of symbolic mutilation in a discourse of exposure and refusal. It is a discourse geared to demystify the illusions bred by a utilitarian commodity-centered society. Its mode of wayward realism seeks to foreground the labor of mutual recognition, collective praxis, and the maternal sensibility against the Manichean theologizing of the "Other," the logic of capital and exchange-value. When capitalism be-gins to decay, the corpus of the project called "becoming-Filipino" mate-rializes in its putrefaction.

Worldly Syncopations

Can you read the secrets of history in my face?
  —*"The Shadow of the Terror"*

We are the living dream of dead men everywhere,
the unquenchable truth that class-memories create. . . .
  —*"If You Want To Know What We Are"*

Charting in *America Is in the Heart* the evolution of his life from childhood to the outbreak of World War II, Bulosan successfully establishes connections between the multiracial proletarian movement in the
United States and over four hundred years of dissidence, protests, and
revolts against colonial impositions in the Philippines. His mosaic of
Filipino lives pays homage to the grassroots initiatives found, for example, in the 1931 Tayug uprising of peasants, which may be interpreted as
an anticipatory emblem for the strikes of multi-ethnic farmworkers in
Hawaii and the West Coast. That nexus, in turn, ruptures U.S. jingoist
patronage.

   AIH, now a classic text of vagrancy and failure, becomes implicitly a
critique of the official assimilationist ideology and the paradigm of immigrant success that apologists of free-enterprise individualism continue to uphold. This is a teleology that up to now serves to underwrite
the distortion and / or exclusion of Bulosan and other Filipino artists
from the mainstream cultural archive. Only a change in the global circumstances that produced their works can undo this status quo.

   Profound geopolitical changes separate this ethnobiography and its
popular-front milieu from the post–Cold War 1990s. Are fascism and
racism dead? Or do we see their resurrection in new disguises? In any
case, today I would stress Bulosan's serviceability as witness to and
conscience of that transitional passage in Filipino life in the United
States. Bulosan returns to what Amilcar Cabral calls "the source" to
recover a submerged tradition of indigenous revolutionary culture, the
deeply rooted insurgent ethos of workers, peasants, and intellectuals
against imperial racism and violence. He recalls the 1931 peasant uprising against landlords, merchant compradors, and bureaucrats—local
agents of the American suzerain and, before that, the 1896–98 insurrection against Spain. One leader of the Tayug uprising, Pedro Calosa, was
in fact a veteran of the 1924 strike of Filipino workers in the Hawaiian
plantations (Sturtevant). It seems a not wholly fortuitous coincidence

that Calosa lived in the same province of Pangasinan where Bulosan was born.

Bulosan's adolescent years were deeply influenced by the survival craft of a large, impoverished family that barely subsisted on a small plot of land. In his letters, collected in *Sound of Falling Light* as well as in *Laughter,* Bulosan describes the earthy, sometimes shrewd, but always carnivalesque spirit of his father trying to outwit landlords, usurers, politicians, and petty bureaucrats in providing for his family. With the father's authority dismantled, Bulosan then begins to focus on the quiet, durable resourcefulness of his mother—that "dynamic little peasant woman" who sold salted fish in the public market of Binalonan and nurtured Bulosan's open, stoic, but adventurous spirit. Her image is sublimated in the samaritanic women who crisscross the fault lines of *AIH,* miscegenating female companions exuberant with ideas and plans. The force of these heterogeneous characters represent, for Bulosan, the "other" half of a schizoid America.

In such representative texts as "Be American," "Story of a Letter," and "As Long as the Grass Shall Grow," (see *On Becoming Filipino*) Bulosan tracks the vicissitudes of migrant alienation and analyzes the predicament of return / self-recovery of the sojourner *manqué.* In the process, he also unfolds those scenes of solidarity with women of various nationalities and other progressive elements occasioned by the search for his brothers, in effect, for meaning in his life. Personal anecdotes thus become synecdoches of collective fate.

Since I have already written at length on the import and architectonics of those stories (see, for example, *Carlos Bulosan; Racial Formations*), suffice it to recall the semiotic dynamics of "Be American." Here, the quest for recognition by a Filipino youth (Consorcio) plots his identity on the objective rhythm of seasonal harvests. This precarious modality of existence, in turn, undermines the concept and fact of private ownership of land and the private appropriation of the fruit (use values) of social labor (San Juan, *Reading the West*). This alien "national," however, destabilizes the foundational logos of business society and must be put in his place. Somehow, Consorcio becomes a journalist fighting for the rights of everyone, "native or foreign born," and goes to jail for his ideas of freedom and peace—the substitute for the citizenship he originally wanted to possess. In a concluding note, the narrator (Consorcio's friend) pronounces an elegiac hymn to the land, "a great mother . . . rolling like a beautiful woman with an overflowing abundance of fecundity and murmurous with her eternal mystery." By way of such unexpected metonymic displacements, Bulosan reminds us of the relevance of Gilles Deleuze's insight that "a society or any collective arrangement is defined first by its points or flows of deterritorialization," its lines of flight (233).

To illustrate further the distinctive cultural praxis embodied in Bulosan's fiction, I offer these brief comments on two stories. They display Bulosan's mode of using the technique of montage to deconstruct the raw materials of experience and reshape them into a teaching-learning artifice or "organon" (to use Bertolt Brecht's term) so as to provoke critical reasoning. This tactic of defamiliarization is performed through the genre of allegory / fantasy, which is designed to undermine the convention of mimetic realism, or at least to unsettle the axioms of orthodox formalism. One virtue of this mode lies in its capacity to subtly fuse two antithetical tendencies, a distanced "imitation" of action and the narrator's passionate critique. This permits the simultaneous exercise of judgment and sympathy. While we grasp difference, we also apprehend the possibilities of synthesis, however heuristic and provisional, which ultimately enables agency and historic intervention.

Just as *AIH* evinced in its fabric the problems of fragmentation and fetishism in a market-centered polity, "Passage Into Life" and "I Would Remember" evoke and in the process deconstruct them. In "Passage," key events in Allos' life between ages five and fourteen register the ravages of feudal greed, suicide, clan violence, poverty, and gratuitous cruelty. It depicts the child's initiation into the reality of a disenchanted world characterized by prejudice and the cash-nexus. How can he survive and continue to trust and hope? Not only the boy's intimacy with nature (section 2) but also his compassion for the weak (sections 5, 6, 12) enable him to confront the catastrophic loss of his father.

The narrator's choric voice foreshadows the encounter with the figure of the stranger and the utopian denouement: "Oh, Allos, hide in the thorns and thickets of the world! . . . Oh, Allos! don't be afraid! The good earth will comfort you in her dark womb!" His greatest fear—his mother's death—is displaced by concern for the plight of his sister and the old Chinese beaten to death; his cry to the dead Chinese—"Wake up, old man. I will tell you we are the same!"—signifies a release from archaic dependency on parent and kins. By juxtaposing scenes of violence and despair with images of solidarity or communion with the natural world, this seemingly arbitrary sequence of episodes sets the stage for Allos' acceptance of the stranger / prophet whose voice echoes the Enlightenment principles of "life, liberty, and the pursuit of happiness":

"No one is really an orphan as long as there is another man living. As long as there is one man living and working and thinking on the earth."

And so the knowledge of death's nonfinality inspires Allos to trans-value his life with a totalizing choice: "Now Allos knew: there in the known world he must go to seek a new life, seek it among the living until he would have enough time to pause and ponder on the mystery of the dead" with "a song of joy warming his whole being until it became the song of all his living dreams." While the figure of the welcoming stranger and the parable in the mountain might suggest a transcendence remote from worldly engagements, what needs foregrounding is how the episodic pattern itself logically produces the strangeness (degrees of alienation and the unknown) and the dialogic contract (the boy seeking answers) that coalesce into the emancipatory vision of the last section.

A variation of this defamiliarizing method is enacted in the second story, "I Would Remember." Here, the problem is how to frame and distance what would otherwise be a horrifying, even morbidly disgusting, scene of Leroy's mutilation: genitals cut, left eye gouged, tongue "sliced into shreds" and entrails "spread on the cool grass." Leroy's slaughter by vigilantes, his "screaming like a pig about to be butchered," was witnessed by the "I" together with several compatriots. The drift toward sensational naturalism is checked here by the narrator, who identifies Leroy as a "stranger" preaching unity and whose life manifests a charismatic aura that detaches the body from the spirit. Leroy, testifies the narrator, "had a way of explaining the meanings of words in utter simplicity, like 'work' which he translated into 'power,' and 'power' into 'security.' I was drawn to him because I felt that he had lived in many places where the courage of men was tested with the cruelest weapons conceivable." Hence, Leroy's dismemberment proves the power of unity: individuals become a community in the act of sharing and struggling together.

Violence thus yields a vision of communicative rationality and a ritual of exchange. Bulosan pursues here the task of linkage, the suturing of that cleavage or split between the uncertainties of life in the United States and the struggle for freedom and dignity in the colonized Philippines. How does history materialize in that fissure between past and present, between the domain of affection and the territory of alienation? What lines of flight can rescue the adolescent soul in its solitary passage? We are engaged at the outset with two traumatic childhood experiences: the mother's dying at the birth of his brother, and his father's killing of the carabao. Although the grandmother's love and sensuous nature assuage the boy's grief, the spectacle of the carabao's slaughter triggers panic: "I wanted to strike my father, but instead, fearing and loving him I climbed out of the pit quickly and ran through the blinding rain to our house."

In the United States, the narrator encounters two deaths before Leroy's in which he discovers a complexity that exceeds the metaphysics of naive humanism: with Marco, it was sincerity, honesty, his gift of laughter; with Crispin, it was gentleness coupled with a redemptive promise, an epiphany of home in exile. Regarding Crispin, "There was something luminous about him, like the strange light that flashes in my mind when I sometimes think of the hills of home. He had been educated and he recited poetry with a sad voice that made me cry. He always spoke of goodness and beauty in the world." The personalities of Marco, Crispin, and LeRoy and their deaths reproduce that uncanny oscillation of fear and love that the narrator felt for his father, who possesses the authority to castrate and kill. We sense in the tone of the discourse not only resignation and intense watchfulness but also the will to affirm something that survives bodily contingency: "When I saw his cruelly tortured body, I thought of my father and the decapitated carabao and the warm blood flowing under our bare feet. And I knew that all my life I would remember Leroy and all the things he taught me about living."

What is achieved by this method of analogic rendering in both stories is not just verisimilitude but also a stance or susceptibility that can absorb the negative and at the same time convert it into material for one's growth. Loss and expenditure become occasions for self-renewal. By probing for contradictions and intervening in the politico-ethical dilemmas of all the victims of democracy, Bulosan's art takes up the challenge of fragmentation, anomic dispersal, reification or reduction to exchange-values, and other dehumanizing symptoms of the Filipino "Babylonian captivity" in the United States.

The Time of Now and Forever

You too were the face of the land, the tongue
Of the people, the voice of time.
    —"Who Saw the Terror"

They are even afraid of our songs of love, my brother.
    —"Song for Chris Mensalvas' Birthday"

When the Japanese struck Pearl Harbor in 1941 and subsequently occupied the Philippines, Bulosan "rediscovered" his homeland as the fountainhead of his creative originality and strength. It was not just a mere return to a mythical origin, a sublation or inversion of the past. He illuminates this conversion experience in "My Education":

> I realized how foolish it was to believe then that I could define roots in terms of places and persons. I knew, then, that I would be as rootless in the Philippines as I was in America, because roots are not physical things, but the quality of faith deeply [ingrained] and clearly understood and integrated in one's life.

In short, roots were "not physical but intellectual and spiritual things," a common faith that Bulosan found in the socialist tradition, a vision of empowering "the wretched of the earth" (in Frantz Fanon's phrase) that transcends nation-state boundaries.

While Bulosan reaffirms the dedication of his work to "the cause of my own people," he also asserts that writing is not self-sufficient and that his sensibility had been nourished by the praxis of class struggles: "I drew inspiration from my active participation in the workers' movement. The most decisive move that the writer could make was to take his stand with the workers" (Bulosan, *Selected Works* 35). These sentiments and thoughts were underscored in his contributions to the 1952 *Yearbook*, in "Letter to a Filipino Woman," "The Writer as Worker," and in two letters to his nephews, written in 1948. In the latter, Bulosan expropriated "the Name of the Father" to express the paramount motivation of his work by resurrecting the primal scene of wholeness before deracination occurred—an imagined exodus from captivity. I would privilege these texts where Bulosan enunciated first principles, as guiding coordinates for any just, rigorous, and substantive appreciation of his achievement.

Earlier, Bulosan had written verses in sympathy with the defenders of the Spanish Republic, which was then beleaguered by reactionary forces. He personified his internationalist creed in the character of Felix Razon—otherwise known as "Felix Rivas" in *The Cry*—who connects the peasant uprising in Tayug, Pangasinan (described in *America*) with the Loyalist (Republican) cause in Spain. Bulosan's commitment to a "popular front" against capitalism in its fascist phase (confirmed by the expansionist militarism of Germany, Italy, and Japan) afforded a philosophical orientation that gave coherence and direction to the nomadic plight he shared with others.

An islander stranded on inhospitable shores, Bulosan was desperately searching for the "heart" or destination of his journey; he found it in the Spanish Civil War, which in some ways was the prelude to World War II. During the war, he affirmed his partisanship via orature and polemic, resulting in three books: *Chorus for America, Letter from America,* and *The Voice of Bataan;* the latter was broadcast overseas by the U.S. Office of War Information. Invited by the exiled government of the Philippine Commonwealth to work in its Washington office, Bulosan opted to remain in the "battlefront" of union organizing. Meanwhile, he contributed to numerous magazines, among them *New Masses, Harper's Bazaar, Town and Country, New Yorker,* and *Arizona Quarterly.*

In my opinion, Bulosan's craftsmanship in the prose genres (fiction, the reflective or familiar essay, and letters) is far superior to his attempts at versification, despite exceptions like "Biography," "In Time of Drought," and "Meeting with a Discoverer." Susan Evangelista has heroically endeavored to present the best case for Bulosan as a "Third World" poet, with emphasis on themes of alienation, internal colonialism, and the lived experience of Filipino immigrants in general, but her argument is vitiated by her downplaying of Bulosan's radical-democratic, socialist vision.

Contrary to the critical doxa, Bulosan's Whitmanesque style exhibited, in such poems as "If You Want To Know What We Are" and "I Want the Wide American Earth" is neither typical nor recurrent. The rhetoric of identification and panoramic catalogue found in those two poems, as well as their Filipinized versions in "Land of the Morning" and "Prologue," springs from the will to valorize the power of multitudes. The poet envisages the serial monads in a market society converging into an irresistible force for change:

we are the subterranean subways
of suffering; we are the will of dignities;
we are the living testament of a flowering race.

But we apprehend that behind this impulse is the quest for secular transcendence, for pleasure-filled alternatives invested in the hitherto unacknowledged labor of "deathless humanity." Except for the instrumental or programmatic verses like *The Voice of Bataan* and the unfinished drama, *Jose Rizal,* Bulosan's poems configure the Horatian injunction to instruct (*prodesse*) and delight (*delectare*) with what I would call the pathos of the folkloric sublime that defines his unique poetic signature.

A majority of his poems meditate on the difficulty of representing the nuances and indeterminacies of exile. They strive to delineate the anxious maneuverings of the native caught in the ravaged cities of the Depression, alarmed by the barbarism of war; his predicament inheres partly in his failure to contrive an objectifying equivalent to his apprehension of disaster. "Biography Between Wars," for instance, stages the reminiscence of the halcyon past in which the death of a friend's husband in Teruel, Spain, and the carnage of war can only be filtered through a surreal perspective:

> Then the planes swarmed like swallows
> And ripped the night with lilies of screaming fire.

Reification blights urban life in "For A Child Dying in a Tenement," anguished by the "terror of plenty." In "Portrait with Cities Falling," the speaker's spiritual crisis is rendered with phantasmagoric intensity; his portrait of an industrial wasteland, however, can only evoke a prophetic longing: "Will they [the headless man and the starlight woman] come to remake the world?" "Letter in Exile" escapes this difficulty of representation via the detour of self-estrangement: the speaker transports himself back to the peaceful islands threatened by enemy planes and then recounts his identification with Jews, Negroes, and with beauty ravished by power, greed, and "the naked blasphemies of money." He counsels his brother: "But all this will come to pass. . . ."

Meanwhile, in "Waking in the 20th Century," Bulosan mediates the exile's predicament by summoning the image of his father, patient and hopeful, plowing the soil against the background of worldwide destruction. At the end the speaker confides to his woman friend that "there will be days when we will stand together," mindful of the antimiscegenation law against Filipinos. Overwhelmed by chaos everywhere, the language of Bulosan's poems during this period becomes repetitive, desultory, extremely uneven. His performance as poet culminates in a bravado gesture: the act of staking "a claim on the world" in "To My Countrymen":

> And across the flaming darkness of life,
> I flung a sword of defiance to give you freedom.

Here, the dramatic protocol of communicating a purpose that will bind together the interlocutors acquires a sublime connotation, when the concept or idea proves unrepresentable. It may be obscured by the contradictions between city and countryside, or between the rapturous past and the tormented present, as hinted in "Biography." Using those few quotes as touchstones, we can speculate that Bulosan intuited the limits of his poetic skill and range (he was heavily influenced by T. S. Eliot, Auden, MacLeish, and other modernists) and chose thereafter to concentrate his energies on cultivating the narrative and expository genres.

But there were also limits of another kind to prosaic sublimations. At the peak of McCarthyism in the 1950s, Bulosan became a blacklisted writer, perhaps the only Filipino writer on the FBI's hit list. He mixed with the wrong people, such as Chris Mensalvas and Ernesto Mangaong, leaders of the International Longshoreman's and Warehouseman's Union (ILWU) Local 37, and dangerous subversives who were scheduled for deportation. (For his inspirational poem "I Want the Wide American Earth," Bulosan seized the pretext of the campaign to defend the two scapegoats of the "Free World.")

Amid this harassment, Bulosan continued to pursue his project of revealing connections, building linkages, demonstrating reciprocities, and fostering alliances via the editorship of the 1952 *Yearbook* of ILWU Local 37 (Taverna). In the *Yearbook,* he wrote: "I believe that the unconditional unity of all workers is our only weapon against the evil designs of imperialist butchers and other profiteers of death and suffering to plunge humanity into a new world war" (21).

Amid the Cold War hysteria, how could the government deport this alleged "communist" agitator, who was commissioned by then-President Franklin Roosevelt to write an essay celebrating the "Four Freedoms"? His praise of populist democracy, "Freedom from Want" (exhibited at the Federal Building in San Francisco in 1943), fulfilled the imperative of oppositional artists capturing strongholds in the terrain of social reproduction (Benjamin, "The Author as Producer"). It succeeded in infiltrating a potentially explosive message that escaped the censors: "But we are not really free unless we use what we produce. So long as the fruit of our labor is denied us, so long will want manifest itself in a world of slaves." Bulosan not only extolled labor and the "desires of anonymous men," but also (with an oblique allusion to a more dangerous manifesto) the right to "serve themselves and each other according to their needs and abilities."

By this time, Bulosan was internationally renowned, the author of best-sellers like *Laughter* (translated into more than a dozen languages) and *America Is in the Heart* (reviewed in the leading trade periodicals),

and listed in *Who's Who in America, Current Biography,* and other direc-
tories of notable personalities. In *Twentieth Century Authors,* his own
account of his uprooting and vagrancy—from birth in the village of
Mangusmana, Binalonan, Pangasinan to his life in Los Angeles—was
reproduced without editorial qualification. He anchored his wandering
with this conviction: "What impelled me to write? The answer is—my
grand dream of equality among men and freedom for all. . . ." Bulosan's
testimony was lucid, controlled, generous. But his claim may sound
banal or premature for an aspiring intellectual from the hinterland
whose literary fortune, together with a generation of "fellow travelers"
and progressive artists around the world, would soon be blasted by the
fury of the Cold War. Nevertheless, I think we need to contextualize his
ambition in historically specific, differential terms.

We might take the distance between two stories, "To a God of Stone"
(1939) and "End of the War" (1944), as a measure of Bulosan's success in
dramatizing the complex predicament of Filipinos (and, metonymically,
of all people of color) in the internal colonies of the metropolis. In the
early story, the narrator's obsession with gambling is interrupted periodically by Dan, a failed and lost spirit, whose idiosyncrasies and
"strange smell of unknown cities" puzzled the narrator. But Bulosan
couldn't decide whether to focus on Dan's alienation or the narrator's;
at one point, his persona muses on his confusion: "What have I done?
Where am I headed for? What do I know about the world?" Meanwhile
Dan kills two musicians—a gesture of absurd revolt, it seems—but the
narrator concludes with the thought of Dan personifying the truth that
"man will always be at the mercy of his invisible creations." The inade-
quacy stares us in the face: Bulosan assumes that a simple mechanical
reproduction of his thoughts plus a portrayal of one derelict would be
enough to epitomize the decay of bourgeois society.

In the later story, however, he succeeds in inventing an "objective
correlative" to concretize a large constellation of ideas and feelings.
Private Pascual Fidel's dream of the surrender of the Japanese in the
Philippines becomes transformed as it circulates into a collective one, a
prophecy of the country's liberation overcoming the limits of fetishized
individualism (typified by Dan and the musicians): "It was a dream that
belonged to no one now. . . ." Gambling, the historic index of Filipino
victimization, is overcome at every instance when the dream becomes
the signifier of exchange between public and private spheres. Meanwhile the American "dream of success" is displaced, and its fraudu-

lence exposed, as the pathos of subaltern innocence is captured in that telltale idiom of simultaneous acquiescence and vexed refusal:

> Ten years I worked peacefully in America, minding my own business, when the *salomabit* come stabbing me at the back. Maybe it is not much I make, but I got the beautiful Ford from Detroit. . . . In the bank I got money—maybe not much, but it is my money. When I see the flag, I take the hat off and I say, "Thank you very much!" I like the color of the flag and I work hard. Why the *salomabit* come?. . . . If only I was there!"

Mess Sergeant Ponso's anger at having been left out, his conflation of dream and reality, his gesture of self-justification, his sense of futility— all these elements of Filipino "becoming" in that transitional conjuncture may be conceived as precisely what Bulosan's vocation sought to engage with humor and humility. He took his bearings with that reflexive critical distance and political sophistication he had gained in almost two decades of loneliness, suffering, and friendships cutting across the barriers of class, gender, nationalities, and race.

Separation and exile always summon their binary opposites: reunion and return. Bulosan continued his role as "tribune" of multi-ethnic workers (including Euro-Americans) in writing for newspapers like *New Masses* and *Commonwealth Times* (founded by Mensalvas and Bulosan in 1936), as well as various periodicals in the Philippines. But as he did so, his conscientization widened to embrace the world system in crisis with the entrenchment of fascism in Europe and Japan. Several poems, such as "Portrait with Cities Falling," "Who Saw the Terror," and "To Laura in Madrid" recorded his loyalty to the socialists and anarchists who were defending the Spanish Republic against the fascist forces of General Francisco Franco.

It was easy for Bulosan to make the connection between the reactionary authoritarianism of the Falangists (who had the support of Filipino landlords / compradors) and the thugs of U.S. agribusiness, who were assisted by the state's ideological apparatus (legislature, courts, prisons) and the military (Bulosan, "Manuel Quezon"). His acceptance of a simplistic version of the united-front strategy explains in part the somewhat melodramatic and sentimental paean to pre–Civil War democracy, as well as his deployment of the utopian metaphor of "America" as a classless and racism-free society; both views pervade the texts of this period. All the rhetoric of democracy and "Four Freedoms" was soon quickly overtaken by McCarthyism.

Emergency: Live Dangerously

> Homeward again under foreign stars. . . .
> —"Landscape With Figures"

> Where I knelt, where I wept, where I lived
> To change the course of history; because I love you.
> —"To My Countrymen"

When Japan occupied the Philippines in 1942–44, Bulosan's attention shifted to the popular resistance to another invader—this time perceived as a more brutal repeat of the Spanish and American conquests. During the war, the Hukbalahaps (acronym for "People's Army Against the Japanese"), guided by the Communist Party of the Philippines, led the underground resistance. When the Huks were suppressed by the U.S. military and its puppet regimes to safeguard the restoration of the old parasitic oligarchy (many of whom collaborated with the enemy, such as Benigno Aquino's father), full-scale people's war erupted in the late 1940s and early 1950s. This period of the Cold War, punctuated by the Korean War, became the time for testing the limits of bourgeois democracy. It was the prelude to large-scale anti-imperialist people's war in Indochina and around the world.

Bulosan reinscribed the exile's predicament in the problematic of "national liberation" in his letters and particularly in his novel, *The Cry,* composed in the last five years of his life. This remarkable novel, unprecedented in portraying the lives of left-wing guerrillas in the Philippines, was directly inspired by his friendship with the imprisoned vernacular poet, Amado V. Hernandez, by his own memory of peasant radicalism in Pangasinan, and by his close association with farmworkers in America, who were veterans of similar struggles. Moreover, I believe that the Huk commander Luis Taruc's autobiography, *Born of the People,* exerted an incalculable influence on Bulosan's thinking, based on his writings of this period.

With the direct intervention of the CIA and the Pentagon in the Philippine military, the United States crippled the Huk insurgency as part of its global strategy to contain the "communist conspiracy" then ascribed to the Soviet Union and China (Bulosan, "Terrorism Rides the Philippines"). Before the Korean War ended, Bulosan was driven to move beyond the parameters of trade-union reformism (rationalized by the U.S. Communist Party's identification of itself with "Americanism").

He was always looking across the Pacific for signs hovering over turbulent tropical shores.

After his stint with ILWU Local 37, he realized that U.S. monopoly capital had become the immediate and long-range threat to the aspiration for justice and independence of Third World peoples. Indeed, the logic of the Cold War compelled a reassessment of his "love affair" with the phantasmal notions of equality and fraternity celebrated in *AIH*. When U.S.-sponsored fascism erupted with renewed virulence in the Philippines, Bulosan had no choice but to enact a long-deferred "return" to the primal scene of dispossession. It was now impossible to resuscitate the America of the Puritans and pioneers whose legitimacy had been rendered suspect, if not refuted and refused, by the transcontinental revolt of people of color, including those in the internal colonies, against western messianic hegemony headed by the United States. With the symbolic capital of American democracy exhausted, what was the alternative then for Bulosan?

A wish-fulfilling trial to respond to that question is made in the story "Homecoming." It is general knowledge that the majority of Filipino bachelors who came to the United States in the 1920s and 1930s never returned to the islands, for the reason that Mariano, the successful sojourner, rehearses in his mind. Paralyzed by anger and fear, however, he is unable to confess the truth: "How could he make them understand that he had failed in America? . . . America had crushed his spirit." We, the readers, understand the plight of the author's surrogate who, after twelve years in the U.S., now believes there is no other place for him in the world but home in the Philippines. A pre-Oedipal fantasy materializes: Mariano "knew that the fate of his mother was in his hands," but, as though castrated, he lacks some organ for unburdening himself of "all the sorrows of his life." The bliss of return, an eternal moment he has been waiting for, overwhelms him: "The mother was in his arms. . . ." Yet he regrets having come home because "he could never make them happy again." After discovering that his father is dead, the reality of his own failure assaults him in the shape of palpable misery at home:

> Now he could understand his mother's deadening solemnity. And Marcela's bitterness. Now it dawned on him that his mother and sisters had suffered the same terrors of poverty, the same humiliations of defeat, that he had suffered in America. He was like a man who had emerged from night into day, and found the light as blinding as darkness. . . . This was the life he had found in America; it was so everywhere in the world. He was confirmed now. He thought when he was in America that it could not be

thus in his father's house. But it was there when he returned to find his sisters wrecked by deprivation. . . .

In chapter 40 of *America*, Bulosan records a dream analogous to this story, which perhaps can help decipher its meaning. Assuming the role of a "Filipino communist" strike leader fleeing from the police, he falls asleep in a bus and dreams of his return to his hometown in the Philippines where he rejoices at seeing his mother and the whole family eating; awakened by "tears of remembrance," he claims that the "tragedy" of his childhood returned in a dream "because I had forgotten it" (283). Could this story be an act of remembering, a reenactment, so as to forestall what had already happened? Is the artist's imagination assuming the role of the redeemer-messiah of the past?

In any case, "Homecoming" performs a symbolic remapping of the world system when he encounters the depredations of the old enemy in the homeland. The climactic event graced by "the vision of his father" as he departs—an ambiguous one since Mariano has usurped his place, only to mark it as preempted by someone else—epitomizes the lesson of the homecoming: "America" now turns out to be one huge self-deception. But it is a hard lesson that can only be symptomatically glimpsed, one which assumes full-bodied articulation in Bulosan's last ambitious work, *The Cry*. (Originally, he planned to write four massive novels covering one hundred years of Philippine history, a tetralogy meant to rival the mammoth dynasty epics of Balzac, Dreiser, and Sholokhov.)

In *The Cry*, Bulosan tries to diagnose what happened to him in the United States—the causes of Filipino self-deception and misrecognition. In general, the novel assists in this task of unraveling the mystery, the absent source of the shock in "Homecoming": namely, the uneven topography of the imperial system and its hierarchical power relations. Alternatively, one can categorize this absent cause as the totality of class/gender relations on a multinational scale, fully present in all of Bulosan's writings in the form of damages wrought upon colonial subjects. While *America* grappled with the antinomy of the real and the ideal—a tension defused only by the advent of war and the united front against world fascism—its protagonist failed to return (if only by anamnesis) to his origin in the indigenous revolutionary tradition of the Filipino masses. In *The Cry* the return is made.

What *The Cry* deploys is the trope or figural schema of homecoming, enacted by members of a guerrilla detachment as preparation for a rendezvous with a certain Felix Rivas, the disfigured bearer/herald of "good tidings" from the United States, whom no one except Dante (the author's alter ego) can recognize. The meeting never takes place. And that is the salient lesson to be learned. What this fabula conveys over and above the immense tragedy of Filipino lives is the *sjuzet* or plot of permanent revolution. This is the subtext in which every character mobilizes the communal "spirit of place" (*genius loci*) of his/her birthplace in order to reconstitute his/her identity by way of wrestling with the demons (promises, disavowals, transgressions) of his/her individual past. For Bulosan subscribed to Marx's axiom that individuality equals the ensemble of social relations at any given time and place.

Through the character of Hassim, Bulosan finally repudiates the aristocratic and even obscurantist idealization of homeland, blood, soil, romanticized childhood, rural harmony, and other kindred mystifications. Instead, he reaffirms the necessity of collectively reinventing the future. And through the demise of Dante, a variation of Mariano and other bitter "old-timers," Bulosan induces a catharsis of the melancholia, narcissism, and diverse sentimental pieties that afflict the text of *America*. The returned exile Dante, however, fails to make the rendezvous with his other half (the disfigured Felix Rivas) when he is killed by his priest brother, Father Bustamante, who has never left home. Bulosan's extinguishing (through death) the schism in Dante's psyche is his trope for the reconciliation of the split psyche, for healing the paranoia and ambivalence complicit in the condition of being an exile/refugee. The authorial intelligence of the novel decides to subsume this problem of the bifurcated subject in the larger goal of enunciating an allegory of national liberation, what Cabral calls "a regaining of the historical personality" of a whole people.

By tapping the resources of autochthonous humor, indigenous rituals of resistance, and a popular memory charged with socialized passions and *ressentiment*, Bulosan finally settles accounts with the duplicitous tricksters and sirens inhabiting the space called "America." His project of "becoming Filipino" in the conqueror's terrain, anticipatory and prefigurative, becomes the only way to realize what the mother, natural abundance, and childhood happiness all represent: freedom, dignity, and recognition of personal worth.

A passage from one of Bulosan's letters may serve to cast light on the novel's title: "I felt that I would be ineffectual if I did not return to my own people. I believed that my work would be more vital and useful if I dedicated it to the cause of my own people" (*Sound* 259). In an earlier essay, he described the Filipino writer's response to the "twists of history," the "labyrinthine circle of revolutionary upsurge and temporary defeat": "Filipino writers went back to their social roots—the peasantry and the proletariat—and began to weave the threads of their folklore with the national tradition. It was only then that cultural activity became a national consciousness." ("The Growth of Philippine Culture" 12–13).

About the time when Bulosan had completed his narrative of the Huk guerrillas articulating their nation's agon in their individual fates, he expressed the fundamental drive of his art in an autobiographical sketch, published a year before he died:

> The question is—what impelled me to write? The answer is—my grand dream of equality among men and freedom for all. To give a literate voice to the voiceless one hundred thousand Filipinos in the United States, Hawaii, and Alaska. Above all and ultimately, to translate the desires and aspirations of the whole Filipino people in the Philippines and abroad in terms relevant to contemporary history. Yes, I have taken unto myself this sole responsibility. (Kunitz 145)

In one letter, Bulosan testified that "what really compelled me to write was to try to understand this country [United States], to find a place in it not only for myself but my people." Since he had already exorcised the specter of the American "dream of success," he was ready to assume a public role. For a decolonizing expatriate writer like Bulosan, whose vocation is complicit with the destiny of his nation, the responsibility is "to find in our national struggle that which has a future," particularly in a time of heightened class conflict. Writing, then, acts as the midwife to cultural renaissance as well as to social transvaluation. The old world is dying, a new world is being born from the ruins of the old—such is Bulosan's crucial insight into the dialectics of historical development. Writing is coeval with the rhythm of the national liberation struggle:

> This is the greatest responsibility of literature in our time: to find in our national struggle that which has a future. Literature is a growing and living thing. We must destroy that which is dying, because it does not die by itself. We must interpret the resistance against the enemy by linking it with the stirring political awakening of the people and those liberating progressive forces that call for a complete social consciousness. ("Letter to a Filipino Woman" 645)

One way of approaching Bulosan's educational value for the generation reared in the putatively hybrid/syncretic milieu of late modernity and globalized capitalism may be suggested by the tone and disposition of the speaking subject in his letters. One can examine the two letters to his nephews Arthur and Fred (see Campomanes and Gernes) and note how Bulosan seeks to negotiate a dialogue or mutual exchange by imagining the questions and responses of his addressees.

He assigns a place of responsibility to Arthur when the image of Arthur's father is evoked as a model of goodness, an inspiration that sustained him in his years of degradation: "my life of terror, my defiance against a system that treated human beings like rotten animals." Juxtaposed with this is an aphorism that spontaneously unfolds from the signifiers of mortality (his mother and grandmother): "We will all die: it is only in the affection that we give to each other when we are still alive that keeps the world moving." One other advice is triggered by the sacrifice of Aurelio for his brother Carlos: "Never forget your family, your town, your people, your country, wherever you go. Your greatness lies in them." In the letter to Fred, Bulosan conceives of the "island" ego rejoining the archipelago by choice: "That is real genius: it is not selfish; it sacrifices itself for the good of the whole community." The context of this remark deals with the significance of Jose Rizal, the Filipino national hero, for the realization of "a free and good Philippines."

Bulosan thus plays the mentor and surrogate father in both letters, through gestures of advising, recalling scenes of his own adolescence, and moralizing about his gambling and the confusion of the times. But he never exaggerates his own status. A tone of understatement may be detected in the way he diverts attention from himself to Rizal or Gorki. And even when he boasts of hoping to leave millions of words behind, he urges Fred to remember the writer as one "who herded carabaos in Mangusmana a long time ago."

Modulating from local details of memory to fabulation, syncopating the fictive with the exhortative and subjunctive, Bulosan performs an act of healing the mutilated psyche by articulating in his letters the liaisons of self and nation, public and private domains, eros and conscience. Such letters, especially those to his American woman friend, not only substantiate the writers' claims but also release—if we can read between the lines and along the margins—those transgressive forces needed to blast what William Blake called the "mind-forged manacles" as well as those venerable institutions and practices that continue to perpetuate the "nightmare of history" for the empire's multitudes.

In his correspondence gathered in *Sound*, we confront Bulosan's alterity, the locus of the civic or "social individual," discernible in this passage from a letter of April 1947: "We are the only expatriates who really lived and worked with the people . . . while we are all alive we must try to understand each other, give each other confidence, help, happiness and goodness." The theme of concern for the Other is further elaborated in a letter to his nephew, wherein he mentions the approaching death of the nephew's mother: "It is good to cry. But don't let sorrow kill your life. We will all die: it is only in the affection that we give to each other when we are still alive that keeps the world moving." In another letter, Bulosan counsels that "we all die . . . any time is as good as any other. . . . But try always to seek the goodness in your fellow man. That is the greatest wealth of all: goodness. And beauty, too. The beauty that you find in all good things." In spite of Bulosan's reiterated faith in life viewed as "a continuum of desire" where the proportion of empathy and rationality, *dulce* and *utile,* are always shifting, the rumor still persists that Bulosan languished in poverty, alcohol, and obscurity.

The whole truth is the tension/fusion of opposites. Bulosan exhibits neither nihilism nor a "sense of foreboding and despair" after the atomic bombs annihilated thousands in Hiroshima and Nagasaki. Instead, a trusting, bold, steady warmth suffuses the following excerpt from a letter of December 1947: "Our task is to live and explore the very roots of life, dig deep into the hidden fountainhead of happiness; and when we die, at last, we must die accepting death as a natural phenomenon and believing also that life is something we borrow and must give back richer when the time comes." Recalling Spinoza's injunction, Bulosan was obsessed with life, not death. Amid the massive destruction of the Korean War and brutalizing counterinsurgency in the Philippines, he pursued the nomadic stance of proposing alternatives—lines of flight, deterritorializing flows. These choices were not utopian in the pejorative sense but were in fact heuristic and realizable because they inhered in the actual everyday praxis of life endowed with meaning by the participation of creative, self-determined, responsible, equal citizens.

Visions of Transcendence

I can't even dream; the whiteness of the land
Skulks in my sleep, stifling my dream. . . .
  —"The Surrounded"

Sleep peacefully, for your labors are done, your pains
Are turned into tales and songs. . . .
  —"Now That You Are Still"

In his fiction, essays, and poetry, Bulosan interrogated the conjuncture of class, gender, race, and ethnicity that underpins the epochal antagonism between capitalism and the world's emancipatory, popular-democratic experiments. In retrospect, the Cold War offered him an opportunity to transcend a narrow bourgeois-nationalist program and envisage a socialist transformation of the empire. (The Filipino community in the United States can be conceived as an "internal colony," despite its lack of a sizable ghetto or *barrio*.)

In the process, the boundary erected by U.S. hegemony between the Southeast Asian writer-exile and his peasant heritage proved artificial when Bulosan encountered racist exclusion and exploitation in the heartland of capital. In addition to *America*, stories like "The Soldier" and "As Long as the Grass Shall Grow" (title inspired by Bulosan's enthusiasm for *Black Elk Speaks*) dramatized the truth of Filipino suffering. They suffered not only class disadvantage, racism, and gender discrimination (antimiscegenation laws condemned them to bachelorhood and they were constantly preyed upon by gamblers, sex merchants, and white supremacists) but also national oppression. In this the Filipinos shared a predicament similar to that of workers of other races and nationalities.

In his voluminous letters, in his novel *The Cry*, and in his essays (like "My Education," "The Growth of Philippine Culture," and "Terrorism Rides the Philippines"), Bulosan argues that the Filipino nationality could not exercise its right of self-determination. It could not do so as long as the Philippines was a dependent colony of a power that claimed to be "democratic" but in practice fostered racial, national, and class discrimination. Overthrowing this unjust system meant cutting its stranglehold on people of color in the dependencies and other subordinate formations, which remain the source of superprofits, cheap labor, and natural resources for transnational corporations (again, Puerto Rico readily comes to mind).

Earlier, I remarked on how Bulosan's hitherto neglected novel, *The Cry*, transports his imagination back to the Philippines to explore what possible ties and reciprocal determinations there might be between peasant-worker insurgency and the Filipino diaspora. One story incorporated in the novel, excerpted here with the title "How My Stories Were Written," rehearses the direction of Bulosan's inquiry. The allegorical resonance of Apo Lacay, the folk sage who resembles the prophet of "Passage into Life," points to the genesis of the historical imagination in the encounter of innocence and experience. Apo Lacay's genealogy brings back to life the primal scene of disinheritance, together with the revitalizing power of narrative:

> Then it seemed to me, watching him lost in thought, he had become a little boy again living all the tales he had told us about a vanished race, listening to the gorgeous laughter of men in the midst of abject poverty and tyranny. For that was the time of his childhood, in the age of great distress and calamity in the land, when the fury of an invading race impaled their hearts in the tragic cross of slavery and ignorance. And that was why they had all become that way, sick in soul and mind, devoid of humanity, living like beasts in the jungle of their captivity. But this man who had survived them all, surviving a full century of change and now living in the first murmurs of a twilight and the dawn of reason and progress, was the sole surviving witness of the cruelty and dehumanization of man by another man, but whose tales were taken for laughter and the foolish words of a lonely old man who had lived beyond his time.

The wisdom of folly incarnated in Apo Lacay's sensibility is exemplary in bridging the gap between (a) the 1898 anti-imperialist resistance to "the fury of an invading race" and (b) the campaign against the anti-communist destruction of militant unions and people's organizations in the 1950s. This mode of apprehending ties, liaisons, and affinities amid disruptions and schisms in the movement's ranks became Bulosan's weapon of endurance and collective self-transmutation. In twenty years, he had persevered in mapping the itinerary of the native / alien in the territory of the enemy / colonizer, leaving marks of his ordeal in forging a new, complex identity for his people, whose novelty and efficacy still are not fully recognized, for reasons discussed earlier.

In 1937, Bulosan believed he was dying in the city hospital in Los Angeles, California. But he was to endure another two decades. He underwent several operations for leg cancer and lung lesions until he was left slightly crippled, one kneecap and one kidney removed, his body frail and vulnerable. Bulosan survived until 11 September 1956. After a night of drinking with a labor lawyer who was a close friend, he wandered the streets of Seattle. At dawn, he was found sprawled on the steps of City Hall, "comatose and in an advanced stage of broncho-pneumonia." Carlos Bulosan was a victim less of neurosis or despair than of cumulative suffering from years of privation and persecution. He died at the height of the Cold War, poor but not entirely obscure. The conviviality and stamina of his creative spirit can be discerned in his "Editorial" in the 1952 Yearbook, where he reaffirmed the union's "uncompromising stand to defend human rights and liberties" against the

"maniacal machinations" of the anticommunist witch-hunts. His audience did not fade because postwar prosperity dispelled the appeal of
the underdog; instead, public concern shifted to civil rights and Third
World national liberation, thus engendering a new, receptive, and susceptible audience.

When the Philippines was granted independence in 1946, the need to
trumpet America's colonial "success" and win allies for the antifascist
cause already had become anachronistic. Bulosan's stories, however,
were reprinted in the Philippines and his legendary aura circulated in
the labor camps, in the subterranean world of the "old timers," in radical circles everywhere. In 1965, Filipino workers in the California vine-
yards, led by Bulosan's contemporaries, Larry Itliong and Philip Vera
Cruz, launched the historic strike that led to the founding of the United
Farm Workers of America. This was the fruit of dangerous ground-
breaking actions initiated in the early 1930s by Bulosan and his associates in the CIO and its predecessors.

Bulosan never compromised his principles, nor his basic commitment
to the socialist vision of world revolution. He reaffirmed this conviction
at every occasion:

> Writing was not sufficient. . . . I drew inspiration from my active participa-
> tion in the workers' movement. The most decisive move that the writer
> could make was to take his stand with the workers. (*Selected Works* 35)

Little could he imagine in those days of fear and betrayal that, after his
death, he would be vindicated and acclaimed as one of the most elo-
quent tribunes of the multiracial working class, here and elsewhere. He
would be honored as a militant chronicler of the multitudes whose
struggles for freedom, equality, and justice would distinguish an era of
unprecedented upheaval across the planet, the import and significance
of which we are just slowly beginning to understand.

Surveying his life and work in this historical framework, I consider
Bulosan a formidable revolutionary artist. His contribution to shaping a
Third World narrative of people's liberation coincides with his project
of resolving the predicament of uprooting and exile, that is, of colonial
subjugation. Whether overseas or at home, this Filipino carried on his
back the burden of history's nightmare in all his travels. Learning from
the rigor of the Depression and the terror of Cold War patriotism, he
worked with others to purge the poison of racist free-enterprise ideology from the mentality and *habitus* of his compatriots.

Colonial ideology in general functions as a seductive, self-rationalizing fantasy—the hallucinations of normal common sense, as it were—shrouding the truths of exploitation and racist exclusion. This ideology, Bulosan never tired of pointing out, reproduces and legitimizes the contradiction between the labor of the many who produce social wealth and the control and distribution of that wealth by a privileged minority. Colonial servitude masquerading as freedom can be remedied only by grounding one's life in the practice of separation, distancing, resistance, and by rooting it in the ethos of a collectivity materializing as an ethicopolitical force from the convergence of individual acts of revolt.

As tribune and chronicler, Bulosan engaged in a praxis of committed writing (tendentious and polemical, if you like), intended to persuade, arouse, and instigate readers to action. He sought to integrate the popular struggles in the heartland of colonial power with those in the "uncivilized" and "untamed" hinterlands. His writings may be deemed a cogent witness to the protracted endeavor of the Filipino masses to free themselves from colonial barbarism, from the unrelenting domination of transnational business. In *America Is in the Heart* and elsewhere, we observed his radicalization and the ripening of his imagination transpire in the gap between the ideals of democracy he had been taught and the violence of the reality he experienced.

Bulosan was a battle-tested combatant in the confrontation between antagonistic classes and interests on several fronts: between the multinational proletariat and the hegemonic power bloc of transnational capital, between Third World subjects and the élite of the industrialized nation-states. To the end of his life, Bulosan conscientiously strove to fuse two powerful tendencies: the political imperative of art (serving the masses through the popularization of egalitarian principles) and the artistic demand for wholeness, delightful release, and magical purposiveness (the ends of usefulness and pleasure). The synthesis he achieved was, in retrospect, an uncompromising but compassionate and lucid critique of the ironies, discrepancies, and paradoxes of Filipino existence in the United States.

Despite his revival in the 1960s and 1970s, and his continuing "prestige" in the field of ethnic studies and other multicultural disciplines, Bulosan actually still remains in the limbo of cultural marginality. Why? Unlike the more notorious expatriate Jose Garcia Villa (now rarely read), and despite his limited success, Bulosan was never really accepted by the U.S. literati. One can say that it was Harriet Monroe, editor of *Poetry*, who discovered Bulosan for American intellectuals and ascribed an "American" reputation to him. Given his association with left-wing intellectuals and radical dissidents before and after the onset of the Cold War, he was immediately suspect, a fringe or provincial author from the boondocks. The answer to our question—why he remains in cultural limbo—hinges on the powerlessness of the Filipino community in the United States, its "silence" and invisibility, its surrender to "creature comforts" and the illusions of consumerism, historically predicated on the subordinate position of the Philippines and its dependent status in the world system of transnationalizing late capitalism.

Within this global framework, Bulosan cannot be categorized simply as another "ethnic" denizen in the currently thriving multicultural mall. The radicalization of his sensibility, from the time he landed in Seattle in 1930 to his death in 1956, enabled Bulosan to traverse the boundaries set by the sectarianism of ethnic closure, the nostalgic melancholy of a wish to return to a mythical past, and the elitism of avant-garde arbiters of taste.

Over two million Filipinos today (1996) constitute the largest segment of the Asian American population in the United States, yet their creative force for social renewal is still either inchoate, repressed, or unacknowledged. Bulosan endeavored to articulate their presence in his account of multiracial conflicts and individual quests for happiness—insisting, however, on the fundamental primacy of social labor or cooperative praxis as the guarantee of liberation for all humans across the barriers of class, gender, nationality, and race.

Because of his radical popular-democratic orientation, Bulosan may be regarded as one of the first consciously multicultural writers in the United States whose profound and consistent involvement in anti-imperialist resistance defies assimilation into the hegemonic liberal pluralist canon. I have cited such attempts at cooptation earlier. It can be argued with more credence that he is one of the first "postcolonial" writers to accomplish the task of inscribing the power of the negative—the multi-accentual speech of "Third World" subalterns—in the archive of western knowledge, questioning its legitimacy, expropriating what was useful, and rewriting the uneven, fractured, dispersed history of the world system from the perspective of its victims.

As long as the Philippines remains a virtual neocolony, and as long as Filipinos remain an oppressed nationality here and around the world (the global diaspora now is five million), Bulosan's texts remain necessary for carrying out the task of elucidating the predicament of the Filipino community and its varying modalities of self-affirmation within the political economy of a "New World Order." Bulosan no doubt will form part of the multiracial but still homogeneous map of a complex and rapidly changing society within which these new settlers—over fifty thousand a year—are bound to regroup, conduct reconnaissance, and calculate their new bearings. The Filipino "alien" surely will find a home in Bulosan's territory, a springboard for future explorations. One of these explorations is that of people of color everywhere claiming their right to be recognized as movers and makers of local/universal history. At the turn of the century, Mark Twain saw as the crucible of the American republic its feat of subjugating the insurgent Filipinos—how "thirty thousand [American soldiers] killed a million [Filipinos]," in Twain's words. This provoked nearly a century of fierce resistance, of which Bulosan's *oeuvre* is one prodigious testimony. This rich, complex dialectic of exchange, of challenge, and of response, whose configuration I have partly traced here, may prove decisive in inventorying the possibilities and fate of the radical democratic transformation of U.S. society in the twenty-first century.

6

Articulating a Third World Modernism: The Case of Jose Garcia Villa

Je dis . . . une fleur . . . l'absente de tous bouquets.
  —*Stephane Mallarmé, 1887*

Nothing conclusive has yet taken place in the world,
the ultimate word of the world and about the world
has not yet been spoken, the world is open and free,
everything is still in the future and will always be
in the future.
  —*Mikhail Bakhtin, 1929*

Jose Garcia Villa, avant-garde artist and modernist poet, is probably the most neglected twentieth-century writer on the planet.

Born on 5 August 1914 in Manila, Philippines, Villa inherited the legacy of three hundred years of Spanish culture transplanted to, and transformed in, an Asian colony of the United States. After three decades of colonial tutelage in the Philippines, Villa immigrated to the United States in 1930. He studied briefly at the University of New Mexico and moved to New York City, now his permanent residence.

Born of the unique encounter between the traditional culture of a Third World country in Asia and the industrial Anglo-European ethos of an emergent world power, Villa almost singlehandedly founded modern writing in English in the Philippines in the 1920s. He inaugurated the first self-conscious theoretical literary and art criticism in the Philippines. He is also distinguished for initiating the project of endeavoring to fuse U.S. modernism (Anderson, Stein, Hemingway) with a nascent, if problematic, Filipino sensibility. He attempted this in his poems, stories, and critical pronouncements, as attested to by *Many*

Voices: Selected Poems and *Poems by Doveglion*. This encounter marked an unusual historic conjuncture: like Ruben Dario's westernizing initiative in Latin America, Villa's aestheticism registered the advent of a heterodox, transgressive creativity. It did so in a milieu characterized by residual feudal or tributary "structures of feeling" that were being altered by the demands of a pragmatic and commercial individualism. This interaction itself was tempered by a peculiar "Malayan/Pacific" *habitus*. One can discern this interface of cultures in the archetypal growth/development motif explored in his collection of stories *Footnote to Youth*.

When Villa transferred to New York, his writings attracted the attention of major critics and writers of the forties and fifties. Despite its ornamental metaphysics and technical idiosyncrasies, Villa's poetry received praise from Conrad Aiken, e.e. cummings, Marianne Moore, Edith Sitwell, David Daiches, Mark Van Doren, Richard Eberhart, Babette Deutsch, Elliot Paul, Irwin Edman, and Horace Gregory. His volumes *Have Come Am Here* and *Volume Two* constitute, for a Filipino audience, world-historical events in the ongoing search for a distinct cultural identity and national autonomy. Leading Filipino critics like Salvador Lopez, Federico Mangahas, Armando Manalo, and Manuel Viray have given testimonials affirming Villa's stature as the foundational Filipino modernist. Given this achievement, Villa was granted the title of "National Artist" from the Marcos dictatorship on 12 June 1973.

But the "alchemy of the word" did not transubstantiate his precarious reputation. Although American critics have acclaimed the innovative breakthrough of his "comma poems" and the use of "reversed consonance" in inventing new poetic rhythms, Villa has lapsed into obscurity since the publication of *Selected Poems and New*. A selection of his love poems entitled *Appassionata Poems in Praise of Love* has not received any serious critical attention. Except for eccentric journalistic pieces during the period of the Marcos regime, Villa has not published anything of worth comparable to his earlier performance. Nonetheless, his enigmatic figure and his obsession with his art, more than his public pronouncements, have exerted a powerful symbolic impact on several generations of Filipino writers who preserve, to some extent, Villa's charismatic legend and aura.

What accounts for the Villa mystique? This essay is a prolegomenon toward exploring this field of ethnopoetics of the diasporic imagination, a treacherous contact zone in the remapping of the U.S. multicultural terrain.

Beyond Orientalism

Critique is always an endless attempt to complete the unfinished and unfinalizable artifact. Confronted with verses like:

And,lay,he,down,the,golden,father,
(Genesis',fist,all,gentle,now)
Between,the,wall,of,China,and,
The,tiger,tree . . .

any reader is bound to expect someone—his brother-reader, this critic, his alter ego—to perform the obligatory *explication de texte,* since texts, especially a poem entitled "The Anchored Angel," do not explain themselves and do not exhibit transparent intentions, cuing the reader on what to say or do next. An academic milieu usually determines how we are going to be constituted (if at all) as readers of Villa in a putative "interpretive community." But I hasten to warn the reader that I will not fulfill that expectation—that is, engage in the traditional routine practice of textual analysis, a *modus operandi* first instituted by the New Criticism and now almost second nature to teachers of literature. Alternatively, I will not perform the ritual of a rigorous dissection of verbal meaning (semiotic, pragmatic) as exemplified by the work of Roman Jakobson and Claude Levi-Strauss. Do we need another interpretation of the text? What do we mean by "text"? Which text?

We all know that those formalist approaches—from Croce to Ransom, from the Chicago neo-Aristotelians to Hartman and Miller—immediately beg certain fundamental questions about the identity of the author, the unitary intent and coherence of form, and the more problematic reception / response of the audience, questions that are implicated in the status of empiricism and humanism in the methodology of contemporary cultural studies. No text (discursive practice, in general) can intelligibly exist outside of its manifold, overlapping contexts, its condition of possibility. And a fine exemplar of this truth is my subject, a nearly anonymous poet in the United States, who is, however, recognized as the inventor of modernist writing in English in the Philippines and one of the subaltern "others" on which American "national" identity depends.

For over half a century now, Villa has lived in Greenwich Village, New York City, where he was acclaimed in the late forties and fifties as one of the leading avant-garde poets. As noted in Chapter 4, he has received numerous prizes and awards, among them a Guggenheim fellowship, American Academy of Arts and Letters Award, a Bollingen fellowship in criticism, and a Shelley Memorial Award for poetry. He was also nominated for the Pulitzer prize in 1943. But, as the platitude goes, times have changed. Today I am quite certain that, except for a handful of area specialists and antiquarians, nobody has heard of Villa, or has even read about him. He is not mentioned in any of the extant literary histories of the United States. Except for one now-defunct anthology on Asian American writing, even critics of multi-ethnic American literature do not find Villa "ethnic" enough to deserve serious attention.

Given the status of Villa as an "endangered species" all by himself, I want to address not only the character of this enigma but also ways of approaching it as a heuristic problem in cultural studies in general. Recent inquiries into "postcolonial" literature, and the foregrounding of racial and ethno-national differences in Third World cultural production vis-à-vis the Eurocentric canon of "world literature," have made necessary the demand for a kind of symptomatic reading (which Althusser and Macherey first theorized) of texts considered marginal, alternative, or oppositional. I include in the category of "texts" the social location of the writer, the shifting contexts of his or her practice, and the contingent reception of his or her works by diverse audiences.

Symptomatic reading was first theorized by Althusser and Macherey. What is symptomatic are the silences, lacunas, and breaks in the text that configure the "Otherness" of its presence on the scene of repression and resistance, what enables it to say what it says, as well as what it does not. The alterity of such signifying practice, its "synthesis of heterogeneous entities" (Della Volpe), is itself emblematic of a larger ethico-political configuration in the world today. Briefly, this sketch of a metacommentary on Villa's performance endeavors to construct the *problematique*, the unconsciousness of discourse, the matrix of its readerly and writerly potential. The discourse in question is not any single text, but "Villa" as the rubric of the imagination inscribed in a specific worldly plot, a complex conjuncture of Western modernity and Third World underdevelopment. "Villa" names the corpus of discursive practices whose textuality is less an essence than a construction of readings and disciplinary glosses that have defined it, made it accessible as knowledge, valorized it, and spelled out its fate as a cultural artifact in modern industrial society.

The Villa problematic, then, involves not just the production of certain texts in the archive. More crucially, it foregrounds its consumption and reproduction by criticism and scholarly discourse: its self-consciousness, its blindness, omission, and oversights can only be understood as effects of the *problematique* that determine the scope of its capacity to know itself, as well as its power to free itself from its own limitations. We are not intending to extract the Logos here, the "true kernel from the mystified shell," so to speak. Our project is to identify the Villa problematic as a literary field (in Bourdieu's sense), where antagonistic cultural forces encounter each other.

In this prolegomenon to Villa, I pose the following questions: Does this encounter between Western and Third World cultures produce mutagenetic phenomena or a cloning process, rather than an authentic synthesis? How can we measure "authenticity"? Can western theory recuperate and consequently neutralize the resources of a transgressive sensibility shaped in a "zone of occult instability" (Fanon)? How was Villa used by majoritarian interests? Can past usage be salvaged for present and future oppositional projects? These are questions that a symptomatic reading will try to examine. This task involves exploring approaches to meaning, identity, and form, each articulated with precisely those specific historical necessities and forces that have been repressed/sublimated by the problematic.

Lest we commit the *faux pas* of the "common reader" in mistaking Villa for a distant cousin of the Mexican Pancho Villa, allow me to indulge in deploying a tactical "metaphysics of presence" by making Villa identify himself, albeit not without equivocation. This point of departure stages the outline of a narrative that, in retrospect, never quite arrives at a peripeteia nor a cathartic denouement. I quote Villa's autobiographical statement from the First Supplement to *Twentieth Century Authors* (Kunitz) that introduces Villa as an "American poet":

> Born in Manila, Philippines, of Philippine parentage. His father was a doctor and was chief of staff for General Aguinaldo in the Philippine revolution against Spain. Villa came to the United States in 1930 and attended the University of New Mexico from which he graduated [with an A.B. in 1932]. He did postgraduate work at Columbia University [where he received an M.A. in 1941]. He is now a permanent resident of the United States.
>
> While an undergraduate at New Mexico he wrote short stories and edited a little magazine *Clay,* which published the early work of Saroyan, Caldwell, William March, David Cornel DeJong, etc. Edward J. O'Brien,

the short story critic, was his first literary encourager and reprinted several of his stories in *The Best Short Stories* annuals, dedicating the 1932 volume to Villa. Scribner's later published a collection of these stories.

Although the short story form was his first literary interest, Villa felt later that it was not his proper métier, as he was not interested in outward events and his tendency was toward more and more concision. He therefore undertook the study of poetry seriously and from 1933 onwards he delved intensively into English and American poetry. He wrote a great deal but did not publish anything until 1942 [factually untrue], when his book of poems *Have Come, Am Here* appeared. It received warm recognition and later Villa was awarded a Guggenheim fellowship and the $1,000 poetry award of the American Academy of Arts and Letters.

Villa has always been interested in technical experiment and in *Have Come, Am Here* he introduced a new rhyming method which he calls 'reversed consonance.' In his next book, *Volume Two,* he introduced the 'comma poems' where the comma is employed as a modulator of line movement. Both experiments are explained in notes to be found in the books.

Recently someone remarked to Villa that he found Villa's poetry 'abstract,' contrary to the general feeling for detail and particularity that characterizes most contemporary poetry. Villa comments: "I realize now that this is true; I had not thought of my work in that light before. The reason for it must be that I am not at all interested in description or outward appearance, nor in the contemporary scene, but in *essence.* A single motive underlies all my work and defines my intention as a serious artist: The search for the metaphysical meaning of man's life in the Universe—the finding of man's selfhood and identity in the mystery of Creation. I use the term *metaphysical* to denote the ethic-philosophic force behind all essential living. The development and unification of the human personality I consider the highest achievement a man can do." (1035–1036)

What is striking in this self-manipulated portrait is how it both reveals and hides facts, claims, and motives. Note how the occasion doubles itself, with Villa quoting himself responding to someone's ad hoc comment. After this mock-interview where Villa simulates the scenario of original rejection of past deeds, experience of lack, and desire for reunion, the editor informs us that Villa is "generally considered to be the first-ranking poet of Filipino origin writing today." To support this estimate, the aristocratic British poet Edith Sitwell is quoted, attributing to Villa "a great, even an astounding, and perfectly original gift."

Villa's early poems were enthusiastically praised for "their freshness" and "imaginative singularity," continues the editor; but his comma poems and "typographical *jeux d'esprit*" have encountered disapproval and skepticism. David Daiches is quoted for noting Villa's "mannerism and self-parody," but qualifies this with a positive judgment: Villa "retains the poet's eye and the poet's ear, and the best poems in this volume have the sharp colors, the cunning verbal precision, and that almost Blake-like combination of innocence and outrage which his earlier poems showed so markedly" (1036).

It is revealing to note that the encyclopedia entry does not mention Villa serving the Philippine government in Washington circa 1942 (mentioned in the jacket of *Have Come, Am Here*) nor his employment in the Columbia University Library. It ends with a mention of Villa's marriage in 1946 to Rosemarie Lamb and their two children. We are also told that Villa is "small, dark, delicate-featured" and that he began working on a "theory of poetry" in 1953 with a Bollingen fellowship.

Villa's locus of enunciation can be said to be inhabited by the twin forces of necessity and chance, by determinate circumstances and gratuitous contingency. Irony and aporia prevail. While Villa was included in poetry anthologies edited by *inter alia* Conrad Aiken[1] and W. H. Auden in the forties and fifties, his reputation seemed to have coincided with their obsolescence. None of the contemporary anthologies of modern American literature published in the sixties and after have included Villa, nor have the literary histories (from Robert Spiller's 1963 *Literary History of the United States* on) ever mentioned him, even in passing.

Aside from the standard New Critical evaluation instanced by Leonard Casper's *New Writing from the Philippines*, the only recent attention given to Villa may be found in Werner Sollor's *Beyond Ethnicity*. For Sollors, Villa's uprooted condition, tellingly juxtaposed with Jean Toomer's predicament, motivated "a radical *formal* response to the ethnic writer's need for a new poetic language" (254); hence the freedom allegedly afforded by the invention of "reversed consonance" whose principle connects fragments like "I am" and "may," "deal" and "lead," in order to renew the question of identity Villa proclaims (*Have Come Am Here* 18):

> Nobody yet knows who I am,
> Nor myself may;
> Nor yet what I deal,
> Nor yet where I lead.

Paradoxically, it is Villa's ethnic difference, not his metaphysical selfhood, that aligns him with the myth of American exceptionalism, with what Sollors calls the "dialectic of the languages of consent and descent." From this perspective, difference reconciles and integrates.

The historical transition from the end of World War II (when Villa's *Have Come Am Here* drew praise from some well-known poets and critics) to the sixties (his last volume of significant poems is *Selected Poems and New*) has been conceived by art critics as the passage from late high modernism to postmodernism. Sollor's perception of Villa as an "ethnic" writer is itself a product of this shift, when the hegemonic canon was first questioned in the early seventies. Seen within this perspective, Villa's modernism was a late comer and an early victim to fashions in the sphere of high bourgeois style and elitist taste.

Why was Villa unable to maneuver any change, thus suffering premature obscurity? What did the American commentators see in Villa's poems that earned him a place, albeit a precarious and transitory one, in the magic circle of modernist icons like Eliot, Pound, and Stevens? How can one explain his disappearance from the Establishment consensus and his persistent invisibility as ethnic protagonist?

Fables of Self-fashioning

To explore answers to these questions, I take as my premise the idea (first enunciated by Etienne Balibar and Pierre Macherey) that literary texts do not have a metaphysical essence or significance by themselves. Rather, they produce fictions that are realized as ideological domination-effects by criticism, which is the discourse of literary ideology. Thus, the literary text is "the agent for the reproduction of ideology in its ensemble," inducing by its aesthetic effects "the production of 'new' discourses which always reproduce (under constantly varied forms) the same ideology (with its contradictions) . . ." (96). The aesthetic effect establishes the rituals of literary consumption and other cultural practices that equate reader and author, author's intentions (one of the literary effects), and interpretations by readers. Balibar and Macherey suggest that "interpretations and commentaries reveal the (literary) aesthetic effect, precisely, in full view. Literariness is what is recognized as such, and it is recognized as such precisely in the time and to the extent that it activates the interpretations, the criticisms and the 'readings' " (97).

Consequently, the focal point of critical analysis should be not the "metaphysics of the text" but the functions and uses to which these are deployed in specific historical conjunctures. As Tony Bennett puts it in *Formalism and Marxism*: "the text must be studied not as an abstraction but in the light of the determinations which, in the course of its history, successively rework that text, producing for it different and historically concrete effects in modifying the conditions of its reception" (158). In other words, the text's multiplicity is a function of its materiality. The translatable cognitive load of social "matter" entails the deferment of analytic closure and the nonidentity of meaning.

Of the most influential commentaries that have constituted Villa not so much as an "American" poet but as a "genius" with "a great, even an astonishing, and perfectly original gift," is Edith Sitwell's introduction to *Selected Poems and New*. Herein she establishes the criteria for inclusion into the canon. Sitwell's hierarchy, however, privileges the "depths of the poet's being," compounded of his blood, spirit, and experience, from which art springs spontaneously and naturally. She sees in Villa's poems the "absolute sensation" which Novalis considers "religious": "All have a strange luminosity—as if they came from the very heart of light—alternating with an equally strange darkness, and this luminosity, this darkness bear a certain resemblance to that in the works of Blake and of Boehme" (xi). Aside from Novalis, Blake, and Boehme, Sitwell invokes St. Catherine of Genoa, Meister Eckhart, Mallarmé (of course), Dr. Carl Jung, and Goethe as resonant, mystical touchstones guaranteeing the genealogy of Villa's "pure poetry." (An earlier version of this introduction compares Villa to Blake and Lorca.) Sitwell isolates lines and phrases that strike her as strange or fiery, a fiction-effect that prohibits rational comprehension, for example:

> I will break God's seamless skull
> And I will break his kissless mouth,
> O I'll break out of His faultless shell
> And fall me upon Eve's gold mouth.

Her judgment is mainly impressionistic: she says that the two words ("golden,father") that end the first line of "The Anchored Angel" "seem sinking as the sun seems to do when it sets into the earth from which all growth arises" (xiii). She ventures a hermeneutic decoding of the lines:

> Between,the,Wall,of,China,and,
> The,tiger,tree (his,centuries,his,
> Aerials,of,light)

as follows: "the Wall of China is Death, seemingly dividing us from another civilisation—the civilisation of the Living, and, also, shielding us
from the dangers of Life. The tiger tree is the infinite growth of the future
arising from that earth, 'the,father,who,made,the,flower,principle.' "
Villa's themes, according to Sitwell, center on the "principle," archetype,
and quintessence—the metaphysical essence that Villa gestures to, a
fiction that escapes complete verbal capture. Language then fails even as
it succeeds; the "mystery of creation" embodies the domination-effect of
subduing any unease or reservation. Sitwell's extravagant reading ascribes to Villa's poems the qualities of "pure poetry": while being beautiful, their strangeness is what transforms them into objects of contempla-
tion and awe.

Sitwell describes the following "divine poem" as one "of an inef-
fable beauty, springing straight from the depths of Being" (*Selected
Poems* 45):

> My most. My most. O my lost!
> O my bright, my ineradicable ghost.
> At whose bright coast God seeks
> Shelter and is lost is lost. O
> Coast of Brightness. O cause of
> Grief. O rose of purest grief.
> O thou in my breast so stark and
> Holy-bright. O thou melancholy
> Light. Me. Me. My own perfidy.
> O my most my most. O the bright
> The beautiful the terrible Accost.

In this judgment, the form of the sensuous in Villa's art thus becomes
"sublime," a phenomenal event transcending the limits of ordinary
metaphor as "determinate abstraction," as polysemic intellectual constructs (Della Volpe 1, 142).

Like Sitwell, Marianne Moore apprehends a "final wisdom" in Villa's
"paradoxical avowals," delicate but forceful, their logic definable only
by analogy: "such writing reminds one of the colors of black ink from a
hog's hair brush in the hand of a Chinese master" (77). Villa is then assimilated to the canon when his temperament is associated with Dante,
Spenser, Blake, and Bunyan. Moore believes that Villa's technique of
reversed consonance affects the content of his poems to the extent that
the numen or charisma is exchangeable: "And would not Everyman—
however camouflaged from himself—be glad to believe that God is

present and is accessible to personality?" (78). Moore extols the "reverence, the raptness, the depth of concentration" in Villa's "bravely deep poems."

Meanwhile, critic David Daiches concurs with Moore's perception of antinomian impulses in Villa: naiveté and cunning, metaphysical elaboration and simplicity, nonsense and myth, all coalesce in the poems in *Have Come, Am Here*. While Villa's mythmaking drive parallel that of Blake and Yeats, Villa's experimental wit evokes that of Gerard Manley Hopkins, George Herbert, Blake, Lewis Carroll, and D. H. Lawrence (79–80). Apropos of the achievement of Villa's *Selected Poems*, Mark Van Doren admires their increased intensity and deepened wit; rich and surprising, Villa "assaults greater subjects and constructs wider worlds" in his "original idiom, so natural yet in its daring so weird." Weird, strange, inexplicable: we encounter here the anticipatory marks, the sacralizing stigmata, of the Kantian sublime.

Sitwell, Moore, Daiches, and others all have registered enthusiastic responses to the verbal texture, diction, phrasing, and imagery of Villa's poems, to what deconstructionists may call their "infinite equivocality," the abyssal vertigo of signifiers in free play. Little concern is paid to their architectonics or overarching designs. Quotes on the jacket of *Have Come, Am Here* underline Villa's "superbly momentous and beautiful articulations" (Raymond Weaver) and "his way of feeling and his imagery are startling in intensity and intimacy" (Peter Monro Jack). Richard Eberhart wonders at Villa's "pure, startling and resounding poetry, informed with so much legerity and fire" so that "the personal is lost in a blaze of linguistic glories." On the basis of Villa's "intense and inventive imagery" as well as "the combination of intellectual fire and cool finished craft," Irwin Edman considers Villa a "poetic genius" akin to Blake, "the most original and genuine poet" in his generation. Like Daiches and Edman, Elliot Paul is struck by Villa's subtle and personal idiom. Although linked with such rebellious moderns as the imagists and symbolists, Villa's individuality keeps company with Blake, Gertrude Stein, T. S. Eliot, and e. e. cummings. Villa is no outsider or alien intruder in the mansion of great "world" (that is, Western) literature.

Following the custom of appraising new writers by comparison with the canonical authors and the received standards, Babette Deutsch holds that Villa's singularity reminds her of Emily Dickinson and Hopkins. The paradoxes and ambiguities (touchstones of aesthetic worth for the New Criticism), as well as the "pure intensity" of the religious poems, all bear "the burning signature of the poetic imagination" (68–

69), which is also manifest in Auden, Dickinson, and the Metaphysical poets. Deutsch notes Villa's relentless humanism when he surpasses Blake by announcing that "God is his miracle, his work, his creation"; in some poems, the young poet "adopts toward Him the attitude of an intimate and peer," as in the poem beginning "The way my ideas think me." Deutsch discerns Villa's pursuit of transcendence via conscious craftsmanship: "Villa is concerned with ultimate things, the self and the universe. . . . He is more interested in himself than in the universe, and he greets the world with a decent urbanity" (70). Clearly, the doctrines of New Critical formalism coalesce with urbane, worldly wise gentility to yield a cosmopolitan poet bereft of class, gender, or ethnic particularities.

But what distinguishes Deutsch from all the other sympathetic commentators is the fact that she is the only one who has taken account of Villa's non-Western origin:

> The fact that he is a native of the Philippines who comes to the English language as a stranger may have helped him to his unusual syntax. But no accident of birth can account for his performance save the ancient *poeta nascitur, non fit*. Even then the adage must be qualified, for though he was undoubtedly born a poet, he has obviously and wisely labored at his art. The result is a group of poems that for all their obscurity, which is sometimes witty, sometimes profound, are luminous and vibrant with the quality of crystal. (71)

Deutsch is troubled with Villa's "unusual syntax." She does not rationalize it as an intentional mode of forging a hybrid, syncretic style of "english," as Bill Ashcroft and his colleagues have demonstrated for non-Western authors in *The Empire Writes Back*. Instead, Deutsch explains Villa's syntax as a defect of being a Filipino native not born to the language. With this sociological inference, Deutsch violates a fundamental axiom of intrinsic criticism.

One can cite here a contrary opinion. In a recent review of Filipino accomplishment in harnessing English for imaginative expression in over half a century, the linguist Andrew Gonzalez evaluates Villa's performance as the most consummate craftsman among pre–World War II writers. According to him, Villa was "the first Filipino poet who took art for art's sake to its logical conclusion and used the resources of a second language to begin innovating with these resources much as a first language speaker does. In the process . . . he embodied the Filipino having perfected his art as form and his mastery of the English language. He

followed his own lights in poetry and as a non-native speaker experi-
mented with the potentialities of the language in the manner of Joyce"
(148).

So far Villa "who hails from the Philippines" has posed no threat to
the orthodox standard of literary excellence in the forties and fifties.
Marianne Moore even counseled those alarmed by his unconventional
attitudes toward religion and bourgeois decorum: "He is not a de-
stroyer, his work is reverent. . . ." While Villa can be domesticated by
New Critical norms, something escapes the reviewers, so that they can
only address his weird carnivalesque affair with language, a practice of
textuality born from excess (the plenitude of the maternal body, the
semiotic chora, in Julia Kristeva's formulation [1982: 182–93]) and separation, a lack or privation that ushers the signifying process. Following
Lacan's schema (1978), Villa's demand for recognition (what he calls
"unification of personality") converts need into unrequitable, infinite
desire.

More than twenty years since the appearance of *Have Come, Am Here,*
which occasioned Villa's entry into the peripheral region of American
poetry, we find a critic who, though doctrinally a formalist, claims to
measure Villa's accomplishment in the context of hypothetical Filipino
values and realities. In evaluating the writers included in his anthology
New Writing from the Philippines, Leonard Casper presumes to see in
Filipino intellectuals like Villa "a peculiar kind of rebelliousness neither
tolerant nor liberating . . . his poetry's near-blasphemy, the unconvinc-
ing pretense at repentance, have some portion of their origin in the
sometimes careless religious observances among Asia's only Christian
people" (106). Villa's stylistic excesses—meager and solipsistic vocabulary, "geometry of narcissism," "essential looseness due to the loss of
substance and consequence," exhibitionistic abuse of the comma, lack
of "specific presence and circumstantial detail"—are proof that Villa
cannot be assigned to the same rank as Donne, e. e. cummings, Seurat,
Picasso, Pound, and Robert Lowell. While not openly admitting it, Casper seeks to reverse Villa's reputation, constituted (as I've detailed earlier) by the celebrations of Sitwell, Moore, Deutsch, Van Doren, Daiches,
and others. Casper relegates Villa to being "the premier poet of the
Philippines," not a distinguished American poet. Villa is no longer a
genius or an original artist, but merely the object of an arrogant imperi-
alizing cult.

Notwithstanding these censures, Casper condescends to include four
poems by Villa. One, from *Selected Poems* (26), is:

Inviting a tiger for a weekend.
The gesture is not heroics but discipline.
The memoirs will be splendid.

Proceed to dazzlement, Augustine.
Banish little birds, graduate to tiger.
Proceed to dazzlement, Augustine.

Any tiger of whatever colour
The same as jewels any stone
Flames always essential morn.

The guest is luminous, peer of Blake.
The host is gallant, eye of Death.
If you will do this you will break

The little religions for my sake.
Invite a tiger for a weekend,
Proceed to dazzlement, Augustine.

In the context of resurgent nationalist resistance to ongoing U.S. imperialist intervention in the Philippines, Casper claims to tutor Filipinos and others who may have been misled by Villa's revolutionary pose: "As an expatriate from the Philippines, he scorns in various disguises his people's most sacred images—the father; the homeland: that residue of ancestor worship visible in oppressive family circles. . . . The arch-rebel may prove to be even more conservative than his society; and far more anachronistic" (105, 110).

Casper's "Orientalism" is grounded more on the most positivistic and dogmatic stereotyping of Filipino culture than on the immanent meanings of the texts he claims to be contextualizing.[2] But what is really at stake in Casper's demotion of Villa? As before, we need to contextualize and situate intertextuality. The vicissitudes of the Cold War intersected with the civil-rights struggles in the fifties, with the worldwide youth revolt and the women's liberation movement, and with the impact of the Cuban revolution and the emerging Cultural Revolution in China in the early sixties. Under the pressure of these events, the climate of critical opinion in the U.S. shifted from the narrow, monolithic formalism of the New Criticism (supplemented with phenomenological insights) to a more historically conscious and self-critical stance—initiated, in particular, by black cultural activists and assorted radicals. Texts no longer can be explicated in their autotelic singularity, divorced from their worldly complicities. Account must be taken of the historical and social specificities (modes of production, ideological interpellations) that enable any discursive practice to signify, to communicate. Meaning is essentially dialogic, multi-accented, and intertextual, an effect of dialectical processes and imbrications.

It is against this background that we should view Casper's attempt to implement his program of revising the Filipino canon. He deploys the traditional New Critical apparatus, refurbished with sociological platitudes to reaffirm the supremacy of an ultimately reactionary, jingoist ideology which was then being challenged in the Philippines and in many decolonizing formations. In the process of carrying out this inherently contradictory project, Casper has to concede that Villa is not a rootless floating spirit, an "unanchored angel" so to speak, without a history or destiny. Casper's version of history, however, is that of the dominant élite. It cannot but occlude the basic contradiction that forms the subtext of Villa's life and works: in one direction, a subaltern artist who adopted the colonizer's tongue for emancipatory individual and (by extrapolation) collective ends, and in the opposite direction, the hegemonic hubris of a polity that reduces people of color to instrumentalized objects and their dignity into commodified labor-power.

In this light, Casper's self-righteous moralizing and the transcendental aesthetics of Sitwell, Moore, and others all conspire to erase Villa's "Otherness" by assimilating it to the homogeneous, totalizing space of Western modernism. Without intending it, both approaches also have precipitated Villa's "disappearance" into a new stage of global capitalism. In this stage, the postmodern compression of time and space no longer may enable a master narrative of national liberation to make sense of Villa's exile from the Philippines, of his solitary struggle for recognition as a poet protesting commodified and reifying capitalist social relations, and of his possible rediscovery as an oppositional Filipino artist by coming generations. He resembles Whitman somewhat who, in the appraisal of C.L.R. James, celebrated the poet's messianic democratizing mission in an age of competitive capitalism (65–66). That lesson in anachronism renders justice to Villa's analogous situation. In retrospect, however, Casper's revision has produced no lasting significant impact.

Except for Deutsch, cited earlier, the only person who had acknowledged the differential nuance that Villa's Filipino origin plays in the economy of his text was Edward J. O'Brien, the editor who furnished the introduction to Villa's 1933 collection of short stories, *Footnote to Youth*. It is beyond question that O'Brien's understanding of the influence of race, culture, and geography is unashamedly empiricist and mechanical. He believes that Villa, endowed with the "Filipino sense of race" fused with "a strong Spanish sense of form and color," was deeply affected by the "severe and stark landscape" of New Mexico where he settled briefly. The severity and "ascetic pattern of the American desert," together with the "stripped dry quality of New Mexican life," O'Brien goes on, coincides with the asceticism, the "classical reticence of form" of the Spanish short story. Into these containers, Villa poured "passionate feeling," "a native sensuousness of perception and expression" (Villa, *Footnote* 3–4). The result is a virginal and lyrical art, quite distinct from that of Sherwood Anderson, whom Villa credits for opening to him "the world of literature and of life itself."

O'Brien intuits or posits a "Filipino sense of race" or "race consciousness" in Villa's fiction, but leaves this unexplained. Although O'Brien claims that the Philippines (a U.S. colony for over thirty years at the time of his writing) is "a totally unrelated civilization," he can nonetheless appreciate the lyrical power of Villa's Filipino tales "where memory takes the place of vision and race consciousness flowers in an unfamiliar kind of art." Unfamiliar and yet somehow quite accessible, even transparent, to O'Brien, who has used the trite pedagogical formulas for containing any possible threat from recalcitrant material and incorporating intractable elements into the centralizing regime of his discourse. Alterity is recognized but only at the expense of recuperating sameness, of foisting identity on the mirage of difference.

Villa's predicament, however, defies easy assimilation into the paradigm of the disenchanted genius. Villa exemplifies the colonized subject who revolts against the philistine milieu of a society divided by caste and class, wherein vulgar commercialism coexists with feudal taboos and religious injunctions, and wherein individual freedom (both of the native subaltern and of the artist as critic of conventional morality) is limited by the political, economic, and cultural backwardness of a dependent formation. What is the alternative?

For three hundred years, the Philippines was a pillaged outpost of the Spanish empire. For thirty years the islands were an annexed territory of the United States (the door to the China market, as the proponents of Manifest Destiny put it), a source of cheap raw materials and labor power as well as a market for finished goods. Thus, the Philippines at the time of Villa's flight had all the characteristics of what is called the uneven and combined development of a peripheral Third World region,

where heterogeneous beliefs, practices, and styles converge in the com-
pressed time-space frame of commodity production for the world market. So, where would this poet, inspired by the utopian tropes of American avant-garde writing and expelled at age twenty-one from the state
university for writing "obscene" poems, flee if not to the metropolis?

Icarus' Flight and *Felix Culpa*

But, I submit there is a more profound complicating factor that charted
Villa's journey to the Empire's heartland. In the Philippines, despite the
defeat of the revolutionary army of the First Philippine Republic under
Emilio Aguinaldo, signifying practices in both Spanish and the vernacular were mobilized against U.S. domination through the first twenty
years of pacification. A culture war complemented the violent pacification of the masses for thirty years. It must be recalled that one of the
most effective ideological instruments for establishing U.S. colonial
domination was the teaching of the English language and its codifica-
tion as a prerequisite for official employment in the bureaucracy and all
state apparatuses. English was also the language of world trade and
industry on which the Filipino compradors and feudal landlords de-
pended for their survival. (Compradors and feudal landlords were two
components of the native élite, the other being the U.S.-tutored bureaucrats who became petty capitalists.)

In due course, writing in English—the prescribed medium of school
and government—functioned as the central ideological signifier for legitimizing U.S. hegemony and its reproduction in the patron-client
transactions between U.S. colonial authority and the Filipino intelligentsia and middle strata. The function of literary practice in English re-
sembled closely that in Central America where, according to John Beverley and Marc Zimmerman "the role of literature was to legitimize the
new oligarchic order, to act as an intermediary between the emerging inadequate 'national' culture represented by the agro-export bourgeoisie and the culture of the metropolitan centers" (41).

Over and beyond the infrastructure, the lure of English literature
overdetermined Villa's rootlessness. He was repelled by the utilitarian
ethic of the colonial milieu and its commodifying logic. Yet, Villa could
not identify with the vernacular culture, despite his nationalist family
background. This expressive formation from below was represented by

the seditious playwrights and other insurrectionary intellectuals whose project was to construct a national-popular subject with an agenda, the first priority of which was the immediate dismantling of the imperial apparatus. Vernacular writers as a group acted as partisans of the independence struggle. Nor could Villa identify with what remained of the indigenized Spanish culture of the Propagandists, from Rizal up to Mabini and Isabelo de los Reyes, whose surviving exponents were nationalists like Claro Recto and the polemicists of *El Renacimiento* and other periodicals in the first two decades of the century. But above all, Villa could not identify with vulgar Americanizers like Trinidad Pardo de Tavera nor with *pensionados* like Carlos Romulo, whose opportunism flourished later in the banal terrorism and corruption of the Marcos dictatorship. In effect, Villa in the halcyon days of the twenties was already stranded in a no-man's land, a heretical/anarchist prophet of the imagination, while still on native ground.

The plight of the *poet maudit* harbors the pathos of the exile caught in a homeland suddenly become alien and inhospitable. While peasants in the *colorums* were staging armed insurrections against predatory caciquism and militant workers were organizing unions in Manila, the adolescent Villa was busy wrestling with the English language, trying to find his unique individual voice, experimenting and pushing the rules of syntax and the conventions of genres to the breaking point. It was the beginning of a lifetime's adventure, the quest for affirming and pursuing a vocation (approximating that of Joyce's persona, Stephen Dedalus). It was a mission of exploring the terrain of the psyche and mapping the boundaries of the imagination, set over against the claims of family, ritual kin, compatriots, and local tradition.

This problematic of the romantic artist evolves differently for Villa because, despite some superficial correspondence, the relation of Ireland and Europe (in Joyce's case) is different from the relation between the Philippines and the United States. One thinks of the contrasting cases of the Peruvian poet Cesar Vallejo's long exile in France and the African/Caribbean intellectual's diaspora in Europe and North America (C.L.R. James, Fanon, Aimé Cesaire). Political refugees from Chile, Haiti, El Salvador, South Africa, Palestine, and the Philippines in the last two decades also come to mind.

As a 1982 interview demonstrates, Villa's rebellion against his parents was traumatic. We find there a replication of Baudelaire and Flaubert's classic *épater les bourgeois* motivation, transposed into a Third World milieu. Situated in its overdetermined social context, Villa's personal predicament becomes an allegory of the Filipino intellectual born into a colonial world. Here, the displacement of Spanish culture (and the Spanish language) and the suppression of the indigenous revolutionary forces (their culture and their plural vernaculars) have closed the paths to restoring the *Propagandista* renaissance of the *ilustrados* (Rizal, del Pilar, Lopez Jaena) and the creative liaison with the dispossessed strata. Synthesis of those traditions into one national-popular culture in the Philippines is still, up to now, an unfinished agenda.

In his stories where the Rizal hero-figure functions as an Imaginary mediation (not Symbolic), Villa certainly understood the need to break out of a collective mirror-stage: the Rizal myth fostered by the colonial ideological state apparatuses bred idiosyncratic characters—Anderson's "grotesques," whose pathos sublimated the aspiration for national sovereignty. In Villa's theater of the soul, the national hero no longer inspires Jacobin violence; instead, he provokes fantasies of requited love, bizarre analogues of integrity, fulfilled desire, and autonomy.

In most of the stories in *Footnote to Youth* wherein "race consciousness" supposedly predominates, we find the cyclical time of patriarchal-feudal society interrupted by the irrational force of sexuality ("Footnote to Youth"), disease and decay ("Given Woman"), and the exorbitance of woman's time ("Valse Triste" and "Malakas"). What we find in Villa's fiction on domestic life—in contrast to the apologues or didactic fables of "Mir-i-Nisa" and "Kamya," which continue an indigenous tradition of folk story-telling—is a displacement of the literary system of emergent social realism. Social realism thrived in the massive production of novels and satirical drama (notably the seditious plays and later the *sarsu-wela*, a theatrical spectacle mixing songs and dances), in the vernacular tongues, which embodied the radical impulse for popular democracy and national independence.

Because Villa used English, the language of privilege identified with the colonial power, and because his experience of subordination occurred not in the directly economic realm but in the more complexly mediated spheres of intellectual and cultural production, he had no use for the code of social realistic representation that aimed to construct a collective agent of social transformation. For Villa, the crisis of representation bedeviling indigenous writers never arose. What was available for Villa under the historical circumstances of Philippine colonial society in the twenties was the western genre / mode of representing the moral and ethical problems of natives as versions of individual psychological experience. This involved the rendering of family, class, and national situations as symptoms of a breakdown in the power of a monadic subjectivity to intervene effectively in specific life-circumstances.

Curiously enough, the paradigm of the transition from rural to urban life—its ordeals and challenges, informing the fiction of Sherwood Anderson and other anti-genteel writers—appealed tremendously to Villa. In any case, the master-plot of experiencing individual anomie, disillusionment, epiphany, and resignation found in many stories written in the twenties and thirties serves as a synecdochic trope for the disempowerment of the Filipino people as a whole. It fragments the nascent community into isolated citizens, governed by the laws of symbolic exchange (labor-power as commodity) within the framework of liberal-democratic ideology and its disciplinary regimes in civil society. This may partly account for the attraction of Villa and his generation to the individualist dramas of the soul in Anderson, Hemingway, and others. Everything in the past has become problematized, or else sublimated into private psychic ordeals.

In the first twenty years of U.S. colonial consolidation and the campaign for hegemonic control of the islands, we are confronted with an interregnum during which the antagonisms between ideological practices, codes, norms, and systems of representation and self-interpretation were still in the process of unfolding. This can account for the hybrid and syncretic nature of Villa's fiction, its mixture of tones ("The Woman Who Looked Like Christ" is the prime exhibit here), and its tendency to mannerism and self-parody (a trait also displayed in the later poems), despite the presence of certain recurrent themes and motifs that give the illusion of coherence.

We have yet to theorize the process of transition from Villa's pre-exilic stage (late 1920s to 1930) to the silence and cunning of the Depression years (1933 to 1942). In this period we encounter the texts of Villa's apprenticeship (many still available only in rare magazines), wherein the influence of the Western tradition (for example, Biblical rhythm) and the indigenous aphoristic / didactic strain consorted easily with his avant-garde impulse of breaking down the syntagmatic chain of discourse (see "Poems from an Unhumble One"; *Selected Poems* 211–13). For this theorizing, the model of metropolis-periphery needs to be modified by stressing the appropriative capacity of the indigenous sensibility more than its reactive defense mechanisms.

I submit that *Footnote to Youth* affords us heuristic insights into Villa's response to the challenge of fragmentation, loss of depth, schizophrenic disjunction—the simultaneous homogenizing and disaggregation of time-space by the power of money and commodity-exchange that were slowly encroaching into the ecological wholeness of Filipino traditional life. What I think will provide the key to Villa's modernism and to his existentialist project of discovering essence ("man's selfhood and identity in the mystery of Creation") may be found in the process of mediation between the colonial mentality of organic contextualization and the dynamics of symbolic exchange in industrial society, which is represented by the way the stories of the transition try to resolve their conflicts. These stories include in particular "Wings and Blue Flame: A Trilogy," as well as "Song I Did Not hear" and "Young Writer in a New Country." These texts capture the crisis of the transition, the passage of the autochthonous sensibility into the intensely commodified world of what David Harvey calls the Fordist compression of time-space in the evolving capitalism of the inter-war period.

Villa confessed that he wrote his prize-winning story "Mir-i-Nisa" to obtain money for his passage from the Philippines to the United States. In the structure of this story, we can see how Villa's conflict with his father—and, by extension, the patriarchal feudal order (*inter alia* the state university and its censors)—is mediated by the form of an ordeal. The daughter Mir-i-Nisa, through her father's help, succeeds in deciding to marry the tame Tasmi instead of the fiery, sweet-tongued Achmed. Achmed's "ingenious" character leads him to lie, to pretend that he found the "pearl"—but it was the illusion that found him out. It is this truth that the mother asks the son not to reveal to his father: the honest and truth-telling father should not know what actually happened, should persevere to live in innocence. This is the collective wisdom of tradition orally transmitted to the generation that is coming of age. It is a wisdom testifying to a solidarity of belief in certain absolute precepts, to a system whose continuity is founded on the distrust of speech unless it is guaranteed by action, on the precedence of clan-based integrity over solitary passion.

The narrative machinery of the fable that Villa inherits from indigenous orature survives as residual ornament in "Malakas" and "Kamya." But it breaks down, or is finally dismantled, in the tales of "grotesques." Examples are "The Woman Who Looked Like Christ," where the desacralizing force of modernity becomes visible, or "Footnote to Youth," where the reproductive urge severs the generations and the father's erstwhile rebellious will is rendered impotent by the uncanny repetition of his own past in his son.

From the brief moment of freedom from Spanish rule to brutal American reprisals, the rapid displacements of time-space offer barriers that are difficult to negotiate. We sense here a glimpse of that futility and dereliction that overtook the generation of Villa's father (Aguinaldo and the *ilustrados* of the Malolos Republic) and inspired the compromising and even opportunist rituals of the "nationalist" politicians surrounding Osmeña and Quezon. Villa's fabulations thus allegorize the élite's vicissitudes as well as the existential quandaries that sooner or later implicate and conscientize sensibilities like Villa's.

Passage in the Labyrinth

Let us accompany the poet halfway in his itinerary. When Villa arrives in the United States at the height of finance-capitalism's catastrophe, he undergoes a fateful metamorphosis: he abandons the subject-position of colonial deracinated/paranoid rebel and tries to construct on the borderline of nomadic space a simulacra of self-reconciliation. Decentered by colonial marginalization, he seeks unity of being, wholeness, recognition as a gifted artist taking advantage of "careers open to talent"—a citizen of the Republic of Humane Letters. However, invested with native *ressentiment*, he also seeks revenge. At the University of New Mexico in Albuquerque, the unresolved contradictions of Villa's personal life—a microcosm of the multilayered antagonisms in colonial society as a whole—begin to be played out. "Profane illumination," in Walter Benjamin's sense (190), overtakes Villa as he consumes the most terrible drug in solitude: the self. The diary-like notations of his life in the artificial environment found in "Wings and Blue Flame: A Trilogy" might strike one as arbitrary, pointless transcription of routine incidents. In fact, Casper condemns its "artificial cellular geometry" as conveying only "the mechanical aftermath of loss," static proclamations of vision and not the unfolding of the process of experience (104).

At the risk of resorting to the imitative fallacy, I suggest that precisely this form of representing Villa's shock of initiation into industrial society attests to the breakdown of realistic continuity that still sutured the spasmodic epiphanies of *Winesburg, Ohio.* (The native's *agon* was mediated by the desert landscape of New Mexico, itself a binary opposite to both the exuberant terrain of the poet's homeland and the urban "wilderness" of New York City.) This impasse prepares the way for the bricolage of reversed consonance, the comma poems, and the attenuated energy of the "Adaptations." Endowed with illocutionary energies, Villa's testimony of abandonment exhibits syncopated rhythms whose gestic import resemble what Bertolt Brecht aimed at in his didactic *Lehrstucke*: "to show human dealings as contradictory, fiercely fought over, full of violence" (116).

History eventually gives way to utopian speculation. What gives coherence to the "Trilogy" is the drama of self-recovery, a process of recuperation operated mainly by metonymic juxtapositions sliding into metaphor. Note the way the protagonist's sense of loss and dispossession, his loneliness, and his apparent lack of control are all gradually overcome by fantasy, by the discovery of metaphor as a means of restoring intelligibility. This discovery of being able to complete the sentence that apostrophizes him as agent ("You . . .") is cathartic in its fortuitousness:

> 31. One night I stopped talking to myself. I was no longer incoherent and the sentence on my lips that began with 'You . . .' got finished.
> 32. The finished sentence was beauteous as a dancer in the dawn. The sentence was finished at night but it was not like the night but like the dawn.

This power of articulation substitutes for the erotic pleasure of caressing Georgia's blond hair:

> 67. After I finished the sentence that was beauteous as a dancer in the dawn I did not care to touch her hair.

The artist assures himself that language heals and restores wholeness. This leads to a self-negation, bidding goodbye to the self alienated from its surroundings, from President Herbert Hoover's home in Palo Alto and the poor crippled woman selling pencils on a sidewalk in California, as well as the "nigger" worker in the Pullman train who behaved automatically "like a machine." The speaker deconstructs the claims of the Cartesian ego implied by the grammatical subject of the sentence:

> 70. I was nowhere. I was now only a shell, a house. The house of myself was empty. (88)

The signs of bondage and suffering in the United States only reflect the father's negativity. His anger sublimates itself into "a gorgeous purple flower" which, kissing the "soft dark hair" of Aurora, becomes "God's white flower." After this epiphanic transformation, Villa confesses: "I was no longer angry with my father."

Throughout the trilogy, the colonial patriarch is the signifier of mutation and of a ruptured identity: "I left myself with my mother because I had always loved her but I took with me the tree of my father, my new love, to the new land—America." By a paradoxical turn, the animus toward the father who separated him from Vi becomes impregnative; the son's imagination refuses any surrogate for the prohibited, tabooed woman in the homeland and mobilizes its own resources in exile. "Warming woman, warming woman," he sings as he suffers in an imagined cold dark room in New York City. It is not the women but the male friends who test his capacity of self-regeneration and catalyzes his resolve; thus, when the impoverished David, who first befriended him, leaves, Villa says: "I died in myself." The trauma of the Oedipal crisis resurrects the maternal body in order to reenact separation and mobilize the ejected psyche to utterance.

In "White Interlude," he affirms the value of pain because he is not a machine: "I am like a great mother wing nourishing loves and never deserting them." Nevertheless, he wonders: "Had I ever been lost to some one? . . . If I were lost to some one how was I to know? Would God whisper to me the beauteous name?—I am waiting for your whisper, God. I am waiting for your whisper." The young artist suffers a sequence of losses: Vi, David, then Wicki, Jack, Johnny. In the last section of the trilogy, "Walk at Night: A Farewell," the protagonist now envisions himself a child "born from the beating of God's wings against blue flame" so that in the pain of his love for Jack and Johnny he undergoes "a silence of death" while he clutches wild flowers lying on the "cool earth's breast" until he is possessed with an ecstatic vision of God's turbulent wings:

I am hungry for You, O God! (60)

Stronger beat God's white wings—stronger blew God's kind winds—stronger God ran His fingers through my hair. And then I knew: *No, no, Johnny!* It is enough to know the Bird is there . . . to know His Wings are beating for me. It is enough . . . it is enough! And then as I turned to Johnny the rain of music was everywhere, in the air and in me, and I was no longer unhappy and the thought of Jack and the walk I had made alone did not hurt any more. And I knew that when I lay on the ground, with the sky wet with stars above me, I was taking Jack out of me and giving him to the earth and to the sky, and white flowers in my hands were my gifts of forgiveness. (61)

This process of canceling the possessive and privatizing libidinal investment is repeated in "Song I Did Not Hear." But this time it is the "I" who substitutes for Jack and who questions Joe Lieberman's friendship: in effect, Lieberman becomes the surrogate for the father whose knowledge kills, and for Christ who redeems. But it was Jack whom the speaker loved the most and who hurt him the most. It is here, in this triadic situation, that Villa's characterization of Jack becomes emblematic of the larger relation between the marginal subject position (cognizant of implicit racial boundaries, the Jewish Lieberman reenacts the father's curse, so that Villa accuses him of Vi's being lost) and the dominant imperial master: "Jack's life was walled thickly and nobody could break into him. The house of his life was strong but it was empty of people. . . . Jack's life was an arena: all soil and no sky: only the unresponsiveness of earth without sky" (256). Villa is ambivalent: he entreats God to purge Jack from his life, but at the same time he wants him "always to be in my life . . . even if it hurts" (258). Is this not the typical dependency syndrome? In the end, despite his praise for God's wisdom whispering to man how difficult love is, and despite his vow that "I will be winged again!" we are left with the lingering doubt that sums up the atomized and alienated condition of life in a world preempted by commodities and money: "And would I have known why I could never enter Jack's life . . . even as Joe Lieberman could not enter mine?" (260–61).

Villa's vocation is unfolded here as rooted in the elision of erotic attachment and the transfer of libidinal cathexis to a new or remade self now assured of its capacity to give, and receive, pleasure. This yields an aesthetic model of self-reconciliation that is given a sharper and more overt formulation in "Young Writer in a New Country." In the homeland, the poet feels in harmony with his natural surroundings. Youth and love and nature blend together until the Law of the Father decrees exile and converts the "plenitude" of language, the full word, into what would become the ludic euphoria of signifiers, relations, perspectives:

> At night, in the new country, I would say to myself: "America, America." I lie in bed quietly, trying to think what it really means. A wind blows through the open window and makes me shiver. America is cold, for the moment that is my thought. In the homeland—never any snow. In the homeland, greenness. O green, O warmth, O bamboos unforgotten—
> What I want to say is that I could not make out anything. I lay in bed, wanting sleep to come, but all the time my lips kept saying: "America, America"—fondling the words, wanting to know what they meant. But nothing got solved in my mind. (300–301)

"America" then symbolizes the valorization of loss and deracination, destroying narcissistic fixation and triggering the "hazardous expenditure inherent in the signifying process" (Kristeva, *Revolution in Poetic Language* 233). Meanwhile, the poet understands that Vi has been changed by Time, that she also aspires for the freedom he enjoys, and that the father is not responsible for lying—it is the mutations occurring in time that eventually dissolve the antinomy between truth and lie. "But Time that hurts also knows how to heal." Abstract symbolic exchange has taken over; a general equivalent of value—Villa's "essence"—is discovered. This is also shown when Villa memorializes David, his first friend, as the figure of impoverished humanity, honored because he lacks the speed of industrial civilization.

Finally, the intertwined discourses of place, body, inheritance, and need culminate in the colonial subject being reborn in the desert of New Mexico (note the reference to the trilogy), where the Oedipal crisis is surmounted in a totalizing myth: the imagination as the ideal solution to the conflict of universal and particular, the polarities of solitary ego and the community of fathers and sons, the antagonisms of subjugated people and imperial lords, of phantasy and the circumscribed body. "America" is the name for the myth:

> Do you see America getting clearer in my mind? Do you see myself getting articulate, getting voice? Little by little calm comes to my mind. Little by little comes my white birth—a cool white birth in a new land.
>
> It was then that my stories were born—of the homeland and the new land. Some of you may have read them—they were cool, afire with coolth.
>
> I, father of tales. Fathering tales I became rooted to the new land. I became lover to the desert. Three tales had healed me.

Now Villa thematizes his role as prophet in the wilderness, passing through the sinful stations of Chicago, Milwaukee, and Washington until he reaches New York City, where he is detained (for ultimate salvaging?). He is thus suspended between those two origins, tired from "daytime movement and nighttime movement"—the circulation of the psyche mimicking "the leveling, equalizing, indifferent operations of the commodity form itself, which respects no unique identity, transgresses all frontiers, melts solidity into air, and profanes the holy" (Eagleton 36).

What Villa accomplishes from here on may be interpreted as a ritual performance to exorcise a transgression, to fulfill an unspoken promise or vow, to appease the furies of what he could have been had he not made the decision to embrace exile into the master's fortress, as it were, from where he could plot his return as the "anchored angel." Assuming the mantle of John the Baptist, the poet incarnates the Furies that would avenge the mother / land from patriarchal rape:

> What I am trying to say is that I left the desert, the desert of my white birth—and now I want to return to it. I want it to enfold me completely, I will surrender, I will never leave it.
>
> But in the homeland, *there* I was young. . . .
>
> Do you get what I am driving you to see? I am crying for the desert, for the peace of the *desert*.
>
> Will the native land forgive? Between your peace and the peace of a strange faraway desert—Between your two peaces—
>
> O tell softly, softly. Forgive softly. (303–4)

All this can perhaps be apprehended as a prologue to "inviting a tiger for a weekend."

We have moved a long way from the narrative continuity of "Mir-i-Nisa" and "Footnote to Youth," the quasi-parables about Rizal's doubles, and the montage of scenes in the trilogy. In "Young Writer in a New Country," a collage of open-ended confessional reverie fails to pass the test that Villa, in an article written in 1936, applies to the short story as a dramatic art: the requirement of a dramatic-unitive principle, organic completeness, finality ("The Contemporary Short Story" 287–88).

But no matter: life's problems must be lived through. And Villa's journey of self-integration seems to have terminated in New York City where, in 1938, the critic Federico Mangahas found Villa living in dire straits but quite obsessed with his being acknowledged as the only worthwhile painter of the Philippines on the basis of four paintings of a face that struck Mangahas enough for him to record the following impression:

> I notice that the face to which he had called my attention was really one and the same thing in every canvas whether of a woman or a child or a man—a highly simplified geometric-like gesture that struck me as a much stylized representation of the artist's face intensely idealised. It must be said to be the human face, perfected in the artist's own, liberated of all human handicaps. (iii)

Narcissus has displaced the Promethean anti-Christ of the "divine poems" as the rumbling of apocalypse is heard from a distance (General Franco's victory in Spain, and Hitler's expansion). It appears that, on the face of the relentless challenge of the fascist Minotaur, Villa has withdrawn to the contemplative study of his persona, his mask, which was the only alternative left after his departure from the desert of New

Mexico whose "windloved sands" stood in stark contrast to the opaque density of the anomic marketplace. The poet becomes enamored of and seduced by the hermaphroditic body of the artist, now an emblem of reconciliation, displacing the subject-object polarity of knowledge in the pleasure of repetition.

In the Beginning Was the Word

Sometime before Mangahas' visit, the leading progressive intellectual Salvador P. Lopez, who had vehemently condemned Villa's early poetry for its solipsistic illogic and obscurantism, conversed with the poet in his Greenwich Village apartment. Although they had opposing agendas and beliefs, Lopez and Villa were united as expatriates in the United States. They shared the collective fate of fellow Filipinos and other people of color (Puerto Ricans, Cubans, Hawaiians, and others). Because both also shared a passionate commitment to art, Lopez was able to elicit this evidence of a double process of awareness and deflection, embodied in Villa's self-conceptualization of his practice:

> It is not true that I am wholly lacking in the "social consciousness" of which you speak. There is no place in all the world where this consciousness is more ubiquitous and powerful than New York. I have been exposed to it continually, and my artist friends here have chided me for what they consider to be my indifference exactly as you have chided me for it back home. But why have I not written poems or stories of social significance? Because I am an artist, and in the kind of art I believe in and to which I have given my whole allegiance, there is no place for anything that has to do with social, economic or political problems. The whole function of the poet is to arouse pleasure in the beautiful. Propaganda does something else. (Lopez, *Literature and Society* 162)

Villa's credo is quite familiar, since Kant's *Critique of Judgment* gave philosophical legitimacy to the division of social labor (mental and manual) and the hierarchization of the faculties that have altered the production and consumption of knowledge since the Renaissance. (Kant, of course, simply elaborated in theory what already had happened since the enclosure movement, the Atlantic slave trade, and the rise of the factory system.) But Lopez would rather examine the texts. He remonstrated with his judgment that some poems which later appeared in *Have Come, Am Here* exhibit semantic thickness or topical worldliness, and they are in his judgment good poems. To this, Villa retorts:

> but not as good as the purely artistic ones I have written. These poems have been written with a purpose, and any purpose other than the creation or celebration of beauty is fatal to poetry as art. They are addressed to the intellect, and the truly beautiful poem should never be addressed to anything but the emotions.
>
> Poetry should approximate painting as closely as possible, and as in painting the greatest canvases are those which have magically caught one mood or aspect at least of beauty, so in poetry the greatest poems are those which, in memorable words, achieve an identical object. (Lopez, *Literature and Society* 163)

In the 1982 interview referenced earlier, Villa reaffirmed his conception of poetry as the expression of organic universals that "touch the essence of life," devoid of descriptive details—a leitmotif of Romantic aesthetics since Coleridge and Croce. Since poetry is designed to evoke pleasure in the manipulation of language, the paramount concern of the artist is the refinement of his craft. By craft is meant form and a repertoire of techniques, not content; craft is all: "If you have the art of writing, whatever you say becomes good. . . . Without technique you have nothing. . . . The select always demand craft. . . . Craft is control. . . . Art is craft before it is meaning. First, craft, then meaning" (Fernandez and Alegre 294, 307). Hewing closely to a technicist construal of Mallarmé's axiom that poems are made of words, not of ideas or meanings, Villa's artisanal mentality (nourished by an archaic ethos of honor) springs from the means/ends rationality of modern bureaucratic administration and pragmatic technocracy. His essentialism—his privileging of craft—is, however, enabled by what he denies: the silence or invisibility of what he deems "content" or raw material is already asserted in the categorization of what is present. (It is generally agreed, however, that forms and techniques have their own historical specificities. T. S. Eliot once said that a modern writer cannot use blank verse any more, since that conventional pattern implies more than itself, implies in fact a whole universe of meanings, beliefs, and practices.)

Villa's inveterate avant-gardism itself, his valorizing of means as ends (form becoming its own substance), can be conceived as symptomatic of the modernist anxiety to defy tradition and aim for the new and the strange.[3] Villa's penchant for performing violations and parodies of rules—for example, reversed consonance, the mechanical use of the comma and other punctuations (to surpass e.e. cummings), as well as playful parodies like "The Emperor's New Sonnet" and the postmodernist pastiche of his adaptations—all exemplify this anxiety:

> If you will do this you will break
> The little religions for my sake.

Like Mallarmé and other artists following Baudelaire's poetics of irrealization, Villa finds the representational logic of classic-expressive realism incapable of dealing with his dilemma: mimesis then gives way to allegory as its ubiquitous double, this duplicity then becoming the demarcating signature of the modern lyric (de Man 185).

We might grasp better Villa's will to "make it new," its subversive motivation, by invoking its theoretical genealogy. The principles concerned are *ostranenie,* aestheticism, and futurism. The Russian Formalist principle of *ostranenie* (defamiliarization or estrangement) may be said to underwrite the avant-garde program of endless experimentalism and innovation, of shocking novelty done for its own sake or to scandalize the philistine bourgeoisie. Aestheticism originally was introduced as a strategy to circumvent the leveling power of the commodity-form and the equalizing abstraction of money in nineteenth-century commercial society. Aestheticism generates both an anticipatory and utopian thrust as well as a nostalgic, reactionary drive. In futurism and its offshoot in high modernism, we find the principle of technical innovation and functionality upheld as the realization of the power of the "esemplastic" imagination to humanize nature and to unleash the potential of the spirit for self-fulfillment in secular life.

In the focus on artisanal finesse and the primacy of charismatic inspiration, we find a retreat to an idealized notion of the Renaissance artist (gifted with divine intuition) or to a handicraft stage of production (glorifying mastery of certain skills). Villa tends to fluctuate between these ideals, at one moment emphasizing the virtue of artisanal skill and at another moment exalting genius. Either way, they function for Villa as modes of sublating the predicament of the Third World artist who is forced to adopt the conqueror's language for ends that he believes transcend the contingencies of birthplace, memories, concrete cultural practices, and unrepeatable experiences of specific times and places.

In effect, Villa from the start conceived himself as the shaman-priest whose individual performance was also a collective ritual (Thomson). Villa's poetic "I" was actually the social ego or public self (as Christopher Caudwell cogently argued for poetry in general in *Illusion and Reality*). But, invariably, Villa misrecognized this voice as his singular, nonconforming subjectivity, his personal daemon, for reasons already discussed. Could this project of transcendence have spelled Villa's disappearance from the U.S. literary scene, a conjuncture dominated by the Cold War ethos of white supremacy?

In the period from the thirties to the fifties, Villa's range of poetic themes and styles was dictated and limited by the ruling standards of the New Criticism and its models: irony and paradox in the Metaphysical poets, Pound's dicta ("make it new"), Eliot's synthesis of encyclopedic references, Joyce's palimpsest for insomniacs, and others. Villa has acknowledged the influence of e.e. cummings, Hopkins, Emily Dickinson, Elinor Wylie, and to some extent Sitwell, Marianne Moore, Wallace Stevens, and Dylan Thomas.

Although Villa's "divine poems" echo Donne, Hopkins, and Dickinson, they deviate in their intent to reenact a stylized psychomachia or internalized fetish-making in order to abolish the hierarchy of institutional religion. The poems seek to reinstate the demiurgic role of the human mind in something like a versification of Feuerbach's humanist reversal of Christianity. Given the subaltern's tendency to mimic the colonizer's repertoire, Villa's antinomianism derives less from the axioms of paradox, ambiguity, and metaphysical conceit than from the project of simultaneously abrogating the hegemonic rule of the English language (symbolic of the colonial predicament) and reappropriating its resources to prove one's autonomy and integrity.

After the premeditated disruption of syntax and grammar as token of his will to assert mastery of the invader's language, Villa's "reversed consonance" and use of the comma deliberately to slow the flow of utterance aim to prove the resourcefulness of his craftsmanship and thus gain avant-garde credentials. Villa wanted to regulate the poem's "verbal density and time movement," a method analogous to Seurat's pointillism)—recall how he bewailed the civilization of speed in the fictive trilogy. In this, he is not scandalizing any critic who is aware that, following Jakobson, the poetic act imposes the paradigmatic axis upon the syntagmatic, the synchronic upon the diachronic process of utterance, and metaphor upon metonymy.

Villa's "Adaptations," however, are less improvisations than they are attempts to uncover "pure poetry" in the debased counters of commercial advertisements and mass media, and to mobilize them in the hope of recuperating the language's authentic voice from the heteroglossia

(Bakhtin) that underlies *Time, Newsweek, The New York Times,* and *Life Magazine.* This is Villa's version of postmodernist performance, of "eventual verse"; its ego-canceling objective is inspired by an anarchist/pacifist politics premised on Buddhist and Taoist cosmology (Mottram 615–16).

American culture, as one hypothetical formulation puts it, is distinguished by a refusal to predicate the present on the sacred authority of an originating covenant. Consequently, every individual act bears its own legitimacy, its "self-born purity of both intention and execution" (Berthoff 661). If this is so, then Villa's habit of inaugurating a series of beginnings puts him squarely in the lineage of Whitman, Pound, the Beat generation (Ginsberg, Frank O'Hara), and Charles Olson. Their creed annuls the ego or person, so that "events do the work" in reenacting poetic utterance (Mottram 612). Here, extreme subjectivism coalesces with mechanical objectivism; the positivist is reconciled with the pragmatist. But is this American exceptionalism (the nonproblematic formulation of which is questionable) consonant with the struggle of people of color (internal colonies of reservations, ghettoes, *barrios,* Chinatowns) whose histories have been interrupted and suppressed by Euro-Anglo violence?

Villa resists this identification with the Whitman/Pound filiation for the simple reason that the world he inhabits has not recognized the presence of his conflicted position, his historical agency, his participation as decolonizing agent. His "divine poems" insistently replay his challenge to "God" to validate his image in the "genius" of the poet-maker (*Selected Poems* 35–41; see in particular his Miltonic/Blakean homage to the rebellious Lucifer in poem #45). One may describe Villa's project as one of inventing the subject position of social agent that Euro-American artists already take as given, to "break the genetic economy" where the "I-Absolute" will spring "in a Time-land of decimals," as he says in "Parthenogenesis of Genius" (*Selected Poems* 114).

Nor can Villa afford to sacrifice whatever piece of territory he has claimed to a universalizing ethnopoetics championed by Jerome Rothenberg and others. This is a "symposium of the whole" that supposedly would include the excluded: "the female, the proletariat, the foreign; the animal and vegetative; the unconscious and the unknown; the criminal and the failure," the bush man, the child, the ape—but not, it seems, a Filipino writer named Jose Garcia Villa (quotes from Mottram 598). Such a new striving for an intercultural sociality in the program of

American postmodernist poetics is clearly attuned to what Fredric Jameson calls the cultural logic of late or multinational capitalism. This is a program symptomatic of what Warner Berthoff calls the distinguishing core theme of American literature: "the dream of an exemption from history, an escape from either continuity or consequence in the cycles of elected experience" (662).

If Villa really is trying to exempt himself from history, then he is as American as, say, Frank O'Hara. O'Hara, invoking Whitman, Hart Crane, and William Carlos Williams, seeks to abolish the "book" and install the poem "at last between two persons." But Villa's project is the opposite. His commitment is precisely to fashion "the book" in Mallarmé's sense, to erase the blank space into which he has been hurled by imperial violence (together with millions of other "unlettered" subjugated others). But, unlike O'Hara and Olson, Villa wants to interpose his signature between "the Wall of China," the past from which he has been disconnected, and "the tiger tree," "the betrayer tree" of modern industrial civilization. If print-capitalism spawns the imagined community of the modern nation-state, then the precursor for this is the metaphysics of "the book."

But in the nonsynchronous levels of a Third World formation, the book competes with other signifying systems, both residual and emergent: oral, cinematic, visual, and gestural/performance arts. Ironically, this book from the *bundok* has to be invented through the mediation of Hopkins' sprung rhythm, the mythological machinery of Christianity where Christ is secularized into a "six-turbined deadlock prince," an Orientalist geography ("Sanskrit of love," "Arabian . . . love flecked eye") and the discoveries of experimental science ("cobalts,love," "Genesis',phosphor"). Using the narrative of the incarnation and eroticizing the passion of Christ as the poet's, "The Anchored Angel" exalts the poet as bearing witness to the hermaphroditic angelic liaison, perhaps the maternal agency—"Genesis',unfissured,spy"—between the spirit ("Verb-verb") and "Christ's,gentle,egg: His,terrific,sperm."

Villa's poem, on the surface, appears remote from the immediate problems of the impoverished colonial artist trying to survive in the heartland of the imperial power, in "the belly of the beast" (as Jose Marti puts it). Yet, in offering a substitute sense of wholeness, ecstasy, and fulfillment realized in the pastiche of mimicry and verbal mockplay, he demarcates a space for the subject of enunciation not just to be represented but to speak and challenge the laws of hegemonic representation. In the transposition of Christian myth to an allegory of the poet's empowerment ("So birthright lanced I hurl my bloodbeat Light"), the signifiers seem to liberate themselves from the signified.

Not the least token of this phantasy of empowerment is the dislocation of the coherence of the syntagmatic chain (via sprung rhythm, parataxis, obscure allusions, distancing idiom, four-stress popular meter) that characterizes Villa's practice. This is a technique that the poststructuralist critic Antony Easthope regards as the chief modernist strategy for abolishing (not just decentering) the transcendental ego, foregrounding the materiality of the signifier as well as the sociohistoric determinants of the writing process, and opening up a subject-position for a community of speakers / readers, the matrix of enunciation and communicative action. In this way, the problematic of aestheticism—the privileging of the self-identical verbal icon—self-destructs in the endless substitutions along the paradigmatic axis so that closure is forfeited. The "book" is a script open to oppositional readings and utopian articulations. A poetics of resistance born from the "disappeared" spirit begins to materialize at this stage of our initiation.

The Ascension of Doveglion

Now we are ready to encounter the strategically "essential" Villa. I propose that Villa's poems be understood as allegorical constructions of a subject-position for the decolonizing artist, a subject responsible for enunciation and not just a recipient of the Establishment's address, commands, and injunctions. In so proposing, I use as a rationale the insights of Theodor Adorno in his provocative essay, "Lyric Poetry and Society." Adorno counters the common-sense notion that lyric poetry is "the untouched virgin word . . . free of the impositions of the everyday world, of usefulness, of the dumb drive for self-preservation." This demand, Adorno writes,

> is in itself social in nature. It implies a protest against a social condition which every individual experiences as hostile, distant, cold, and oppressive; and this social condition impresses itself on the poetic form in a negative way: the more heavily social conditions weigh, the more unrelentingly the poem resists, refusing to give in to any heteronomy, and constituting itself purely according to its own particular laws. Its detachment from naked existence becomes the measure of the world's falsity and meanness. Protesting against these conditions, the poem proclaims the

dream of a world in which things would be different. The idiosyncrasy of poetic thought, opposing the overpowering force of material things, is a form of reaction against the reification of the world, against the rule of the wares of commerce over people which has been spreading since the beginning of the modern era—which, since the Industrial Revolution, has established itself as the ruling force in life. Even Rilke's 'cult of things' [recall Williams' slogan of 'back to the thing itself!' which inspired Olson and a whole generation of American poets; Rilke is one of Villa's favorite poets] belongs to this form of idiosyncracy, as an attempt to bring the alien objects into subjectively pure expression and dissolve them there—to give their alienness metaphysical credit. *The aesthetic weakness of this cult of things, the cryptic gesture, the mixing of religion and decorative handicraft, betrays at once the genuine power of reification that can no longer be painted over with a lyric aura, and can no longer be comprehended.* (58–59)

I have italicized the last sentence as a sharp exposé of Villa's glorification of technique or craft for its own sake—a repression of the "political unconscious" and its agenda of refusal. How is the lyric poem to be construed as a critique and subversion of modern society, in the midst of which reification inflicts its toll the more it is denied or ignored, where aestheticizing individualism (the fetishism of objects and artifacts) is the revealing index of its subordination to its Other? Adorno defines the lyric form in general:

> What we mean by lyric ... has within it, in its 'purest' form, the quality of a break or rupture. The subjective being that makes itself heard in lyric poetry is one which defines and expresses itself as something opposed to the collective and the realm of objectivity. While its expressive gesture is directed toward, it is not intimately at one with nature. It has, so to speak, lost nature and seeks to recreate it through personification and through descent into the subjective being itself. Only after a transformation into human form can nature regain anew that which man's rule over her has taken away. Even lyrical creations which are untouched by conventional, material existence, by the crude world of material objects, owe their high worth to the power the subjective being within them has, in overcoming its alienation, to evoke an image of the natural world. Their pure subjectivity, apparently flawless, without breaks and full of harmony, actually witnesses to the opposite, to a suffering caused by existence foreign to the subject, as much as it shows the subject's love toward that existence. (59)

There is no doubt that Villa's poems no longer can evoke that "image of the natural world" still discernible in the early poems. In fact, the theme of dispossession (as in the first poem quoted earlier), together with the poet's struggle to overcome the loss, to challenge fate, and to assert his control by means of thaumaturgic speech, is what pervades the majority of his poems. What is evoked is the scenario of discovery of creative power, together with the force that stifles it, intimated in "The Anchored Angel," the realization of autonomy. What is precipitated in the texts are historical forces that oppose alienation and reification—both the reality-effect and domination-effect are staged and given utterance.

By virtue of its own subjectivity, Adorno argues, lyric poetry as a genre possesses this objective content: "it has this objectivity only if its withdrawal into itself and away from the social surface is motivated by social forces over and beyond the head of its author" (62). One social force is linguistic form, which confirms the proposition that individual and society, subject and object, are comprehended only in the process of their dialectical interaction. One can apply this observation to the speaker/persona of Villa's poems: "the subject negates both his naked, isolated opposition to society as well as his mere functioning within rationally organized society" (63). The silences and gaps contoured by the problematic and disclosed by the reader's deciphering intuition can be apprehended in the imagery, diction, rhythm, and design of the poems. By this linkage of presence and absence, Villa's poems can be grasped as "the subjective expression of a social antagonism," the elements of which I sketched earlier.[4]

Finally, I cite an anecdotal crux, a dialogic counterpoint to the biographical statement that was my point of departure for this meditation on the case of a "disappeared" Third World artist.[5] In his 1982 interview, Villa was asked whether it is true that American critics consider him an American poet. He replied: not true, as witnessed by his being denied the Bollingen Prize in 1949 because he was not an American citizen; instead Wallace Stevens won the prize. The epithet "American" is reduced to its juridical/legal signification. Another injury Villa resents: unlike Conrad Aiken, W. H. Auden and Selden Rodman, Oscar Williams refused to include Villa in his anthology because Villa was not, legally speaking, an American. When asked whether Villa considers himself a Filipino—of all metaphysical questions!—Villa gives an over-determined response that epitomizes the ethico-symbolic instability of the Filipino diaspora in the United States: "Yes, I am a Filipino, but an American resident" (308).[6] (Incidentally, in this interview, Villa also mentioned his preference for two philosophers celebrated in the existentialist shrine: Nicholas Berdyaev and Friedrich Nietzsche.)

In the *fin de siècle* postmodern era, the era of a late-capitalist "New

World Order," Villa remains disappeared partly by choice and partly by the asymmetrical global picture in which the Philippines (which identifies him as its "National Artist") remains a neocolonial dependency of the United States, Japan, and the consortium of interests represented by the International Monetary Fund/World Bank. Why he chooses to do so may be illuminated by an artifact/manifesto entitled ",,A Composition,," published in 1953 but probably written in the time when the Hukbalahap uprising in the Philippines was being suppressed by the CIA-backed government of Ramon Magsaysay and when the carnage of the war in Korea—the gateway to Vietnam—was subtly and painstakingly marking the demise of *pax Americana.* I present this exhibit (virtually inaccessible to the general public) to counterbalance the suasive resonance of the early autobiographical document.

> My name is Jose, my name is Villa.
> I was born on the island of Manila, in the city of Luzon.
> My true name is Doveglion.
> My business is ascension.
>
>   I was born on the island of Manila, in the city of Luzon. My country is the Country of Doveglion.
>   The Country of Doveglion is a strange country: Boundaries it has none— and yet boundaries it has:
>   Subhumans cannot live there.
>   Only the *Earth Angels,* the true humans, may live there. These perceive my rigors, my perils and fervors, my hazards and possibles, my graces and invincibles, and claim my citizenship: them I greet.

One immediately discerns in this opening section the thematic drive to offend commensensical taste and mock quotidian appearances. It is a provocative response to the immigration officer, the police, the tax collector, the interdictions of the law, performed through a series of antitheses and inversions and delivered in a confessional rhythm of repetition with incremental variation. The bardic tone can be construed as both parodic and pontifical, at once naive and disingenuous. By scrambling literal geography and codes of stereotyping, the speaker achieves geopolitical if not moral "high ground": he seeks to mimic here the colonial displacement of the native whose aspiration for national independence has been suppressed by diplomatic trickery and violence. To compensate for such a loss, the poet proclaims his demiurgic gift; words create and demarcate a country from what is now surveilled and disciplined terrain. In the beginning was speech, then habitat, then flora and fauna. Amalgamating precolonial and colonial times, the poet's fusion of the emblematic figures of dove, eagle, and lion in his pseudonym "Doveglion" (alluding to both classical mythology and Christian iconography) betokens the incarnational thaumaturgy of speech, its integrative and foundational power. Fusion implies separation; contraries beget each other; consequently, boundaries are nullified. We subsist in the autonomous realm of signifiers that produce meaning by difference and opposition—an insight derived not from Saussure but from the "savage war" between Filipino revolutionaries and U.S. invaders.

Walter Benjamin once noted that modernist art originated from "the disintegration of the aura [of traditional art] in the experience of shock" induced by urban crowds, with the chaotic fragmentation and ephemerality of the metropolis leading to a loss of the capacity for meaningful experience (*Illuminations* 194; compare Williams, *Politics of Modernism*). For Villa and his contemporaries, the shock-effect came from the violence of U.S. aggression and the extinguishing of a nascent interpretive community. Their response to that crisis assumed the form of a reactionary repudiation of the commercial ethos and an aristocratic pride in the ability to terrorize the American *compadres* of the native comprador and bureaucratic elite. Denied citizenship, they sought recognition from the iconoclastic rebels of the Lost Generation, from the stigmatized avant-garde and its international style. Deprived of an independent homeland, they ("the voyager, ransomer and parablist I") traversed national borders like the exiled or deported *Propagandistas* of the *fin de siècle* in search of new sensoriums to legitimize their transgressive hopes and desires.

What is striking in the second section is its syntax of affirmation and negation. Its rhetoric captures the ambivalence of the middle stratum caught between the plebeian masses and the feudal oligarchy. This register-shift may also be glossed as a mimesis of the paradox epitomized by the colonizer William Howard Taft proclaiming "Philippines for Filipinos." Appearances become truly deceptive. In any event, the subjugated natives are compelled to negotiate their terms of survival and compromise. Space (the conquered archipelago) modulates into a place that is imagined—not the "imagined community" of recent postcolonial scholarship but a hypothetical or invented field of discourse inhabited by androgynous figures: Earth Angels. The inspiration here may be William Blake or, more plausibly, the canonization of secular heroes like Rizal and Bonifacio by millenarian movements in the rural areas. In any case, the now fashionable "politics of recognition" (induced by postmodern reflections on the libertarian ideals of Rousseau, Hegel, and the European Enlightenment) stages its bizarre twist: the substance of the "I" is confirmed and validated by his own creation, the "true humans" who claim his citizenship and who appreciate his authentic labors, qualities, pathos, potentiality, and so on. There is a semblance of dialogue, but it is only the mirage of a dramatized soliloquy. And so, while the colonized subaltern (recall that the archipelago was given commonwealth status in 1935 after Villa had already settled in New Mexico, preparing his passage to New York City) existed in a limbo of indeterminacy, neither citizen nor alien, Villa resolves that dilemma here by the artifice of the strange "Country of Doveglion."

The next sections elaborate the configuration of this locality with its own symptomatic landmarks. Following the inaugural trope of inversion, we find here a translation of place into "movement," the mutation of abandonment into allegiance. God's rebellious angels find refuge in Doveglion's territory (the number of angels represents the poet's age), while the four quarters of the planet lose their fixity and become reversible. This in turn prefigures the approaching domination of money, exchange value, the cash nexus in colonial life. Doveglion then names the scenario of revolt against imperial authority and the newly discovered haven of dissidents. Space is transfigured by time. Instead of stasis, motion or process defines Doveglion's domain: "A country that *moves to follow Fire!*" Its authentic ontology inheres in this pursuit. The poet condemns other countries as "husk," mired in entrepreneurial machinations and vulgar politics, in racist exclusions and class exploitation. This precept of "learning to move" can be read as Villa's version of the slogan of Western modernism: "Make it new."

This text thus reveals itself as an allegory of naming and inhabiting, of the modality of acquiring a style of citizenship by claiming a vocation. Vocation equals identity. The text then syncopates self and community through the mediation of metaphor and the play of tropes. In *Illusion and Reality*, the great Marxist critic Christopher Caudwell observes that a lyric poem is actually not a cry of the solitary psyche but the "organized emotion" of a collectivity, "feelings controlled by the social ego" (220). Society, in particular its system of signs or signifying practice, is the objective medium through which artist and audience communicate; the signifying artifice transforms the poet's private experience into a socially shared one (Caudwell, *Romance and Realism* 35). The function of poetic expression then is distinctively productive, if not practical: the projection of a desired "phantastic object" that becomes more real or realizable as the poem is enacted or performed by readers and listeners. Such cultural practice coincides with its cognitive and pedagogical function: instructing oneself and others by mapping the texture and contours of the real, its limits and possibilities.

Another way of formulating the principle of transformative criticism that I am illustrating here is to categorize a poem as a social act. From this perspective, the poet socializes his personal experience through imagery and rhythms that enact the dynamic process of collective labor, inscribing his fantasies in the phenomenal world and transforming reality through such utopian extrapolations (Thomson, *Marxism and Poetry* 66; *Human Essence* 73). In this context, Villa's apostrophe to the "I," coeval here with the esemplastic imagination (praised by Coleridge and the German romantic philosophers, with an antecedent in the Platonic *daimon*), is really a trope for the missing society or community from which aesthetic practice derives its import and significance. What is lacking or absent then signals closure. Villa strives to unite the "I's direct temporal flower" with art's "permanent flower"; he envisions conjoining the temporal and the permanent not in a worldly "house"—he has already rejected the "husk"—but in the ambiguous fold of "death": "Conjugator death will illuminate and bloom it, as corsair death will end it." Uncannily anticipating death, the site of pleasure and fulfillment, the imagination still has the last word.

Despite the slippage of signifiers and the aporias that provide counterpoint in every sentence, the animating passion of this testimonial prose poem is unequivocal: "The soul is my grand dominion, my grand possession." From a historical-materialist viewpoint, this soul conceived by poetry cannot be individual, since the poetic act de-individualizes the private, ego-centered experience by passing it through the linguistic catalyst. Poetic expression synthesizes the heterogeneous materials of feelings, thoughts, intuitions, hopes, and other affects to reveal the common interests of otherwise disparate and antagonistic individuals. It constructs the ground of solidarity that binds individuals who would otherwise float like atoms or fragments in a market-oriented competitive milieu. This, I submit, is the political economy of form that frames Villa's metaphysics.

At first glance, the poet's grandiloquent focus on the "I" may suggest his will to apotheosize the bourgeois illusion of individual freedom, the Cartesian self-identical consciousness characteristic of capitalism since the time of Baudelaire and Flaubert. This suggestion provides the alibi for the recurrent accusation that Villa is a narcissist akin to the surrealists who regard the self as a "terrible drug" taken in solitude (Benjamin, *Reflections* 190). But this is now a banal reflex reaction. In this text, the charge of solipsist withdrawal is disposed by a more nuanced and responsible reading. Villa in fact painstakingly separates his "I of Identity, the Eye of Eternity" from the conceited, vainglorious, rhetorical "I" of the petty-bourgeois sensibility. With somewhat elitist aplomb, he draws the boundary—and here Doveglion's country enacts its immigration law, its customs regulation, its naturalization rule—between the speculative "I" of the imagination and the empirical "I" of private property and profit making. I consider the following passage the synapse or semantic crux of this composition, the central preoccupation of writing as performance of naming oneself and renouncing alien tutelage:

> The I of Identity, the eye of Eternity, is the *ore*-I, the fundamentalizer I. The I that cannot discontinue itself: the truefarer amazer I. The voyager, ransomer and parablist I: the I that accosts and marauds eternity—the covenantal I. This is the ,,I,, I write about, the true and classic I, the I of the Upward Gravity.

The last phrase, "Upward Gravity," distills the antinomic and ludic pathos of Villa's career, its ultimately counterhegemonic telos. Since this radicalizing "I" is associated with the destructive / creative power of the imagination, the source of conceptual and figurative discriminations between, say, core and husk or light and darkness (offering the possibilities of meaning through the binary *combinatoire*), what we are really witnessing here is the vast amorphous field of energies that Emile Durkheim designated as the source of collective representations: society, the matrix of distinctions and demarcations (sacred / profane). What Villa's "I" in effect adumbrates and signifies is the possibility of socius, the organic community, absent in the colonial possession of the United States and submerged in the vernacular culture and everyday practices of the peasantry and plebeian masses. Any act of reclamation or recovery requires a turning upside down of the colonial, tributary system together with its patronage apparatuses that produce and reproduce the subordination of the subjugated populace, their ironically "civilized" dehumanization.

It is clear then that beyond the themes of nominating self and others, of locating habitats, and of establishing allegiances and directions, the speaking subject in this text exploits both literal and symbolic levels of reference. In effect, Villa (more precisely his persona or speaking surrogate) is concerned more with the condition of possibility of fashioning poetic utterance through the vehicle of a collective struggle for the right to speak, for participatory democracy. This project of gaining status as speaking subject is at once social and personal. "Ascension," the spatial trajectory that overcomes political and social barriers with "Upward Gravity," is to be translated as spiritual development, inward progress (according to the author's footnote). Conversely, "Earth Angels" challenge the traditional motif of psychic growth by first valorizing perception (evoked by visual images, the play on "eye" and "I") and then undercutting it by privileging the genius of poetic utterance: "Conjugator death will illuminate and bloom it, as corsair death will end it." What we confront here is the spectacle or the self-narrating *gestus* (in Brecht's parlance) in which Villa compensates for the absence of homeland and sympathetic audience: the ritual of celebrating the poet's skill, faculty, intellect as self-sufficient and self-contained. In this ritual that we share with the poet lies the "political unconscious" of this *l'art pour l'art* exercise designed to resist commodity fetishism and the anonymous market (Fischer), an act of resistance still distinguishable from Mallarmé's retreat into utter uselessness and the nihilism of fascist art.

Villa concludes with the return to the obsession with identity linked with vocation. He refuses the limitation of realistic biography, since "All my Pure shall beggar and defy biography." Is this a return to essentialism, to idealist mystification? Language, for Villa, seems so impoverished that the reiteration of "flower," "eternity," and other mantra-like words suffices to cover the blankness of the sheet of paper. The word "Pure" has no exact denotation. The gap between "ambition" and "eternity" is too wide; chance or necessity takes over to determine whether the "italic flower" will appear or not. What does it mean for the speaker to declare: "The main thing always is that I *lived* / The First Eternity"? In retrospect, the last three lines indicate that this "First Eternity" involves the "temporal flower," the performance of living as experienced and memorialized by the poet who has baptized himself "Doveglion." The name and virtues of the creative intellect conflated in Doveglion function as the author of the subject bereft of a nation-state, "Jose Garcia Villa," who is no longer confined to any island or city worth locating in the imperial map.

Overall, the structure of this testimony can be grasped as a parodic and seriocomic rehearsal of the usual response to a demand for passport or identification papers from a "third world" traveller (now personified as "Overseas Contract Workers," diasporic alter egos) by Western border patrols. It encompasses the quest for the opportunity/capacity for naming oneself, locating one's presence in a symbolic environment, and entitling oneself with a vocation. The poet's "ascension" is strictly secular or "terrestrial" (to use Cesar Vallejo's term [13]), even though the vocabulary or idiom deployed recalls an archaic past, and even though Doveglion's country, with its kaleidoscopic properties of "hazards and possibles," occupies an uncharted realm between a fabled heaven and the subhuman region. The artist's vocation concerns movement—from refusal and desertion to finding true allegiance, from abandoning a "husk country" to following "Fire." It concerns defining an "I" that subsumes opposites, contraries, tensions between the temporal and the eternal, between the lone "voyager" and the "covenantal I," in the reconciling trope of "the I of the Upward Gravity." Art and eternity become synonymous in this discourse of configuring the shape and temper of the poetic vocation, an intertextual topos where the right of the speaking subject (I/We) to actualize self-determination materializes.

My agenda here is to challenge the New Critical hermeneutic of reifying Villa's texts as "verbal icons" or "autotelic" museum pieces, a strategy of seeking to exorcise even the minuscule traces of an oppositional impulse and weaker pulses of emancipatory motivation. What I have attempted here is to sketch the groundwork, necessarily heuristic and exploratory, for interpreting and evaluating Villa's *oeuvre* as a representation of the public sphere of the cultural encounter between the Philippines and the United States, an instance of the conflicted transactions between periphery and core in the capitalist world system. Whether one agrees with Villa's public statements about art, politics, and other topics is less important. In my view, the vital and substantive question we need to grapple with is whether Villa, to paraphrase Antonio Gramsci (112), has been able to externalize, objectify, and historicize his phantasms. Viewed as articulations of the complex ethico-political forces of his time, Villa's poems reveal both their expressive and mimetic dimensions, their dialogistic (in Bakhtin's sense) and documentary resonance implied by the interrogations that they enact, such as: Who is the speaking subject? Where is s/he coming from? To whom is the utterance addressed? What is the intent and purpose of such utterance? And what are the historical-ideological relations that constitute the site and conditions of the utterance?

If "biography" is indeed annulled, can we doubt that this is Villa speaking/writing? We confront a spectacle of appearance and disappearance, an uncanny happening in which the protean emblems of dove-eagle-lion (Doveglion) merge and separate in the production of poetic discourse ascribed to a single name: Jose Garcia Villa.

What is at stake depends on what we have salvaged here: a myth of self-identity? a testimony of ethnogenesis? the voice of national liberation willing its transcendence from imperial exchange-value founded on logocentric, instrumental reason? A mimicry of the Enlightenment ideal of humanist emancipation, as indicated by the transposition of "ascension" to "man's inner development"? The deconstruction of the atomized, self-acquisitive, monadic ego of business society? Is it Lyotard's *differend* (Villa's "Earth Angels") exploding both the imperatives of universality and identity? Finally, is this the essentializing speech of the unnameable "disappeared," archetype of the exile and nomadic stranger in modernist writing? Or is it the unrepresentable trace of Desire well-nigh beyond the reach of language, of critical theory, of the norms of postmodern civility and academic liberal exchange under the aegis of which I, we, presume to speak?

7

Allegories of the Nation in the Postmodern World

The spirit, strength, and intelligence of the people are miraculous. But truth should be their beacon and guide at all times. This awakening to truth will lead to complete liberation. . . . It is possible that the artist may surrender and be mute in order to survive, but that spells surely the death of his art. . . . Like Antaeus in mythology who fought Hercules, the artist must needs stand always on solid earth, his feet on the soil, because from the heat and power of the soil spring the life and strength of his body.
—*Amado V. Hernandez, 1964*

On the threshold of a new millennium, we gaze at the crossroad before us, at once familiar and strange, beckoning with hope and nostalgia. The post–Cold War era we inhabit today was inaugurated by the United Nation's bombing of Iraq for occupying the territory of another nation-state (Kuwait). Thus, we may be as far removed from the Enlightenment vision of a unitary world culture (expressed, for example, in Goethe's notion of a *Weltliteratur*) as we were in the years when this century opened, with the Boer War in South Africa, the Boxer Rebellion against foreign incursions in China, and the Spanish-American War. Our postmodern conjuncture is, in fact, distinguished by ethnic particularisms and their protean assemblages; by the valorization of the aleatory, contingent, fragmentary, and heterogeneous.

Indeed, the ideal of internationalism presupposes a plurality of nation-states asymmetrically ranked in a conflict-ridden global market of human labor and natural resources. It thrives on national differences, since "world interdependence has diffused balance of power considerations and transformed them into a balance of terror" (Smith, *Theories of Nationalism* 196). War among capitalists breeds nations as "communities of fate" (Bauer). As long as the ethnic archive persists amid the homogenizing secular ideals of modernization and liberal individualism that inform the policies of most states—an order grounded on exchange-value and the logic of capital accumulation—nationalism will remain a major, if not decisive, force shaping the economic, political, and ideological contours of the late-capitalist world system.

Nationalism as a global phenomenon is thus a historically determinate process of group-identity formation with multi-accented manifestations and ramifications. In the context of a resurgent Filipino nationalism, we might review the key themes of the preceding chapters, in particular, how a "minor" writing (as defined by Deleuze and Guattari, *Kafka*) becomes a nomad "walking a tightrope," how literature as "desiring-machine" introduces dysfunction in the system and destroys the normal circuits of material and symbolic production.

Within the world system of hierarchical nation-states, one finds a pattern of ranking that openly discriminates among the various national literatures. Born from the violence of colonial occupation, Filipino writing in English has never been recognized by American arbiters of taste, upholding canonical standards. The anomalous and nonexistent position of Filipino writing in English in U.S. literary history explodes the myth of cultural pluralism and questions the claim of transhistorical universality attached to its cultural icons and myths. "Difference" in the asymmetrical marketplace, after all, is what constitutes the dominant mode of U.S. self-identification. Its reifying power seems infinite, until it encounters the refusal of the outcast, the pariah, the "lazy native," the "terrorist," "illegal aliens," and the communist—all enemies of the "American Way of Life."

To democratize the liberal marketplace as the first stage in reordering priorities, we need to problematize the received consensus of American cultural history, just as we need to criticize and understand the position of reactionary nativism and the chauvinism of the "international style." Is there room for the much-touted syncreticity and hybridity of post-colonial writing within Western disciplinary regimes of "high" critical theorizing?

After surveying the texts of U.S. critics who judge Filipino writers, one would have to argue that Filipino writers (excluded also from the attention of Commonwealth postcolonial scholarship) can offer a challenge to canonical U.S. criticism. The narrative telos of this axiology is predicated on the exclusion of its subaltern "Others," on which it depends for recognition and self-validation. As part of the excluded "others," Filipino writers implicitly problematize the possibility, in late capitalism, of composing an official U.S. "national" literary history in a space constituted by "polymorphously perverse" nationalities, ethnic/racial communities, and other internal colonies within the nation-state territory.

In the context of transnational literatures written in English, one can ask: can there be a reciprocal and mutually creative dialogue between the neocolonized Filipino imagination and the "power/knowledge" machine of the hegemonic geopolitical bloc? Is it possible to expect a rupture from this bloc and a challenge from the hypothesized subjugated subject? To clear the ground for a response, I would like to present a résumé of what the previous chapters have elaborated in some detail and in the process highlight the pivotal stages in the unfolding of the complex "dialectics of Philippines-U.S. literary relations."

Narrative of Surveillance and Misrecognition

When the United States occupied the Philippines by military force in 1898, a Filipino nation had already been germinating in over two hundred revolts against Spanish colonialism. Filipino intellectuals of the Propaganda Movement (1872–96) had already implanted the Enlightenment principles of rationality, civic humanism, and autonomy (sovereignty of the masses of peasants and workers) in the program of the revolutionary forces of the *Katipunan* (the association that spearheaded the 1896 insurrection against Spain) and the first Philippine Republic.

At the outset, the propagandists—Jose Rizal, Marcelo H. Del Pilar, Graciano Lopez Jaena, and others—used the Spanish language to appeal to an enlightened local and European audience in demanding reforms. With the aim of conscientization, Rizal's novels, *Noli Me Tangere* (1887) and *El Filibusterismo* (1891), incorporated all the resources of irony, satire, heteroglossia (inspired by Cervantes and Rabelais), and the conventions of European realism to criticize the abuses of the Church and arouse the spirit of self-reliance and sense of dignity in the subjugated natives. For his subversive and heretical imagination, Rizal was executed—a sacrifice which serves as the foundational event for all Filipino writing.

Although a whole generation of insurrectionist writers (the most distinguished being Claro Recto) created a "minor" literature in Spanish, only Rizal registered in the minds of liberal Spaniards like Miguel de Unamuno, a precursor of modern existentialism. In effect, Hispanization failed. In 1985, when I visited Havana, Cuba, I found reprints of Rizal's two novels widely disseminated and avidly read—a cross-cultural recuperation, it seems, of a popular counter-memory shared by two peoples inhabiting two distant continents but victimized by the same Western hubris.

A retrospective glance is helpful here. Just as a Filipino nation was being born, entangled in the toils of demotic vernacular speech, U.S. imperial arrogance intervened. Its conquest of hegemony or consensual rule was literally accomplished through the deployment of English as the official medium of business, schooling, and government. This pedagogical strategy was designed to cultivate an intelligentsia, a middle strata divorced from its roots in the plebeian masses, who would service the ideological apparatus of Anglo-Saxon supremacy. Americanization was mediated through English, sanctioned as the language of prestige and aspiration.

Meanwhile, the vernacular writers (the true organic intellectuals of an emergent *populus*), who voiced the majority will for national sovereignty against U.S. "Manifest Destiny," sustained the libertarian Jacobin heritage of the Propagandists. Witness to this were Lope K. Santos, author of the first "social realist"—more precisely, anarcho-syndicalist—novel *Banaag at Sikat* (1906), and Isabelo de los Reyes, founder of the first labor union and of the Philippine Independent Church. Both were influenced deeply by Victor Hugo, Proudhon, Bakunin, and the socialist movement inspired by Marx and Engels. As I argued in the previous chapters, and in *Reading the West/Writing the East*, "vernacular discourse articulated a process of dissolving the interiority of the coherent, unitary subject" (91). This was accomplished in texts that dramatized the breakdown of taboos or territorializing codes and the release of Desire in the sociolibidinal economy of violence and delirium. Eventually, the subject of discipline empowered itself as the subject of Desire in the locus of its anarchic utterance.

While U.S. imperial power, in general, preserved the tributary order via the institutionalization of patronage in all levels of society, the use of English by apprentice-writers fostered individualism through the modality of aesthetic, sacramentalizing vanguardism. Individual liberation displaced the dream of national sovereignty. The overt but subterranean influence of the "Lost Generation" (Anderson, Hemingway, Stein) on Villa and his contemporaries shaped the content and direction of Philippine writing in English from the twenties to the sixties. Internationalism in this case took the form of imitation of U.S. styles of personal revolt against alienation in a compradorized, bureaucratic society. While Villa enacted the role of the aborigine as Prometheus and achieved a measure of recognition by the U.S. New Criticism in the fifties, he has never been included in the mainstream cultural canon (Lopez, "Literature and Society" 11). In encyclopedias and other reference books, Villa has always been identified as a "Filipino" writer. Interred in the pantheon of formalist mannerism, his ethnic signature survives only in his name.

A breakthrough occurred in the thirties. It was the global crisis of capitalism and the intense peasant dissidence throughout the islands that impelled Salvador P. Lopez, Teodoro Agoncillo, and others to mount a challenge to U.S. hegemonic authority and the threat of oligarchic fascism by establishing the left-oriented Philippine Writers League (1939–41). For them, "nation" signified the working people, the producers of social wealth, whose alignment with the antifascist insurgency in Europe and Asia invested with apocalyptic *Jetztzeit* (Walter Benjamin's term) the solidarity of all the victims of capital in every nation. For the first time, the insurrectionary legacy of 1896 was rediscovered, vindicated, and renewed.

We find this stance of nationalist internationalism vibrant in the fiction of Manuel Arguilla and Arturo Rotor, in the novels of Juan C. Laya, in the essays of Jose Lansang, Salvador P. Lopez, Angel Baking, Renato Constantino, and in the massive testimonies of Bulosan. For the first time, writers in English united with the vernacular artists (among others, Jose Corazon de Jesus, Faustino Aguilar, and Amado V. Hernandez) to affirm the dialectical interaction between cultural praxis and radical mobilization, even though the protest against continuing U.S. domination had to be sublimated into the worldwide united front against fascism.

One instructive conjuncture may be adduced here to illustrate the dialectic of metropolis and periphery that informs the complex, oscillating alignment of political and ideological forces in the former colony. When Arturo Rotor wrote his essay "Our Literary Heritage" in 1940 to exhort his fellow writers to respond to the needs of the working masses, he invoked as models of committed intellectuals the names of Ralph Waldo Emerson, when he publicly combatted slavery, and Thomas Mann, when he admonished artists "to seek [Right, Good, and Truth not only in art but also] in the politico-social sphere as well, and establish a relation between his thought and the political will of his time" (21). Rotor ended his nationalist (and by the same token, inter-nationalist) manifesto vindicating literature's *raison d'être* by quoting Maxim

Gorki: "[literature] must at last embark upon its epic role, the role of an inner force which firmly welds people in the knowledge of the community of their suffering and desires, the awareness of the unity of their striving for a beautiful free life" (23). In this way, Filipino vernacular allegory may be said to harmonize its pitch and rhythm with others from North and South (now replacing East and West), speaking tongues whose intelligibility is guaranteed by our sharing common planetary needs, the political unconscious of all art.

The theory of Filipino national allegory emanates from within the problematic of the struggle for self-determination, in the hiatus between what is desired and what is exigent. It is conceived in the synergism between the project of liberating the homeland (from Japanese invaders) and the defense of popular democracy everywhere. It thus sublates bourgeois chauvinism in the heuristic trope of the national democratic revolution.

The chief practitioner of this allegorizing mode is Carlos Bulosan, a worker-exile in the United States, whose exemplary life and work I discussed in Chapter 5. His now-classic ethnobiography, *America Is in the Heart*, synthesized the indigenous tradition of antifeudal revolt in the Philippines with the multiracial workers' uprising against racist exploitation on the U.S. West Coast and Hawaii. Bulosan's art expressed his partisanship for popular/radical democracy. It demonstrated his faith in the intelligence of people of color—Reason's cunning, in the old adage—rooted in cooperative labor. His sympathy with Republican Spain besieged by fascism coincided with his union organizing against white supremacist violence in the U.S. and Japanese militarism ravaging his homeland.

Because Bulosan's sensibility was deeply anchored in the proletarian struggles of his time, he was able to capture the latent transformative impulses in his milieu as well as the emancipatory vision of the realist-populist strain in U.S. literature: from Whitman to Twain, Dreiser to Richard Wright. The prime exhibit here is Bulosan's novel, *The Cry and the Dedication* (first published in 1972 in a Canadian edition with the title *The Power of the People*), the pedagogical motivation of which was to render in parabolic episodes the dynamics between the Huk uprising against U.S. imperialism and its comprador agents, and the farmworkers' agitation in the U.S. for equality and justice. In contrast, the aesthetes who emulated Villa can only gesture toward, or parody, U.S. neoconservative styles and banalities ranging from the compromised liberalism of the welfare state to the slogans of religious fundamentalism, *laissez-faire* utilitarianism, and packaged postmodern fads fresh from the dream factories of California.

Despite Bulosan's achievement, it remains the case that the vision of a nation-in-the-making sedimented in Filipino writing in English cannot be fully assayed except in antithesis to the metropolis. Since the sixties, however, the metropolitan paradigm and its claim of truthfully representing the "Filipino" has entered a period of protracted crisis. For American critical arbiters, Filipino writing in whatever language remains negligible, at best peripheral. Filipino writers who are combatting the realism of the center, the pathos of the status quo, have not refused to abandon the theme of national / class emancipation, the now-contested Enlightenment project of modernity given a subaltern inflection. Consequently, they have not been so easily coopted by paternalistic concessions and assimilated to the neoliberal multicultural "chain of equivalence." U.S. neoliberal ideology may accord formal rights to Filipino cultural identity, but does so only to deny recognition of its substantive worth.

Missionaries of "postcolonial" orthodoxy ensconced in U.S. universities are celebrating their incommensurabilities as the part of Commonwealth / British literature that really matters. But, so far, they have not claimed to appropriate Philippine writing in English as an illustration of what the authors of *The Empire Writes Back* call a "hybridized" or "syncretic" phenomenon (Ashcroft, Griffiths, and Tiffin 180, 196).[1] The reason is not far to seek: whether in the United States or in the Philippines, Filipino writers cannot escape the vocation of resistance against neocolonial (not postcolonial) forces crystallized, for example, by the International Monetary Fund / World Bank, guarantors of predatory corporate forays around the world. Filipino writers cannot shirk the task of reinventing their nation anew in a world where the "internationalism" of the transnational corporations seeks to impose a mandate of Eurocentric supremacy.

This program of reconfiguring what Gramsci calls the "national-popular"—not the state that has instrumentalized the nation—is not nationalist, in the vulgar sense of seeking to preserve ethnic purity or to instigate a cult of linguistic uniqueness. Rather, it is "nationalist" in defense of the integrity of the work-process in a specific time-place. This nationalism inheres in affirming the dignity and worth of workers and peasants that so far constitute the nation / people for-itself, the axis of equivalence around which reciprocal interactions of class, gender, sexuality, and other categories find their shifting valence.

Whenever U.S. experts on the Philippines pronounce judgment on our literary achievement, the implicit standard may be seen to originate from the notion of "tutelage." In sum, U.S. knowledge-production of the truth about the "Filipino" rests in part on the organic metaphor of parent-child and tributary-stream, a figural strategy whose repetition endows U.S. culture with inexhaustible recuperative reach. In the 1969 *Area Handbook for the Philippines*, we read: "For the first two decades of the American occupation the short story suffered from a stiltedness of style when written in English, but, after the authors went through a period of practice in acquiring the idiom, excellent writing began to emerge" (Chaffee 140). This is repeated in subsequent editions, as well as the citation of authors (Villa, Romulo, Joaquin, Gonzalez) who acquired visibility by being published in the United States. One example of the way U.S. critical discourse occludes the reality of resistance to its client regime, the Marcos dictatorship, is by the simple tactic of omission. Consider this: after 1972, "themes shifted from social comment to a search for self-awareness and personal identification" (Vreeland 148). What actually happened was that "social comment" *faced with government censorship* either stopped, turned Aesopian, or went underground. Further, the U.S. retrogressive will to categorize and subjugate its clients can be illustrated by the well-intentioned but patronizing comments of Donald Keene in a 1962 review of an anthology of modern Filipino short stories: "we are certainly fortunate that there are now Filipinos who can speak to us beautifully in our own language . . . [this collection] is an admirable testimony to the emergence of another important branch of English literature" (44).

One response to this strategy of incorporation by subsumption is the privileging of contradictions inscribed in the site of what is alter/native, the Other of paranoid mastery. One can venture the proposition that Philippine writing is not a "branch" of American or English literature; it is *sui generis*. This is not just a matter of "differences 'within' English writing" or embedded national traditions that postcolonial dogmatism considers "the first and most vital stage in the process of rejecting the claims of the centre to exclusivity" (Ashcroft, Griffiths, and Tiffin 17).

Nick Joaquin, the virtuoso romanticizer of the petty-bourgeois Filipino, formulates the genealogy of his maturation as a process of awakening to the claims of the unlettered folk and the pious gentry. After describing the itinerary of his education in the worship of American and British authors (from Dickens to Willa Cather), he finally discovers the Philippine folk-Catholic milieu of rituals and festivals that then furnishes the raw materials for his imagination ("The Way We Were" 4–5). While rightly denouncing the mechanical imitation of U.S. standards and styles, Joaquin seeks to locate the authenticity of Filipino creativity in a folk version of Christianity lodged in the psyche of characters who resist commodity fetishism—in *The Woman Who Had Two Navels, Portrait of the Artist as Filipino,* and *Cave and Shadows* (San Juan, *Subversions*).

More problematic than this essentialist quest for an indigenous *genius loci* subordinated to Eurocentric Christianity is Joaquin's idea of tradition as a cumulative inventory of the colonial past. To illustrate, Rizal was produced by 300 years of Spanish culture; Villa by 400 years of Westernization (add about 100 years of American colonial tutelage), a frame of reference that includes for Joaquin "Adam and Eve, Abraham, Venus, St. Peter, Cinderella, and the Doce Pares" ("The Filipino" 42). So Joaquin contends that "if Philippine writing in English is to be justified at all, it will have to assert its continuity with that particular process and development" of absorbing the Western episteme and the anxiety of the self-deluded Cartesian ego. Rather than a radical rupture with the past, Joaquin's empiricist naiveté posits a libidinal investment in European forms, values, knowledge—a cosmopolitan instrumentalism that replicates the less-subtle conditionalities of the IMF/World Bank. Such a mimicry of colonial icons and paradigms springs from a myth of self-apprehension characterized by a claim to vindicate modern urban culture, signs of *différance* so highly prized by the current high priests of "postcolonial" discourse (hatched in the Indian subcontinent, Australia, and Canada) reacting to the master narratives of bourgeois freedom and progress.[2]

Reservations and doubts interrupt here to pose the following questions: What would differentiate this tenet of syncretism from the doctrine of liberal pluralism (either post-Keynesian or post-Fordist) under which the "New World Order" of the U.S., Japan, and the European Community seeks to redivide the world into their respective spheres of influence? Is nationalism (often interpreted as a mode of "ethnic cleansing") the genuine alternative? Is ethnocentric nativism—a return to the *pasyon,* millenarian rituals, and other sectarian or autarchic practices—a viable option? Can, for example, Virgilio Enriquez's quest for an indigenous *sikolohiyang Pilipino* centered on *kapwa,* an immanent worldview—a strategic essentialism that provokes deconstruction as well as historicizing discrimination—be harnessed to yield a new, highly nuanced poetics of Filipino creativity? How has the Filipino writer succeeded in transcending the either/or dilemma of choosing between abrogation through appropriation, or unilaterally privileging the indigenous? Is Samir Amin's universalist resolution of this predicament (proposed in *Eurocentrism*) a cogent way of breaking through the impasse?

Boundaries/Displacements Otherwise

In essence, the conflict over language situated in its worldly habitat is a struggle over renegotiating hegemony. From what place of enunciation will the national identity and the people's historic destiny be spoken? Who will articulate and represent the sovereignty of the nation, the collective aspirations of the Filipino people?

Virgilio Enriquez and Elizabeth Protacio-Marcelino have forcefully presented the nationalist perspective in the context of a broadly based mass movement for genuine political, economic, and cultural liberation. They advance the view that the possession of a national language is an essential precondition for autonomy. They assert that the continued use of English in an American-oriented educational system (textbooks, curriculum, methodology, and so forth) not only suppresses the democratic aspirations of the Filipino masses but also "undermines Filipino values and orientation and perpetuates the miseducation and captivity of the minds of the Filipino people to the colonial outlook" (3). For them, the English language symbolizes the belief in the superiority of American culture, values, and life-styles, as we have noted earlier. Thus, English can serve only the exploitative, profit-seeking ends of American power. To eradicate the persisting effects of an inherited dependency syndrome manifest in the neocolonial structures of the economy, government, schools, and in the institutions of civil society, linguistic nationalism must be promoted to insure the cultural survival and to preserve the unique ethos and physiognomy of the Filipino people.

Pursuing the logic of this pedagogical and heuristic endeavor, Enriquez and Protacio-Marcelino demonstrate their case by showing how American psychologists have insidiously diagnosed the Filipino character as an embodiment of certain behavioral patterns (like *utang na loob* or *hiya*) based on a perverted, basically Eurocentric, construal of their meanings and contexts of reference. Enrique argues that research in psychology should proceed by searching for the "right words" in the vernacular languages that "will truly reflect the sentiments, values and aspirations of the Filipino people," and not through superimposing

Western concepts. He illustrates how the repertoire of significations condensed in the word *kapwa*, for example, captures a truly indigenous mode of social interaction. Vernacular usage, in effect, registers the mutations of what is both national and popular. The genius of the native languages is thus envisaged to be the most accurate reflection as well as artificer of the Filipino psyche, contextualized in its interface with local and global environments. Here in this micropolitics of psychosocial linguistics, it seems that the Whorf-Sapir hypothesis of language as shaper of one's world view is resurrected with a vengeance.

Now, it is precisely this hypothesis that Filipino writers in English seem to have implicitly rejected when they chose English as their privileged medium of artistic expression. Of course, as everyone knows, the choice is not a genuine free choice, given the constraints of dysfunctional literacy, limited access to resources like channels of publication, audience, rewards, and so forth. On the other hand, the choice of English conveys more than the cathexis of a mere aesthetic/personal decision. A politics/ethics of signification is implied. No one has really explored this terrain of personal responsibility and complicity of vocation, a task with stakes larger and more profound than the ethical resonance of balancing individual rights, duties, and pleasures.

In assessing the fate of English as a literary medium in the Philippines for the last half-century, the noted linguist Andrew Gonzalez has reached an ambiguous but ultimately ironic conclusion. He has documented the process whereby the code or signaling system of the English language "was transferred without its cultural matrix," resulting in a variety of Filipino English with distinctive speech patterns in accord with "Pilipino styles of thought." This is a phenomenon underlying the development of diverse kinds of "english" (as sociolinguists put it)— conceived now as an international idiom, no longer fixated on a British or American model—spoken and used in Jamaica, India, South Africa, Australia, New Zealand, Canada, and elsewhere. A genre called "world literature written in English" is even proposed by humanitarian fellow travelers to abolish the invidious distinction between margin and center in the geopolitical reckoning of nation-states, between the canonical and the optional/elective, between what is major and what is minor.

On the Philippine scene, this encounter between the alien and the indigenous triggered a curious mutagenesis. When it comes to discourse patterns evinced in Filipino prose, Gonzalez notes the phenomenon of a new contextualization of English, the "transplantation of English structures and poetic discourse applied to a new environment, a new cultural matrix" (148). Since the indigenous discourse conventions and techniques of a native tradition have all been practically destroyed by Spanish and American colonization, the formerly trammelled creativity of Filipino writers has been released in their appropriation of a new language and the need to innovate within this new system. In the process, however, their imagination has been circumscribed by its strict adherence to Western canonical standards. Discourse structure and grammatical code are all foreign; only the reference hierarchy, themes or topoi, and their cultural matrix are Filipino. Hence, Gonzalez observes that Filipinos write poetry in the English language concerning Philippine topics and realities and themes, "but there is no Filipino art form to speak of as transferred from the indigenous culture to the new tongue. There are no traces in this literary language born of academic and English schooling and modeled on the poetic experiments of America, of the local traditions of versification and poesy" (149). What results, then, is a "monstrous" production, an enigmatic sport defying the wisdom of taxonomists. Is this proof of "indigenous creativity"? Or is it unwarranted to call it self-induced alienation and schizoid gestures of a pathological case?

Obviously, Gonzalez's mode of divorcing form from content, separating diverse signifying practices from changing historical circumstances, essentially fails in its attempt to grasp that peculiarly Filipino "creativity" he is positing. The alloy seems inferior compared to the pure ingredients. I acknowledge Gonzalez's linguistic expertise in canvassing conformities and deviations to the code. However, it is necessary to underscore his inadequacies. For one, his account ignores the whole contextual field of writing practices that critics like Voloshinov/Bakhtin and linguists like Jakobson, Halliday, Ferrucio-Landi, and other social semioticians have brought to our attention, particularly in the last two decades.[3]

Indeed, Filipino writers read the West—the tradition-sanctioned discourses of Shakespeare, Wordsworth, T. S. Eliot, Faulkner, and Hemingway, according to canonical standards—but they write their hermeneutic responses with an embodied, place-indexed signature. As I have indicated earlier and will elaborate later, this dialogic conjuncture derives from the historical specificity of the Philippines as the only U.S. colony in Asia at the turn of the century, a focal point of condensation and displacement for numerous conflicting political, ideological, economic, and social trends. The Philippines, conceived as the site of contradictory forces and heterogeneous actors with their own transitional genealogies, is what underlies the antinomic but ultimately conciliatory art of Nick Joaquin (already examined in a materialist critique of his major texts in *Subversions of Desire*). Likewise, the prodigious artifacts made by Bulosan cannot be properly understood without appreciating how the rhythm of oral storytelling and the calculated inversions of folklore pervade the stories in *The Laughter of My Father*. Nor can one comprehend his syncretic alchemy of mapping events in *America Is in the Heart*, which combine picaresque motifs and autobiographical notations, without contextualizing it in the experience of peasant unrest in Pangasinan and the resistance of migrant labor to racist violence on the U.S. West Coast—the existential "lived experience" of Filipinos in the master's territory. (I have thoroughly explored both aspects in my *Carlos Bulosan and the Imagination of the Class Struggle* and in countless essays; see Chapter 5 in the present work.)

The same applies to the prison writings of Father Ed de la Torre, Jose Maria Sison, and others incarcerated by the national-security state; and to recent oppositional texts and emergent cultural practices, particularly in the spheres of musical and theatrical performances (see Van Erven); and in what has now become in our fractured milieu the now hegemonic cultural signifiers of universal commodification: film and TV. One example of recent work, whose form is conditioned by historic impulses and circumstantial pressures, is the underground novel *Hulagpos* (Break Away, 1980). It is a realistic but also polemical critique of the Marcos martial-law regime. While the plot is ostensibly patterned after Jose Rizal's *Noli Me Tangere*, its technique of montage—abrupt cuts and syncopated juxtaposition of incidents—and collage of characters clearly derive from, *inter alia*, the method of the serialized novels in the weekly comic books and underground pictorials popular among the masses today and from the techniques of the avant-garde cinema.

Allegories of Aliens, Nomads, Monsters

It might be instructive to briefly sketch the dialectical crossbreeding between the autochthonous tradition and modern Filipino writing in English, using three examples. The three I have selected are a poem by Villa, a short story passage from Arguilla, and a *sarsuwela* by Tiongson. I suggest that, contrary to Gonzalez's positing of a dichotomy between native sensibility and alien tongue, a subtle intertextual symbiosis actually obtains in the play of locutionary forces.

228 ALLEGORIES OF THE NATION

In this sense, Jose Garcia Villa's poetic art, long held to be an exercise in imitation of modernist styles to the point of mannerism and parody, cannot be reduced to a matter of eccentric prosody such as "reversed consonance" or "sprung rhythm." Again, here, form and substance cannot be so easily disjoined. Villa is the exemplary case of the offspring of *ilustrado* gentry who rejects his class origin, yet paradoxically glorifies the caste privilege of the artist. This cannot be understood except as a revolt, principally against the commercial, materialistic, philistine mores and manners of colonial society. Despite his ultra-vanguardist exhibitionism, Villa's art cannot deny the influence of over three hundred years of Spanish-Malayan cultural interaction (on Villa's career, see Chapter 6).

Villa's representative texts in *Selected Poems and New* exhibit a characteristic surface of aphoristic verbal play and quasi-parody (even pastiche) of metaphysical conceits. If we compare the design and texture of these texts with the native tradition of didactic and allegorical indirection—from the pre-Christian riddles, oratory, song, and *dagli* (vignette), to Balagtas' epic *Florante at Laura*, to the satires of Rizal and M. H. Del Pilar—we can begin to understand how and why his individualist revolt in the sterile milieu of the twenties and thirties assumed the form it took: exile, adoption of masks, aristocratic ventriloquism, and other eccentric poses.

Whatever the merits of Villa's response to his dilemma, the persistence of generic conventions in his poetry seems to override changing social contexts. As a provisional orientation, it may be helpful to illustrate a still-undefined genealogy of modernist Filipino writing by comparing the tropological scheme of two poems. These are the first stanza of Villa's poem No. 123 (Villa, *Selected Poems* 101): and a poem dating to precolonial times, when Indian, Arabic, and Chinese cultural currents blended in the Malayan aesthetic intelligence (Lumbera 9). First, Villa's unmistakable verse:

What,is,defeat?
    Broken,victory.
Darkest,sanctuary,
    But,solider,far,
Than,the,triumphal,star.

And the precolonial verse, in Tagalog (originally transcribed by a Spanish priest-lexicographer):

Ang sugat ay kung tinanggap
di daramdamin ang antak
ang aayaw at di mayag
galos lamang magnanaknak.

Freely translated:

When one submits oneself
to wounding,
the intensest pain is bearable;
when one is unwilling,
even the merest scratch can fester.

As for the invention of an authentic Filipino discourse in the short story, anchored in the peasant *habitus* (Bourdieu's term) and the ethical forms of subjectivity in a kinship-based organic community, it might be sufficient to present a synecdochic example. Consider the nuanced tonality and figurative resonance of this passage from Manuel Arguilla's "A Son is Born." His peculiar mix would be difficult to find in Chekhov, Maupassant, Hemingway, or any other Western practitioner of this art:

My mother's face was small in the growing dusk of the evening, small and lined, wisps of straight, dry hair falling across it from her head. I could see the brown specks on my mother's cheekbones, the result of working long under the sun. She looked down upon Berting and me and her eyes held a light that I dimly felt sprung from the love she bore us, her children. I could not bear her gaze any longer. It filled me with a longing to be good and kind to her. I looked down at my arms and I was full of shame and of regret. (Lumbera 177)

My third example of the amphibious-but-recuperative nature of neocolonial discourse production is different from the first two instances. Here, the linguistic code of English is seized, dismantled, and then refunctioned to serve emancipatory ends, when it is incorporated into a modernized form of the *sarsuwela*. This is a theatrical spectacle that mixes songs and dances, with a melodramatic plot of threatened romantic love suturing the unraveled "thickness" of contemporary social and political issues. Introduced by the Spaniards in the nineteenth century as a popular form of entertainment, it has been Filipinized by major artists like Severino Reyes, Vicente Soto, Mena Pecson Crisologo, and others.

This passage from Nicanor Tiongson's *Pilipinas Circa 1907* is a rewriting or adaptation of Reyes' 1907 play of the same title. It has been cross-fertilized by the "seditious" drama and novels of the first decade, the paramount cultural signifiers of anticolonial resistance to U.S. aggression. In Tiongson's script, the anticipated overcoming of American economic-political power is symbolically enacted by the ironic chorus of modernizing "girls," part of which I quote below. The second stanza may be read as an emblematic specimen of counter-hegemonic renegotiation of the dominant linguistic code:

Ba't nga ba may Pilipino
[Why are there Filipinos]
Na masyadong atrasado
[Who are still so backward]
Dumaong na'ng Amerikano
[The Americans have already landed]
Ay! pusakal pa ring Indio!
[But my, they're still wild Indios!]

I do not know to them
I do not know to them
We do not know to them!
Kundi kay William Mckinley
[If not for William McKinley]
We are still swinging from a tree
Walang statue of liberty
[We wouldn't have a statue of liberty]
(Tiongson, *Pilipinas* 46–47)

Given this complex historical background, absent in most literary histories, writing in English in the Philippines is no doubt an ideological practice firmly imbricated in the conflicts and problems of subaltern existence. If we deploy a historical contextualization of the field of writing practices, we will see that English is only one "language game," or one choice in the means of cultural production amid a space where electronic visual communication (television, video, cinema), together with its protean "commodity aesthetics" (Haug), predominates. In fact, Filipino English can be construed as only one kind of vernacular with a fairly limited, and even shrinking, audience within a decolonizing but assuredly not yet postcolonial site of antagonisms. The sign, indeed, is one strategic arena of political struggle.

Writing finds itself historicized, so to speak, without knowing it. Unless the production of such discourse is historically situated, one cannot grasp its power of producing meaning and also comprehend what Foucault calls the knowledge/power *combinatoire* and its dual effects of inhibiting and in the same breath mobilizing people into action. This imperative of contextualizing aesthetic form becomes more compelling if we accept Earl Miner's theory that Asian poetics is fundamentally affective-expressive rather than mimetic or dramatic like European poetics in general, a distinction originating from incommensurable cultural-social disparities (82–87). Conversely, Third World mimesis, unlike the Western kind, can be deciphered as ultimately allegorical and collective in meaning and motivation, as Fredric Jameson has so persuasively argued (see also Gugelberger).

This is why I suggest that it is imperative to situate Filipino literary expression in the specific historical convergence of political, economic, and ideological forces—the transition from colonial dependency to the initial stages of national-popular autonomy—as I have outlined above. Everyone recognizes the axiom that the linguistic system (Saussure's *langue*) is self-contained, a differential system of signifiers structured in binary oppositions. But it is also the case that (as Voloshinov/Bakhtin has shown) *parole* or utterance is what sets the system in motion and generates meaning among interlocutors in the speech community (65–106). Speech acts or performances of enunciation are social, not individual phenomena. In other words, discourse is always intertextual and complicit; the world, the concrete historical life-situation of speakers and horizon of listeners, is a necessary constitutive element of the semantic structure of any utterance (Todorov 41–45).

Consequently, it follows that the character of any discourse cannot be fully understood without reference to its intertextuality, its axiological embeddedness in social process, its social filiations and networks. To separate code from the context of enunciation is thus to annul discourse, to negate utterance in its modalities of communication and artistic expression. In the social text foregrounded here, the conjuncture of colonial occupation, the twin aspects of U.S. hegemony and Filipino resistance are two moments or phases of the same event.

This is the reason why I would strongly endorse the deployment of what Mary Louise Pratt calls a "linguistics of contact" instead of the conventional "linguistics of community" (or its late-capitalist variant, the "communicative action" of Habermas). I advocate a linguistics of contact in order to displace the "normative vision of a unified and homogeneous social world" and to accentuate instead "the relationality of social differentiation" (Pratt 59). Dialectics, then, instead of functional empiricism. This mode of linguistic comprehension would decenter a self-identical community, foregrounding instead "the operation of language across lines of social differentiation." It would focus on modes and zones of contact between dominant and dominated groups and on "how such speakers [with multiple identities] constitute each other relationally and in difference, how they enact differences in language" (60). Tiongson's *sarsuwela*, Villa's poems, and Bulosan's fiction may thus be conceived as attempts to explore the operation of an aesthetics of contact and disjunction between U.S. hegemonic apparatus and Filipino strategies of resistance.

Undoing Scripts, Unsettling Contracts

Initiatives for a renewal of national allegory (Jameson, *Marxism and Form*), the renaissance of the radical-democratic imagination, might be witnessed in a critique of what I might call mendicant, culinary nationalism—the ideology and culture of the "New Society" of the Marcos regime—drawn up by progressive intellectuals just after the February 1986 insurrection.

In Africa and Asia after the sixties, the triumph of élite nationalism led to a catastrophic disillusionment of writers who expected the radical transformation of society after independence. But what the "passive revolution" (Chatterjee) ushered in was neither national-popular liberation nor relief from the humiliations inflicted by white racial supremacy. Instead, it was neocolonialism. During the Marcos dictatorship, pseudohistorical propaganda and self-serving kitsch that manipulated symbols of the archaic tributary / feudal past tried to project the regime as an embodiment of the nation's "authentic identity." In truth, however, it was a client state obsessed with "national security" and the demonology of anticommunism. This was standard Cold War obscurantism and unconscionable mass deception. Nicanor Tiongson and others exposed how the ethos of communal cooperation called *bayanihan* or *kapitbahayan* was ascribed by the state to the *barangay* (the pre-Spanish village government) as its "soul." This ethnic mediation was designed to function as the political base for the authoritarian political party, *Kilusang Bagong Lipunan* (53).

In 1969, Imelda Marcos raided the public treasury to build her pet project, the aristocratic and extravagant edifice called the "Cultural Center of the Philippines," which she designated as the "Sanctuary of the Filipino Soul." These icons, symbols, and accoutrements of Marcos' "Filipino Ideology" might have fooled the regime's narrow circle of cronies and compradors, but it was easily recognized by most Filipinos as mystification and apologetics for corrupt kleptocratic despotism, as well as marks of subservience to Western and Japanese transnational interests. Lino Brocka, then the leading progressive filmmaker, pointed out that such "nation-building means trying to give a 'beautiful' picture of the country, trying not to disturb people, not to make them angry by depicting the truth to them" (Tiongson 57). This understanding was shared by most artists, who aligned themselves with the platform and principles of the National Democratic Front (NDF). The NDF's alter/native project of constructing a "democratic and scientific culture" via popular participation of the broad masses insured that nationalism of the kind that disappointed many African writers (like Chinua Achebe and Ayi Kwei Armah) would not be a substitute for a thoroughgoing social transformation that would be brought about by a change in property-relations and redistribution of social wealth/power. Such a change would, by necessity, entail the assertion of national sovereignty against U.S. impositions in particular (Diokno). Above all, it would prioritize the control of a circumscribed space or territory, without which the Filipino people could not contribute to the community of states claiming to represent nations.

Thus, we come back to the paradox that the internationalism of Goethe, Condorcet, and Marx conjured: for "national one-sidedness and narrow-mindedness" (to quote the *Communist Manifesto*) to be eradicated, what is required is precisely nationalism (albeit a utopian and overdetermined one) conceived not just as a collective primordial sentiment but as a mode of organizing a collectivity. It is neither the concept of the nation-people nor its radical-democratic articulation that is problematic. Rather, it is the comprador or client state that manipulates the "nation" and its accompanying symbolic capital as its instrument for profit accumulation and maintenance of prestige.

Within the Marxist tradition, one finds a rich and complex archive of controversies on "the national question," from Lenin, Trotsky, Luxemburg, and Otto Bauer to Mao Tse-tung, C.L.R. James, Che Guevarra, Edward Kardelj, and Amilcar Cabral. Surveying this field, Michael Löwy concludes that the principle of self-determination centers on a given community's act of deciding consciously to constitute itself as a nation (157). But, before judging one nationalism as legitimate and another as suspect (if not reactionary), Löwy advises us to undertake "concrete analysis of each concrete situation" relative to the goal of defeating international capitalism. In his study of ethno-nationalism in Britain, Tom Nairn counseled us about the Janus-faced nature of historical nationalisms that are reducible neither to the simplistic notion of "imagined communities" nor to the fascist *Volksgeist*.

Whatever the ambiguity of this phenomenon, the idea of the nation in its spatio-temporal concreteness cannot be exorcised from thought without eliminating the historicist temper of modernity. As noted before, nationalism and its corollary, the nation-state, are energized by a teleology of the conquest of necessity by reason, of humanity's tortuous progress toward freedom. This position has been questioned by postmodern thinking. It is also questioned by Regis Debray, who believes that the idea (or ideal-type) of the nation, which for Marxists would be rendered obsolete by the advent of communism, is permanent and irreducible. For Debray, the idea of a nation is necessary to thwart entropy and death by establishing boundaries and, thus, identity through difference. Claiming to be more materialist than Marx, Debray insists that the universalizing thrust of bourgeois-analytic reason (as instanced by Amin's book mentioned earlier, or the messianic thrust of Fanon's Third World advocacy) ignores the reality of contemporary developments. Specifically, it ignores the resurgence of identity politics in the forms of ethnic separatism, regional schisms, sexual nonconformity, and so on. We are witnessing

> a growing interdependence of the conditions of economic production and exchange, comporting a trend toward uniformity; yet this is dialectically accompanied by a new multiplication of cultural diversity. . . . Equality is never identity. . . . What we are seeing now is indeed a growing divergence of cultural identities, a search for specificity as the other face of emerging globalism. ("Marxism and the National Question" 31)

Such a schematic mapping of the present world system, a recapitulation of the principle of "uneven and unequal development," is enabled by the very contradictions of late capitalism. In this totalizing regime of exchange value, there are multiple antagonisms that overdetermine sectoral class struggles across the boundaries of metropolis and periphery. From the perspective of oppressed people of color, the primary contradiction is still between the advanced industrial centers, with their shifting tactics of negotiating compromises or using force, and their subjects within and outside their borders. These victims, both communities and peoples, are heterogeneous and polyethnic, with a commonality of sharing the historic fate of domination by mainly Western civilization. This shared experience underpins the sociolibidinal economy of their individual quests for recognition as world-historical peoples, responsible for shaping "national" communities of interests and desires.

On the terrain of an uneven and disaggregated social formation, writing in the Philippines stages, in rhetoric and narrative, an emergent popular agenda or "structure of feeling." It proceeds by refunctioning residual forms (such as the *dupluhan* and *zarzuela*, which are folk theatrical genres) and rehabilitating marginalized conventions. The intent is to subvert the aestheticist idealism authorized by U.S. disciplinary regimes as well as the commodified imports and imitations from Japan, Europe, and elsewhere. Anachronism somehow becomes a timely principle of subversion. By the logic of engaging in counter-hegemonic prefigurations, the resistance assumes the modality of revitalizing indigenous cultural practices, so as to constitute an oppositional, transformative narrative of their return with new effectivities. What distinguishes this tendency is a rigorous selectiveness evinced, not just in the adaptation of Western genres (for example, Brecht's epic distancing, retooled in PETA productions like *Buwan at Baril*), or in the feminist abrogation of neocolonial / feudal patriarchy (as in Lualhati Bautista's *Bata, Bata . . . Paano Ka Ginawa?* and other vernacular experiments). The selectivity is also evinced in the invention of a distinctive colloquial, satiric sensorium.

Nor is this innovative resourcefulness fully registered in the creation of a new style of tracking the metamorphosis of the migratory sensibility, as in Jose Dalisay, Jr.'s novel *Killing Time in a Warm Place*. Rather, it can be discerned in the project of contriving a national-popular idiom addressed not to the *Volk* (Herder, Fichte) but to a resurgent *sambayanan* (*populus*). An allegorizing strategy of storytelling is explored. Its point of departure is an alter / native sensibility rooted in acts of decolonizing intransigence, in ruses of heterological simulation, in a critique of the illusions propagated by the world system of transnational capital. This "emergent" form of textual production (Godzich) exemplifies the popular-democratic praxis of signification occurring in schools, churches, families, unions, professional organizations of the middle strata, and other loci of the public sphere.

The praxis of alter / native writing interrogates the "post" in "postcolonial" theory. We observe this in the partisan texts of Emmanuel Lacaba, Estrella Consolacion, Levy Balgos de la Cruz, Jason Montana, Edberto Villegas, and others. They all strive to actualize what Father Ed de la Torre calls "incarnation politics." They instantiate a theology of liberation indivisible from the daily acts of resistance against a client state that has sacrificed the nation-people to profitmaking (De la Torre, *Philippines*).

This project of enunciating the colonized subject "becoming-Filipino" is not nationalist, in the orthodox sense of legitimizing a state wherein the nation is hostage to traders and entrepreneurs ready to sell it to the highest bidder. Its actualization of nationalism is prophetic because it materializes in everyday acts of popular refusal. The nation appealed to here condenses a multiplicity of resistances across gender, class, ethnicity, location, sexuality, age, and so on. In this context, the nation then would signify a "concrete universal" that embodies solidarity with other oppressed communities who are engaged in fighting the same enemy. Such unity with others is premised on the socially constructed differences of peoples, including those whose histories have not yet been written, only sung; or those whose narratives have been interrupted by the West's "civilizing mission". We appreciate differences that are invested with value to the extent that they can be mediated or translated for the recognition of others and our mutual enrichment. How is the Other fully recognized? One provisional answer: by transposing the mimesis of the Self (the parasitic colonizer within) into an allegory of its own constitution and self-reproduction.

What distinguishes the oppositional temper in vernacular writing, as described earlier, is the collective project of constructing a popular-democratic mode of expression combining a unique sensibility which signifies a Filipino identity-in-the-making with a theoretical understanding of its situatedness in the world system of late capitalism. What deserves priority for future investigators is to describe concretely how this project of national-popular articulation may be conceived as a "concrete universal" that embodies supranational impulses of solidarity. It definitely is neither a chauvinism of ethnic superiority, nor essentialized "racial" singularity. On the contrary, it is premised mainly on an internationalism of peoples of color. This ecumenical alliance grants the historical differences of peoples (including those presumably "without a history," subjugated people of color), but it derives from a commonality of principles centered on liberty, justice, peace, ecological caring, and concern for sustaining life on this planet. These principles were once designated "humanist," but are nowexpropriated as mere ornament in the liberal marketplace.

Fanon enunciated this dialectical insight concisely in this thesis: "It is at the heart of *national* consciousness that *international* consciousness lives and grows" (italics added; 248). National independence and popular sovereignty are fundamental requirements for this transcendent vision to live and flourish. The struggle for people's liberation thus explodes the circumscribing ethnocentrism/racism of bourgeois and comprador variants of nationalism and opens up the space for intercultural exchanges across once-sacrosanct geopolitical boundaries.

What I have in mind can perhaps be suggested by Edward Said's hermeneutics of the culminating moment of the decolonization process plotted by Fanon. This is the moment of liberation, "a transformation of social consciousness beyond national consciousness" ("Reflections" 83). It is exemplified in Pablo Neruda's poems, in Aimé Cesaire's *Cahier d'un retour*, in the life and work of the Filipino revolutionary poet Amado V. Hernandez, as well as by the deeds of nationalist martyrs like Alex Boncayao, Frank Navarro, Maria Lorena Barros, and others. Because of the general reification of social life today, we cannot as yet fully comprehend the dynamics of this transformation without the mediation of allegory: Neruda evokes through Machu Picchu the heroic resistance of the aborigines, while Cesaire's surreal strophes evoke the promise of Negritude in utopian rhythms. What does the Philippines have to offer to the commonwealth of the disinherited, insurgent multitudes?

Crisis of Commodity Fetishism

Because the Filipino experience mediates two complicitous if irreconcilable spaces, it is necessary not only to demystify neocolonial myths, but also expose the insidious working of the entire commodity system that we have inherited and continue to inhabit. In this connection, I have just examined many stories and reports of Filipina migrant laborers around the world in my quest of a symbolic economy of national identity (on this, more later). Structured by the contradiction between use value and exchange value intrinsic to capital accumulation, the narratives of overseas contract workers (domestics like Flor Contemplacion and hundreds of thousands of her compatriots) are pervaded by the ironies of uneven development and asymmetrical causality (Bottomore 502–3). Instead of acting as "free laborers," whose value is measured by socially necessary labor time, according to the orthodox Marxist paradigm, these women are treated as virtual slaves in the context of generalized commodity exchange. Both the use value and exchange value of their commodity (labor power) seem dissolved in this ambiguous zone of

existence. This singular political economy of Filipina existence is registered in truncated and disrupted narratives of their experience. Fetishism of money collapses memory into a vision of an apocalypse of wealth
(consumer goods), punctuated by the devaluation of bodies and the
dissolution of logical / rational causality. Commodity fetishism equals
death—and the contingencies of postmodern textuality.[4]

Unfortunately, *in medias res* we find ourselves caught in a geopolitical "repetition compulsion" with a new twist: Filipinos, in particular
women, have now emerged as the new serfs in what Arjun Appadurai
describes as the disjunctive but also synthesizing "ethnoscape" of the
postmodern global cultural economy (329). In this new life-world, the
archive of national self-identification literally becomes engendered
within an intertextual network that defies mere aesthetic categorization. We are confronted here with the birth of a new type of what I call
dissident, anti-postcolonial allegory. What is unique about this new
form of expression is that it fuses both modalities of "emergency" (in
Walter Benjamin's sense) and "emergent" (in Wlad Godzich's formulation) writing in a genre whose provenance and trajectory I can only
schematically draw here. From a narratological framework, this genre
can be viewed as a late-modern allegorizing of Filipino cultural production vis-à-vis the fate of *pax Americana* in decline.

While the patrons of a triumphalist "New World Order" celebrated
freedom and democracy for the subjects of the erstwhile "Evil Empire,"
thousands of people of color were displaced from the oil-rich Arab
states during the Gulf War. Prominent among the victims of this reassertion of Western imperial hegemony were Third World contract laborers,
primarily women located in the often conflated spheres of material
production and social reproduction. Not only in the Middle East but in
Europe, Hong Kong, Japan, and elsewhere, the drive to resolve the
crisis of accumulation that began in the seventies continues in the shape
of flexible, post-Fordist production and the accelerated proletarianiza-
tion of dependent / peripheral formations.

Given the exacerbated uneven development of the world system, the
patriarchal capitalism of the industrialized nation-states (and its neocolonial client regimes) has been able to displace the crisis by exploiting
the reserve army of female labor outside their national boundaries for
unprecedented bargain prices. As Robert Miles observes, "labour migration accentuated the process of uneven development of the world
capitalist economy" (*Racism* 60) and paradoxically intensified the contradictions at the heart of the accumulation crisis. The expenditure of

refeudalized concrete labor, whose use value is measured by a dras- ·
tically reduced price, constitutes the necessary condition for sustained
profitmaking. Both use value and exchange value are relational categories that operate within the logic of accumulation. Their tension produces uneven development.

Why the diaspora of Third World workers? Samir Amin explains:
"The world capitalist system embodies a structure of labor-market seg-
mentation wherein workers in peripheral countries receive no more
than one-sixth of the wages received by their counterparts in the advanced industrial center" ("Class Structure" 26).

This global process of late capitalism acquires symbolic expression in
the stories of Filipino women whose textualization of their individual
and collective experiences reveals both the pathos of commodity fetishism and the possibilities of distancing and counterhegemonic reversal
(see Orozco; Parel; Maglipon). We begin with the dream of the unemployed Filipina to advance her lot by crossing terrestrial boundaries and
earning a few dollars with which she secures the right to inhabit the
dream world of a consumer's paradise overseas—even if vicariously,
because what she earns is really enjoyed by her parents, children, or
relatives in the impoverished homeland. Her life is suspended in a zone
between ascetic solitude (the present), deracination and wandering (the
past), and convivial reunion with her family (the future). What kind of
intelligible and coherent recounting (*sjuzet*) can be constructed from this
situation (*fabula*) of indeterminacy?

According to Isabel Taylor Escoda, an expert on the plight of Hong
Kong *amahs* as "Filipino chattel," the archetype of the Wandering Jew
has now been replaced by that of "the Filipina Servant Abroad." This of
course is part of a global process: geographical mobility of laborers
adjusts the wage rate to its average value and helps balance profit accumulation worldwide (Harvey). But this process is in truth profoundly
contradictory, engendering its own eventual dissolution. The plot begins with the breakdown of realistic representation; from then on, everything is possible.

The logic of remembering for Filipino contracted labor overseas parodies the Western epic form: ushering us *in medias res*, where events
soon acquire fantastic proportions, we see how beginnings assume an
apocryphal coloring. Soon the denouement becomes problematic, *non
sequitur*, even undecidable. Transcendence is not "always already" waiting for us. The protagonist of this narrative tries to acquire adequate
means to gain happiness from "donor" societies (money is the mediator

for security and success). But this quest is quickly foiled, and she finds herself deceived and shortchanged. She is angry, enraged, terrified— terror lurks behind every State apparatus keeping track of her movements. With the prospect of being deported, she is swiftly reduced to mute despair. She tries to accomplish the task she has assumed for the sake of family and kin by physical resistance and cunning ruses of self-defense, by sheer motion impelled by the reversal or peripeteia that has overtaken her. But, contrary to the usual expectations, the shock of recognition never fully materializes because many of these women return drugged, still mesmerized by the amount of consumer durables their meager savings had allowed them to bring home. The condition of virtual "slavery" (as Bridget Anderson documents it) for many Filipina contract workers sheds light on why their testimonies are composed of flashbacks, regressive loops, and analeptic withdrawals to scenes of privation that need to be revisited in order to induce a catharsis of the trauma.

In retrospect, the migrant women's contract is really with their vision of what their version of "mother right" signifies: togetherness, belonging, pleasure. Because there is no cure for their desire, their search for dignity and happiness, they will not give up their imagined utopia of material fulfillment for family and children. So they are eager to venture out again, since local conditions provide no substitute way of fulfilling dreams of consumption. This actantial model may be trite and hackneyed, but the interest lies in its distortion and displacement by individual experiences of change. Agonistically toned oral narratives give way to solipsistic textuality (Ong)—one obvious effect of commodification. Although the mass media impose their reifying conventions, the genre of migrant female labor narratives exhibits its performance as symptom of, and protest against, the logos of general equivalence (Goux).

In 1992, Raymond Bonner wrote an article for *The New Yorker* (16 November issue) that described in detail the horrendous plight of female migrant labor in Kuwait—about 71,000 domestic servants from India, the Philippines, Bangladesh, and Sri Lanka. Of the 25,000 women from the Philippines, 2,000 so far had fled from the brutality of working long hours for meager pay, virtually imprisoned, often subjected to arbitrary physical violence (including rape), and even killed. There was, for instance, the case of Jenny Casanova, 30 years old, mother of three daughters left in the Philippines, beaten for days by her employer's wife, who finally sought the refuge of the Philippine Embassy. She began work at 5:30 A.M., was allowed to sit down during the day only for meals, took care of four children, and did all the cooking and cleaning. She had no day off, not even for church. Another case was Shirley, who worked from 6 A.M. to 9 P.M., was paid fifty cents an hour for 15 hours a day, 6 days per week, with one day off. She fled after two weeks. And there was Josephine, hit by a 29-year old son and threatened with death.

The labor laws of Kuwait and other Gulf states do not cover such domestic workers who, in the absence of a valid contract, virtually become chattel slaves to those who "buy" them from unscrupulous recruiting agencies. Unless "released" by her employer, it is practically impossible for a woman to secure another visa; hence she becomes desperate and physically fights back. If she succeeds in escaping, she can claim the right to the solidarity of victims, not excluding fugitives and refugees and other outcasts who stake their lives for freedom and self-determination.

When Bonner interviewed these "domestic helpers," to use the honorific euphemism, the Philippine Embassy had become a home for battered women and runaways. Kuwait, newly liberated from the Iraqi invaders, was a country where only Kuwaitis, who constitute 28 percent of the population, can vote and exercise the rights of citizenship. Of the labor force, 80 percent was non-Kuwaiti; every Kuwaiti family had five or six servants. But these statistics do not really provide the context or theoretical framework necessary for understanding the anecdotes of oppression and exploitation—from swindling and insult to rape and daily battering—that characterize the lives of thousands of women of color scattered all over the globe (Mirkinson).

One study confirmed the empirical observations of many that the vast majority of workers in the Gulf suffer for lack of protection for their basic human rights "due to the absence of clearly defined legal rights, the ineffectiveness of local courts and administrative procedures" (Owen). Completely dependent on their institutional or individual sponsors, who confiscate their passports as soon as they arrive in the host country, these workers are maltreated, exploited, abused, beaten, and even killed. According to *Women in the World: An International Atlas*, this new phenomenon of migrant women—the poorest of the world's impoverished populations—are "triply burdened by race, class and gender barriers" (Seager and Olson 17; see also Vickers).

An interview with one Filipina reveals a different view. She had worked in a garment factory in the islands for eight years, and then left for Kuwait. After two years of working in a jewelry store she married the owner, a military man who worked for the Kuwait National Petroleum Company. She was converted to Islam, which earned her 2,000 dinars on the spot. Semaya Muhammad Mokhtar (formerly Shirley Arrieta) now owns a BMW and testifies to her good fortune as a citizen of Kuwait, just before Saddam Hussein's tanks rolled in:

> Imagine a place so clean, where if you get sick all is taken care of for free. There is no place like Kuwait. If you're a Kuwaiti, not only do you not pay any taxes, you can borrow money to set up a business. No taxes. Where in the world will you find a place where they give you money to set up a business, and you don't have to pay taxes? If you give birth to a child, you also get money. Just to show you the strength of the dinar, 10 dinars is enough to fill your grocery bags; you'd have a hard time lugging them home. . . . My purpose there when I left our country was to marry a Kuwaiti, because once you're married to one, one was certain to live in great comfort. But one disadvantage was their men want their wives to stay home (Laurel 4).

Semaya Mokhtar's narrative exemplifies the fulfillment of a quest that departs from the conventional pattern of women who alienate their time and energies to provide for an extended family left at home. But where is home? Filipinos who return to the Philippines at Christmastime are eager to go back to Kuwait where, although problems beset them, they unanimously concur that "over there we have money, and that makes a big difference." They frankly confess their motivation: "The money is the attraction, nothing else, and it's as simple as that." They cheer at the mention of the exchange rate: "If you've tasted earning three thousand pesos a month [in dinars], and your husband is just a jeepney driver, I think even you can bear the loneliness" (Laurel 5). The key motif of petty accumulation shrivels the montage of events into an apocalypse of redemption from oppression based on class, gender, race, and nationality.

For many Filipinos who have been forced to sell their labor-power abroad, Saudi Arabia has become a symbol of the new path to a simulacrum of prosperity, even if the affluence is superficial and transitory. Many seem to agree with this belief, expressed in the early eighties: "This 'Saudi Juice' has really helped our country a lot. . . . Many things have changed in our lives. Before, only the rich can afford to eat good food. Now, the rich can be equaled by someone who has gone to Saudi Arabia" (Catholic Institute for International Relations 79). By 1992, this "juice" seemed to have gone sour, at least in Kuwait, where 367 Fil-

ipinas sought refuge in the Philippine Embassy, each reporting physical, sexual, or psychological abuse at the hands of their employers. One
badly cut and bruised Filipina stated that her boss had thrown her out
of a two-story window (see Kelley).

Such examples of wayward and self-deconstructing accounts spun by
veteran domestics generate the inverse of Freytag's "pyramid" (Shipley
189). They serve as anticlimactic glosses to an anachronistic, nonlinear
pattern of development wherein the commodity-form (whose substance is comprised of the bodies of Filipino women) is assigned a price
quite out of proportion to the surplus value it adds to their product. The
price is the reproduction of class inequality and a hierarchical political
economy of racialized gender/sexuality. There may be utopian varia-
tions in the unfolding of these vicissitudes, as in the sporadic cases of
women who marry their penitent employers (a case of life imitating the
Gothic romance!). But here, too, domestic labor continues with a new
disguise, where production (household chores) and reproduction (pro-
creation, caring) are fused.

In general, the quantitative schema of the transformation of com-
modity→money→commodity hides the qualitative relation of exploitation
and subordination in metropolitan civil societies. Value as a social relation is occluded by the exchange of the commodity labor-power, now
converted into abstract labor in order to be measured in terms of alienated time. Hermeneutic inquiry can easily demonstrate how the material relations between humans mediated by the money wage always
become fetishized, acquiring an enigmatic life of their own. Within the
geopolitical parameter of uneven development in the world system,
one can reflect on the fact that it is the sex/gender contradiction that
functions to disrupt commodity-fetishism and reification, revealing in
the process the limits of patriarchal Eurocentric power.

The feminist scholar Cynthia Enloe has observed that the unprecedented production of narratives by women is either due to their new
self-confidence and awareness of their rights, or to the fact that Kuwaiti
men have grown more violent after the cessation of the Gulf War (185).
People magazine popularized the stories of the Kuwaiti families' atro-
cious and barbaric conduct toward these hapless denizens. The most
notorious case of abuse might be illustrated by the person of Lorna
Laraquel, 44, who worked as the maid of Sheikha Latifa Abdullah Jaber
al-Sabah, a Princess in the royal family. According to one testimony, the
Sheikha forced Laraquel to eat her meals off the floor. She also once
threatened to cut off the Filipina's hands and tongue and gouge out her

eye. While traveling in Egypt in February 1992, Laraquel felt that she could no longer tolerate the abuse and stabbed her mistress to death with a kitchen knife. As of this writing, she had been condemned to death in Egypt.

In a *USA Today* report (21–23 February 1992), the version of the event employs a sanitized style:

> Foreign workers are bracing for more violence after the stabbing death of a member of Kuwait's ruling family by a Filipina housekeeper. Lourana Crow Rafaeil, 44, is accused of murdering Sheikha Latifa Abdullah Al-Jaber Al-Sabah last week in Cairo after she refused Rafaeil's request to travel to the Philippines. Kuwaiti and other Arab newspapers are calling the foreign workers untrustworthy, and even branding them as prostitutes.

With her name altered at every mention of the incident in various publications, Lourana / Lorna's agency is operationalized: she becomes an emblem of an irrepressible resistance and her story an exemplum of vindication. She becomes the archetypal victim warning of retribution, a stand-in for all subalterns smoldering with vindictive *ressentiment*. Her mutilated figure registers and mocks at the same time the claims of bourgeois realism and surveillance.

Meanwhile, many Filipinos continue to feel no alternative to the misery in the Philippines, except to seek employment abroad. Despite repeated humiliation, hunger, brutal abuse, and solitary confinement culminating in rape or murder, these new "modern-day heroes" (to quote former President Corazon Aquino's ironic praise of the islands' most lucrative exported merchandise) seem incapable of learning the lesson of refusal. Could it be naiveté, ignorance, or sheer bullheadedness? Or could it be a deeply ingrained susceptibility to fantasy and hallucinations of "making it"?

One answer is given by Ricardo Lee and Gil Portes' film *Bukas . . . May Pangarap* (1984); the script depicts a man from the peasantry who was swindled by a recruiter. After being deported from Saudi Arabia, Udong (the main protagonist) returns to his family and struggles to earn a living. Somehow feeling guilty for the failure of her husband's adventure in Saudi Arabia, his wife Mering kills herself. After her burial, Udong offers himself to another recruiter (not connected with "Saudi") so he can feed his children and pay back his debts. It is the end of the rope for him; the only way out is to sell himself again at a price higher than what he can get in the Philippines. Reminded by his brother of his being swindled before, his subsequent "loss of face" and the suicide of his wife, Udong seems unable to summon up the courage needed to give up his dream (or delusion?) of being able to earn enough to support his family and wipe away his debts by going abroad. The siren overseas beckons; desire for proving one's worth, one's honor, to kins, loved ones in the family and community, pushes each individual Filipino to try his or her luck, even risk life itself, in the hazards of playing the game of the global marketplace.

It becomes evident that the seduction exercised on millions of Filipino men and women occurs in the space of a wrecked or stagnant Philippine economy, massive damage due to plunder by transnational corporations aided by the IMF / World Bank and the unconscionable greed of the comprador élite. Freedom to sell one's labor power to anyone who will buy it is a freedom that crosses, nay, overturns national boundaries and seems to leap barriers of all kinds. But soon, one discovers the concrete limits of this freedom. It is accomplished with the mediation of petrodollars, Japanese yen, or any viable European currency. Its use-value is precisely its exchange-value, its translation into commodities. When these merchants of their own bodies find time to reflect and attempt to reconstitute their identity, the montage of their fragmented lives revolves around the post office (the medium of communication with relatives and provincemates) and the bank, the two loci where there crystallizes the diegesis of the world system as a metanarrative of the global circulation of finance capital.

In the Middle East, petrodollars purchase the labor-power of migrant workers, not only to build infrastructure, but to sustain and reproduce the patriarchal structures of power in tributary or feudal social formations. But more important is the exchange of their time and energies—or put another way, the exchange of their bodies, appraised and traded as consumer goods or as disposables—for money (which never really corresponds to what is socially necessary to reproduce their human capacities, not to speak of their singular lives). This provides the foreign exchange needed to bail out the native élite and to sustain their criminal lifestyles, the oligarchic comprador bloc that has mortgaged the future of neocolonial Philippines to the IMF / World Bank and financial consortiums of the West.

Opposites are indeed united here, but costs and benefits are never equalized, despite the short-term relief of debt payments. The whole symbolic lawfulness of the world market, with its quotidian logic of buying / selling, disintegrates. In its wake, the vicissitudes of the migrant *récit* replay the breakdown of all traditional narrative paradigms.

The case of Flor Contemplacion and Delia Maga witness to a cata-strophic waste, an "expense of spirit" and flesh, that devastates any emergent plot or residual narrative configuration that purports to give meaning to these women's lives, subverting the psychic economy of sublimation and "hyper-real" carnival that defines contemporary neo–Social Darwinist consumerism. Is this the lesson inferrable from the circulation of social energies in the latest saga of Filipino migrant labor?

We have seen how the socially necessary labor time needed to pro-duce the power to work—the value of women's labor power—has been reduced to the minimum. The condition of serfdom already alluded to is worsened by bourgeois illusions of ego-centered liberty—for exam-ple, the ideology that everything is normal, natural, in the competitive marketplace. In this milieu, the "free" laborer collapses all of time into the expenditure of labor power that is measured and translated into money wage. The time left to recuperate or reproduce that same labor power is either absent or left to coincide with the purchased time. In short, production and reproduction of the worker's life have become identical. The value of abstract labor is represented by the money com-modity, by its exchange into consumer goods. Money, as social power and as the form of value (not as money capital) and the commodities to which it is equivalent, conceals the social meaning of value itself, in-cluding the value of pleasure and happiness for social individuals. It also hides the character of private labor and the social relations between workers and their employers.

The market system—the commercial exchange of the capacity-to-labor as a commodity—seems to dictate the price of quantities of use values expended by these racialized and sexualized "slaves." But it is actually the political and economic domination of the Philippines by the United States, Japan, and the industrialized states of the "North" (to-gether with their Arab clients) that explains how the exchange value of the women's capacity to produce value results in their degradation, their dehumanization. Both the conditions of work, as well as the inten-sity of the labor process—symptomized by the gaps, absences, and eli-sions in the women's recollection of their experiences—are wholly con-trolled by the employers, who are citizens of powerful nation-states, and who can manipulate their governments and international agencies in the service of global capital.

In these narratives of spatial adventure, we find a temporal process that deconstructs the Eurocentric paradigm of the "free laborer" emerg-ing from the dissolution of feudal serfdom. Inserted into the force-field

of antagonisms in the world system, with its sex-gendered and racialized class hierarchies, women from the Philippines and elsewhere are
reduced to modern-day slaves (see Anderson; Javate-De Dios). Their
bodies become commodities, the exchange of which is severely delimited by their virtual "ownership" by Western or Japanese businessmen
and gangsters. This situation exists, even while the institutional framework that defines the status of overseas contract workers superimposes
the mirage of the "free" circulation of labor power exchanging according to fair market prices.

This disjunction between the classic model of the free market of commodities and the tributary relations between nation-states—the underdeveloped peripheries like the Philippines, which supply cheap labor—
has configured the plots of women's stories into either a pathetic or
sentimental one. They are pathetic in that a sequence of misfortunes
cuts down our protagonists, who do not deserve such suffering and so
arouse our sympathy. They are sentimental in that, despite the blows of
adversities, our attractive and weak protagonists enjoy a semblance of
relief—through marriage or safe return to the homeland (Ducrot and
Todorov).

Women's agency here confounds orthodox determinations. We
scarcely find any plots of education or revelation, since most of these
women seem not to have absorbed the lesson of avoiding repetition.
Instead we find them confessing their desire either to return to the same
place of misfortune, or to travel to another place where tales of opportunities abound. At the very least, a change occurs in their specific
attitudes, but not in their central belief that the economic improvement
of their lives cannot happen in their homeland but must occur abroad.
This perception matches the reality of unrelenting immiseration, which
in turn hides the dangers of exploitation abroad. Some women are
tested, reformed, and enlightened; others become disillusioned. Rarely
do these veterans give warning to their compatriots to desist from exploring unknown, alienating territory. So, in effect, the commodity-
fetishism of the system of dependency continues to mediate the dispersal of libidinal investments by people of color. We see this in narratives
where the process of mediation of their lives is determined by a combination of brute physical force, coercive patriarchal norms, callous neglect of governments, and—last but not least—the philanthropy of hyp-
ocritical moralists.

I insert here a few concluding remarks on the play of value in the
plight of Filipina migrant workers. This is a prolegomenon to under-

standing the drama of wide-ranging aesthetic and cultural transformations that are overtaking the Filipino people today, as they finally try to break away from U.S. hegemony at the threshold of the twenty-first century.

In the *Grundrisse,* Marx emphasized that "society does not consist of individuals; it expresses the sum of connections and relationships in which individuals find themselves. . . . [Thus,] to be a slave or to be a citizen are social determinations." Likewise, to be a Filipina migrant laborer in the domestic sphere today is to be determined in a geopolitical hierarchy, where the fact of being located as (1) Filipino, (2) female, (3) worker, and (4) domestic/household slave, produces texts that can be read simultaneously as symptoms of a new global political economy of accumulation and as allegories of resistance. In transnational capitalism, the productive consumption of labor power as the prime commodity (abstract, quantitatively comparable) that is exchanged has been marked by gender, sexuality, region/locality, and nationality in order to reduce the labor needed to reproduce it and therefore maximize surplus value (unpaid labor).

What is "socially necessary" becomes politically defined: Third World women are paid subsistence wages, even starved as prisoners of their employers, denied basic rights, abused, raped, and even killed (Sklair). Female domestic and sexual labor-power yields a use value (a product) whose market price as commodity is depreciated because of its property as (1) female, and (2) as subaltern impoverished nationality (Filipina, Sri Lankan, Bangladeshi). The unequal division of international labor and the abundant supply of such cheap "Third World" hands in the world market, as well as the hegemonic pressures of the centers of finance capital, all converge. They reverse the ascribed, putative leveling power of abstract exchange value (money as "universal social property") and make the expropriated use-value reinforce tributary or semifeudal hierarchical relations.

In the classic narrative plot of accumulation and mastery (progress), $M_1 \rightarrow C \rightarrow M_2$, exchange value grows by consuming labor-power. But for the stories recounted by migrant female domestic workers (contracted overseas labor), the plot evokes the order of simple or petty commodity production: $C \rightarrow M \rightarrow C$. The fetishism of exchange-value is destroyed by the constant and immediate conversion of money into consumer goods. The textuality of servitude and death in the policed domestic sphere dissolves with the purchasing power of whatever wage is received: "the power that each individual exercises over others' activity or over social wealth exists in her as the owner of exchange values, money" (Marx 66).

Orgies of consumption, spectacles of expenditure, aim to celebrate use value and to overcome, through spasmodic shopping sprees, and by an evocation of utopian finality, the death drive that is prefigured in the postmodern sublime. Its text is nothing else but the infinite circulation of signifiers of difference—circulation as an end in itself. Such female narratives of diaspora and return, replicated endlessly in our estimate, may be parables of autochthonous energies attempting to transform the market and the commodity form into signs of the anticipated transcendence of use value per se, commodities valorized as aesthetic objects and as instruments to negate their exchange value. At the very least, when these women either strike back or escape from their multiple confinements, their narratives begin to interrupt the flow of warm bodies into the market. They signal a crisis in the global traffic of differences and heterogeneities that genuinely challenge the rule of racist and sexist capital.

Amelioration of these women's suffering and a halt to the traffic of contracted domestics and sexual "slaves" (the latter particularly in Japan) will surely begin when and if a critical mass of women from the Philippines and other Third World countries are conscienticized enough to organize and revolt against the whole system. Lacking this, we can for the moment be consoled by one woman's quest for happiness and freedom—I have in mind the fate of Lorna Laraquel, Maricris Sioson, Maria Victoria Suller, Delia Chavez, Melita Garcia, and hundreds more, all condemned by a whole system of racist exploitation and oppression, whose testimonies remain to be exhumed and liberated from the archive of an unjust and iniquitous "New World Order."

In a play entitled *Pitik-Bulag Sa Buwan ng Pebrero* (1989), Ricardo Lee captured the existential predicament of women such as Lorna Laraquel, Flor Contemplacion, and others, who so far remain invisible and silent to most people. As a rule, they can only articulate their struggles in letters to friends and kins for fear of losing their jobs. Their deaths succeed in releasing these letters to the general public—but too late to intervene in rescuing them. The power of indigenous women's agency can be felt in the language of Yolly who, in a recognizably Brechtian defamiliarizing style, narrates and simultaneously reflects on her life as a Filipina "dancer" in Japan:

Nagputa ako hanggang gusto nila. Pinag-aral ko lahat. May malaking aquar-
ium, nakababad kami d'on sa tubig, may mga numero sa dibdib, parang mga
ipinagbibiling isda. Tiniis ko lahat. Nag-cultural dance ako nang naka-bikini.
Nakipag-sex nang may nanonood. Nilaspag-laspag nila ako, lahat na nang bagay
ay pumasok sa katawan ko, pero lagi pa rin akong at your service, omese, anything
you say. Nakakulong kami, may kandado at bantay, pinupurga sa contraceptives
at penicillin, binubugbog kapag nagreklamo. Kagaya ni Esper ay marami rin
akong hiwa at pilat sa katawan. Tinanggap ko lahat nang mga iyan. May naka-
plaster na ngiti sa mga labi ko pero putang ina, sabi ng dibdib ko, putang ina.

(I became a whore up to the hilt. I studied everything. They had a large
aquarium, there we were immersed in the water, with numbers on our
chests, like fish being hawked. I endured everything. I did cultural dances
with a bikini. I had sexual intercourse with spectators around. I was thoroughly bruised, almost all kinds of objects penetrated my body, but I was
still at your service, yes, anything you say. We were imprisoned, with lock
and guard, purged with contraceptives and penicillin, beaten up if you
complain. Like Esper [a "mail order bride" beaten up by her Australian
master], I have many cuts and scars all over my body. I accepted all these.
There was a smile plastered on my lips but son of a bitch, my chest cried
out, son of a bitch.)

The authentic closure to all these aborted, dispersed, vertiginous narratives cannot be found in the individual fates of the speakers or characters involved. Rather, it is suspended in the larger diasporic agon of
Filipina domestic workers, the latest epiphany of which is the execution
of a "modern slave" in Singapore.

On 17 March, Singapore's government hanged Flor Contemplacion
for the alleged killing of a fellow maid and her four-year old charge.
Despite the patent implausibility of such an accusation, belied by witnesses who testified that Contemplacion was innocent (she was, according to some reports, tortured by the Singaporean police and forced to
confess to the alleged crime), her story was given no credence—even by
the Filipino officials who, doubting Contemplacion's own disavowal,
made the motion of setting up its own bureaucratic inquisition. But
millions of Filipinos, outraged by such injustice, exploded into rallies of
indignation all over the islands; urban guerrillas as well as local town
and provincial administrators threatened Singaporeans, their lives and
properties, in a gesture of protest. In response to President Fidel Ramos'
plea for clemency, the Singaporean president was quoted as saying that
his cabinet "found no special circumstances to justify commutation of
her sentence" and cited Section 302 of Singapore's penal code to the

effect that anyone convicted of murder is meted the death penalty "regardless of nationality" (*Philippine News*, 15–21 March 1995, A6). It was a classic tautology to wash bloody hands and also conceal the real criminals. Ramos, of course, assumed that the woman was guilty. In the version of the incident in Singapore's newspapers, Contemplacion was portrayed as hearing voices that told her to kill the Filipina maid and the Singaporean boy—obviously, a self-induced *deus ex machina* invented by apologists. In a last-ditch effort, the Philippine government appealed to the United Nations to intervene, but apparently this gesture was meant only to appease the infuriated citizens (*Philippine News*, 22–28 March 1995, A1, A14).

In the immediate aftermath, the Ramos administration mounted an all-out display of concern for our latter-day "national heroes," hundreds of thousands of contract workers exploited and brutalized daily in Singapore, Hong Kong, Tokyo, and other cities in the Middle East, Europe, North America, and elsewhere. Somehow we want to affirm our national dignity, our conscience, our sense of solidarity. Rallies, vigils, flag-burning, funeral marches, massive protests, and unrelenting cries for vengeance—these interruptions of the tragicomic plot in which our compatriots are entangled seem to betoken the impending collapse of the entire symbolic economy of globalized labor-exchange on which the ideology of individual success through work, thrift, and self-sacrifice rests. Empathy is no longer needed, vicarious identification no longer avails. The shock of recognition we experience does not spring from peripeteia or reversal but from our encounter with state power, the terror of state violence.

Finally, the sacrifice of bodies for the sake of Gross National Product and IMF / World Bank conditionalities—in other words, the sacrifice of sensuous use value for the abstracted or reified exchange value—now has found a precise corporeal embodiment in the hanging of Flor Contemplacion by the rabidly self-righteous authoritarian regime of Singapore. Their worship of the Commodity / Money fetish eludes the interpretive capacity of rational communicative action. Indeed, there are no more stories or tales to recount at this point, only this uncanny quiet of the vigil, whispers of something being mounted, intimations of "the fire next time. . . ."

Afterword

It was as if many of us Filipinos were living behind hidden identities for fear of
associating with the realities of our lives, our real names, and therefore, our real
identities. . . . We need the truth more than we need heroes.
   —*Philip Vera Cruz, 1977*

Let us take our bearings, where we came from and in what direction we
are heading. So far, we have charted the discursive terrain where the
salient contradictions of our time involving race, ethnicity, class, nationality, and so on are refracted in a multilayered fabric of textuality
open for interpretation, critique, and ecumenical dialogue. My intervention here should be deemed a prologue to a substantial and more
nuanced inventory of the historical specificities of the Philippine social
formation that would determine the various modes of cultural production and appropriation pivoting around the event called "becoming-
Filipino." Less ethnogenesis than alter/native *poiesis,* the goal is to convert the "state-nation" (Smith, *Theories of Nationalism* 189–90) to an
evolving national-popular site of dialogue and praxis.

   Such a reconnaissance of a Third World people's struggle to define
and validate its agency is, in effect, a task of reconstituting the nation
and its reinscription in the syntax of the world community. In so doing,
we encounter ourselves in others, who enrich and complete us. We engage in a provocative and catalyzing exchange with voices from other
societies, using a constantly revised lexicon of "communicative reason"
(to borrow Habermas' terminology)—a polylogue, or exchange oriented toward a fusion of horizons, where all can equally participate in
the creation of purpose and value.

   My proposal of an alter/native poetics as a hypothetical paradigm for Third World cultures depends, of course, on the peculiarities of each nation's history. What seems imperative now is to insist on a more dialectical comprehension of the global process, one that subsumes both the United States and the Philippines in the text of a world system crisscrossed by antinomies, schisms, and contradictions, and so on. Cultural representations are constructed and deconstructed along lines of race, class, gender, and ethnicity that seem to defy the boundaries of the traditional disciplines.

There is, I might suggest at this point, a felicitous correspondence between the subject-position of writers in the Philippines and their counterparts in Latin American societies, given the historical parallels in their colonial domination by Spain and by their subordination to U.S. economic-military supremacy. Investigating the literary institution as an ideological practice in Central American revolutions, John Beverley and Marc Zimmerman remark that "the ideological centrality of literature in Latin America has to do with the effects of colonialism and capitalist combined and uneven development in the region, which have left intact and/or specially marked elements of earlier cultural formations that have become extinct or marginal in the metropolis" (15).

I concur with this stress on the uneven, nonsynchronized field of forces—textual practice or symbolic inscription being one force—where precisely a hegemonic politics relative to local circumstances becomes the only feasible long-range strategy for confronting a militarily and economically superior enemy. (To forestall misunderstanding, I should like to stress here that I take "hegemony" to imply varying proportions or ratios of the war of maneuver and war of position, privileging neither, the mix being dependent on the social field of forces at any given time.)

Unlike Ruben Dario's *modernismo* or Ernesto Cardenal's Christian-Marxist repertoire of prophetic jeremiads and exempla, no contemporary cultural text—except perhaps the writings of former political prisoners like Sison, Angel Baking, and Karl Gaspar; interviews of quasi-charismatic personalities like Bernabe Buscayno or Father Edicio de la Torre; or certain poems of Amado V. Hernandez—so far has exercised the role of a central ideological signifier, one that could generate a national-popular culture with overwhelming mass appeal, one strong enough to mobilize an intraclass bloc that could successfully challenge the U.S.-supported oligarchic machine and the military-ideological agencies at its command. A likely candidate for this status would be the cinema-texts of Lino Brocka and of Kidlat Tahimik (if the latter's films are thoroughly popularized), or the lore of myth and filmic aura surrounding certain personalities like ex–movie star Senator Joseph Estrada.

But the future cannot be totally mortgaged to past or present achievement. In this interregnum, I consider the primary and urgent task of criticism to be the revitalization of oppositional texts and the invention of a wide range of disruptive practices that would fulfill the function of such a charismatic signifier. This is needed in a highly disintegrated society that is nevertheless structured in dominance by the reactionary apparatus of terror and the state's dependence on foreign financing and investment. Without this emancipatory practice of critical reading/ writing and its mediation of meaning, literary texts can be used to advance the ends of reproducing exploitative social relations and reinforcing the victims' *ressentiment*. This expropriative praxis entails the risk of historicism, of invoking a teleology based on superimposed values and convictions. However, since everyone is implicated in historical becoming, and one is forced to take sides (sometimes without knowing it) in a struggle whose stakes are life or slow death for millions of Filipinos, I take this risk. It is a small price one must pay for unfolding the power of literature—the submerged Orphic voices prophesying the revenge of the oppressed generations in limbo, victims of injustice and ruthless calculation of profit; prophesying the fulfillment of dreams, hopes, desires: justice for the living and the dead—not only in interpreting our personal and communal experiences, but also in changing the direction of our lives together with others.

A convergence of my position as a Filipino intellectual based in the metropolis and an unprecedented nationalist resurgence in the Philippines situates my critical commentaries and researches as necessary interventions in the realm of cultural politics. In the process of comparative cultural investigation, the margin and center, like the inside and outside, ultimately coalesce. It is now generally acknowledged that any person engaged in a critical commentary on Philippine culture and society is always a participant in the arena of ongoing political and ideological antagonisms encompassing two polities, the United States and the Philippines.

The essays gathered here function as a heuristic reconnaissance of the terrain for my larger ongoing project of assessing English writing in its historical inscription. This undertaking is modest, however; it is basically revisionist in a sense antithetical to that of Karnow's *In Our Image* and mainstream scholarship mentioned at the outset. It is heretical and dissident in conceiving of literature in the Philippines as an ideological practice of national liberation, the paradigm of an alternative "emergency" politics with a national-popular agenda. It is fundamentally counterhegemonic because it strives to articulate the Filipino subversion of the "received," legitimizing identity imposed on it by the metropolitan power and reproduced daily by local and transnational institutions. Finally, it is oppositional in its effort to construct a sovereign Filipino identity, multiple and protean, in the process of rereading and rewriting the U.S. inscription of the Filipino subject-position in the text of Western metaphysics and its fetishizing instrumentalities.

Revision, then, is a form of what Nietzsche calls "creative destruction." In this otherwise reconstructive task, I share the burden of responsibility with my Filipino brothers and sisters in numerous organizations in the homeland, in Europe and elsewhere, committed to egalitarian social justice, participatory democracy, and true national independence.

Illustrated in my recent books *Allegories of Resistance, From the Masses, to the Masses,* and *Hegemony and Strategies of Transgression,* I have often taken as a point of departure a seditious perspective in the critique of texts and writers. My aim is to recover what has been repressed, and to help release/unleash energies that constitute the historical-materialist agency of the working masses, the fundamental stratum or matrix of any cultural artifact. I hold that the practice of writing in Third World formations like the Philippines cannot be understood unless it is contextualized in specific historic conjunctures, unless it is situated in the uneven and unsynchronized political economy of a dependent society. My primary interest involves both substance and method: how writing practices, which are acts of signifying as well as referencing, reflect the struggles of popular forces, even as the specific texts themselves mediate between conflicting ideologies, either on the side of oppression and neocolonial hegemony, or on the side of transgression and popular democracy. Conflicted sensibilities of authors and a heteroglossia (to use Bakhtin's term) or polyphony of world views are registered in the choice of literary forms, genres, styles, and imagery that highlight specific problems or thematize urgent exigencies gripping whole communities.

In this light, the engaged critic necessarily has to conceive of the peculiar configuration of texts generated by revolutionary changes in decolonizing societies where the imagination becomes the arena or field of competing ideologies and political forces. These texts mediate the ideology, politics, economics, and culture of specific historic conjunctures, while at the same time articulating the feelings and thoughts of the oppressed (Fanon's multitudinous "wretched of the earth") and inscribing their presence in a palimpsest decipherable by those readers whose "horizon of expectation" affords empathy and alterity.

Nor is this approach one-sided in its partisan stand for national liberation struggles of Third World peoples. As critique and transformative metacommentary, the decolonizing approach to which I subscribe conducts a dialogic if contentious and skeptical exchange with Western theorizing, whether neoconservative and liberal or neo-Marxist and poststructuralist in tendency. Neither compromise nor reconciliation, but a play of contradictions and the idea of transformation fused with practice, are the initial objectives we should strive to attain.

Despite the unavoidably particularizing impulse of constructing indigenous signifiers (the context-specific vernaculars) of each national or regional literature, a partisan of anti-imperialist theory from the *bundok* shares a general orientation with all those who have nonelective affinities in being victims of colonial power, in facing common obstacles in the present (there is nothing postcolonial about the Northern hegemony of capitalist-industrial powers over the poor nations of the South), and those who entertain visions of a cooperative future. This does not signify a leveling or homogenizing orientation, in which differences that really matter are erased. Indeed, all determination is negation (Spinoza), so a negative hermeneutics that questions everyone's referentiality and logic except itself is indeed a sorry affair, if not downright fraudulent. What is needed is a dialogic—more precisely a dialectical—horizon of communication, sustained by mutually supportive reciprocal goals.

Can Filipino writers, given the confluence of Asian, Spanish, and Anglo-Saxon imprints on their collective psyches, really choose to be singular and idiosyncratic? How could that be demonstrated in living practice? These essays, in fact, explore the conjunction and disjunction between a Eurocentric discourse of autonomy (initiated by bourgeois Enlightenment thought) and an embattled Asian sensibility that is trying to define itself in opposition, trying to assert what in retrospect could be original or indigenous, relationally speaking. Reckoning globally, I take comfort in the thought that this is not a solitary enterprise. In the community of Third World intellectuals and partisan activists, I have found inspiration in the models of solidarity personified by Frantz Fanon, Amilcar Cabral, Lu Hsun, Che Guevarra, C.L.R. James, Adolfo Sanchez Vasquez, George Jackson (to cite only the most publicized names), and numerous Asian, Latin American, and African combatants for popular democracy and socialist internationalism. But without being necessarily sectarian about it, some tactical demarcations with those claiming a theoretical edge sometimes needs to be drawn.

Within the framework of dependency / world-systems analysis, Australian critics Ashcroft, Griffiths, and Tiffin have espoused an anti-Empire position with commendable erudition and rhetorical force. They have emphasized the hybrid and syncretic nature of postcolonial writing (mainly Commonwealth writers, from former British possessions) in their theoretical synthesis, *The Empire Writes Back*. I agree with their basic thesis of a dialectical relationship between metropolitan and peripheral cultures, and with the impossibility of recuperating "an absolute precolonial cultural purity." But I disagree with the corollary belief that it is impossible to create a national formation geared to realizing autonomy within the given hegemonic global system—even after the collapse of a so-called socialist Soviet Union in the post–Persian Gulf War, in the grisly hard times of the "New World Order" of capital.

Needless to say, Ashcroft and colleagues ignore the Third World outside the Commonwealth. For example, they have nothing to say about the rich, diverse cultures of the American Indians in the north and south, nor do they manifest any awareness that something is going on in their neighbors' space (Indonesia, Timor, New Caledonia, the Philippines), or in Cuba, Palestine, and other sites of fierce anti-imperialist struggles. "The Empire" is clearly delimited by the authors' national experience. This is where the centrality of the category "nation" for literary theory intrudes (also its corollaries: national democracy and national liberation). Whether through mimetic or allegorical modes, in either imaginary or symbolic registers or both, the quest for national autonomy (even though the postmodern configuration of "nation" appears problematic) seems inescapable (see Bhabha). Will subaltern, minority, postcolonial discourse always be reactive, a vertiginous psychodrama of resistance? Is there no possibility for the *novum* (after Bloch) to materialize in symbolic exchange? If there are no closures and no beginnings either, the power of capital in the New World Order *in medias res* will always win.

Whatever the answers to those questions, I hold that it is not enough simply to multiply ingenious deconstructive re-readings and rewritings of the European or American historical and fictional records. Ashcroft, et al. claim to legislate what Third World / postcolonial artists should do: "These subversive manoeuvres [mentioned before], rather than the construction of essentially national or regional alternatives, are the characteristic features of the postcolonial text. Postcolonial literatures/ cultures are constituted in counter-discursive rather than homologous practices" (196). The guerilla-writer in the jungles of Peru or Timor queries: why "rather than"? Is there no room for the homology of *testimonio*—those of Rigoberta Menchu or of Domitila Barrios de Chungara? A foreclosing judgment seems to punctuate the aporia of postcolonial normative speculation and immediately suspends dialogue. Is it possible that, here once again, we are confronting the imperial hubris of Western logocentrism and power, resurrected in the guise of unsolicited "friendly" advice?

But can we, "the hewers of wood and drawers of water," not decide for ourselves? Is a clean break foreclosed? Are all the boundaries fixed? Can we not stake new ground? What indeed are the real stakes in this antifoundational discourse? Whose lives are on the line confronting imperial power? Of course, we—if I may presume to use this editorial pronoun—in the decolonizing societies of the Third World understand the historical predicament and susceptibilities of a settler state like Australia and its "White Australia" heritage (Miles, *Racism* 90–98). Consequently, despite our own scholarly interest in "advanced" theory, we have no illusions about the heterogeneity and radical Otherness of postcolonial theory arising even from the pulpits of the sub-metropolitan centers. But reversals and disruptions that clear the ground are bound to happen, as Gramsci observes: "A historical moment . . . is rich in contradictions. It acquires a personality, it is a moment of development in that some basic activity of life dominates others and represents a historical 'advance'" (Thibaudeau 19). What historical experience has shown is that interventions from new social agencies are bound to erupt in places least expected, not necessarily weak links, so we remain vigilant and hopeful that the changes going on will not repeat the narratives of the past.

In the ongoing *perestroika* of the whole planet, the coordinates of periphery and core constantly are being scrambled. Icons are recurrently destroyed; cries of convulsive birth pangs resound. Subterranean rumblings charged with "auguries of innocence and of experience" can be heard, even from seemingly pacified frontiers like Timor, "zones of occult instability" (Fanon's phrase) like Bosnia, Peru, Chechnya, Chiapas, Kurdistan, and large parts of the Amerindian regions. I am hopeful that, from the struggles of peoples in Haiti and El Salvador, South Africa, Palestine, Northern Ireland, Guatemala, and other outposts of the Empire, new theories and practices of popular resistance art will spring—

not just one or two but many. Only then will a real dialogue or colloquy with the West begin. As Ernst Bloch and Walter Benjamin have discovered in the darkest days of European fascism, the new is permanently possible. And in the fullness of time, it will blast the continuum of history.

In the meantime, I urge partisans of the emancipatory imagination in the contested borderlands—whether inner cities in the industrial North, or free trade zones in South Korea, or the desert of Saudi Arabia—to engage in inventing new modes of renegotiating the terms of the hegemonic transnational discourse embracing "justice," "democracy," and "freedom," and articulating them toward a collective project of national-popular liberation. This oppositional task is unavoidable if we want to challenge the disciplinary regimes of imperial power and their liberal or even "libertarian" surrogates. It can be synchronized or merged with that of producing transformative, liminal, and utopian discourses and practices.

One task in this project is propaedeutic or heuristic in nature: the effort to draw up a provisional cognitive mapping of one terrain in which the fates of two cultures, two peoples, have been joined. We need a radical, deconstructive rewriting of how U.S. hegemonic culture has read and "produced" the Filipino (more precisely, the "truth/knowledge" concerning the Filipino). We need understanding of how the subaltern, engendered by interlocking cultures (albeit ones that are polarized and originally discordant, including the Malayan, Chinese, Arabic, Spanish, and North American), finally has begun to speak and act (perhaps to curse, like Caliban) in a new language, a strange and bewildering speech inscribed in oral or written texts, gestures, body movements, songs, cinematic and video images, weapons native and imported—all signs of a new beginning.

Notes

Introduction

1. An instance of this dependency is the Filipino historian Gregorio Zaide, who is considered a nationalist in some circles, but whose textbook *History of the Filipino People* (1971 edition) contains this apologia for U.S. imperialism: "It was the policy of America to govern the Philippines for the happiness and welfare of our people and to train us in the ways of democracy so that someday we shall be worthy of independence." Again, another Filipino, Narciso Ramos, Secretary of Foreign Affairs under Marcos in the late sixties, is utilized to plead the case of the dominant superpower.

But these two positions, I argue, are not really idiosyncratic. They share assumptions with many élite intellectuals and differ only in degree from the thinking of their colleagues. These include, for example, the late ambassador Leon Maria Guerrero, a Marcos adviser, who blamed his countrymen for "quiet desperation" in welcoming the reactionary dictatorship (*New York Times*, 24 November 1973), and Raul Manglapus, minister of foreign affairs during the Aquino administration, who invoked America's "conscience" as a force that granted Filipinos their independence in 1946 and would again intervene (as it did in 1986) to restore and "save democracy for the Filipinos" (*New York Times*, 4 October 1973). Uneven development proves again to be a fertile breeding ground for subalterns of all stripes and disguises.

2. The fabrication of apologias has become fashionable in the wake of February 1986. In a review of *The Philippines Reader*, edited by Daniel B. Schirmer and Stephen Shalom, the noted anthropologist Fred Eggan—a member of the first generation of American Filipinologists who produced bits of the official knowledge about tribal Filipinos for universal consumption—condemned the book as "good propaganda but poor history." Eggan's brand of history, to be sure, is not the long nightmare of colonial oppression and exploitation of the benighted "tribes" of the archipelago, but one characterized by "unusual liberalism and benevolence." He cites Narciso Ramos' statement as proof: "American policy

was explicitly intended for the happiness, peace and prosperity of the people of the Philippine islands" (20; for the view of Protestant missionaries, see Clymer).

What about other statements by prestigious Filipinos who say the opposite? Interviewed in 1984 by Princeton University scholar Richard Falk about the impact of U.S. policy, ex-senator Jose Diokno declared: "With its military bases, the United States has made the Philippines a neocolony. It is in part because of U.S. bases that we do not have full control over our lives or our destinies" (442). For all practical purposes, such dissenting voices have been silenced or censored by the fiat of the fabled Philippines-U.S. "special relations." In the final reckoning, Eggan faults the Filipinos for their failure to come up to the American standard of modernization. Had Dean Worcester and other "enlightened" administrators who patronized the non-Christian tribes continued to exert power and influence, Eggan muses, Filipinos would not have misbegotten the horrendous Marcos regime, which in hindsight the country fully deserved! With few qualifications, this is the same message offered by two Filipinologists of Cold War vintage, Carl H. Lande and Richard Hooley. In an article in *Foreign Affairs,* they conclude their assessment of what happened in the Philippines before and after Marcos' overthrow by invoking that structure of attitude and reference signified by the phrase "the old patronage game" (1107). For them, it is the key to explaining the cause of the massive and seemingly intractable problems that afflict Filipinos.

It is revealing that in both articles, the impact of U.S. Cold War policies is either absent or occluded, from MacArthur's restoration of the collaborationist élite to the Magsaysay/CIA-manipulated campaign against the Huk insurgency (see Richardson xxii–xxiii). (President Ramon Magsaysay [1953–57], with CIA backing, is usually credited with reforms that deflected mass support for the Huk rebels.) Instead, a culturalist mode of explanation supervenes. The reproduction, circulation, and reinforcement of the doctrine of normative clientelism, somehow insulated from the critical winds of historical change, appears to be an index of the abysmal degeneration of Philippine studies in the United States at the present time. But, one might ask, when has this area study ever been free of covert pressures from above and released from the blandishments and chicaneries of philanthropists and corporate business?

3. In the field of cultural inquiry, the performance of U.S. Filipinologists has grown more dreadful, if not contemptible. I can only speculate that this is due to the perception that the Philippines is becoming more independent and recalcitrant, thanks to thousands of Filipinos dead, tortured, up in arms, malnourished, or in jail. Another hypothesis is the loss of control and security as the empire fades away. One recent example displays the proverbial arrogance and smug philistinism of "experienced hands" in colonial affairs. Undeterred by factual errors and simplifications, Morton Netzorg, merchant of assorted Filipiniana, tries to put down Bulosan's resourceful and inventive retelling of folk narratives, *The Laughter of My Father,* with the comment that the stories "purport

to be tall tales about his wacky father, and wacky neighbours and wacky relatives in rural Luzon" (177). In the same breath, Netzorg expends just enough animal spirits to describe Stevan Javellana's powerful realist novel, *Without Seeing the Dawn,* as "a flawed but substantive work," delivering his *obiter dictum:* "the book was overpraised because here at last (and after quite a few false starts) was a novel in English by a self-coached Filipino—indubitably, unquestionably and by any standard a novel" (177).

What we have here is not at all, as colleagues suggest, a matter of policing the circulation of the "traumatic memory" of American colonialism as the reason for the marginalization of Philippine studies and the "invisibility" of Filipinos as protagonists of world-historical importance. It is rather a special variant of Alzheimer's disease, as though the islands were still a territorial possession and the Filipinos benighted wards of the Bureau of Indian Affairs. On the other hand, this performance may not be so culpable as the deeds of some crass opportunists who assisted the Marcos dictatorship. Among the mercenary propagandists, two may be cited here: Sarah Caldwell of the Opera Company of Boston was paid at least $200,000 by Mrs. Imelda Marcos for her complicity in cultural matters (*The Boston Globe,* 20 November 1982), and Hartzell Spence wrote Marcos' autobiography, *For Every Tear A Victory* (*New York Times,* 3 November 1988).

4. Failure to understand this fundamental truth leads to a repetition of the same mistake committed by some scholars who take public pronouncements as equivalent to the reality. A recent case comes to mind. Antonio Contreras aptly advises Robin Broad and John Cavanagh, authors of *Plundering Paradise: The Struggle for the Environment in the Philippines,* not to take the superficial claims of NGOs (non-governmental organizations) and other "new social movements" as unequivocal harbingers of grassroots democracy: "The élites have found new ways to coopt radical alternatives and NGOs are becoming part of this reactionary politics. This is seen in state-sanctioned 'people-oriented' programs designed more to control than to empower, and carried out through NGOs more interested in the money which the government offers through these programs than in sustainable development" (139). In effect, the putative radical or alternative politics of the NGOs become not alternatives to the system but "alternative types of organizing within the system" and "hegemony is re-established when former oppositions are transformed into mere differences."

5. Here is an example of how this ideology of postmodern chic versatility is played out in a tourist guidebook, wherein we encounter a now-stereotypical congealing and virtual commodification of the Filipino "essence":

Given four hundred years of Hispanization, it is predictable that the visitor should see (or think he sees) certain traits that the Filipino has in common with the Mexican, the Peruvian, the Argentinian and all the other *indios* of Madre España's former colonies. A touch of the *mañana* syndrome; volatility, capriciousness, rhetoric; an instinctive style and flair; the pursuit of all fads and fashions with avid enjoyment; a feeling for music and rhythm that puts Filipino groups at the top of the bill in nightclubs throughout Asia. . . . There is much contrariness, even contradiction, in the Pinoy (as the Filipino calls himself colloquially). But the combination of Malay warmth and generosity, the ingredient of Latin temperament, the sudden shifts from Utopian optimism to moody fatalism, the mixture of brashness and grace, makes the Filipino's a hard act to follow (Mayuga and Yuson 14).

The act is neither unique nor inimitable. Peoples displaced or transported across borders—slaves, refugees, emigres, fugitives, exiles—and forced to live by cannibalizing cultures and carnivalizing them as well, may be said to exhibit this contrariness, this mirage of the versatile actor and the ingratiating player. Nonetheless, this is one contemporary version of what we have become as a result of the struggle to endure colonial domination and still retain our humanity. But it is definitely not a version that expresses the clamor of millions of workers and peasants for justice and equality.

Chapter I

1. "Civilize 'em with a Krag." The quote is a line from a famous marching song of American soldiers engaged in the Philippine pacification campaigns of this century's first decade. The Krag was a government military rifle of the era. "Boondocks" is American slang for rough country, dense bush, or jungle, according to *Webster's Third New International Dictionary*, 1976. The term comes from *bundok*, the Tagalog word for mountain, mimicked by by American soldiers during the Filipino-American War of 1989–1903.

While most textbooks use the year 1902 as the end of the Philippine "insurrection" following President Theodore Roosevelt's pronouncement (Graff 171), I use 1903 to decenter official historiography for the following reasons: after Aguinaldo's capture, the Philippine Republic continued its armed resistance under General Miguel Malvar, who surrendered in 1902, and General Luciano San Miguel, who died in combat on March 28, 1903 (Constantino, *History* 253). Historical records testify that even after the demise of Macario Sakay's "Tagalog Republic" (1902–05) and the hanging of Sakay in 1907, numerous uprisings occurred until 1910. In fact, political prisoners were executed for sedition by the U.S. military until 1914. The year 1903 also marks the first massive May Day demonstration by Filipino workers against U.S. imperialism in front of Malacanang Palace.

For an early version of this chapter, consult San Juan, *Ruptures, Schisms, Interventions: Cultural Revolution in the Third World* (21–37); see also San Juan, *Only by Struggle: Reflections on Philippine Culture, Politics and Society in a Time of Civil War*. One can illustrate here the effectivity of ideological determinants in a cultural formation such as the Philippines during Spanish rule (1565–1898) with reference to the mediating organ of textual authority as a means of producing and reproducing subalternity. Backed by the state's coercive might, the Roman Catholic Church legitimized its extortionary pastoral care of its flock through the institution of the *auctores* (approved religious texts) by controlling educational institutions and the apparatus of communication (printing press, censorship, enforced illiteracy for peasants and workers, selected admission to schools, and so on). Imitation of medieval romances was allowed so that the natives could display their originality and verbal astuteness within the framework of this sanitized generic convention. In this milieu, a poet like Francisco Balagtas (1788–1862) derived his authority not so much from his genius as from the folkloric aura of the *corrido* and the ceremonial pattern of its reception. Balagtas was not an author, properly speaking, but a practitioner of a ritual or *habitus* of the community safely guarded by the inquisitorial agencies of the Church. On the other hand, as Dolores Feria has shown, the case of Leona Florentino (the mother of anarcho-syndicalist Isabelo de los Reyes) demonstrates how the feminist hubris can override colonial-patriarchal closure and (to quote Hegel) "be at home with itself in its otherness" (Feria, "The Florentino Umbilicus").

2. The testimonials of support are found in Senator Richard Lugar, "Stand by Cory Aquino," *The Washington Post National Weekly Edition* (29 September 1986: 29). For earlier accounts, see Stephen Solarz, "Press for Philippine Reforms," *The New York Times* (8 August 1984: A23) and U.S. Senate Staff Report to Select Committee on Intelligence, *The Philippines: A Situation Report 1 November 1985* (Washington, D.C., 1985). See also my *Crisis in the Philippines*, particularly the Introduction and Chapter One.

3. See also Barrows' revealing testimony to Congress, reproduced in Graff (159–65).

4. On the U.S. literary culture and milieu at the turn of the century, see Howard Mumford Jones, "Introduction" to W. C. Brownell, *American Prose Masters* (Cambridge, MA, 1909, reissued 1967: vii–xi).

5. On the orthodox conception of "tutelage," see among others Stanley. On the politics of the language question from the viewpoint of the colonial power, see Hayden (583–603). For a contemporary Filipino response, see Enriquez and his articles in Rogelia Pe-Pua's *Sikolohiyang Pilipino* (5–21, 64–82, 120–30). One of the projects I proposed in the late seventies was entitled "Dialectics of Influence: U.S.-Philippines Literary Confrontations 1900–1972"; its partial realization has been disseminated in books previous to this one: *Toward a People's Literature: Essays in the Dialectics of Praxis and Contradiction in Philippine Writing, Writing and National Liberation,* and *Reading the West/Writing the East: Studies in Comparative Literature and Culture,* among others.

Originally I designed my analysis—an open-ended application of hermeneutic comparatist approaches—to focus on specific texts as symptomatic products of the colonial/neocolonial experience. I sought to ground the speculative inquiry on the concrete historical reality of the lives of key writers being investigated, their familial / class conflicts, and the sociopolitical tensions subtending them. The effect of U.S. hegemony (by which I mean consent-of-the-ruled, negotiated through compromise and ultimately enforced by coercion) from the first decades of this century up to the seventies (from Sherwood Anderson to the New Criticism and Cold War "humanism," followed by neoconservative trends masked in postmodern trappings) would be thoroughly examined and appraised. With ideas and idioms migrating to / from metropolis to periphery, the critic can plot a distanciating / overturning movement of reading and interpretation in order to reveal the underlying grid of structures and relations between "lived" production and hegemonic representation.

6. For the general temper of the milieu, see Gossett (287–459) and Spiller et al. (789–1106).

7. Howells' review of Rizal's novels is in *Harper's Monthly Magazine* (April 1901: 805–06).

8. Compare the views of George Weightman, "The Philippine Intellectual Élite in the Post-Independence Period," *Solidarity* (January 1970: 20–25). The early sixties, one may recall, witnessed also the celebration of the Beatles and Marshall McLuhan's electronic "global village." Taylor had no cause to worry. We can see how "the semiotic of capitalist valorization"—to use Felix Guattari's phrase—operates in this vulgar mercantile fashion. Examples include a leading Filipino novelist, Bienvenido Santos, proudly declaring in 1976 that he was qualified for American citizenship because he could sing the "Star Spangled Banner from memory as if I have been singing it all my life, which indeed I have"; and the practice of Filipino writers up to now seeking validation by trying to get into the prestigious U.S. journals (as did their predecessors in claiming recognition when their works appeared in *Pacific Spectator, Partisan Review, Poetry,* and others) or by achieving publication of their books in New York City.

9. Stegner's mystification becomes more pronounced when compared to the accounts of resistance before and after the years of the Huk uprising, as found in "Tatang"; see also Kerkvliet and Allen. Stegner's oblique strategy of salvaging an obsolescent hegemonic discourse may be seen in Casper's entry on the Philippines in the *Encyclopedia of Poetry and Poetics,* a symptom of neocolonial aggression that needs recapitulation here. In his contribution, Casper unreservedly condemns Filipino writers for their "chauvinistic" imitation of Whitman and for their "sentimentality and wordiness," in the same breath that he conjures a peculiarly American "emphasis on the dramatic and concrete." U.S. expertise again flaunts its imperious and reductive mode of knowledge-production when it cranks out historically false statements—for example, that in the thirties "except for a small group of writers producing in Tagalog the vernaculars were seldom used for literary expression." Nothing can be further from the truth. On the whole, Casper denigrates the vernacular while pretending to objectively judge Filipino poets who write in English. Casper's "indiscriminate" distortions are not unique, one might add. They replicate mainstream scholarly

wisdom typified by the 1972 and 1976 editions of the *Area Handbook for the Philippines,* a major authoritative source of "scientific knowledge" for the U.S. government. These works assign to the urban élite the task of forging a national culture, premised on the functionalist bias that "artistic traditions were not an assimilated whole but more a layering of cultural contributions."

Chapter 2

1. American literary personalities other than Hemingway had greater impact—for example, Sherwood Anderson and Edgar Snow, among others—but the social and historical contexts of Hemingway's visit explain his "overdetermined" presence then, just as, during the Cold War era, the lecture tours of William Faulkner and Sidney Hook acquired more than just an individual resonance.

2. See also Weisstein, Shaw, Corstius, and Clements. It is possible to argue, as does Francois Jost (41–61), that we should not confuse authorial influence with immanent similarity or analogy of circumstances so as to avoid imputing to the ideas of a few intellects an exaggerated power over vast cultural processes. I agree with this viewpoint and its historical sense of heterogeneity / plurality; but in the sphere of analyzing the relationship between metropolis and periphery, between colonizing power and subaltern peoples, we cannot treat each entity of this dialectical complex as autonomous or separate. And here I disagree with the perspectivism of Nietzschean deconstructionists who act as though the Philippines was and is a genuinely independent nation-state like France or the United States. Cultural studies dealing with peripheralized societies cannot ignore direct and mediated linkages with the totality of Western hegemonic culture. This culture exerts a systemic pressure on the subordinate formation and its symbolic codes and repertoire of representations, even while we grant that subjugated peoples are able under the circumstances to preserve their historic agency by subverting, transvaluing, or decoding the instruments of their subjection and inscribing their signature in them. "Postcolonial" is less malapropism than a euphemistic coverup by latterday Gunga Dins in postcolonial regalia.

3. For a critique of dependency theory and anatomy of neocolonialism, see Katz, Woddis, and Magdoff. For the Philippine case, the standard references are Guerrero, Lichauco, and Constantino.

4. See also Kolko (*Triumph of Conservatism*) and Lasch. Lasch notes that by the mid-twenties, socialist and populist radicalism in the U.S. was dead. A recent cogent explanation of the U.S. imperialist ethos, building on the previous works of Sweezy, Baran, Amin, Appleman Williams, and Eqbal Ahmad, is Parenti's *Against Empire.*

5. For the ideological orientation of the Spanish-speaking writers, as well as those of the vernacular tongues, see Majul and San Juan, *The Radical Tradition.*

6. I am proposing this dialectical approach, based on the Gramscian problematic of hegemony and the distinction between wars of position and wars of maneuver presented in *Selections from the Prison Notebooks*. See also Williams. On interpellation, see Laclau 100–42. For linguistic and cultural capital, see Bourdieu and Passeron.

7. In 1926, Professor Cristino Jamias, a respected member of this first generation of American-trained teachers of English, wrote: "In our universities, we must emphasize mind-building. . . . Culture, which means a study and live interest in things of the mind. The tenacity to think will give us the real directors of destiny—an aristocracy of mind, an intellectual minority, unleading, unled" (Yabes 39). The Westernization of the Filipino intelligentsia is the subject of many investigations, among them Renato Constantino, "Part I" of *Neocolonial Identity and Counter-Consciousness*.

8. The classic text of the 1930s literary renaissance is Salvador P. Lopez's *Literature and Society*. See also Ordoñez ("Literature under the Commonwealth"). For a retrospective evaluation by Lopez himself, see his "Literature and Society—A Literary Past Revisited," in Bresnahan 6–17; and also "The Writer in a Society in Crisis."

9. For a eulogistic account of Hartendorp's role, see Marsella.

10. See the essays by Bruce Franklin and Richard Ohmann in Kampf and Lauter. For the British inflection of New Critical elitism, see Raymond Williams, *Writing in Society* 177–228.

11. See also Viray's "Writers Without Readers." Viray's historical sensibility deteriorates when he composes his later piece, "Racial Heritage," in Guthrie.

12. See Bernad's bleak prognosis for English in "Philippine Literature in English: Some Sociological Considerations," which curiously contradicts and deflates his own Americanizing drive in an earlier piece, "Literature in the Philippines."

13. See Marcuse; Wolff; and Lukacs.

14. The last three terms—Orientalizing scope, intensity, and persistence—are taken from Malek; see also Aijaz Ahmad, *In Theory*. In addition to Edward Said's well-known works, other Third World critiques of cultural imperialism are Fanon, Ngugi, C. L. R. James, and Amin. See also the pertinent selections in the two volumes of *Communication and Class Struggle*, edited by Mattelart and Siegelaub.

15. For a sampling of American anti-imperialist writing, see Bresnahan, *In Time of Hesitation* and Zwick. For the itinerary of American "Filipinologists," see the series on Philippine Studies published by the Center for Southeast Asian Studies, Northern Illinois University. A self-righteous defense of U.S. imperialism is in Gleeck. One observes how the scholarly findings self-destruct when they are popularized in such references as Chafee, Steinberg, and Roces.

16. The *Area Handbook for the Philippines* cited previously (Chaffee) propagates such fraudulent statements as: "Despite heroic attempts to sustain it, the [Tag-

alog] novel gradually died" (140); and "except for a small group of writers producing in Tagalog, the vernaculars were seldom used for literary expression" (141). Such gross errors explain why teachers and run-of-the-mill commentators have been misled and misinformed. Although aware of the rich and accumulating vernacular writing in the Philippines, John Echols for the most part endorses Stegner's opinions in his essay, "The Background of Literatures in Southeast Asia and the Philippines," in Guthrie 1953: 133–63.

17. The documentation on repression and militarization during the Marcos regime is voluminous. Because of space limitations, I can cite only the following texts: Amnesty International, International Commission of Jurists, Permanent People's Tribunal, Lawyers Committee for International Human Rights, and Poole and Vanzi. For recent reports of human rights violations under the Aquino dispensation, see Amnesty International, *Human Rights Violations and the Labor Movement*, June 1991, and *"Disappearances" in the Context of Counterinsurgency*, February 1991; and for a general assessment, see Thomas O'Brien.

18. A massive corpus of counter-arguments has already been produced, among them: Feria, *The Long Stag Party*; Teodoro and San Juan. A revitalized scholarship on the vernaculars is illustrated by Reyes, Mojares, Lumbera, and San Juan. I sketch the genealogy and archive of the revolutionary cultural tradition, a sequel to my earlier *The Radical Tradition* and *Toward A People's Literature* in the following: *Writing and National Liberation, Reading the West/Writing the East*, and *Allegories of Resistance*. The historical context has been ably recapitulated in Agoncillo and in Constantino and Constantino.

19. See Magno, Rivera, and Villegas.

20. See also Ferrucio Rossi-Landi. These trends, born from the crisis of institutional representation and shaped by the pre-positional strategy to circumvent and disrupt, may be observed in the activities conducted by various legal organizations. Among them are Center for Women's Resources, Nationalist Alliance, Kilusang Mayo Uno, Task Force Detainees, Institute for Popular Democracy, Gabriela, and numerous Christian base communities; see San Juan (*Crisis*), Aguilar, Canlas et al., Davis.

The project of overall renewal now is being accomplished by the multifarious organizing enterprises of the New People's Army, guided by the Communist party of the Philippines; the Bangsa Moro Army, led by the Moro National Liberation Front; the Cordillera Front of the Igorots; and other sectoral affiliates of the National Democratic Front in the Philippines and around the world.

Chapter 3

1. Unfortunately, even a recent dramatization of the typical worker's life in Hawaii, entitled *Istorya ni Bonipasyo* (*Bonipasyo's Story: Hawaii Is Like Paradise*), although it foregrounds the activist drive, fails to make the connection with the

national-democratic resistance in the Philippines. As a symptom of the deeply sedimented "colonial mentality" of this "transported" peasant community, the play glorifies the bourgeois work ethic now ascribed as part of the natives' "cultural baggage"—a strange but revealing conflation!

2. The use of "P" instead of "F" for Filipino was introduced by some Filipino activists in the late sixties on the premise that the sound for "F" in English is not found in any of the Filipino languages and therefore a nationalist identity politics needs to revise the spelling of the designation for immigrants from the Philippines. This practice did not really become popular. After 1987, however, the official term (as stipulated by the 1987 Constitution) for the emergent national language in the Philippines became "Filipino," not "Pilipino," in the interest of subsuming more than seventy languages and dialects used by the total population. For international communication, I opt for the more ecumenical "Filipino" instead of the symbolic, separatist "Pilipino" in the English usage.

Chapter 4

1. Takaki, *From Different Shores* (4).

2. Takaki, *Strangers* (324).

3. Eric Chock, another name listed by Amy Ling, identifies himself as a Hawaiian writer and resident (Ruoff and Ward 362). The Filipinos in Hawaii, condemned to almost castelike conditions, constitute a community significantly different from Filipinos on the mainland. For a survey of the writing by Hawaiian Ilocanos, see Somera.

4. Aside from serving as Director of the Peace Corps in the Philippines (1961–63), Fuchs was Executive Director of the Select Commission on Immigration and Refugee Policy under President Carter. Another mode of recuperation is exemplified by Stanley ("The Manongs" 4), who insists on the "relatively libertarian character of U.S. rule."

5. In 1946, 6,000 Filipino workers were imported to Hawaii to counter an industrywide strike—proof once more that the Philippines is an "inside" factor in the U.S. imperial polity (Philippine Center for Immigrant Rights 6).

To the early contingents of Filipino workers belongs the honor of spearheading the first and most resolute labor militancy in Hawaii in modern U.S. history. According to Sucheng Chan, after the 1882 Chinese Exclusion Act and the Gentleman's Agreement of 1907 limiting the entry of Japanese labor, Filipinos became the predominant agricultural labor force in Hawaii: "Not surprisingly, they became the main Asian immigrant group to engage in labor militancy. Moreover, as Beechert has noted, they did so in politically repressive environments with criminal syndicalist laws" (87).

While Bulosan does not claim to describe, for instance, the epic strikes of 1924 in Hawaii's Hanapepe plantation and of 1937 in Puunene, the scenes of union organizing and strikes in America function as an allegorical emblem of all such instances of either sporadic or organized resistance by masses of people of color. Bulosan's life covers four major episodes in the Filipino workers' history: the action of the Agricultural Workers Industrial Union–Trade Union Unity League in 1930, the formation of the Filipino Labor Union in 1933, the affiliation of the Alaska Cannery Workers Union with the CIO in 1937, and the establishment of the Filipino Agricultural Workers Association in 1939.

In the late thirties, 25 percent of Filipinos were service workers, 9 percent were in the salmon canneries and 60 percent in agriculture (Takaki, *From Different Shores* 316–18; Catholic Institute for International Relations 36).

6. Aside from Sam Tagatac's experimental "The New Anak" (Peñaranda's "Dark Fiesta" deals with native rituals and folk beliefs in the Philippines), the Flips will include only the Flip poets—some of those in *Without Names* (Ancheta), and some in Bruchac's collection. I will not repeat here the bibliographic data of Filipino-American authors found in Cheung and Yogi's excellent reference guide.

In fairness to the Flips, I should state here that Serafin Malay Syquia's poems and his essay "Politics and Poetry" (Navarro 87–89) represent a crucial intervention that seeks to reclaim an "America" reconstituted by people of color. At a time when leaders of the community were rejecting Bulosan's socialist vision and the legacy of the Manongs, Syquia and his comrades were striving to reconnect, via their ethnic rebellion, with the insurgency in the neocolony—an emancipatory project of opening up the space prematurely closed by Santos' conciliatory acceptance of the status quo, Gonzalez's myths of restoration, and Villa's patrician withdrawal.

7. I take issue with the bias of functionalist, positivist social science in my book *Racial Formations/Critical Transformations*. The assimilationist doctrine of the ethnic paradigm, with its ahistorical empiricism, has vitiated practically most studies of the Filipino community in the United States. Typical is Pido's *The Pilipinos in America*, littered with such blanket pronouncements as "Pilipinos fear alienation" (35). Far more insightful are articles such as Aurora Fernandez, "Pilipino Immigrants," *East Wind* 34–36; and Teresita Urian (written by Mila de Guzman), "Into the Light," *Katipunan* (10–11).

8. Occeña's pioneering effort can be supplemented and corrected by regional, archival studies made by Barbara Posadas, Ruben Alcantara, Edwin Almirol, Antonio Pido, and revisionary archival work now being done by younger scholars.

9. "Asian-American" as an operational bureaucratic designation is misleading because of the widely disparate historical experiences of the groups concerned and because it tends to covertly privilege one or two of its elements (as in the MLA surveys I've cited). However, Occeña points out that both self-recognition and societal recognition of the peoples involved stem from their integration into U.S. society "on the bases of inequality vis-à-vis whites; subjected to vari-

ous forms of racial and national discrimination and constituted as an oppressed strata of U.S. society" (29). But, because the Asian and Pacific Islands peoples, from their arrival through today, have not amalgamated to form one distinct nationality, it is best to discard the label "Asian-American" and use the specific name of each nationality to forestall homogenizing ascriptions like "super-minority," "model minority," etc.

10. Until 1946, Filipinos did not have the right to become naturalized U.S. citizens. Nor could they marry whites in California until 1948, nor own land until 1956 (Philippine Center for Immigrant Rights 8–9, 15–16).

11. This trend is discernible in the Flips' statement of identity politics. The Flips descend mainly from the relatively conservative formation of the second wave of Filipino immigrants (numbering about thirty thousand), comprised of war veterans who enjoyed some privileges (Catholic Institute for International Relations 41–42). Their codewords that registered anxiety toward "melting pot" miscegenation are found in phrases like "cathartic stage of ethnic awareness" and "maintaining ethnic awareness." But by juxtaposing inside / outside without historical qualifications, they replicate what they want to negate: including the Same / excluding the Other.

12. Although Solberg is correct in pointing out the interdependence of Fili-pino-American writing and indigenous Filipino writing in English, his ascrip-tion of a myth-making function to Bulosan and others is misleading (which explains, for instance, Buaken's failure to produce a unified narrative from his own fragmented life). The reason surfaces thus: the myth's regime of truth turns out to be a discourse of cooptation as "the Filipino dream of independence fades into the American dream of equality and freedom" (56).

13. Gonzalez's mercantile mentality typically contrives an apologia for the Cordova volume (xi) when he cites the white master's endorsement of his ser-vant: "My servant was a Manilla man." In this way, the stereotype of Filipinos in the thirties as "wonderful servants" (Takaki, Strangers 317) is repeated and reinforced.

14. To illumine the deceptive stoicism of Santos' closure in his stories "The Day the Dancers Came" or "Scent of Apples," it would be instructive to com-pare the ending of J. C. Dionisio's "Cannery Episode" (413), where the narrator captures the discipline and strength of the "Alaskeros" on the face of a horrible mutilation of one of their compatriots. We also find in Pete's character (reflected by the choric narrator) an embodiment of revolt against the inhumane system, a subject position typically absent in Santos' and Gonzalez's fiction.

15. Elaine Kim dismisses Villa as non-ethnic (288). Bulosan's judgment of Villa reflects my own earlier polemical evaluation (People's Literature 73–76). For Bulosan, Villa "is somewhat in line with Baudelaire and Rimbaud, for these two appeared when French poetry had already reached its vortex and was on the downgrade. Naturally they were great apostles of the poetry of decay. When we speak of literature as a continuous tradition, a growing cultural movement, Villa

is out of place and time." Villa does not represent "the growth of our literature"; rather he "expresses a declining culture after it has reached its height" (*Writings* 151).

16. Here I approximate the first mode of incorporation via commodity form that Hebdige outlines (94–96). The ideological mode of incorporation I exemplify in my remarks on Bulosan, Santos, and Villa.

17. Only two of over two hundred photos depict Filipinos on strike in Cordova (76, 81). Most are photos of families and relatives of the editor and the kin-related staff of the Demonstration Project. Comparing the text of the section on "Alaska Canneries" with a contemporary account of the dismal conditions by Emeterio Cruz, one notices the textual and iconographic techniques of neutralization and obfuscation deployed by Cordova's album, the cut-off point of which is 1963, a revealing date that marks the resurgence of radical activism in the Filipino community. In featuring Hilario Moncado (183), Cordova commits an act of partiality and censorship, one of many, when he fails to mention Moncado's notorious opposition to Filipino workers' demands for justice (Chan 76, 89).

Cordova's inadequacies include his false generalizations on religion (167) and his embarrassing eulogy for one million Filipinos who died during World War II for the sake of "Americanism" (221). But these amateurish mistakes descend to unwitting racism when he lumps *inter alia* Lincoln, The Lone Ranger, Superman, Charlie Chan, and Martin Luther King, Jr. together (230).

A similar reservation can be made of otherwise instructive documentaries like *In No One's Shadow*, wherein the cinematic sequence focuses on the normal adjustment of the Filipino immigrant despite all odds. This selective method of fetishizing individual success stories conceals the institutional structures and historical contingencies that qualified and limited such individual lives. The ideology of the image and its system of verisimilitude need to be elucidated and criticized as a determining apparatus that produces a deformed Filipino subjectivity ripe for hegemonic reproduction.

18. A modest attempt has been made by the Philippine Center for Immigrant Rights in New York City to revive the example of *Letters in Exile* with the publication of their pamphlet, "Filipinos in the USA." But no major initiative has been taken to organize the Filipino community on the basis of its nationality and its unique response to continuing U.S. domination since the demise in the eighties of various socialist formations with Filipino leadership or active involvement.

19. Except for Puerto Ricans. In another essay, I argue that U.S. cultural history cannot be fully inventoried and assayed without registering the symptomatic absence in it of Filipinos and Puerto Ricans as colonized subjects. Operating in the field of American English, the Filipino interruption of U.S. monologism is unique, insofar as it demarcates the limits of the imperial episteme, its canonical inscriptions, and its reflexive frame of reference.

20. This is a play directed by Behn Cervantes, who adapted materials from

Virgilio Felipe's M.A. thesis, "What You Like to Know: An Oral History of Bonipasyo," presented in Hawaii in late 1991. The assimilationist rationale for this event may be perceived from this statement in the program notes: "The Hawaii [the chief protagonist] was lured to as 'paradise' seems harsh and full of hardships, but is compensated for by Bonipasyo's rightful pride in the conviction that his toil and sacrifice made Hawaii." Whose Hawaii?

21. Fermin Tobera, a 22-year old worker, was killed during the anti-Filipino riot in Watsonville, California, on 22 January 1930; his body was interred in the Philippines on 2 February, marked as "National Humiliation Day" (Quinsaat 55, 57; for a contemporary estimate of the Watsonville situation, see Buaken 97–107). Silme Domingo and Gene Viernes were anti-Marcos union activists and officials of the International Longshoremen's and Warehousemen's Union, Local 37, in Seattle, Washington; Bulosan edited their 1952 *Yearbook*. The two were slain on 1 June 1981 by killers hired by pro-Marcos elements and corrupt union operatives (Churchill). It is alleged that the FBI and CIA were involved in this affair.

22. By "anti-canon," I mean a mode of resisting standardization by the dominant Euro-American ideology and by the conservative aura of a comprador-bourgeois Filipino tradition. On the problematic of the canon, I have consulted Weimann, Guillory, and Scholes.

23. Berger inflects the theme of exile in this century of banishment by suggesting that "Only worldwide solidarity can transcend modern homelessness" (67).

Chapter 6

1. Aiken's Modern Library anthology (*Twentieth Century American Poetry*) includes the following poems by Villa: "There Came You Wishing Me," "Be Beautiful, Noble, Like the Antique Ant," "God Said, 'I Made a Man,'" "Now, If You Will Look in My Brain," "My Mouth Is Very Quiet," "The Way My Ideas Think Me," "Saw God Dead but Laughing," and "Mostly Are We Mostless" (396–400).

2. One Filipino critic, Rolando Tinio, seems to follow Casper's footsteps when he confesses difficulty in sympathizing with Villa's universe, "a universe completely evacuated of values which we can easily recognize as human. The landscape is completely antiseptic, like Mondrian" (724). Less adversarial, although still mainly negative, is L. M. Grow's recent appraisal (326–44).

3. On the nature of Villa's avant-gardism, these remarks by Eduardo Sanguineti on Baudelaire are illuminating: "We see in the prostitution of which Baudelaire speaks a two-fold tendency which is intrinsic to the avant-garde. It expresses a heroic and pathetic straining for an immaculate product, which would be free of the immediate interplay of demand and supply, and which would, basically, be commercially enviable. At the same time and through pre-

cisely the same gesture, it expresses the cynical dexterity of the 'hidden persuader' launching on the art-market a commodity which might achieve instantaneous success, through sheer surprise and audacity, in competition with the feeble products of those who are less astute and less free from prejudices" (390–91).

4. Adorno's "dialectical" deciphering of the worldliness of poetic form finds support in Hayden White's remarks on the social function of literature in bourgeois society and how literature as a commodity "reflects" the social conditions of its production: "Considered as a commodity, the literary work would reflect the social conditions under which it was *produced,* the various conditions under which it was *exchanged,* and the various conditions under which it was *used.* Considered as a piece of historical evidence for the illumination of the social structures and processes of an earlier time, however, it is the *exchange function* that is crucial. It is the literary text which enters into the exchange system prevailing in a given society" (376).

5. The term "disappeared," a literal translation of *desaparecidos,* refers to persons kidnapped and killed by the military in Latin America (especially in Argentina, Chile, and El Salvador). The word is a contribution of the Third World to the English language. The same goes for "salvaged" in the sense of abducted and murdered, applied in the Philippines to political dissenters or prisoners who disappear and reappear later as corpses. A reversal is operated on the English word to make its meaning conform to the horrendous reality of a neocolonial truth, vis-à-vis the fact that English is the language of business and the military, both institutions complicit with the U.S. in exploiting and oppressing the majority of seventy million Filipinos.

6. Public records show that Villa has made only three visits to the Philippines, one in 1937 for two months, the second in 1962 when he was awarded a *doctorate honoris causa* by the Far Eastern University, and the third sometime in the seventies. During his 1962 visit, this "Filipino who made good" was reported to have said: "I feel haunted by my country! During my visit I feel in love with my country and my people. It was a very good realization, to have rediscovered myself as a Filipino." A phantom of essentialist humanism?

Chapter 7

1. Writing from the Australian end of the British empire, Ashcroft, Griffiths, and Tiffin in *The Empire Writes Back* consider the United States as the first postcolonial society to develop a "national" literature. This is an astonishing claim from the viewpoint of Puerto Ricans, Cubans, Hawaiians, Native Americans, and other former subjects. They not only believe that the United States is "first" in this, but also that the U.S. can be "the model for all later postcolonial writing." Such an exorbitant proposition is either a joke in bad taste, or an ironic trope to

outrage "politically correct" fellow travelers. Can the United States ever be postcolonial, by any stretch of the imagination?

Ashcroft and his colleagues have formulated a statement that functions like a mirror-image of the U.S. discourse of pacification I alluded to earlier, a rhetoric of the "civilizing mission" used to legitimate the violent subjugation of Filipinos—"thirty thousand killed a million"—in the first three decades of this century. On certain appropriate occasions, the victims of "postcolonial" writers like Emerson and Bellow may still commemorate the ideals of the Enlightenment, the U.S. Declaration of Independence, and so forth; but to celebrate U.S. culture as a paragon for the Third World simply exceeds the limits of liberal tolerance and utilitarian prudence.

2. Perhaps we can draw a lesson from a recent case. One testimony of the havoc that the internalized fictions of Western/white supremacy can inflict may be seen in the introduction to a 1993 anthology of Philippine literature in English, entitled *Brown River, White Ocean*. The editor, Luis Francia, claims to address "the disparities in dissemination" between Third World literatures and those of the West by regurgitating the myth of "Benevolent Assimilation." He states that Filipinos should be grateful to U.S. colonial occupation, not only for democracy but also for English, allegedly a "unifying language" (contrary to the historical record and what sociolinguists have convincingly demonstrated). Francia says: "By enabling Filipinos of proletarian background to go not just to grammar school but all the way to university, the American occupation seemed downright revolutionary" (x).

Too bad for Sakay and his comrades, and all the other million peasants who did not take advantage of that golden opportunity and so did not grow up with English as their native tongue. I wonder what the generation of Pedro Calosa and Salud Algabre, leaders of the Tayug and the Sakdal revolts, respectively (see Sturtevant), were doing during those first three decades when the Thomasites taught Romulo and the oligarchic élite their ABCs? While English has been "ingrained into our writers consciousness" and even "blended with the landscape," according to Francia, the modern Filipino, however, is a "confusion"— "somewhat like a Cubist painting with blurry lines" (xiii). We are told that Filipino society is a hodgepodge and its literary artifacts are "portmanteaus," garbage seemingly floating down the puny "brown river" to be swallowed up finally in the all-encompassing "white ocean."

Such unfortunate tropes of dependency and subservience are nonetheless appropriate in capturing the pathos of this editor who, while asserting that "whatever Philippine writers write about, whether they intend to or not, reveals them as being ineluctably Filipino" (xiii–xiv), also hopes that from the anarchy and presumed multicultural jumble the Filipino will "forge a new identity" (xix). These egregious inconsistencies and *non sequiturs* may perhaps be claimed as signifiers of the virtue of being a multicultural, if commodified, product of U.S. hegemony and the Philippine neocolonial milieu. While the editor hopes to

achieve "a creative subversion of the Thomasites' efforts," the naive endorsement of the conqueror's "civilizing mission" and the fatuous praise of assimilation engenders the opposite: an apology for servitude. The lessons of Twain and
other American anti-imperialists, not to speak of Apolinario Mabini, Isabelo de
los Reyes, Juan Abad, Aurelio Tolentino, and all the "seditious" intellectuals
who were imprisoned, deported, tortured, or killed have been forgotten or
ignored.

The lesson distilled in Paulo Freire's insight found in *The Pedagogy of the
Oppressed* is appropriate here: "The true focus of revolutionary change is never
merely the oppressive situation which we seek to escape, but that piece of the
oppressor which is planted deep within each of us, and which know only the
oppressor's tactic's, the oppressor's relationships" (51).

3. In my books, especially *Toward a People's Literature*, *Only By Struggle*, and
Writing and National Liberation, I analyze classic texts like Juan C. Laya's *His
Native Soil*, Stevan Javellana's *Without Seeing the Dawn*, and other deviant or
nonconformist texts. Especially in *Subversions of Desire*, I provide substantive
metacommentaries on the major writings of Nick Joaquin, by consensus the
leading Filipino writer in English. In these works, I concretize the parameters of
the "sign," a privileged locus of ideological contestation, within the "uneven
and combined development" of the Philippine social formation. The previous
chapters have endeavored to recapitulate this complex interweaving of history,
ideology, and form, implicating a metropolitan power, the United States, in the
fate of its former colony in Asia, the Philippines, and of at least two million
Filipinos scattered over the North American continent.

4. "Death," in this context, signifies the negation of conscious sensuous praxis
integral to the full development of the person in a future communist society,
accompanied by the unleashing of the powers of the body (whose immortality
is theorized by the materialist philosopher Baruch Spinoza). What prevails in
the postmodern world is the heteroglossia of mass consumerism, the babble of
reified success.

Works Cited

Adorno, Theodor W. "Lyric Poetry and Society." *Telos* 20 (Summer 1974): 56–71.
—— and Max Horkheimer. *Dialectic of Enlightenment*. New York: Continuum, 1972.
Agcaoili, T. D., ed. *Philippine Writing*. Manila: Archipelago House, 1953.
Agoncillo, Teodoro. *Filipino Nationalism 1872–1970*. Quezon City: R. P. Garcia Publishing, 1974.
Aguilar, Delia D. *The Feminist Challenge*. Manila: Asian Social Institute, 1988.
——. *Filipino Housewives Speak*. Manila: Institute of Women's Studies, St. Scholastica's College, 1991.
Aguilar–San Juan, Karin, ed. *The State of Asian America*. Boston: South End Press, 1994.
Ahmad, Aijaz. *In Theory: Classes, Nations, Literatures*. New York: Verso, 1992.
——. "The Politics of Literary Postcoloniality." *Race and Class* 36.3 (1995): 1–20.
Ahmad, Eqbal. *Political Culture and Foreign Policy: Notes on American Interventions in the Third World*. Washington: Institute for Policy Studies, 1982.
Aiken, Conrad, ed. *Twentieth-Century American Poetry*. New York: Random House, 1944.
Alavi, Hamza, and Theodor Shanin, eds. *Introduction to the Sociology of "Developing Societies."* New York: Monthly Review Press, 1982.
Alegre, Edilberto, and Doreen Fernandez. *The Writer and His Milieu*. Manila: De La Salle University Press, 1984.
Allen, James S. *The Philippine Left on the Eve of World War II*. Minneapolis: MEP Publications, 1993.
Alquizola, Marilyn. "Subversion or Affirmation: The Text and Subtext of 'America Is in the Heart.'" In *Asian Americans: Comparative and Global Perspectives*, edited by Shirley Hune et al., 199–209. Pullman: Washington State University Press, 1991.
Althusser, Louis. *Lenin and Philosophy and Other Essays*. London: New Left Books, 1971.

Amin, Samir. "The Class Structure of the Contemporary Imperialist System." *Monthly Review* 31.8 (1980): 9–26.

———. *Eurocentrism.* New York: Monthly Review Press, 1989.

Amnesty International. *"Disappearances" in the Context of Counterinsurgency.* New York: AIM, February 1991.

———. *Human Rights Violations and the Labor Movement.* New York: AIM, June 1991.

———. *Reports on the Philippines* (22 November–5 December 1975). New York: AIM, 1981.

———. *Reports on the Philippines* (11–28 November 1981). New York: AIM, 1981.

Ancheta, Shirley, et al., eds. *Without Names.* San Francisco: Kearney Street Workshop, 1985.

Anderson, Benedict. "Cacique Democracy in the Philippines: Origins and Dreams." *New Left Review* 169 (May–June 1988): 3–33.

Anderson, Bridget. *Britain's Secret Slaves.* London: Anti-Slavery International, 1993.

Appadurai, Arjun. "Disjuncture and Difference in the Global Cultural Economy." In *Colonial Discourse and Post-Colonial Theory,* ed. Patrick Williams and Laura Chrisman, 324–39. New York: Columbia University Press, 1994.

Appel, Benjamin. *Fortress in the Rice.* New York: Bobbs-Merrill, 1951.

Arguilla, Manuel, Esteban Nedruda, and Teodoro Agoncillo, eds. *Literature under the Commonwealth.* Manila: Alberto Florentino, 1973 (reprint of 1940 edition).

Ashcroft, Bill, Gareth Griffiths, and Helen Tiffin. *The Empire Writes Back.* New York: Routledge, 1989.

Baker, Carlos. *Ernest Hemingway.* Princeton, NJ: Princeton University Press, 1969.

Bakhtin, M. M. *The Dialogic Imagination.* Austin: University of Texas Press, 1981.

Balibar, Étienne, and Pierre Macherey. "On Literature as Ideological Form." In *Untying the Text,* ed. Robert Young. New York: Routledge and Kegan Paul, 1981.

Bauer, Otto. "National Character and the Idea of the Nation." In *Essential Works of Socialism,* ed. Irving Howe. New York: Bantam Books, 1970.

Bautista, Cirilo. "Conversation with Jose Garcia Villa." *Archipelago* 8 (August 1979): 30–31.

Bautista, Lualhati. "Lorena." *Midweek* 5 April 1989: 24–27, 44.

Bauzon, Kenneth E. *Liberalism and the Quest for Islamic Identity in the Philippines.* Durham, NC: The Acorn Press, 1991.

BAYAN International. *The Truth About the Ramos Regime.* Los Angeles: Philippine Peasant Support Network, 1974.

Benjamin, Walter. "The Author as Producer." In *The Essential Frankfurt School Reader,* ed. Andrew Arato and Eike Gebhardt, 254–69. New York: Continuum, 1988.

———. *Illuminations.* New York: Schocken, 1969.

——. *Reflections.* New York: Harcourt Brace Jovanovich, 1978.

Bennett, Tony. *Formalism and Marxism.* New York: Methuen, 1979.

Berger, John. *And Our Faces, My Heart, Brief as Photos.* New York: Pantheon, 1984.

Bernad, Miguel. "Literature in the Philippines." *Thought* 37 (Autumn 1962): 437–48.

——. "Philippine Literature in English: Some Sociological Considerations." In *Literature and Society in Southeast Asia,* ed. Tham Seong Chee. Singapore: National University, 1981.

Berthoff, Warner. "Continuity in Discontinuity: Literature in the American Situation." In Vol. 9, *American Literature,* of the *New Pelican Guide to English Literature,* ed. Boris Ford. New York: Penguin, 1988.

Berting, Jan. "An Appraisal of Functionalist Theories in Relation to Race and Colonial Societies." In *Sociological Theories: Race and Colonialism.* Paris: UNESCO, 1980.

Beverley, John, and Marc Zimmerman. *Literature and Politics in the Central American Revolutions.* Austin: University of Texas Press, 1990.

Blount, James H. *The American Occupation of the Philippines, 1898–1912.* 1912. New York: Oriole Editions, 1973.

Bhabha, Homi, ed. *Nation and Narration.* New York: Routledge, 1990.

Bock, Deborah, et al., eds. *Pearls.* Springfield, VA: Educational Film Center, 1979.

Bogardus, Emory. "Anti-Filipino Race Riots." In *Letters in Exile,* ed. Jesse Quinsaat. Los Angeles: UCLA Asian American Studies Center, 1976.

Bottomore, Tom, ed. *A Dictionary of Marxist Thought.* Cambridge, MA: Harvard University Press, 1983.

Bourdieu, Pierre, and Jean-Claude Passeron. *Reproduction in Education, Society and Culture.* Beverly Hills: Sage, 1977.

Boyce, James K. *The Philippines: The Political Economy of Growth and Impoverishment in the Marcos Era.* Honolulu: University of Hawaii Press, 1993.

Bradley, Harriet. "Changing Social Divisions: Class, Gender and Race." In *Social and Cultural Forms of Modernity,* ed. Robert Bocock and Kenneth Thompson. London: Polity Press, 1992.

Brecht, Bertolt. *Brecht on Theater.* Trans. John Willett. New York: Hill and Wang, 1964.

Bresnahan, Mary I. *Finding Our Feet: Understanding Crosscultural Discourse.* New York: University Press of America, 1991.

Bresnahan, Roger. *In Time of Hesitation.* Quezon City: New Day Press, 1981.

——, ed. *Literature and Society: Cross-Cultural Perspectives.* Manila: USIS, 1976.

Bresnan, John, ed. *Crisis in the Philippines: The Marcos Era and Beyond.* Princeton, NJ: Princeton University Press, 1986.

Bruchac, Joseph, ed. *Breaking Silence: An Anthology of Contemporary Asian American Poets.* Greenfield Center, NY: Greenfield Review Press, 1983.

Buaken, Manuel. *I Have Lived with the American People.* Caldwell, Idaho: Caxton Printers, 1946.

Bulosan, Carlos. *America Is in the Heart.* 1946. Reprint. Seattle: University of Washington Press, 1973.

——. *The Cry and the Dedication*, ed. E. San Juan, Jr. Philadelphia: Temple University Press, 1995. Another version, *The Power of the People*, was published in Manila in 1986.

——. "The Growth of Philippine Culture." *The Teachers' Journal* (May–June 1941): 1–18.

——. "I Am Not a Laughing Man." *The Writer* 59 (May 1946): 143–45.

——. *If You Want to Know What We Are: A Carlos Bulosan Reader*, ed. E. San Juan, Jr. Minneapolis: West End Press, 1983.

——. "Labor and Capital: The Coming Catastrophe." *Commonwealth Times* (15 June 1937): 1.

——. *The Laughter of My Father.* New York: Harcourt, 1944.

——. "Letter To a Filipino Woman." *The New Republic* 8 November 1943: 645–46.

——. "Manuel Quezon—The Good Fight." *Bataan Magazine* (August 1944): 13–15.

——. *On Becoming Filipino: Selected Writings of Carlos Bulasan*, ed. E. San Juan, Jr. Philadelphia: Temple University Press, 1995.

——. *The Philippines Is in the Heart.* Quezon City: New Day Press, 1978.

——. *The Power of Money and Other Stories.* Manila: Kalikasan, 1990.

——. *The Power of the People.* Manila: National Book Store, 1986.

——. *Selected Works and Letters*, ed. E. San Juan, Jr., and Ninotchka Rosca. Honolulu: Friends of the Filipino People, 1982.

——. *Sound of Falling Light*, ed. Dolores Feria. Quezon City: University of the Philippines Press, 1960.

——. "Terrorism Rides the Philippines." In *1952 Yearbook, ILWU Local 37*, ed. by Carlos Bulosan. Seattle: International Longshoreman's and Warehouseman's Union, 1952.

——. "To a God of Stone." *Amerasia Journal* 6.1 (May 1979): 61–68.

——. "To Whom It May Concern." *1952 Yearbook.* Seattle: International Longshoreman's and Warehouseman's Union, 1952.

——. *Writings of Carlos Bulosan*, ed. E. San Juan, Jr. *Amerasia Journal* 6.1 (Special Issue: May 1979).

Buss, Claude A. *Cory Aquino and the People of the Philippines.* Stanford: Stanford Alumni Association, 1987.

Cabezas, Amado, and Gary Kawaguchi. "Race, Gender and Class for Filipino Americans." In *A Look Beyond the Model Minority Image*, ed. Grace Yun. New York: Minority Rights Group, 1989.

Cabral, Amilcar. *Return to the Source: Selected Speeches.* New York: Monthly Review Press, 1973.

Callinicos, Alex. *Against Postmodernism: A Marxist Critique.* New York: St. Martin's Press, 1989.

Campomanes, Oscar, and Todd Gernes. "Two Letters from America: Carlos Bulosan and the Act of Writing." *MELUS* 15.3 (Fall 1988): 15–46.

Canlas, Mamerto, Mariano Miranda, Jr., and James Putzel. *Land, Poverty and Politics in the Philippines*. London: Catholic Institute for International Relations, 1988.

Capulong, Romeo. "U.S. Intervention Still the Main Problem of the Filipino People After Marcos." Talk given at the National Lawyers Guild National Convention at Denver Colorado, 11–16 June 1986. New York: PHILCIR Educational Services Program.

Carbo, Nick. *Running Amok*. Woonsocket, RI: Mango Press, 1992.

Cariño, Benjamin. *The New Filipino Immigrants to the United States*. Honolulu: East-West Center, 1990.

Casper, Leonard. "Introduction" to *Scent of Apples* by Bienvenido Santos. Seattle: University of Washington Press, 1979.

——. *New Writing from the Philippines*. Syracuse: University of Syracuse Press, 1966.

——. "Philippine Poetry." In *Encyclopedia of Poetry and Poetics*, ed. Alex Preminger. Princeton, NJ: Princeton University Press, 1965.

Catholic Institute for International Relations [CIIR], ed. *The Labour Trade: Filipino Migrant Workers Around the World*. London: Catholic Institute for International Relations, 1987.

Caudwell, Christopher. *Illusion and Reality*. London: Lawrence and Wishart, 1946.

——. *Romance and Realism*. Princeton, NJ: Princeton University Press, 1970.

Chaffee, Fredric and others. *Area Handbook for the Philippines*. Washington: U.S. Government Printing Office, 1969.

Chan, Sucheng. *Asian Americans: An Interpretive History*. Boston: Twayne Publishers, 1991.

Chapman, William. *Inside the Philippine Revolution*. New York: W. W. Norton, 1987.

Chatterjee, Partha. *Nationalist Thought and the Colonial World*. London: Zed Books, 1986.

Cheung, King-kok and Stan Yogi, eds. *Asian American Literature*. New York: Modern Language Association of America, 1988.

Chomsky, Noam. *The New World Order*. Westfield, NJ: Open Magazine Pamphlet Series, 1991.

Church, A. Timothy. *Filipino Personality: A Review of Research and Writings*. Manila: De la Salle University Press, 1986.

Churchill, Thomas. *Triumph Over Marcos*. Seattle: Open Hand Publishing, 1995.

Cingranelli, David Louis. *Ethics, American Foreign Policy, and the Third World*. New York: St. Martin's Press, 1993.

Clements, Robert. *Comparative Literature as Academic Discipline*. New York: Modern Language Association of America, 1978.

Clymer, Kenton J. *Protestant Missionaries in the Philippines, 1898–1916*. Urbana: University of Illinois Press, 1986.

Constantino, Renato. *A History of the Philippines.* New York: Monthly Review Press, 1975.

———. "The Miseducation of the Filipino." In *The Philippines Reader,* ed. Daniel B. Schirmer and Stephen Shalom. Boston: South End Press, 1987.

———. *The Nationalist Alternative.* Quezon City: Nationalist Foundation, 1979.

———. *Neocolonial Identity and Counter-Consciousness.* New York: Monthly Review Press, 1978.

———. *The Philippines: A Past Revisited.* Quezon City: Tala Publishing Services, 1975.

——— and Letizia R. Constantino. *The Philippines: The Continuing Past.* Quezon City: Nationalist Foundation, 1978.

Contreras, Antonio. "Review of Robin Broad and John Cavanagh's 'Plundering Paradise: The Struggle for the Environment in the Philippines.'" *Capitalism, Nature, Socialism* 5 (March 1994): 137–40.

Cordova, Fred. *Filipinos: Forgotten Asian Americans.* Dubuque, IA: Kendall Hunt, 1983.

Corstius, Jan Brandt. *Introduction to the Comparative Study of Literature.* New York: Random House, 1968.

Covi, Giovanna. "Soggettività decolonizzate, teorìe storicizzate: *la cyborg* nelle Filippine." *Femminile e maschile tra pensiero e discorso,* ed. P. Corin et al. Trento: Università dagli Studi di Trento, 1995.

Cruz, Emeterio C. "Filipino Life in the Alaskan Fish Canneries." *Philippine Magazine* 30 (June 1933): 45–48.

d'Alpuget, Blanche. "Philippine Dream Feast." *New York Times Book Review:* 25 March 1990: 1, 38.

Daniels, Roger and Harry Kitano. *American Racism: Exploration of the Nature of Prejudice.* Englewood Cliffs, NJ: Prentice-Hall, 1970.

Davis, Leonard. *Revolutionary Struggle in the Philippines.* London: Macmillan, 1989.

Debray, Regis. "Marxism and the National Question." *New Left Review* 105 (September–October 1977): 25–41.

De la Torre, Father Edicio. *The Philippines: Christians and the Politics of Liberation.* CIIR Justice Papers No. 9. London: Catholic Institute for International Relations, 1986.

———. *Touching Ground, Taking Root.* London: Catholic Institute for International Relations, 1986.

Deleuze, Gilles. *The Deleuze Reader,* ed. Constantin Boundas. New York: Columbia University Press, 1993.

——— and Felix Guattari. *Anti-Oedipus: Capitalism and Schizophrenia.* Minneapolis: University of Minnesota Press, 1982.

———. *Kafka: Toward a Minor Literature.* Minneapolis: University of Minnesota Press, 1986.

———. *On the Line.* New York: Semiotext(e), Inc., 1983.

———. *A Thousand Plateaus.* Minneapolis: University of Minnesota Press, 1987.

Della Volpe, Galvano. *Critique of Taste*. London: Verso, 1978.

de Man, Paul. *Blindness and Insight*. Minneapolis: University of Minnesota Press, 1983.

Demetillo, Ricaredo. "Dimensions and Responsibilities of Philippine Literary Criticism." *The Literary Apprentice* 47 (November 1974): 63–67.

Deutsch, Babette. "Critical Essay." In *Poems 55* by Jose Garcia Villa. Manila: Alberto Florentino, 1962.

de Vera, Arleen. "Without Parallel: The Local 7 Deportation Cases, 1949–1955." *Amerasia Journal* 20.2 (1994): 1–26.

Diokno, Jose. *Anti-Americanism*. Quezon City: Kaakbay, 1984.

Dionisio, J. C. "Cannery Episode." *Philippine Magazine* (August 1936): 397, 412–13.

Dorlik, Arif. *After the Revolution*. Hanover: Wesleyan University Press, 1984.

Doctorow, E. L. *Ragtime*. New York: Bantam, 1975.

Doerner, William. "To America with Skills." *Time* 8 July 1985: 42–44.

Ducrot, Oswald and Tzvetan Todorov. *Encyclopedic Directory of the Sciences of Language*, trans. Catherine Porter. Baltimore: Johns Hopkins University Press, 1979.

Eagleton, Terry. *Literary Theory*. Minneapolis: University of Minnesota Press, 1983.

Easthope, Antony. *Poetry As Discourse*. London: Methuen, 1983.

Eggan, Fred. "The Philippines in the Twentieth Century: A Study in Contrasts." *Reviews in Anthropology* 20 (1991): 13–23.

Enloe, Cynthia. *The Morning After*. Berkeley: University of California Press, 1993.

Enriquez, Virgilio. *From Colonial to Liberation Psychology: The Philippine Experience*. Quezon City: University of the Philippines Press, 1992.

—— and Elizabeth Protacio-Marcelino. *Neo-Colonial Politics and Language Struggle in the Philippines*. Quezon City: Akademya ng Sikolohiyang Pilipino, 1984–1989.

Escoda, Isabel Taylor. *Letters from Hong Kong*. Manila: Bookmark, 1989.

Espiritu, Yen Le. "The Intersection of Race, Ethnicity, and Class: The Multiple Identities of Second-Generation Filipinos." *Identities* 1 (1994): 249–73.

Evangelista, Susan. *Carlos Bulosan and His Poetry*. Quezon City: Ateneo de Manila University Press, 1985.

Evasco, Marjorie, Aurora Javate de Dios, and Flor Caagusan, eds. *Women's Springbook*. Quezon City: Women's Resource and Research Center, 1990.

Falk, Richard. "Views from Manila and Washington." *World Policy Journal* (Winter 1984): 419–45.

Fanon, Frantz. *The Wretched of the Earth*. New York: Grove Press, 1968.

Feleo-Gonzalez, Marina. *A Song For Manong*. Daly City, CA: Likha Promotions, 1988.

Feria, Dolores. "Bulosan's Power, Bulosan's People." *The Manila Times* 28 April 1991: 7–8.

——. "Carlos Bulosan: Gentle Genius." *Comment* 1 (1957): 57–64.

——. "The Florentino Umbilicus: Isabelo de los Reyes' 'El Folklore Filipino.'" In *The Long Stag Party*. Manila: Institute of Women's Studies, 1991.

Fernandez, Doreen G. "Paths of Policy: Art and Culture in the Aquino Government." *Midweek* 18 May 1988: 31–36.

—— and Edilberto Alegre. *The Writer and His Milieu*. Manila: De La Salle University Press, 1986.

FIDES (Forum for Interdisciplinary Endeavors and Studies). *Religion and Society: Towards a Theology of Struggle*. Manila: FIDES, 1988.

Fischer, Ernst. *The Necessity of Art*. Baltimore: Penguin Books, 1963.

Fitzgerald, F. Scott. *The Last Tycoon*. New York: Scribners, 1941.

Forbes, William Cameron. *The Philippine Islands*. 2 vols. Boston: Houghton Mifflin, 1928.

Foucault, Michel. *The Foucault Reader*. New York: Pantheon, 1984.

Francia, Luis, ed. *Brown River, White Ocean*. Brunswick, NJ: Rutgers University Press, 1993.

Franklin, H. Bruce. *War Stars*. New York: Oxford University Press, 1986.

Freire, Paulo. *Pedagogy of the Oppressed*. New York: Herder and Herder, 1972.

Friedman, Edward, and Mark Selden, eds. *America's Asia: Dissenting Essays on Asian-American Relations*. New York: Vintage, 1971.

Friend, Theodore. *Between Two Empires: The Ordeal of the Philippines, 1929–1946*. New Haven: Yale University Press, 1965.

Fuchs, Lawrence H. *The American Kaleidoscope: Race, Ethnicity, and the Civic Culture*. Hanover: University Press of New England, 1991.

Garcia, Ed, and Francisco Nemezo. *The Sovereign Quest*. Quezon City: Claretian Publications, 1988.

Gleeck, Lewis. *American Institutions in the Philippines 1898–1941*. Manila: Philippine Historical Society, 1976.

Godelier, Maurice. *The Mental and the Material*. London: Verso, 1986.

Godzich, Wlad. "Emergent Literature in the Field of Comparative Literature." In *The Comparative Perspective on Literature*, ed. Clayton Koelb and Susan Noakes, 18–36. Ithaca, NY: Cornell University Press, 1988.

Goldberg, David. *Racist Culture*. London: Blackwell, 1994

Gomez, Alexander. "Filipinos for Sale." *Liberation International* 5.1 (January–February 1993): 9–11.

Goncharov, Ivan. "Ten Days in Manila." *Archipelago* 20 (August 1975): 8–16; (September 1975): 39–46.

Gonzalea, Juan L. *Racial and Ethnic Groups in America*. Dubuque, IA: Kendall/Hunt Publishing Co., 1993.

Gonzalez, Andrew. "Poetic Imperialism or Indigenous Creativity? Philippine Literature in English." In *Discourse Across Cultures*, ed. Larry Smith. New York: Prentice Hall, 1987.

Gonzalez, N. V. M. "The Long Harvest." *Midweek* 23 May 1990: 25–26, 28.

Gossett, Thomas. *Race: The History of an Idea in America*. New York: Schocken Books, 1965.

Goux, Jean-Joseph. *Symbolic Economies: After Marx and Freud*. Ithaca, NY: Cornell University Press, 1990.

Graff, Henry, ed. *American Imperialism and the Philippine Insurrection*. Boston: Houghton Mifflin, 1969.

Gramsci, Antonio. *Selections from Cultural Writings*, ed. David Forgacs. Cambridge, MA: Harvard University Press, 1985.

——. *Selections from the Prison Notebooks*. New York: International Publishers, 1971.

Grow, L. M. "Jose Garcia Villa: The Poetry of Calibration." *World Literature Written in English* 27.2 (1987): 326–44.

Guerrero, Amado. *Philippine Society and Revolution*. Hong Kong: Ta Kung Pao, 1971.

Gugelberger, Georg. "Decolonizing the Canon: Considerations of Third World Literature." *New Literary History* 22 (Summer 1991): 505–24.

Guillen, Claudio. *The Challenge of Comparative Literature*. Cambridge, MA: Harvard University Press, 1993.

Guillory, John. "Canon." In *Critical Terms for Literary Study*, ed. Frank Lentricchia and Thomas McLaughlin. Chicago: University of Chicago Press, 1990.

Guthrie, George, ed. *Six Perspectives on the Philippines*. Manila: Bookmark, 1953.

Habermas, Jurgen. "What Does Socialism Mean Today?" *New Left Review* 183 (September–October 1990): 3–21.

Hagedorn, Jessica. *Dogeaters*. New York: Pantheon, 1989.

Harlow, Barbara. *Resistance Literature*. New York: Methuen, 1987.

Harvey, David. *The Condition of Postmodernity*. Cambridge: Blackwell, 1989.

Hayden, Joseph Ralston. *The Philippines: A Study in National Development*. New York: Macmillan, 1942.

Hebdige, Dick. *Subculture: The Meaning of Style*. London: Methuen, 1979.

Hofstadter, Richard. *The Paranoid Style in American Politics and Other Essays*. New York: Vintage, 1967.

Hosillos, Lucila. *Philippine-American Literary Relations 1898–1941*. Quezon City: University of the Philippines Press, 1969.

International Commission of Jurists. *The Decline of Democracy in the Philippines*. Geneva: ICJ, 1977.

James, C.L.R. *American Civilization*. Cambridge, MA: Blackwell, 1993.

——. "Colonialism and National Liberation in Africa: The Gold Coast Revolution." In *National Liberation: Revolution in the Third World*, ed. Norman Miller and Roderick Aya. New York: Free Press, 1971.

Jameson, Fredric. *Marxism and Form*. Princeton, NJ: Princeton University Press, 1971.

——. *The Geopolitical Aesthetic: Cinema and Space in the World System*. Bloomington: Indiana University Press, 1992.

——. "Third World Literature in the Era of Multinational Capitalism." *Social Text* 15 (1986): 65–88.

Javate-de Dios, Aurora. "Japayuki-San: Filipinas at Risk." In *Filipino Women Overseas Contract Workers . . . At What Cost?* ed. Ruby Palma Beltran and Aurora Javate de Dios, 39–58. Manila: Women in Development Foundation, 1992.

——, Petronilo Daroy, and Lorna Kalaw-Tirol, eds. *Dictatorship and Revolution.* Manila: Conspectus, 1988.

Joaquin, Nick. "Culture as History." *The Manila Review* 3 (1975): 12–25.

——. "The Filipino as English Fictionist." In *Literature and Social Justice,* ed. Leopoldo Yabes. Manila: Philippine Center of PEN, 1982.

——. *The Language of the Street.* Manila: National Book Store, 1980.

——. *Manila: Sin City? and Other Chronicles.* Manila: National Book Store, 1980.

——. "The Way We Were." In *Writers and Their Milieu,* ed. Edilberto Alegre and Doreen Fernandez. Manila: De La Salle University Press, 1987.

Jolipa, Nora. "Philippine Literary Criticism in Spanish: A Tradition of Commitment." *Philippine Social Sciences and Humanities Review* 45.1–4 (January–December 1981): 333–44.

Jones, Gareth Stedman. "The Specificity of U.S. Imperialism." *New Left Review* 60 (March–April 1970): 1–23.

Jost, Francois. *Introduction to Comparative Literature.* Indianapolis: Bobbs-Merrill, 1974.

Kampf, Louis and Paul Lauter, eds. *The Politics of Literature.* New York: Pantheon, 1972.

Kaplan, Amy and Donald Pease, eds. *Cultures of United States Imperialism.* Durham, NC: Duke University Press, 1993.

Karnow, Stanley. *In Our Image: America's Empire in the Philippines.* New York: Random House, 1989.

Katz, Stephen. *Marxism, Africa, and Social Class.* No. 14, Occasional Monograph Series. Montreal: McGill University, 1980.

Keene, Donald. "Native Voice in Foreign Tongue." *Saturday Review of Literature* (6 October 1962): 44.

Kelley, Jack. "Kuwaitis Are 'Treating Us Like Animals.'" *USA Today,* 21–23 February 1992: 1A–2A.

Kerkvliet, Benedict J. *The Huk Rebellion.* Berkeley: University of California Press, 1977.

Kim, Elaine. *Asian American Literature: An Introduction to the Writings and Their Social Context.* Philadelphia: Temple University Press, 1982.

Kitano, Harry, and Roger Daniels. *Asian Americans: Emerging Minorities.* Englewood Cliffs, NJ: Prentice-Hall, 1988.

Klare, Michael T., and Peter Kornbluh, eds. *Low Intensity Warfare.* Quezon City: Ken Incorporated, 1988.

Kolko, Gabriel. *Main Currents in Modern American History.* New York: Pantheon Books, 1976.

——. *The Triumph of Conservatism*. New York: Harper, 1963.

Korsch, Karl. "Independence Comes to the Philippines." *Alternative* (1965), translated by Mark Ritter in *Midweek* (6 June 1990): 40–42.

Kristeva, Julia. *Revolution in Poetic Language*. New York: Columbia University Press, 1984.

——. *Strangers to Ourselves*. New York: Columbia University Press, 1991.

——. "Women's Time." In *Feminist Theory*, ed. Nannerl Keohane et al. Chicago: University of Chicago Press, 1982. Also in *The Kristeva Reader*, ed. Toril Moi, 187–213. New York: Columbia University Press, 1986.

Kunitz, Stanley J., ed. "Carlos Bulosan." In *Twentieth Century Authors*. First Supplement, 144–45. New York: H. W. Wilson, 1955.

Lacan, Jacques. *The Four Fundamental Concepts of Psychoanalysis*. New York: W. W. Norton, 1978.

Laclau, Ernesto. *Politics and Ideology in Marxist Theory*. London: New Left Books, 1977.

Lande, Carl, and Richard Hooley. "Aquino Takes Charge." *Foreign Affairs* 64.5 (Summer 1986): 1087–1107.

Lasch, Christopher. *The Agony of the American Left*. New York: Vintage, 1963.

Laurel, R. Kwan. "Migrant Workers' Christmas." *Midweek* (December 1990): 3–5.

Lauter, Paul, ed. *The Heath Anthology of American Literature*. Boston: Heath, 1990.

Lawyers Committee for International Human Rights. *The Philippines: A Country in Crisis*. New York: Lawyers Committee, 1983.

Lee, Ricardo. *Bukas . . . May Pangarap* [*Tomorrow . . . A Dream Exists*.] Quezon City: Markenprint, 1984.

——. *Pitik-Bulag Sa Buwan ng Pebrero* [*Fantasies in the Month of February*]. Quezon City: Kalikasan Publications, 1989.

Leonard, John. "The Literary View." *The New York Times Book Review* (12 March 1978): 48–49.

Lichauco, Alejandro. *The Lichauco Paper: Imperialism in the Philippines*. New York: Monthly Review Press, 1973.

Lim, Shirley Geok-lin. "The Ambivalent American: American Literature on the Cusp." In *Reading the Literatures of Asian America*, ed. Shirley Geok-lin Lim and Amy Ling. Philadelphia: Temple University Press, 1992.

Lopez, Salvador P. *Literature and Society*. Manila: University Publishing, 1940.

——. "Literature and Society—A Literary Past Revisited." In *Literature and Society: Cross-Cultural Perspectives*, ed. Roger Bresnahan. Manila: USIS, 1976.

——. "The Writer in a Society in Crisis." *Philippine Collegian* 12 May 1982: 4–5.

Lowe, Lisa. "Heterogeneity, Hybridity, Multiplicity: Marking Asian American Differences." *Diaspora* 1,1 (Spring 1991): 24–43.

Löwy, Michael. "Marxism and the National Question." In *Revolution and Class Struggle: A Reader in Marxist Politics*, ed. Robin Blackburn. Sussex: Harvester Press, 1978.

Lukács, Georg. *History and Class Consciousness*. London: Merlin Press, 1971.

Lumbera, Bienvenido. *Revaluations*. Quezon City: Index, 1984.

—— and Cynthia N. Lumbera. *Philippine Literature: A History and Anthology*. Manila: National Book Store, 1982.

Mabini, Apolinario. "In Response to General Bell." In *Philippine Literature: A History and Anthology*, ed. Bienvenido Lumbera and Cynthia N. Lumbera, 98–101. Manila: National Bookstore, 1982.

Machery, Pierre. *A Theory of Literary Production*. New York: Routledge, 1978.

Magdoff, Harry. *The Age of Imperialism*. New York: Monthly Review Press, 1969.

Maglipon, Jo-Ann Q. *The Filipina Migrant: Braving the Exile*. Hong Kong: Mission for Filipino Migrant Workers, 1990.

Magno, Alex. "Developmentalism and the 'New Society': The Repressive Ideology of Underdevelopment." *Third World Studies Papers*. Quezon City: University of the Philippines, 1983.

Majul, Cesar. *The Political and Constitutional Ideas of the Philippine Revolution*. Quezon City: University of the Philippines Press, 1967.

Malek, Anouar Abdel. "Geopolitics and National Movements: An Essay on the Dialectics of Imperialism." In *Radical Geography*, ed. Richard Peet. Chicago: Maaroufa Press, 1977.

Mangahas, Federico. "Personal Introduction." In *Poems by Doveglion* by Jose Garcia Villa, ii–vi. Manila: Philippine Writers League, 1941.

Marcos, Ferdinand. "Our Vision of Human Settlements." *Philippines Quarterly* 8 (June 1976): 4–5, 64.

Marcuse, Herbert. "The Affirmative Character of Culture." *Negations*. Boston: Beacon, 1968.

Marsella, Joy. "Some Contributions of the 'Philippine Magazine' to the Development of Philippine Culture." *Philippine Studies* 17 (April 1969): 297–331.

Marx, Karl. *Marx's Grundrisse*, ed. David McLellan. New York: Macmillan, 1971.

Mattelart, Armand, and Seth Siegelaub, eds. *Communication and Class Struggle*. Vols. 1 and 2. New York: International General, 1979 and 1983.

May, Glenn Anthony. *Social Engineering in the Philippines*. Westport, CT: Greenwood Press, 1980.

May, J. R. and Francisco Nemenzo, eds. *The Philippines after Marcos*. London: Croon Helm, 1984.

Mayuga, Sylvia, and Alfred Yuson. "In the Wrong Waters." In *Philippines*, created and designed by Hans Johannes Hoefer. Hong Kong: Apa Productions, 1980.

McClintock, Anne. "The Angel of Progress: Pitfalls of the Term 'Post-Colonialism.'" In *Colonial Discourse and Post-Colonial Theory*, ed. Patrick Williams and Laura Chrisman. New York: Columbia University Press, 1994.

McWilliams, Carey. Introduction to *America Is in the Heart* by Carlos Bulosan, vii–xxiv. Seattle: University of Washington Press, 1973.

——. *Brothers Under the Skin*. Boston: Little, Brown, 1964.

Melendy, H. Brett. *Asians in America*. 1977. Reprint. New York: Hippocrene Books, 1981.

———. "Filipinos." In *Harvard Encyclopedia of American Ethnic Groups*, ed. Stephan Thernstrom, 354–62. Cambridge, MA: Harvard University Press, 1980.

Miles, Robert. "Labour Migration, Racism and Capital Accumulation in Western Europe Since 1945: An Overview." *Capital and Class* 28 (Spring 1986): 49–86.

———. *Racism*. London: Routledge, 1989.

Miller, Stuart Creighton. *"Benevolent Assimilation": The American Conquest of the Philippines 1899–1903*. New Haven, CT: Yale University Press, 1982.

Min, Pyong Gap, ed., *Asian Americans*. London: Sage Publications, Inc., 1995.

Miner, Earl. *Comparative Poetics*. Princeton, NJ: Princeton University Press, 1990.

Mirkinson, Judith. "Red Light, Green Light: The Global Trafficking of Women." *Breakthrough* 18.1 (Spring 1994): 10–15.

Mojares, Resil. *Origins and Rise of the Filipino Novel*. Quezon City: University of the Philippines Press, 1983.

———. "Sojourners, Immigrants, Sharecroppers: Philippine Writing in English Today." *Asian and Pacific Quarterly* 16 (Spring 1984): 39–43.

Mottram, Eric. " 'Forget About Being Original': Recent American Poetics." In *American Literature*, ed. Boris Ford. New York: Penguin, 1988.

Navarro, Jovina, ed. *Diwang Pilipino*. Davis, CA: Asian American Studies, 1974.

Nearing, Scott and Joseph Freeman. *Dollar Diplomacy*. 1925. Reprint. New York: Monthly Review Press, 1966.

Nee, Victor, and Jimy Sanders. "The Road to Parity: Determinants of the Socioeconomic Achievements of Asian Americans." *Ethnic and Racial Studies* 8.1 (January 1985): 75–93.

Netzorg, Morton J. "The Philippines in Mass-Market Novels." In *Asia in Western Fiction*, ed. Robin Winks and James Rush. Honolulu: University of Hawaii Press, 1990.

O'Brien, Edward J. Introduction to *Footnote to Youth* by Jose Garcia Villa. New York: Scribners, 1933.

O'Brien, Thomas. *Crisis and Instability: The Philippines Enters the Nineties*. Davao City: Philippine International Forum, 1990.

Occeña, Bruce. "The Filipino Nationality in the U.S.: An Overview." *Line of March* (Fall 1985): 29–41.

O'Hare, William P., and Judy C. Felt. *Asian Americans: America's Fastest Growing Minority Group*. Washington: Population Reference Bureau, 1991.

Ong, Walter. *Orality and Literacy*. London: Methuen, 1982.

Ordoñez, Elmer. "Literature Under the Commonwealth." *Philippine Social Science* 28 (December 1963): 395–407.

———. "People's Culture." *Midweek*, 20 July 1988: 34–35.

Orozco, Wilhelmina. *Economic Refugees: Voyage of the Commoditized*. Pamphlet Series No. 1. Manila: Philippine Women's Research Collective, 1985.

Owen, Roger. "The Conditions Experienced by Migrant Workers in the Gulf." *IDOC Internazionale* 16 (November–December 1985): 4–8.

Paine, Robert. *Second Thoughts About Barth's Models*. London: Royal Anthropological Institute of Great Britain and Ireland, 1974.

Pajaron, Ding. " 'Dogeaters' Is a Sumptuous Feast." *Katipunan* (June 1990): 17, 20.

Palumbo-Liu, David. "Closure as Capitulation: The Ideology of Healing in Asian American Literature." Manuscript, 1991.

Parel, Tezza O. "Japayuki." *Midweek* 12 April 1989: 8–12.

Parenti, Michael. *Against Empire*. San Francisco: City Lights Books, 1995.

Parry, Benita, "Signs of Our Times." *Third Text* (1994): 5–24.

Patel, Dinker. "Asian Americans: A Growing Force." In *Race and Ethnic Relation [19]92/[19]93*, ed. John Kromkowski. Guilford, CT: Dushkin Publishing Group, 1992.

Pe-Pua, Rogelia, ed. *Sikolohiyang Pilipino*. Quezon City: University of the Philippines Press, 1989.

Peñaranda, Oscar, Serafin Syquia, and Sam Tagatac. "An Introduction to Filipino-American Literature." In *Aiiieeeee!* ed. Frank Chin et al. New York: Anchor Books, 1975.

Permanent People's Tribunal. *Philippines: Repression and Resistance*. London: Filipino People's Committee, 1981.

Philippine Center for Immigrant Rights. *Filipinos in the USA*. New York: PhilCir, 1985.

Pido, Antonio J. A. *The Pilipinos in America: Macro/Micro Dimensions of Immigration and Integration*. New York: Center for Migration Studies, 1986.

Poole, Fred and Max Vanzi. *Revolution in the Philippines*. New York: McGraw-Hill, 1984.

Posadas, Barbara. "At a Crossroad: Filipino American History and the Old-Timers' Generation." *Amerasia Journal* 13.1 (1986/87): 85–97.

Pratt, Mary Louise. "Linguistic Utopias." *The Linguistics of Writing*. New York: Methuen, 1989.

Preminger, Alex, ed. *Encyclopedia of Poetry and Poetics*. Princeton, NJ: Princeton University Press, 1964.

Putzel, James. *Captive Land: The Politics of Agrarian Reform in the Philippines*. New York: Monthly Review Press, 1992.

Quinsaat, Jesse, ed. *Letters in Exile*. Los Angeles: UCLA Asian American Studies Center, 1976.

Radhakrishnan, R. "Ethnicity in an Age of Diaspora." *Transition* 54 (1992): 104–15.

Rafael, Vicente. *Contracting Colonialism*. Quezon City: Ateneo de Manila University Press, 1988.

——. "Patronage and Pornography: Ideology and Spectatorship in the Early Marcos Years." *Comparative Studies in Society and History* 32 (April 1990): 280–304.

Requiza, Moreno. "Immigrant Adaptation of Filipinos in the Mid-Atlantic States." *Amauan Notebook* 2.1 (Spring 1981): 25–28.

Reyes, Soledad. *Nobelang Tagalog 1905–1975.* Quezon City: Ateneo University Press, 1982.

——. *The Romance Mode in Philippine Popular Literature.* Manila: De La Salle University Press, 1991.

Richardson, Jim. Introduction to *The Philippines.* Oxford: Clio Press, 1989.

Rivera, Temario and others. *Symposium: Feudalism and Capitalism in the Philippines.* Quezon City: University of the Philippines Press, 1982.

Rizal, Jose. "Filipinas Dentro de Cien Años" ["The Philippines a Century Hence"]. 1890. *Rizal.* Manila: Comision Nacional del Centenario de Jose Rizal, 1961.

Robinson, Cedric. "Ota Benga's Flight Through Geronimo's Eyes: Tales of Science and Multiculturalism." In *Multiculturalism: A Critical Reader,* ed. David Goldberg. Oxford: Blackwell, 1994.

Roces, Alfredo and Grace. *Philippines: Culture Shock!* Singapore: Times Book International, 1985.

Rodil, B. R. *The Lumad and Moro of Mindanao.* Minority Rights Group Intervention Report. London: Minority Rights Group, 1993.

Rossi-Landi, Ferrucio. *Language As Work and Trade.* South Hadley, MA: Bergin and Garvey, 1983.

Rotor, Arturo. "Our Literary Heritage." In *Literature Under the Commonwealth,* ed. Manuel Arguilla and others. 1940. Reprint. Manila: Alberto Florentino, 1973.

Ruoff, A. LaVonne Brown, and Jerry Ward, eds. *Redefining American Literary History.* New York: Modern Language Association of America, 1990.

Said, Edward. *Beginnings: Intention and Method.* New York: Columbia University Press, 1975.

——. *Orientalism.* New York: Pantheon, 1979.

——. "Reflections on Exile." In *Out There: Marginalization and Contemporary Culture,* ed. Russell Ferguson and others. New York: New Museum of Contemporary Art, 1990.

——. *The World, The Text, and the Critic.* Cambridge, MA: Harvard University Press, 1983.

——. "Yeats and Decolonization." In *Nationalism, Colonialism, and Literature,* ed. Terry Eagleton, Fredric Jameson, and Edward Said. Minneapolis: University of Minnesota Press, 1990.

Sanguineti, Eduardo. "The Sociology of the Avant-Garde." In *Sociology of Literature and Drama,* ed. Elizabeth and Tom Burns. London: Penguin Education, 1973.

San Juan, E. *Allegories of Resistance.* Quezon City: University of the Philippines Press, 1994.

——. "Beyond Identity Politics: The Predicament of the Asian American Writer in Late Capitalism." *American Literary History* (Fall 1991): 542–65.

——. *Bulosan: An Introduction with Selections.* Manila: National Book Store, 1983.

——. *Carlos Bulosan and the Imagination of the Class Struggle.* Quezon City: University of the Philippines Press, 1972.

——. *Crisis in the Philippines: The Making of a Revolution.* South Hadley, MA: Bergin and Garvey, 1986.

——. *From the Masses, to the Masses: Third World Literature and Revolution.* Minneapolis, MN: Marxist Educational Press, 1994.

——. *From People to Nation: Essays in Cultural Politics.* Manila: Asian Social Institute, 1990.

——. *Hegemony and Strategies of Transgression.* Albany: State University of New York Press, 1995.

——. *Introduction to Modern Pilipino Literature.* Boston: Twayne, 1974.

——. "Mapping the Boundaries: The Filipino Writer in the U.S.A." *The Journal of Ethnic Studies* 19.1 (Spring 1991): 117–31.

——. *Only by Struggle: Reflections on Philippine Culture, Politics and Society in a Time of Civil War.* Manila: Kalikasan, 1988.

——. "On the Limits of 'Postcolonial' Theory: Trespassing Letters from the 'Third World'." *ARIEL* 26.3 (July 1995): 89–116.

——. *A Preface to Philippine Literature.* Quezon City: Phoenix Press, 1971.

——. *Racial Formations/Critical Transformations: Articulations of Power in Ethnic and Racial Studies in the United States.* Atlantic Highlands, NJ: Humanities Press, 1992.

——. *The Radical Tradition in Philippine Literature.* Quezon City: Manalapaz Publishing, 1971.

——. *Reading the West/Writing the East: Studies in Comparative Literature and Culture.* New York: Peter Lang, 1992.

——. *Ruptures, Schisms, Interventions: Cultural Revolution in the Third World.* Manila: De La Salle University Press, 1988.

——. *Subversions of Desire: Prolegomena to Nick Joaquin.* Quezon City: Ateneo de Manila University Press and University of Hawaii Press, 1988.

——. *Toward a People's Literature: Essays in the Dialectics of Praxis and Contradiction in Philippine Writing.* Quezon City: University of the Philippines Press, 1984.

——. *Writing and National Liberation.* Quezon City: University of the Philippines Press, 1991.

Santos, Bienvenido. *Scent of Apples.* Seattle: University of Washington Press, 1979.

Scharlin, Craig, and Lilia Villanueva. *Philip Vera Cruz: A Personal History of Filipino Immigrants and the Farmworkers Movement.* Los Angeles: UCLA Asian American Studies Center, 1992.

Schipper, Mineke. *Beyond the Boundaries.* London: Allison and Busby, 1989.

Schirmer, Daniel Boone, and Stephen Shalom, eds. *The Philippines Reader.* Boston: South End Press, 1987.

Scholes, Robert. "Canonicity and Textuality." In *Introduction to Scholarship in*

Modern Languages and Literatures, ed. Joseph Gibaldi. New York: Modern Language Association of America, 1992.

Scott, William Henry. *Of Igorots and Independence.* Baguio City: ERA, 1993.

Seager, Joni, and Ann Olson. *Women in the World: An International Atlas.* New York: Simon and Schuster, 1986.

Shaw, J. T. "Literary Indebtedness and Comparative Literary Studies." In *Comparative Literature,* ed. Newton Stallknecht and Horst Frenz. Carbondale: Southern Illinois University Press, 1961.

Sheridan, Richard Brinsley. *The Filipino Martyrs.* 1900. Reprint. Quezon City: Malaya Books, 1970.

Shipley, Joseph T., ed. *Dictionary of World Literature.* Paterson, NJ: Littlefield, Adams, 1962.

Sison, Jose Maria. *Philippine Crisis and Revolution.* Ten lectures delivered at the Asian Center, University of the Philippines, Quezon City, April–May 1986.

——. *Prison and Beyond: Selected Poems 1958–83.* Manila: Free Sison Committee, 1984.

Skinner, Michelle Cruz. *Balikbayan: A Filipino Homecoming.* Honolulu: Bess Press, 1988.

Sklair, Leslie. *Sociology of the Global System.* Baltimore: Johns Hopkins University, 1991.

Smith, Anthony. *Nationalism in the Twentieth Century.* New York: New York University Press, 1979.

——. *Theories of Nationalism.* New York: Harper and Row, 1971.

Smith, Joseph. *Portrait of a Cold Warrior.* New York: Ballantine Books, 1976.

Smith, Neil. *Uneven Development.* New York: Basil Blackwell, 1984.

Solberg, S. E. "An Introduction to Filipino American Literature." In *Aiiieeeee!* ed. Frank Chin et al. New York: Mentor Book, 1991.

Sollors, Werner. *Beyond Ethnicity.* New York: Oxford University Press, 1986.

Somera, Rene. "Between Two Worlds: The Hawaii Ilocano Immigrant Experience." *Diliman Review* (January–February 1982): 54–59.

Spiller, Robert E., et al., eds. *Literary History of the United States.* New York: Oxford University Press, 1963.

Stanley, Peter. *A Nation in the Making: The Philippines and the United States, 1899–1921.* Cambridge, MA: Harvard University Press, 1974.

——. "The Manongs of California." *Philippine U.S. Free Press* (November 1985): 4, 7–8, 45.

Stauffer, Robert B. *The Marcos Regime: Failure of Transnational Developmentalism and Hegemony-Building From Above and Outside.* Research Monograph No. 23. Sydney, Australia: Transnational Corporations Research Project, 1985.

——. "Philippine Democracy: Contradictions of Third World Redemocratization." Paper presented at Philippine Studies Colloquium, University of Hawaii, 4 May 1990.

——. "Review of Peter Stanley, 'Reappraising an Empire.'" *Journal of Asian and African Studies* 12.1–2 (1987): 103–4.

Stegner, Wallace. *One Nation*. Boston: Houghton Mifflin, 1945.

——. "Renaissance in Many Tongues." *Saturday Review of Literature* 34 (4 August 1951): 52–53.

Steinberg, David Joel. *The Philippines: A Singular and a Plural Place*. Boulder, CO: Westview Press, 1982.

Strobel, Leny Mendoza. "A Personal Story: On Becoming a Split Filipina Subject. *Amerasia Journal* 19.3 (1993): 117–30.

Sturtevant, David. *Popular Uprisings in the Philippines 1840–1940*. Ithaca, NY: Cornell University Press, 1976.

Sussman, Gerald. "What 'Hearts of Darkness' Left Out." *Guardian* (29 April 1992): 19.

Tañada, Wigberto. "Senator Tañada Addresses Security Issues." *Philippine Witness* 50 (October 1994–March 1995): 5–9.

Takaki, Ronald, ed. *From Different Shores*. New York: Oxford University Press, 1987.

——. *Strangers From A Different Shore: A History of Asian Americans*. Boston: Little, Brown, 1989.

Tarr, Peter. "Learning to Love Imperialism." *The Nation* 5 June 1989: 779–84.

"Tatang." *Sa Tungki ng Ilong ng Kaaway: Talambuhay ni Tatang*. Manila: LINANG [Movement for the Development of Revolutionary Literature and Art in the Countryside], 1988.

Tauli-Corpuz, Victoria. "Environment and Development: The Indigenous Peoples' Perspective." *Philippines Development Briefing* 2 (November 1992): 1–15.

Taverna, Odette. "Josephine Patrick." *Midweek* 11 March 1992: 19–21.

Taylor, Anne. "Father Ed de la Torre and the Theology of Struggle." *Asian Times* 7 August 1987: 19–21.

Taylor, Charles. *Multiculturalism and "The Politics of Recognition."* Princeton: NJ: Princeton University Press, 1992.

Taylor, George. *The Philippines and the United States: Problems of Partnership*. New York: Praeger, 1964.

Teodoro, Luis, and E. San Juan. *Two Perspectives on Philippine Literature and Society*. Honolulu: University of Hawaii Center for Philippine Studies, 1981.

Thibaudeau, Jean. "Preliminary Notes on the Prison Writings of Gramsci: The Place of Literature in Marxian Theory." *Praxis* 3 (1976): 3–29.

Thomson, George. *The Human Essence*. London: China Policy Study Group, 1974.

——. *Marxism and Poetry*. London: Lawrence and Wishart, 1947.

Tiempo, Edith. "The Creative Temper, Provoked and Challenged, Triumphed." *Panorama* 6 January 1980: 26–27.

Tinio, Rolando. "Villa's Values; Or, The Poet You Cannot Always Make Out, Or Succeed in Liking Once You're Able to." In *Brown Heritage,* ed. Antonio Manuud. Quezon City: Ateneo de Manila University Press, 1967.

Tiongson, Nicanor. *Pilipinas Circa 1907*. Quezon City: Philippine Educational Theater Association, 1985.

——, ed. *The Politics of Culture: The Philippine Experience*. Manila: Philippine Educational Theater Association, 1984.

——, Maria Luisa Doronila, Alice Guillermo and Fe Mangahas. "The Ideology and Culture of the New Society." In *Syntheses: Before and Beyond February 1986*, 49–65. Quezon City: Interdisciplinary Forum of the University of the Philippines, 1986.

Todorov, Tzvetan. *Mikhail Bakhtin*. Minneapolis: University of Minnesota Press, 1984.

Twain, Mark. *Mark Twain's Weapons of Satire*, ed. Jim Zwick. Syracuse, NY: Syracuse University Press, 1992.

——. "Thirty Thousand Killed a Million." *The Atlantic Monthly* (April 1992): 52–65.

Urian, Teresita (as told to Mila de Guzman). "Into the Light." *Katipunan* (October 1991): 10–11.

U.S. Commission on Civil Rights. *Civil Rights Issues Facing Asian Americans in the 1990s*. Washington: U.S. Commission on Civil Rights, 1992.

Vallejo, Cesar. *The Mayakovsky Case*. Willimantic, CT: Curbstone Press, 1982.

Van Erven, Eugene. *The Playful Revolution*. Bloomington: Indiana University Press, 1992.

Veneracion, Jaime. *Agos ng Dugong Kayumanggi*. Quezon City: Educational Forum, 1987.

Vera Cruz, Philip [with Craig Scharlin and Lilia V. Villanueva]. *Philip Vera Cruz*. Los Angeles: UCLA Labor Center, Institute of Industrial Relations, 1992.

Vickers, Jeanne. *Women and the World Economic Crisis*. London: Zed Books, 1993.

Vidal, Gore. *The Decline and Fall of the American Empire*. Berkeley: Odonian Press, 1986–92.

Villa, Jose Garcia. "The Contemporary Short Story." In *Filipino Essays in English*, ed. Leopoldo Y. Yabes. Quezon City: University of the Philippines Press, 1962. (First published in *Prairie Schooner*, Fall 1936.)

——. *Footnote to Youth. Tales of the Philippines and Others*. New York: Scribners, 1933.

——. *Selected Poems and New*. New York: McDowell Obolensky, 1958.

——. *Volume Two*. New York: New Directions, 1949.

Villanueva, Marianne. *Ginseng and Other Tales from Manila*. Corvallis, OR: Calyx Books, 1991.

Villapando, Venny. "The Business of Selling Mail-Order Brides." In *Making Waves*, ed. Asian Women United of California. Boston: Beacon Press, 1989.

Villegas, Edberto M. *Studies in Philippine Political Economy*. Manila: n.p., 1983.

Villones, Rebecca. "Filipino Workers in Silicon Valley." In *Asian Americans in the United States*, ed. Alexander Yamato, Soo-Young Chin, Wendy Ng, and Joel Franks. Vol. 2. Dubuque, IA: Kendall/Hunt, 1993.

Viray, Manuel. "Certain Influences in Filipino Writing." *The Pacific Spectator* 6 (Summer 1952): 298–305.

——. "Writers Without Readers." *Philippine Review* (June 1952): 16–29.

Voloshinov, V. N. [Mikhail Bakhtin]. *Marxism and the Philosophy of Language.* Cambridge, MA: Harvard University Press, 1986.

Vreeland, Nena, et al., eds. *Area Handbook for the Philippines.* Washington: U.S. Government Printing Office, 1976.

Wand, David Hsin-Fu, ed. *Asian American Heritage.* New York: Washington Square Press, 1974.

Weightman, George. "Sociology in the Philippines." *International Review of Modern Sociology* 17 (Spring 1987): 35–62.

Weimann, Robert. *Structure and Society in Literary History.* Baltimore: Johns Hopkins University Press, 1984.

Weisstein, Ulrich. *Comparative Literature and Literary Theory.* Bloomington, IN: University of Indiana Press, 1973.

White, Hayden. "Literature and Social Action: Reflections on the Reflection Theory of Literary Art." *New Literary History* 12.2 (Winter 1980): 363–80.

Williams, Raymond. *The Country and the City.* New York: Macmillan, 1973.

——. *Marxism and Literature.* New York: Oxford University Press, 1977.

——. *The Politics of Modernism.* London: Verso, 1989.

——. *Writing in Society.* London: Verso, 1984.

Williams, William Appleman. *The Tragedy of American Diplomacy.* New York: Dell Publishing, 1962.

Woddis, Jack. *Introduction to Neo-Colonialism.* New York: International Publishers, 1967.

Wolff, Janet. "Culture." In *A Dictionary of Marxist Thought,* ed. Tom Bottomore. Cambridge, MA: Harvard University Press, 1983.

Wolff, Leon. *Little Brown Brother.* Garden City, NY: Doubleday, 1961.

Wong, Sau-ling Cynthia. *Reading Asian American Literature: From Necessity to Extravagance.* Princeton: Princeton University Press, 1993.

Yabes, Leopoldo, ed. *Filipino Essays in English.* Vol. 1. Quezon City: University of the Philippines Press, 1954.

Zinn, Howard. *A People's History of the United States.* New York: Harper, 1980.

——. *The Twentieth Century.* New York: Harper and Row, 1992.

Zwick, James, ed. *Mark Twain's Weapons of Satire.* Syracuse, NY: Syracuse University Press, 1992.

Index

Hernandez, Amado V., 49, 54, 73, 158, 215, 219, 237, 253
Harris, Joel Chandler, 56
Harris, Wilson, 39
Harrison, William Burton, 59
Harte, Bret, 33
Hartendorp, A. V. H., 34, 58, 60
Hartman, Geoffrey, 173
Harvey, David, 191, 239
Hegel, Friedrich, 145, 209
Heine, Heinrich, 40
Hellman, Lillian, 134
Hemingway, Ernest, 25, 33, 40, 47, 51–52, 65, 76, 171, 190, 218, 226, 229
Henry, O., 33, 58
Herbert, George, 181
Herder, Johann Gottfried, 235
Hicks, Granville, 40
Hikmet, Nazim, 134
Hirsch, E. D., 76
Hobbes, Thomas, 74
Hofstadter, Richard, 3, 26
Holmes, Oliver Wendell, 28, 57
Hook, Sidney, 42, 48, 59
Hoover, Herbert, 193
Hopkins, Gerard Manley, 181, 201, 203
Horace, 73, 153, 164
Hosillos, Lucila, 56
Howells, William Dean, 24, 40, 49, 69, 88, 105
Hugo, Victor, 218
Huneker, James, 34
Huntington, Samuel, 74

Ilagan, Hermogenes, 54
Irving, Washington, 34, 56
Itliong, Larry, 81, 130, 167

Jacinto, Emilio, 54
Jack, Peter Monro, 181
Jackson, George, 46, 67, 86, 256
Jaena, Graciano Lopez, 33, 189, 217
Jagor, Feodor, 70
Jakobson, Roman, 173, 201, 226
Jalandoni, Magdalena, 54, 73
James, C. L. R., 6, 14, 21, 67, 185, 188, 233, 256

James, Henry, 65, 76
James, William, 69, 105
Jameson, Fredric, 11, 203, 231, 232
Javellana, Stevan, 106
Jefferson, Thomas, 28, 76
Jesus, Jose Corazon de, 54, 73, 219
Joaquin, Nick, 51–52, 72–73, 222–23, 227
Jones, Gareth Stedman, 3
Jopson, Ed, 65
Joyce, James, 118, 182, 188, 201
Jung, Carl, 179

Kant, Immanuel, 34, 181, 198
Kaplan, Amy, 4
Kardelj, Edward, 233
Karnow, Stanley, 5–9, 12, 70, 109, 234
Keene, Donald, 222
Keesing, Felix, 45
Keynes, John Maynard, 35, 223
Kim, Elaine, 111–12
Kingston, Maxine Hong, 88
Kipling, Rudyard, 3, 26
Kolko, Gabriel, 3, 56
Korsch, Karl, 6–7
Kristeva, Julia, 117, 145, 183, 196
Kroeber, Alfred, 45

Lacaba, Emmanuel, 65, 235
Lacan, Jacques, 136, 183, 195
Lamb, Rosemarie, 177
Lansang, Jose, 49, 219
Laraquel, Lorna, 103, 243–44, 249
Lardner, Ring, 33, 58
Lauter, Paul, 111
Lawrence, D. H., 181
Laya, Juan C., 219
Leaño, Fernando, 29
Lee, Ricardo, 244, 249
Lenin, Vladimir, 89, 134, 233
Leonard, John, 170
Levi-Strauss, Claude, 173
Lewis, Sinclair, 33, 62
Lim-Wilson, Fatima, 127
Ling, Amy, 111
Linmark, R. Zamora, 127
Litiatco, Alfredo E., 58
Lodge, Henry Cabot, 80